REMINISCENCES

This is a volume in the Arno Press collection

THE DEVELOPMENT OF CONTEMPORARY ACCOUNTING THOUGHT

See last pages of this volume for a complete list of titles.

REMINISCENCES

GÉRARD VAN DE LINDE

ARNO PRESS
A New York Times Company
New York • 1978

Editorial Supervision: LUCILLE MAIORCA

Reprint Edition 1978 by Arno Press Inc.

Reprinted by permission of Gee & Co., Publishers Ltd.

Reprinted from a copy in the American Institute
of Certified Public Accountants Library

THE DEVELOPMENT OF CONTEMPORARY ACCOUNTING THOUGHT
ISBN for complete set: 0-405-10891-5
See last pages of this volume for titles.

Manufactured in the United States of America

Library of Congress Cataloging in Publication Data

Van De Linde, Gérard, 1840-
Reminiscences.

(The Development of contemporary accounting thought)
Reprint of the 1917 ed. published by Gee & Co., London.
1. Accounting--Great Britain--History. 2. Van De Linda, Gérard, 1840- 3. Accountants--Great Britain--Biography. I. Series.
HF5616.G7V36 1978 657'.092'4 [B] 77-87290
ISBN 0-405-10917-2

Very sincerely yours.
Gérard van de Linde

REMINISCENCES

BY

GÉRARD VAN DE LINDE, F.C.A.

PRICE 12s. 6d. NET.

LONDON:
GEE & CO. (PUBLISHERS) LTD., 34 MOORGATE STREET, E.C. 2.

1917.

PREFACE.

I HAVE already written thirteen books and papers as detailed at the end of this Volume under the head of "Works by the same Author."

As it has already been pointed out to me on more than one occasion that thirteen is an unlucky number, I have now written the present work, "REMINISCENCES," the proceeds of which I purpose devoting to the funds of The Chartered Accountants' Benevolent Association, in which, for over thirty years, I have taken the greatest possible interest, helping it in every possible way.

I trust that my voluntary endeavours (a labour of love) will meet with adequate success, thus helping once more to benefit this very worthy charity.

GERARD VAN DE LINDE.

CONTENTS.

CHAPTER I.

My Parentage and Early Days.

I WAS born at Wellington House, Stoke Newington, on 9 May 1840. My father, the Rev. Gérard van de Linde, was born at Rotterdam and educated at the University of Leyden, the Students' Club of which was called "MINERVA." He was Poet Laureate of Holland, and a personal friend of the old King and Queen there. The Queen often came over to London, staying at Claridge's Hotel; when there, she always took an opportunity of sending for me to have tea with her, giving me a tip on leaving.

My father's volume of poems, entitled *Gedichten van den Schoolmeester,* by *Gerrit van de Linde Janszoon,* his full Dutch name, is known throughout the whole of Holland, from the palace to the cottage, and the following complimentary notice from an unknown writer, which appeared in the London "*Echo*" of 12 September 1895, and was reproduced in "*The Accountant*" of 21 September 1895, will show my readers in what esteem its author was held :—

A Dutch Ingoldsby.

Great men live and die, and, generally, it is posterity, rather than their contemporaries, that discovers the true value of their work. An apt instance of this truism is afforded in the following paragraph which we reprint from a recent issue of *The Echo* [of 12th inst.] :—

A contemporary of Barham, and bearing a stronger resemblance to that singular genius than any of his imitators, Gerrit van de Linde may well be called the Dutch "Ingoldsby." It would be as impossible to translate his verses as it would be to translate the "Ingoldsby Legends," so much are the two alike in the delicate handling of the language, the wealth of rhymes, the *jeux de mots*, and the apparent nonchalance and facility, which was the result of laborious art. It was remarkable that van de Linde should have retained so marvellous a mastery over his mother-tongue, for all his work was done in England. He came over here soon after he left the University of Leyden, intending to go to the Cape, but he stayed in London, became completely Anglicised, and ended his days here, dying at Cromwell House, Highgate, on 27 January, 1858. He gathered around him a large circle of English friends, and his table-talk, full of ripe thought and wide learning, and flashing with wit, was listened to by his guests with as much delight as that of another brilliant dweller in Highgate, Samuel Taylor Coleridge. At the University he had been famous for the ease and elegance with which he expressed himself, his ready imitation of dialects, and his power of investing an anecdote or a story with irresistible drollery. Although his choice of subjects was different, the treatment and the turn of mind gives them a place in the same niche of one's literary memory as the "Ingoldsby Legends." In the "Natural History for the Young," the "Abridged Roman History," and the "Fables," there is a piquancy, a collocation of heterogeneous notions, a prestidigitation in the management of words that impart to them a flavour all their own. Van de Linde, like "Ingoldsby," was not voluminous. The smallness of his literary legacy is atoned for by its polish and precision.

The name at once struck us as being familiar ("Gerrit" is the Dutch for "Gerard"), and accordingly we instituted inquiries which have revealed to us the interesting information that the "Dutch Ingoldsby" who is so highly eulogised by the unknown writer of the above paragraph is none other than the late father of the well-known accountant whose name is a household word among accountant students throughout the country. A demonstration of the great law of heredity is offered by the fact that the distinctive feature in the character of both father and son appears to be a love of writing for its own sake—neither have sought to turn their undoubted talent to their own pecuniary advantage. The son, however, has been more fortunate than the father in this respect, at least, that his warm-hearted geniality and ready talent are even now well known and justly appreciated not merely by a large circle of personal friends, but also by the vast majority of those who are, or hope at some future time to be, his colleagues in the profession of accountancy.

When my wife, daughter, and I went over to Holland in the summer of 1912, we stayed first at Amsterdam at the Hotel Amstel, and then at the Hague at the Old Doelen. When we reached the Dutch frontier, arriving there from Germany, the Custom House officer touched his hat, and pointing to our nine pieces of luggage asked me if I was the son of the Poet Laureate; and when I said I was, he immediately bowed and passed everything, seeing us into a reserved first-class carriage on the train, which we had all to ourselves till we arrived at our destination (Amsterdam).

At both of the above Hotels we were treated right royally, and one night, while we were staying at the "Old Doelen" at the Hague, a gentleman came round and presented his card. He said that he had heard I was staying there, and he wished to make our acquaintance, as his great-uncle, a former Professor at the University of Leyden, had had the honour of passing my father for clerical honours.

The old hall porter, too, quite remembered both my father and myself very well, for we stopped there in 1855, some sixty years back, while visiting the Hague and its wonderful galleries.

While at the Hague we went over one afternoon to Leyden, looking in at the University, where the Head of it took us all over, and, with the greatest respect, showed me my father's old desk with his initials carved by him on the same, as also on the staircase. It appears they are all proud of this memento of my father's, treasuring it (as well as all connected with him) very highly.

From the University we went on to my father's old club, the "*Minerva*," and, sending in my card, a deputation of the students came down into the hall; receiving us with open arms, they took us upstairs into their sanctum (ladies as a rule excluded), gave us a magnificent tea, and me a really excellent box of cigars, which I thoroughly enjoyed. Then they escorted us as a body to the station, where there was nearly an uproar by the way they shouted when our train went off. However, when the station-master was told who we were, he made no complaint, and I believe even joined in the shouting and waving of hands.

My mother, a French lady of the name of Caroline Marie Eve Monteuuis, came of an old French noble stock, and our crest and motto are those of her family. The crest is a lion holding an anchor, and the motto, "*Espoir supporte*" ("*Hope maintains*"), I value very much, endeavouring to live up to its precepts, as also to one my dear mother was very fond of impressing upon me. That was "*Noblesse oblige.*" I do not translate it because it reads best in French.

My mother's brother, Monsieur l'Abbé Isidore Monteuuis, was born at Marquise in the year 1800.

In 1825 he was appointed Curé (Vicar) of Guines (the scene of the Field of the Cloth of Gold, where our King Henry VIII of England and Francis I of France met).

My uncle was indeed a grand simple-minded man, who might over and over again have been made a Bishop, but he preferred to remain a simple Curé in his own beloved village, and so he always steadily declined; in the year 1875 we celebrated his jubilee of fifty years' active work at Guines. His real titles were "*Monsieur l'Abbé Monteuuis, Curé Doyen et Chanoine Honoraire, de Guines.*" We all went over and attended his jubilee. It was indeed a wonderful event and a truly touching sight to watch his gentle, loving ways with all there, rich and poor, old and young, alike.

The following year (1876) the dear old man died, to the great grief of his parishioners and numerous friends. I generally used to visit him during my Christmas holidays, sometimes alone, and sometimes accompanied by my sister; while in the summer he often used to come to us at Cromwell House, Highgate.

As it was found that the air of Stoke Newington did not suit my dear mother, who needed a more bracing, purer atmosphere, we moved early in 1843 to Cromwell House, the Bank, Highgate, staying there until Michaelmas 1858, when my mother disposed of the school, buying a house, 11 St. John's Park, Upper Holloway, and living there; it was only about a mile down from our dear old home at Highgate, where my dear father died on 27 January 1858, as already mentioned.

My father was an accomplished linguist, speaking quite fluently Latin, Greek, English, French, and Dutch—five languages. My mother spoke Italian, French, and English, the last always with a slightly broken accent; in fact, my French clients all declare that I take after her, speaking English all right, but all the same they say they can readily detect the French accent. I never contradict them, for it pleases them and does me no harm; *au contraire*, it identifies me all the more with them, and, as Shakespeare says, "One touch of nature makes the whole world kin." I might mention, as far as I am concerned, that I still understand Latin quite well, but have forgotten my Greek. French and English come quite naturally to me (we spoke French habitually in our family until I was eight years old), and in the course of my travels I have learned Portuguese (rather thoroughly), Spanish, Italian, and Hindustani (when in India in 1866-7), but no Dutch.

When his scholastic duties were finally over for the day, which (including evening prayer and supper) was about 8.30 p.m., my father used to invite me into his library, where we had a pleasant hour's recreation over dominoes (the old-fashioned game) or cribbage, till 9.30 p.m., when we had a quiet little supper together, and then at 10 p.m. I went up to bed. We had no gas in the bedrooms, so in the winter time (being always an early riser) I undertook the duty of going into the various bedrooms at about 6.30 a.m. and lighting the candles, for we all had to be down and in the schoolroom at 7 a.m. for preparation of our lessons. This lasted an hour till 8 a.m., when we had morning prayer, at which my father always officiated, then breakfast and a run in the playground till 9 a.m., when we went into school again. I remember one winter's morning, after I had lighted the candles, one of the fellows jumped out of bed and was going to begin to dress when all of a sudden he remembered something and jumped into bed again. "What's that for, Johnson?" I said, "Oh," he replied, "I am ill and have to stay in bed." "All right, my boy, remember you are in for a dose of castor oil," I replied. That settled him; he jumped out of bed again and was soon dressed. Castor oil was the sovereign remedy my dear mother always gave the fellows, myself included, when anything was the matter with us. She considered it an infallible cure for every ailment. Oh, how we all loathed it, but we had to take it whether we were really ill or only just shamming. Being a vegetable and not a mineral medicine it certainly did not do us much harm if it did not do us much good. We stayed in school from 9 till 11 a.m., when we had a quarter of an hour's run in the playground until 11.15 a.m. We then went into school again till 1 p.m., dinner-time. After dinner, in the playground again till 3 p.m., going into school again till 5 p.m., then tea and playground till 7 p.m., when we had preparation for an hour till 8 p.m., evening prayers, at which my father again officiated, then supper and bed at 8.30 p.m. But in winter, instead of going into school at 3 p.m., we stayed out till 4 p.m., then went into school till 6 p.m., when we had tea, and school again at 7 p.m. Wednesday and Saturday we had half-holiday, when in summer we played cricket. We had an excellent cricket ground in a large field in Maiden Lane, just opposite Cromwell House. Rounders we played in our own playground, a game we all much enjoyed. At the bottom of the playground was a fruit orchard and garden, which my father divided up into allotments for the fellows to cultivate. These allotments were under the supervision of M. de la Hylais, who was a splendid gardener himself and stimulated us to vie with each other as to who should have the best garden, to which there was a prize attaching; so altogether our fellows' gardens, including my own, were a great success and kept us out of mischief. One thing my father would not stand at any price, and that was "loafing." Woe betide any chap whom he caught at it—he never tried it on again; once was sufficient. "No more loafing for me, thank you; I have had quite enough"—that is what the culprit (or, shall I say, victim?) said; and he meant it, too. All this kept us thoroughly fit and up to the mark; we did not require much castor oil.

My dear mother had a sweet voice and used to charm us all with her lovely singing. I remember three of her favourites, and ours too—(*a*) "Ma Normandie"; (*b*) "Voltigez Hirondelles," and (*c*) "Coucou," the gem of the lot. One of our chaps (Gibbs), who afterwards had a Government appointment abroad, was humming the tune one day, when a stranger accosted him, saying, "Excuse me, but I think I heard you humming "'Coucou' just now; did not Madame van de Linde, "of Cromwell House, Highgate, teach it you?" "Why, "of course she did," replied Gibbs, "but how did you "know?" "Simply because she taught it me also, for I too am an old Cromwellian," was the reply, and that was the commencement of a lasting friendship between these two dear "old Cromwellians."

Highgate is very little changed since we first went to live there (now over 72 years ago). It is in three distinct parishes: the Bank, where we lived, is in Hornsey parish; opposite it is St. Pancras Parish; while just a little south of it, with the boundary, Maiden Lane, is Islington Parish; St. Michael's Church in the Grove is in St. Pancras Parish (the third parish). It is replete with historical reminiscences of the most interesting and unique character. I will instance a few of them in three different categories:—Remarkable Buildings, Remarkable Personages, and Quaint Customs.

Cromwell House, on Highgate Bank, where we lived from 1843 to 1858, a magnificent red brick mansion, standing in its own grounds, was built by Cromwell about the year 1620. as a residence for General Ireton, who married his daughter, and was one of the commanders of the Roundhead Army. Oliver Cromwell also used it occasionally as a residence for himself. There was a subterranean passage from this house to the Mansion House, which cropped up in our coal-cellar, where one day our page boy accidentally moved the trap-door leading down to it. As he nearly broke his leg my father had it bricked up, much to the consternation of learned antiquaries, who regarded it as sacrilege. Cromwell House was built and internally ornamented to suit the taste of its military occupant. The staircase, of handsome proportions, is richly decorated with oaken carved figures in costume, members of the General's army, while the balustrades are filled in with devices emblematical of warfare. On the ceiling of the drawing-room are the arms of General Ireton, and the ceilings of the other principal rooms are similarly lavishly enriched. From the Belvedere, the platform on the top of the mansion, may be seen a perfect panorama of the surrounding country, rivalling, if indeed not surpassing, that from "The Spaniards" at Hampstead, commanding also a grand and extensive view all around.

The Mansion House was built by Sir William Ashurst, Lord Mayor of London in 1694, and also commanded a fine view of the country for many miles as well as over the Metropolis; the chestnut staircase, from a design of Inigo Jones, the noble doorway, carvings, and tapestried chambers being well worthy of admiration. It was for years occupied by Sir Alan Chambre, one of the Justices of the Common Pleas, who was almost the last occupant of it as a private residence. It was taken down in 1830, and the new church, St. Michael's, was erected upon its site, and consecrated by the Bishop of London, 8 Nov. 1832. The architect, Mr. Lewis Vulliamy, and the Incumbent, the Rev. Thomas Henry Causton, M.A., were great friends of my late father, who identified himself with all the parish work. Reverting again to the Mansion House, the stone doorway with the coat of arms was afterwards placed by Mr. Thomas Townsend as an entry to his house in the High Street, Highgate, while the arms carved in wood went to Mr. John Thompson, of Frognall, Hampstead, and deposited amongst his most extraordinary collection of antiquities.

Lauderdale House, built in 1600, was for many years the residence of the Earls of Lauderdale; the entrance hall still in its primitive state, with the delightful terrace on the southern side and the walls of the garden, testify the fact that they belong to ancient days. The mansion was formerly the residence of Nell Gwynne, the mistress of Charles II, and mother of the first Duke of St. Albans. Nell Gwynne, wishing to obtain a title for her son, seeing the King on the terrace below the window of the room she was in with the child, held it out of the window, at the same time calling to the King: "If you do not do something for this brat, I will drop him," to which the King immediately replied, "Save the Earl of Burford." A stone tablet in the entrance hall refers to and confirms this historical fact—a perfect romance, indeed.

When we lived at Cromwell House, Lauderdale House was for many years the residence of Sir Richard and Lady Bethell (afterwards Lord and Lady Westbury), with whom my parents were very friendly; in fact, Lady Bethell was repeatedly sending over to my mother for the loan of our cook whenever they gave any special banquet. When the Bethells left they were replaced by Mr. and Mrs. James Yates, with whom we as a family were all very friendly. He was a great antiquarian, to whom I again refer on two separate occasions.

Lauderdale House and magnificent grounds were acquired by my old friend the late Sir Sydney H. Waterlow, the latter being incorporated with his own grounds at Fairseat. Before his death he made over Lauderdale House and adjoining grounds as a free gift to Highgate—a magnificent gift indeed; it is now known as Waterlow Park, and is very judiciously administered by the London County Council.

Ken Wood, in Hampstead Lane, between Highgate and Hampstead, was in 1780 the country residence of Viscount Stormont, Chief Justice of the King's Bench, and created a peer of England in 1792 under the title of Earl of Mansfield. The year 1780 is identified with the Gordon Riots of that year. Lord George Gordon (more or less an enthusiastic maniac) had for his adherents the very scum of the Metropolis, whose watchword (like that of our present adversaries) was "Plunder" (without the "Kultur," by the way). As one of His Majesty's Judges, Viscount Stormont had necessarily to enforce the law against numbers of these miscreants, and this he did with such resolute impartiality and justice as to infuriate the mob against him. They began on 6 June 1780 by burning his house in Bloomsbury Square to the ground, a loss of over £30,000 (a considerable sum in those days). His valuable library alone cost £10,000, comprising the choicest collection of scarce manuscripts ever known in the possession of an individual; all was destroyed, together with his Judge's Note Books—a great loss to the Bar.

Lord and Lady Stormont were at the house at the time, and only escaped by hastily quitting it. Infuriated by this and many unchecked excesses, the mob gave the word of command, "Ken Wood," intending that the mansion there should share a similar fate as the one in Bloomsbury Square. The route of the rioters was through Hampstead to the "Spaniards' Tavern" in Hampstead Lane, then kept by one Giles Thomas. Quickly learning their object, he promptly urged them to refresh themselves freely, and threw the house open to them, taking care at the same time to mix their liquors thoroughly. Just then, Dr. William Wetherell (grandfather of our old Highgate friend), who attended the family, happened to ride up, and with great presence of mind backed up the landlord, Giles Thomas, in his unbounded lavish hospitality.

Then whispering to the landlord to keep his guests well in hand, he rode off at full speed to the Horse Guards, returning with a detachment in an incredibly short space of time through Milfield Farm Lane, thus intercepting their approach northward, and opportunely presenting a bold front to the rabble, who by that time had congregated in the road, which then passed within a few paces of the mansion. The rebel mob was quickly routed, and instantly returned in great disorder to London, the leading ringleaders being taken prisoners by the Guards. Lord George Gordon, their President, was taken prisoner at the same time, remaining in the Tower of London until 1 February 1781, when he was tried at Westminster for High Treason. He was declared to be not guilty on the ground of absence of proof of his having called the multitude together with any traitorous unlawful intentions, so he was set at liberty. For seven years he remained comparatively quiet, when in 1788 he wrote an infamous libel on the Queen of France. Being indicted for the libel he was found guilty and fled to Holland. But the Burgomaster of Amsterdam shipped him back to Harwich. Having been excommunicated by the Archbishop of Canterbury, he made a public profession of the Jewish religion, was arrested and cast into prison, where he died in his cell, on 1 November 1793, being then only forty-three years of age.

My father was very friendly with the late Earl of Mansfield, sending me over repeatedly to Ken Wood with messages for his Lordship, who invariably received me with uniform kindness and consideration.

King William IV paid a visit to Ken Wood on 23 July 1835, with several members of the Royal Family, the Duke of Wellington, and many of the nobility. They were accorded a right royal welcome in every sense of the word. The Earl of Mansfield gave them a grand entertainment, and a triumphal arch was erected on Hampstead Heath, where the King received an address of welcome. It was indeed a gala day for both Highgate and Hampstead.

Arundel House (on the Bank and close to our old home) was the residence of the Earls of Arundel, and the place of imprisonment of Lady Arabella Stuart in 1611. It was also the scene of the last moments of the great Lord Bacon, who died there on 9 April 1626, aged 66; he was a guest at the time of the Earl of Arundel. It was taken down in 1825 and replaced by a modern building, the garden at the back overlooking the grounds of Cromwell House.

Fitzroy House, the seat of Lord Southampton, adjoined Ken Wood, and was built in 1780. The Earl of Buckinghamshire resided there in 1811. The Mansion was taken down in 1828, and the grounds divided up for the erection of some very handsome houses and grounds. My old friend Mr. William Gladstone (first cousin of the great statesman, and senior partner of Messrs. Thomson, Bonar & Co.) resided there, and we often partook of his hospitality; it was he who gave me my start in the City in November 1858 (nine months after my father's death), and was always a very kind friend to us all, as was also his wife, Mrs. Gladstone. Years afterwards, his son, Cecil Gladstone, came into my office to learn business and its ways. Another old friend of mine living in Fitzroy Park was Colonel Josiah Wilkinson, to whom I more especially refer in the next paragraph.

At Holly Lodge, the seat of Baroness Burdett-Coutts, we attended many pleasant garden parties. In 1859, when the Volunteer movement was started, I became an original volunteer in the 14th Middlesex—commanded by Colonel Josiah Wilkinson, with Captain Frederick Whinney and Lieutenant Benjamin Greene Lake. It was at Holly Lodge that Colonel Wilkinson, on the occasion of a garden party there, presented me with the Queen's shilling, enlisting me there and then. We used to drill in Holly Lodge Park, spending many happy, profitably healthful, days there, all most enjoyable.

In those days the Baroness had not received her title, but was known as Miss Angela Burdett Coutts, the senior partner until the day of her death of Coutts & Co.'s Bank.

I sat next to the Baroness, shortly before her death, at the Mansion House at a meeting of the Gordon Memorial College of Khartoum, presided over by Lord Salisbury. Her ladyship was, as usual, very genial, and talked with delight of our old Highgate days.

At West Lodge, my old friend, Sir William Bodkin, Assistant Judge, lived, while his friend, Mr. Joseph Payne, the Deputy Assistant Judge, occupied a cottage adjoining. Both these gentlemen were staunch friends and practical philanthropists, ardent admirers of the noble Lord Shaftesbury and Ragged Schools. Their greatest enjoyment was to give garden parties in Sir William's magnificent grounds, and to get the numerous guests to entertain the Ragged School children. We were always invited and made a point of being present. It was busy work looking after these children, who had for each and all of us one title, that of "Teacher." Miss Bodkin, Sir William's daughter, too, was a great help in every way. She was quite in her element with them all.

While Her Majesty, the late Queen Victoria, accompanied by her mother, the Duchess of Kent, was on 6 July 1837 (soon after her accession) taking an airing, descending Highgate Hill on the west side, the horses became restive, and on arriving near the "Fox and Crown" set off at a fearful pace down the steep hill; but their progress was happily arrested by the prompt assistance of the landlord, Mr. Turner, who at great personal risk stopped the horses, thus saving the royal party from a most serious accident. His services were requited by the grant of a licence to use the royal arms in front of his house, and in addition a suitable present was forwarded to him. "The Fox and Crown" was for many years a show place in Highgate, until, quite recently, my old friend Mr. John Scrimgeour bought it and razed it to the ground, to the consternation of many old inhabitants of Highgate, who looked upon it as another act of sacrilege.

Heading the list of remarkable personages of Highgate comes Samuel Taylor Coleridge, one of the most distinguished poets and philosophers of his time. He died 27 July 1834 at the house of the late Mr. Gillman, at Pemberton Row, Highgate, where he had resided for the last nineteen years of his life, and a marble tablet to his memory has been erected in St. Michael's Church.

George Morland, the celebrated animal painter, was, until shortly before his death, a very frequent guest at the Bull Inn, where many of his choicest productions were painted, and sold, as soon as finished, for his bare maintenance. It was only after his death that their real value was appreciated, and now they fetch very high prices from eager connoisseurs to enrich their galleries. Just as it is easy to recognise the paintings of Wouverman by the *white horse* in each of them, so it is equally easy to spot a George Morland by the *white horse and white pig* he almost invariably painted in all his pictures. Some years ago, when staying at Palermo in Sicily, I visited there the King's quaint Chinese pagoda palace, "La Favorita." The ground floor had in it a huge picture gallery, the paintings mostly by one artist. I inquired of the porter the name of the artist; he could not tell me, except that he was an Englishman. "In that case, my friend, his name is George Morland," I said; and the porter told me I was right, for that was his name.

Andrew Marvell, born 1620, died on the Bank, Highgate, in 1678; he was the author of many well-known poems, chiefly of a satirical nature, and of several prose works, mostly against Prelacy and Imposture in matters of religion. The Countess of Huntingdon resided at Highgate in 1663. Dr. Sacheverel, a notoriously libellous preacher, some time minister of St. Saviour's, Southwark, died 5 June 1724 at his house in the Grove. His portrait was once engraved, with the initials "S. T. P.," signifying "Sacræ Theologiæ Professor." Three or four persons were looking at a print of the portrait in a shop window, and one of them inquired the meaning of "S. T. P." The Rev. Thomas Bradbury, a popular and influential Nonconformist minister, passing by at the time and hearing the question asked, at once replied, "Stupid troublesome puppy," and then passed on. General Monk, who was created Duke of Albemarle for his services in restoring Charles II to the throne, drew up his forces on Finchley Common, 3 February 1660, where the Guards halted when marching towards Scotland during the rebellion of 1745. Hogarth has immortalised this occurrence in his wonderful painting recording the fact.

Hogarth, during his apprenticeship, visited Highgate one Sunday with two or three boon companions. The weather being hot, they went into a public-house, where a quarrel soon after arose between some persons in the same room. They came to nasty blows, one man striking the other with a quart pot, making the blood flow freely. Hogarth immediately drew out his pencil, reproducing on the spot the full scene, with exact likenesses of the combatants and onlookers. Taking my cue from "*David Copperfield*" I should say that Dickens knew his Highgate very well, often riding or walking over there in the early morning.

The quaintest of all the Highgate customs is that known as The Highgate Oath—

"It's a custom at Highgate, that all who go through,
"Must be sworn on the horns, sir! and so, sir, must you!
"Bring the horns! shut the door! now, sir, take off your hat!
"When you come here again, don't forget to mind that!"

I confess to my shame that although I have kissed the "Blarney Stone" hanging down head foremost from the parapet of the old square tower of Blarney Castle, near St. Anne's, some six miles from Cork, I have never yet been sworn on the horns at Highgate. But, notwithstanding, I know something about it.

The landlord swearing in the novice proclaims in a loud voice, as follows: "Upstanding and uncovered! Silence!" Then he addresses the novice he is swearing:—

"*Take notice what I now say unto you, for that is the* "*first word of your oath, mind that!*" *&c. &c.*

. . . .

. . . .

"*You must not eat brown bread while you can get* "*white, except you like the brown best. You must not* "*drink small beer while you can get strong, except you* "*like the small the best. You must not kiss the maid* "*while you can kiss the mistress, except you like the* "*maid the best, but sooner than lose a good chance you* "*may kiss them both.*" *&c. &c.*

. . . .

"*I have now to acquaint you with your privilege as* "*a freeman of this place. If at any time you are going* "*through Highgate and want to rest yourself and see* "*a pig lying in a ditch, you have liberty to kick her out,* "*but if you see three lying together you must only kick* "*out the middle one and lie between the other two.* "*God save the King.*"

This important privilege of the freeman of Highgate was first discovered by one Joyce a blacksmith, who some ninety years ago kept The Coach and Horses, but the custom probably first originated at The Gate House Inn, by the Gate House itself, but all the other public houses enjoyed the privilege more or less and got fat over it. Considering that in 1826 there were no less than 19 licensed public-houses in this small hamlet, they all of them did a roaring trade, for in those days it was the great coach road to London, upwards of 80 stages stopping every day at the old Red Lion Inn, and out of every five passengers three were sworn. The horns, fixed on a pole of about 5 feet high, were erected by placing the pole upright on the ground, near the person to be sworn. There was one circumstance essential for a freeman of Highgate to remember, "and *that* is the first word of your oath, mind *that*." The swearer-in wore a black gown, mask, and wig, accompanied by his clerk, who carried the horns.

Another favourite trick of the innkeepers at Highgate was to produce a huge glass globe with a long funnel at one end, broad where it joined the globe and tapering at the end. This globe they would fill with beer and produce it to a newly-fledged novice, telling him that if he could drink the contents without spilling a drop he would not be charged for the drink. On making the attempt he found he could not get a drop out without tilting his head right back, when suddenly without the slightest warning the whole of the contents would rush out and drench him thoroughly.

1 May was always a gala day and a full holiday at Highgate, for three reasons:—(*a*) It was "Sweeps' Day," and any amount of processions of sweeps paraded the hamlet to the great admiration of the beholders.

(*b*) John and Elizabeth Wilson, the proprietors of the "Favourite Omnibuses," made a grand display, the horses having new ribbons, the coachmen and conductors, rosettes, with everything new, spick and span, to match. It was indeed a sight worth seeing. (*c*) Being a general holiday there was a good deal of horse and donkey riding to Hampstead Heath and back, we, the inmates of Cromwell House, coming in for our fair share. But the hacks had to be bespoken weeks beforehand, being in great demand.

November 5th, "Guy Fawkes' Day," was observed in all its glory at Highgate, rivalling if not surpassing Lewes. We at Cromwell House always had our guy and huge bonfire, the guy always personating some notorious character of the day. I remember, during the Crimean War in 1855, it was the Emperor Nicholas of Russia, with whom we were then at war, our allies being the French, Italians, and Turks. I well remember the battles of the Alma, Balaclava, Inkerman, and Sebastopol, and the eventual capture of the Crimea. As it turned out, we backed the wrong horse. We should have got Russia as our ally, and Turkey as our opponent —as is happening now.

One of my father's friends was Sir Alexander Cockburn, Lord Chief Justice of England. When he was Attorney-General he often came to our house at Highgate to dinner. I remember, on one occasion, my father thought it would be nice to have Dr. George Croly, the Rector of St. Stephen's, Walbrook, to meet him, but it turned out to be an unfortunate mistake, for both being brilliant speakers and somewhat egotistical, they did not get on at all well together, as one was always interrupting the other. I remember, when they left, Sir Alexander Cockburn said to my father: "I am always "happy to come to your house, van de Linde, but never "invite that wild Irishman again, for I cannot stand "him"; and Dr. Croly made a similar request to my mother. I remember on that occasion my mother prepared the wine beforehand. In those days very little champagne was drunk, the principal wines being Chateau Margaux claret (which my father used to get specially over from Holland—the Dutch being great claret drinkers of the best kind), and port and sherry. To save time my mother got the butler (Henri Dubois) to decant the port and sherry, which he did. My mother then said to him: "Henri, we will put the wine back into the cellar—it will keep cooler there." To which Henri replied, "Yes, madam, and fuller, too."

Sir Alexander Cockburn, as Attorney-General, made himself celebrated in the well-known poisoning case, Dr. Palmer, the Rugeley practitioner, being found guilty and hanged entirely through Sir Alexander Cockburn's wonderful acumen and very special gift of grasping the smallest details—the poison used by the prisoner Palmer being of an extra subtle kind. On that occasion Sir Alexander Cockburn invited my parents to go and hear him speak, but they felt the whole thing was too gruesome, and so they courteously declined. However, later on, when he became Lord Chief Justice (I think after my father's death) my mother on one occasion went and heard a celebrated case he was judging, but she came back very disappointed and never attended his Court again, although he repeatedly invited her to do so.

Another friend of ours was Mr. William Scrimgeour, the manager of the Union Bank, London, who lived at the Bank—four doors higher up from Cromwell House. When I got older, Mr. Scrimgeour often used to invite me after church on a Sunday to early dinner at his house. I remember on one occasion meeting there the notorious Pullinger, who was at that time the bank's chief accountant. At dessert Pullinger left the room for a minute or two, when someone said to Mr. Scrimgeour, "What a splendid fellow Pullinger is; he seems to be devoted to you, besides being a good man of business." "Oh, yes," said Mr. Scrimgeour, "he is my factotum; "I don't know what I should do without him. Poor "fellow, he works so hard that he never takes a holiday. "However, to-morrow he must take one as he has to be "away for a funeral." Pullinger attended that funeral, when a strange thing happened at the Bank. For some reason or other the Bank of England pass-book was required and could not be found, so they sent round to the Bank of England to know if it was there, and the Bank sent it on. On comparing the pass-book the balance was found to be very much below that appearing in the books of the Union Bank. It turned out that Pullinger had for some time past made a habit of robbing the bank and having two pass-books—one containing fictitious entries, which he filled up for the use of Mr. Scrimgeour and the directors; the real Bank of England one he kept locked up, so that no one had access to it but himself. The locksmith was sent for, the desk was forced open, and the fictitious pass-book was found in it. He confessed his pilferings, was given into custody, tried, found guilty, and sent to prison. On his release he retired, a ruined man, to Boulogne, where he died shortly afterwards in very abject and miserable circumstances.

Another great friend of our family was Mr. Mark Beauchamp Peacock, the solicitor to the Post Office; we as children often used to go to his lovely house and grounds in Southwood Lane, where the two daughters loaded us with delicious fruit, especially apples, of which we were very fond. These two daughters on the same day married, respectively, Mr. Charles Hansard Keene (first cousin of Charles Keene, the famous *Punch* artist) and the Rev. George Weldon, at St. Michael's Church, Highgate; my sister was bridesmaid at their wedding. The engagement between Miss Peacock and Mr. Weldon was of rather a romantic nature. They both met as guests at a wedding at which the Rev. Mr. Nelson, his vicar, officiated, sitting together at the breakfast. Mr. Nelson had already married the eldest Miss Peacock. Miss Peacock had cold fowl for lunch, and wishing to have some other cold dish on the same plate, Mr. Weldon (in order to relieve her of the chicken bones on her plate) said to her quite innocently: "Will you lay your bones beside my bones?" at which they both smiled, and then and there became great friends and were engaged shortly after, just about the same time as Mr. Keene became engaged to the third sister.

My father was a member of the Royal Society of Arts and a pretty constant attendant at its meetings, and he very often took me with him. Sitting just in front of him, and also a pretty regular attendant, was Prince Albert, known later on as the Prince Consort, the consort of our late Queen Victoria. The Prince got to know my father and me by sight, and always gave us a friendly nod. One evening he turned round to my father and said, " Mr. van de Linde, I understand you "and my friend, Mr. Harry Chester, are both of you "recognised authorities upon National Schools and " Cottage Garden Allotments." On my father modestly replying that he thought he knew something about them, the Prince added : " Well, if you don't mind the trouble, " I want you and Mr. Chester to come down to me, say " next Wednesday. Mr. Chester tells me that day will " suit him, so I hope it will you as well, and, if so, I will " expect you both on that morning at Windsor." My father bowed his acquiescence. The train and everything being fixed up, they duly started together; a Royal carriage met them at Slough railway station and took them to Windsor Castle, where the Prince met them and they all three spent a happy unceremonious day together, the Prince lunching with them, sending them back to Slough in the same way, and thanking them both warmly for the valuable information they had given him and which he fully hoped to profit by, and I believe he did thoroughly.

My brother-in-law, the late Thomas Sidney Cooper, R.A. (we married sisters), had a similar experience with Royalty, for during the summer of 1848 he received a letter from a lady-in-waiting informing him that Her Majesty Queen Victoria required his presence at Osborne to paint a picture for her from her own stock, and that, if convenient to him, she wished him to go down immediately to the Isle of Wight and commence work as soon as possible. He accordingly started very shortly after, putting up at an hotel at East Cowes, and going over to Osborne, where Mr. Toward, the steward, received him, giving him full instructions, also showing him the animals to be painted. He accordingly grouped them in his own mind, setting to work the next morning. He painted for several hours each day, lunching at Barton Farm, where the steward and servants paid him every attention, returning each afternoon to his hotel at East Cowes on the completion of his day's work, enjoying in the evenings the fresh sea air and the lovely coast scenery. On the fourth day the Prince paid him a visit, admired his pictures, the manner of the grouping and the style in which he was painting the animals, adding kind appreciative remarks. A day or two after, his Royal Highness came again, dressed in a tweed suit and with a very large umbrella, as it was pouring with rain. He gave him his hand and said the Queen would like him to go round to Osborne House that afternoon at 2.30 to show her the picture, so he and the bailiff went up together at the appointed time. He was received in the hall, and in the course of a few moments the dining-room door opened and the children came out laughing and joyous, running up the grand staircase. Her Majesty and the Prince then came forward, the latter saying, "Mr. Cooper, the Queen." He bowed low and her Majesty bowed in return. He then followed her and the Prince into the grand drawing-room, on the table of which Sidney Cooper placed his picture. As soon as the Queen saw it she exclaimed, "Oh, yes; that is my Buffie!" the pet name she had given her cow from its having a largely-developed "dewlap," and therefore in that respect resembling a buffalo, but its proper name was "Victoria." The Queen so very much admired the picture that she was fully a quarter of an hour examining its different points, making intelligent and pertinent remarks as to its execution. Just as he had thanked Her Majesty for her graciousness and was about to leave, Prince Albert suddenly asked him, "How about those "dock leaves you are introducing in the picture, Mr. "Cooper?" and on Sidney explaining to him that such accessories were considered allowable to avoid as much as possible the monotony of grass and earth,

"Well," said the Prince, jocosely, "they are beauti-"fully painted, and doubtless help to relieve the "monotony, but they are not evidence of good farming!" Upon which the Queen, smiling apprecia-tively and shaking her finger at the Prince, said: "How "about the little pool of water in which the heifer's hind "legs are standing?"

"Oh," said the Prince laughing, "I think it a "beautiful artistic idea, giving a stamp of nature to "the scene."

"Yes," said the Queen, "but it is not evidence of good draining," at which they all three laughed heartily. As a matter of fact, the Queen loved farming, and the Prince then was endeavouring to make a complete work of the drainage throughout the whole estate. Sidney Cooper, too, was a practical farmer himself, so they were all three a well-matched trio, understanding thoroughly what they were about, and that made the incident all the more interesting.

It may be remembered that 1851 was the year of the first great exhibition in Hyde Park, and I visited it with my parents. We had the pleasure of seeing the

Duke of Wellington there, very much bowed down with age. The following year, 1852, he died, and my father and I attended his lying-in-state at Apsley House, followed a day or two afterwards by his public funeral at St. Paul's Cathedral, where we saw the procession pass, from a window in Ludgate Hill.

My father was fond of taking me to places of interest, and among others he took me one Sunday to the Savoy Chapel Royal, where the old Duke of Cambridge had his pew, being a regular worshipper there, taking part most strenuously in the service. For instance, when the clergyman said "Let us pray," the old Duke would say, in a loud voice, "By all means." This reminds me of a similar incident that occurred when my sister was confirmed at St. Michael's, Highgate. The Rev. Thomas Henry Causton was then dead and was replaced by the Rev. C. B. Dalton, who, as it happened, married the daughter of the then Bishop of London. Dr. Croly, the well-known preacher at St. Stephen's, Walbrook, attended, and was invited to take part in the procession, but he said he preferred being with his friends the van de Linde's; so Mr. Dalton very kindly put us all in the gallery, just overlooking the vestry. When the procession came out headed by the Bishop of London, and followed by Mr. Dalton, Dr. Croly said in a loud voice so that all could hear: "Clever chap, that Dalton; he married the Bishop's daughter." In spite of the sacred surroundings, I am afraid an audible titter went round the amused assembly.

On another occasion my father took me to the Tower to London to hear Canon Melvill, the Golden Lecturer. It was rather a quaint sight to see the troops parading outside the chapel playing secular hymns until they entered the Tower, when all was proper again.

My father and I now and then lunched or dined in the City, generally either at the Chapter Coffee House or else at The George and Vulture (Pickwick's Inn) in George Yard. We followed the usual custom prevailing in those days, which was to personally select and buy our chop or steak at Banister's and our roll each at Leman's, leave them at the chop house, ordering our regular table, and getting the cook to grill chop or steak for us on our arrival, the waiter serving it all up on regulation pewter plates, with delicious mealy potatoes in their jackets, peas (when in season), cheese and butter, washed down with a grand tankard of their special London porter—a feast for the gods indeed. The George and Vulture, though still called by that name, is now, I think, better known as Thomas's Chop House. The old gridiron cook and head waiter, who used to wait on the late Charles Dickens, have only died within a few years past. This was a wonderful fellow in making up your bill. "Steak, 1s." "But I did not have a steak, I had a chop." "All the same, Sir, chop 1s., potatoes 2d.—fourteen pence, 1s. 4d."—evidently taking the pence for "pfennigs" and the shillings for "marks" on the decimal system. It was useless to argue with him; better give it up at once, for he always had his way. But all that is nearly sixty years ago. Since then times have changed, and the custom some years ago dropped out of favour. Banister's are no longer there and Leman's have removed from their palatial establishment in Threadneedle Street to a very modest shop in St. Swithin's Lane, but the quality of their bread and biscuits is just as high-class as ever, also, perhaps, not in such great demand as formerly. In those days a favourite restaurant was Pursell's in Cornhill. Whenever my mother went to the City she took me there to lunch, especially for the delicious chocolate and cream, which she thoroughly enjoyed, together with a horseshoe roll and pat of fresh butter. But Pursell's, too, has disappeared.

The Ship and Turtle in Leadenhall Street (or "Painter's" as originally known), a favourite resort of the late King Edward when Prince of Wales, is still there, though somewhat shorn of its ancient glory. You still get, in all its perfection, turtle soup, and after having regaled your inner man on this luxury you can, after lunch, by adjourning downstairs to the lounge for your cup of coffee and cigar, feast your eyes upon the real live article swimming in numbers in the huge tanks with glass sides, filling up the whole length of the lounge. Birch's (Ring and Brymers), in Cornhill, is another celebrated place for real turtle and other soups; their meat patties, oyster patties, and other similar pastry are just a dream. They do a huge business outside in public catering, standing at the top of the tree—no one can approach them.

Another favourite resort was, and still is, the old Cheshire Cheese in Fleet Street, with Dr. Johnson's old original seat still there in evidence. The huge pudding containing steak, kidneys, larks, mushrooms, oysters, &c. &c., and generally on hand every Wednesday at one o'clock, is well worth trying. The Cheshire cheese, too, finishing the repast, is the best of its kind. Before the manager cuts it, he asks about six guests present to mark on the door the height they think it is, and they do so. He then puts the cheese on the floor by the side of the marks, when it turns out that the marks are mostly all of them wrong. I used to drop in there occasionally, but it was rather too much of a function for me, better suited in fact for commercial travellers with more leisure time to spare. The same remark applies to the ordinary one got at Billingsgate—any quantity of fish in all variety (reminding one of the Old Ship dinner, Greenwich), followed by two or three joints, vegetables, cheese and butter: all for the modest sum of one shilling per head. Pimm's and Sweeting's, both noted for their celebrated oysters, are ancient landmarks still well to the front and going as strong as ever.

My first visit to Holland was in the summer of 1848. My father was a great friend of Captain Dunlop, the captain of the old "Batavier," and his daughter, Kate Dunlop, had been staying a month with us on a visit. My father took my sister, aged five years old, and myself, aged eight, to see Miss Dunlop off as far as Gravesend, where we were supposed to leave the steamer, but when we got to Gravesend, Captain Dunlop said to my father that we had better go on the whole way, and we did, staying at Captain Dunlop's house, "Slephelling," adjoining Fyenoord, opposite Rotterdam, and visiting from there the city of Rotterdam, my father's old house, and the Cathedral Church of St. Nicholas, returning, two days after, home again, having thoroughly enjoyed our excursion, which we used to say was "all by ourselves."

Three years later I went to Holland for the second time, again accompanied by my father, and on that occasion

I wore a black silk hat and a short Eton jacket, while all the boys and men in Rotterdam and Holland generally wore blue blouses and caps, so that I with my tall hat created rather a sensation, and the boys used to follow me shouting out :—

" *Hoed, waar ga ye met den jongen naar toe?*"

which being interpreted means :—" *Hat, where are you taking that little boy to?*"

Mr. Aart Veder (an old college friend of my father's), living at Rotterdam with a country seat near Arnheim, having no children of his own, wished to adopt me as his heir, and that I should go and live with him. My father, out of old friendship to Mr. Veder, rather liked the idea, but neither my mother, my sister, nor myself were very keen on it. However, the next time my father and I were at Rotterdam, he half gave his consent, and it was arranged that a very great banquet should be given at Mr. Veder's house in Rotterdam, where all his friends had been notified, and I should be introduced as his recognised heir. All went well until a certain dish came round, and seeing no salt on the table, I asked the butler to bring me some salt. Unwittingly this was a very great insult to Mr. Veder's celebrated chef, because he was supposed to season his dishes so skilfully that they needed neither salt, pepper, mustard, nor any other condiment. Mr. Veder was furious, and requested my father to give me a thrashing, which my father refused to do. The meeting broke up, and I never enjoyed the inheritance. I must say I did not regret it. The following year, Mr. Veder calmed down and suggested that my sister should take the place originally intended for me, but my sister absolutely refused, and we were all very glad that she did so. I suppose everyone knows Voltaire's cynical remark about the Dutch and the three C.'s: "*Canards, canaux, canaille*"—most unjust, to say the least of it.

In the late autumn of 1857 my father had to attend a Catholic funeral abroad. The church was cold and damp; he caught a chill standing on the cold stone slabs, with nothing but a narrow cane-bottomed chair to sit upon and with no stool for his feet. He came home thoroughly ill and had to go to bed, but he was soon up again, and in spite of the doctor's orders would attend school as usual. He insisted, too, on my mother, much against her will, going over for the Christmas holidays to her relations in France, while I stayed at home to nurse and look after him, which I certainly did to the best of my ability, for my father and I were great chums, more like brothers than father and son.

In the middle of January, 1858, he got evidently weaker. I sent for our old practitioner and neighbour, Dr. Moger, but as he was unfortunately away, I sent for Dr. Richardson, also close by, who came over at once and nursed him most conscientiously and skilfully; no one could have been kinder or more attentive. He pronounced my father to be very ill, so we moved him upstairs into the largest bedroom on the first floor—The Chinese Room—where he had a roaring fire and every comfort, with a screen to keep off any draught. Dr. Richardson sent him a skilled nurse, while I had my own bedroom adjoining with the door communicating generally wide open.

But my dear father, though still keeping up as far as he was able his cheerful spirits and pleasant genial smile, got no better; so, on the morning of 24 January 1858, I telegraphed my mother to come home at once, and she arrived from Boulogne early the next day, 25 January, and from that moment never left his bedside. They were indeed a devoted couple, each vieing with the other in practising noble acts of Christian self-denial. It was, of course, this unselfishness on my father's part that impelled him to insist upon my mother going to Boulogne for those Christmas holidays, for he felt that she needed a thorough rest and change. This same self-denying feeling on his part actuated him, in his daily letters to her, to write in a bright, cheerful spirit, never once leading her to think he was so ill as he turned out to be, for in this respect he even kept me in the dark, although I was his constant companion. So when my mother hurriedly arrived back that morning of the 25th, she was terribly shocked at seeing his altered emaciated appearance; it was indeed a trying ordeal for her. But all hope was now gone, and about 6.30 on the morning of 27 January 1858 my dear father breathed his last.

That very day the school reopened; the masters had already arrived, so in hurried consultation with them it was arranged that the headmaster should interview the parents as they brought their sons back, explain to them the situation and that we were keeping on the school, at any rate for the present, giving the parents the option of taking their sons back home or of leaving them with us. I am proud to say that not one of the parents held back. On the contrary they one and all, while expressing their deepest sympathy in our heavy bereavement, assured the headmaster that they left their sons at Cromwell House with the very greatest confidence and without one single misgiving. This was indeed a great cheer and comfort to my beloved mother, and in fact to all of us.

My dear father was shortly afterwards buried at Hornsey Churchyard—Hornsey was really our parish—and it seemed to me that the whole of Highgate turned out to honour his memory.

CHAPTER II.

THE CITY IN THE 'SIXTIES.

MY dear father had insured his life for a certain sum which at his death was to enable me to go to one of the Universities (Oxford or Cambridge) with a view to my being eventually ordained and taking holy orders in the Church of England. The Rev. John Bradley Dyne, the Headmaster of the Cholmondeley Grammar School, Highgate, on hearing of this, at once came forward with the very generous offer to himself coach me and efficiently prepare me for going up to the University. My mother and I both thanked him very warmly, and taking him aside, while renewing to him my very heartfelt thanks, I explained that for many cogent reasons I must give up all idea of carrying the matter any further, as I felt that—at present, at any rate—my place was at home. He thoroughly understood my position, assuring me that he respected me for it; adding that if at any time he could be of any use to me I was to go to him at once, for, being a very old and attached friend of my father's, he felt he had a right to act towards me *in loco parentis*. We all were deeply touched and encouraged by this. I, too, felt that I had taken the right course, and never once regretted having done so. Things gradually settled down, all going on smoothly and working harmoniously, till just before the Midsummer holidays I had a thorough nervous breakdown; so when the holidays came on, by the advice of Dr. Thomas Hodgkin and our own old friend, Dr. Moger, it was decided that I should go abroad, with no settled plan beforehand, but just to take things as they came, and go wherever my inclination led me.

I started on my foreign peregrinations in due course, reaching Dunkirk, where my cousin Isidore Monteuuis and his wife gave me a hearty welcome, and I stayed at their house all the time I was there. The morning after my arrival, strolling by the seashore, I came to the swimming bath, and asked the owner, an old officer of the first Napoleon, whether he would teach me to swim. He agreed, and I was to go there every morning for an hour's lesson, which I did. When I got out of the water, he never allowed me to dry myself with a towel, but made me run about and dry naturally, which I did; and that I find is the proper course to adopt. After I had taken six lessons and was standing on the board with the rope round my waist he said to me "*Cry 'Vive l'Empereur,'*" and I did so, when he at once pushed me into deep water, without any helping rope, and said "Now you can swim," and I found I could.

That expression as above, "*Cry 'Vive l'Empereur,'*" although applying to Napoleon III, the then Emperor of the French, might almost have applied to the great Napoleon I, for many in those days maintained he was still alive. I remember when travelling from Boulogne to Marquise to visit my dear mother's native place (where a celebrated marble quarry still bears her name, "*la carrière Caroline*"), I had to travel by the diligence, the drivers of which were mostly old soldiers of Napoleon I, and they always referred to their great hero with the greatest veneration. One of them lent me a book entitled "*L'histoire de Napoléon racontée par un de ses anciens soldats*," and referring to the practice of impaling a prisoner then prevalent in the East, he described the mode of inflicting the last penalty of death thus:—

> "*On vous prie très poliment de vous asseoir sur la pointe d'une baïonnette qui est la manière de guillotiner dans ces pays là.*"

When I went to my uncle l'abbé's place at Guines, I generally went by steamer from London to Calais, and from there found my way to the Hotel Dessin, or as Sterne in his "Sentimental Journey" calls it, "Hotel Dessein" (with an *e*), from whence the proprietor sent me off to Guines in the first market cart going that way. All this is now done by train, but in those days we had to rely upon the diligences, and very comfortable travelling they were, too. It was a great treat sitting next the driver, and hearing him talk of olden days, all of the deepest interest to me. It used to be bitterly cold travelling in the winter, but we had plenty of wraps and managed to keep ourselves comfortably warm. I never thought of going inside; I quite loathed the very idea of such a thing. These old French diligences remind one of the hackneyed old story of Julius Cæsar invading Gaul (or France) "*Summa diligentia,*" which the intelligent schoolboy just back from his summer holiday in those parts translated as "on the top of the diligence" —bright youth that he was.

When I got back home my dear mother called me privately into the study and told me that my recent serious illness, from which I had only just barely recovered, had set her seriously thinking, and she had decided to sell the school and all its belongings on very advantageous terms to the Rev. Henry Stretton, and that the transfer would take place the ensuing Michaelmas Day (1858). When Dr. Dyne heard of this he expressed his thorough approval, and again reverted to the coaching scheme, but this we again gratefully declined accepting. We left, therefore, dear old Cromwell House on Michaelmas Day, 1858, and went down to live at 11 St. John's Park, Upper Holloway, but still keeping in full touch with our staunch old Highgate friends, with whom we remained just as affectionately attached as ever; and the link has never yet been broken.

As we had thus given up the school and left Cromwell House, I might at the time have truly said of myself, "Othello's occupation's gone," and it behoved me to set about getting another, and so not be a burden to my dear mother, who already had to pay for the schooling of my sister and two brothers. In order to help my attaining this laudable end our Highgate friends came forward to see what they could do towards it. Among these kind friends were the dowager Countess of Dufferin and her son, the late Earl of Dufferin, who recently died; they sat immediately behind us in church. Then came Mr. and Mrs. William Gladstone (who with their family sat immediately in front of us), Mr. Robert John Lodge, and Sir Sydney H. Waterlow. But it was Mr. William Gladstone, the great City magnate, who succeeded; he was simply indefatigable. His first offer was that I should accept a very good post in the West Indies, but we had to decline it with thanks, as I felt just then that I could not leave my dear mother. Nothing daunted, the next morning he got his wife to call on us to invite us both up to dinner that very evening, saying that their carriage would fetch us at 7, and take us back after dinner. We were just a quiet party of six—Mr. and Mrs. Gladstone, their two sons (William and Bob), and our two selves (my mother and myself). The new offer was this: that I should at once enter the office, as assistant secretary, at a commencing salary of £80 a year, of the Recife and Sao Francisco Pernambuco Railway Company, at 199 Gresham House, Old Broad Street. Of course, we at once joyfully and thankfully accepted it, so it was arranged that I should walk up that very next morning to Fitzroy Park, get there at 8.30, breakfast with Mr. Gladstone, and he would then drive me to the office of the Pernambuco Railway, introduce me to the secretary, Mr. W. H. Bellamy (the witty author of "The Gay Cavalier," "Simon the Cellarer," and other splendid songs), so that I should at once enter upon my new duties. I, of course, fell in with all these kind arrangements, and was up at Fitzroy Park the next morning in very good time: everything went off quite satisfactorily according to programme. I found my new master, Mr. Bellamy, a most genial, kind, practical man, so having duly introduced me to him, Mr. Gladstone left us, saying he would call for me at 1 and take me to lunch. His office was in 57½ Old Broad Street, just opposite the entrance to Gresham House, where our office was on the third floor. The chairman's office was on the ground floor, 62 Gresham House. His name was Mr. Robert Benson, senior partner of Robert Benson & Co. Mr. Gladstone, according to promise, turned up for me a little before 1, and the chairman happening to be with the secretary in the board-room, Mr. Gladstone took me in and introduced me in very flattering terms to the chairman, who at once took to me, and from that day he became my friend, the friendship lasting till he died in April 1875.

Mr. Gladstone took me to lunch at Joe's, the then celebrated chop-house in Finch Lane. Our lunch consisted of a delicious thick loin chop grilled before our eyes and served hot on a pewter plate, a couple of mealy potatoes in their jackets, bread, cheese, and a pat of butter, with half a pint of their celebrated London porter, drawn before our eyes in two pewter pint tankards, so that we each got full measure, and with the froth on the top. He then took me back, leaving me at the entrance of Gresham House, and saying that he would call for me that afternoon at 5 and drive me home, which he very kindly did. Of course, all this attention on his part very much impressed Mr. Bellamy and my fellow clerks, certainly having the effect Mr. Gladstone wished it to have with them, and so I was launched in my new career under the most favourable auspices possible. Our office hours were 10 to 5 (including Saturdays), with a short interval for lunch, but later on, when I got to know the ropes better, I managed as a rule to get away a little before 2 on Saturdays, inventing some plausible excuse, which Mr. Bellamy cut short by saying, "I understand you, van de Linde, in spite of your explanations, so cut along," and I cut.

My general plan was to leave our house, 11 St. John's Park, Upper Holloway, a little before 9 o'clock, to walk from there to the Highbury Station on the North London Railway, taking from there the half-past nine train to

Fenchurch Street, which got me comfortably to the office by 10 o'clock sharp, but Sir Sydney Waterlow getting to hear of this, used very kindly to manage to overtake me in his victoria and pair just as I had left Holloway Church and was walking in the Holloway Road. His offices being in Great Winchester Street, he used to drop me in Broad Street for Gresham House, on his way there. Mr. Robert Benson, the Chairman of the Pernambuco Railway (as I mentioned before), took a great fancy to me, and would never write any important letters to the Brazilian Minister in London without first showing me the letter, often getting me to fair copy the same for him, for he had a shocking handwriting, almost illegible. I remember on one occasion, being in a hurry to keep another appointment, he wrote his firm's name (Robert Benson & Co.) on a slip of paper, to be lithographed on a circular that was being sent out. The printers printed it upside down, and it went out thus unnoticed. One of his partners said to his senior, "Benson, I strongly advise you in future to sign your name standing on your head." Mr. Benson smiled, taking it all in very good part.

One morning I had to go out, and when I came back I found Mr. Benson waiting with a letter to the Brazilian Minister, which in my absence he had got one of the other clerks to fair copy for him. He showed it to me, asking me whether it was all right. I just glanced at it, and said: "No, Mr. Benson, it is all wrong." "Why, what's the matter?" he said. "Well," I said, "you "have referred to 'the Emperor of Brazil' as 'the "Emperor of the Brazils,' which won't do at all, for "he would consider it as a direct insult." "Dear me, "van de Linde, you are quite right. I am indeed "thankful that you discovered that awful mistake in "time," and he got me to re-write the letter for him. Ever after that I invariably wrote all his letters for him. I remember on that occasion he was a very long time deciding whether to put "nevertheless, notwithstanding" or "notwithstanding, nevertheless." I don't know now how we eventually settled this knotty point, and which combination we adopted. I leave my readers to choose whichever they think best. "You pays your money and you takes your choice," as the showman used to say. My personal attention on the Chairman very often interfered with my regular luncheon hour, but I did not mind that a bit. On those occasions Mr. Bellamy took me into his private room, giving me delicious cheese, fresh butter, Leman's biscuits, and an excellent glass of brown sherry—this, in fact, was the Board's invariable lunch. When I had my regular time I used to go and have lunch at Joe's chop-house in Finch Lane, but, when rather pressed, I would run over to Mabey's luncheon room in Gresham House, Bishopsgate Street end. Mabey in those days also kept the refreshment rooms at the Stock Exchange, whilst his brother catered in the Captains' room for Lloyd's over the Royal Exchange: in later years I lunched there regularly, as I very frequently had occasion to go up to Lloyd's.

Our office staff, besides Mr. W. H. Bellamy as secretary and myself as assistant secretary, consisted of Mr. Underwood Price Harris (chief accountant) and Barnes (his deputy), with a youngster. The Transfer department was managed by Robert Armour Gutteridge (brother-in-law to Harris—the two always quarrelling, although really great friends) and a youngster. When Gutteridge went to his lunch, Barnes temporarily took charge of the Transfer office, always an imaginary grievance with Harris, though it really didn't matter one iota, as the accountant's department was certainly not overworked, their really only busy time being when the Brazilian mail came in, either once a fortnight or once a month, I forget which. So, one day, Harris (nursing his grievance) went into Mr. Bellamy's office and asked if I could not take Barnes' place. Mr. Bellamy rather demurred, but Mr. Benson, happening to be in the room, said: "Oh, I think it will be all right, Bellamy. Anyhow, we might try," and I accordingly took up this temporary work in the Transfer office. My very first day resulted in a great score for me, for a transfer coming in executed by Underwood Price Harris I found to be full of mistakes, and took it into Mr. Bellamy to know what I should do. Mr. Benson was there and asked to see the transfer, and I showed it him. He had Harris in and made him correct it on the spot, the Chairman giving him a good blowing up, and telling him that "if it hadn't been for van de Linde, the consequences "might have been very serious." Poor Harris slunk out with "a flea in his ear," as the saying is, and I fancy rather regretted having thrust me into this temporary post of responsibility. However, he didn't dare to vent his spite against me, knowing that I was fully backed up by the Secretary, the Chairman, Mr. Gladstone, and by the Board generally.

We used to have a lot of official documents in Portuguese sent over from Brazil, which had to be given outside for translation. As these were more or less of a private nature, Mr. Benson and Mr. Bellamy both thought it would be well if these translations could be done in the office, and accordingly the staff was notified that any of us who liked to go in to study Portuguese might do so, and at the end of, say, three months the successful candidate would be appointed as official translator at a remunerative fee, while his out-of pocket expenses would be refunded him on a liberal scale. Accordingly the two youngsters and myself decided to go in for this, repairing twice a week between 5 and 6 p.m. to a very snuffy old man who gave us an hour's lesson at 1s. a lesson each—that is to say, 2s. a week for each of us. When Mr. Gladstone heard of this, he at once told me to go up to breakfast at his house the following morning, informing Mr. Bellamy that I should probably be late in arriving the next day at the office. I accordingly went up to Fitzroy Park, and after breakfast Mr. Gladstone drove me to the Portuguese Financial Agency in London Wall, asking to see there Mr. Da Costa Ricci, an attaché to the Portuguese Embassy, who had been specially recommended to him by the Portuguese Ambassador.

"Good morning, Mr. Da Costa Ricci," said Mr. Gladstone, "I want to introduce you to my great "friend, Mr. Gérard van de Linde, to whom I under-"stand you are very kindly going to give lessons "in Portuguese." "Certainly, Mr. Gladstone, I shall "be most happy to do so, and I suggest his coming twice "a week to me here from 9 till 10 in the morning; I "guarantee that, if he sticks to it, he will in three months' "time from now be able to undertake the post of official "translator to the Pernambuco Railway." "Thank you, Mr. Da Costa Ricci, that's splendid," said Mr. Gladstone, "nothing could be better." "But, Mr. Da Costa Ricci," said I, "what will your fee be?" "7s. 6d. an hour, or 15s. a week" (rather different to 2s. a week). I just jumped at this sudden rise from 2s. a week, but Mr. Gladstone. anticipating me, said, "And "very reasonable, too, Mr. Da Costa Ricci, so you may "expect van de Linde to-morrow morning at 9 o'clock. "Come along, van de Linde," and off we went.

Many years afterwards, about the year 1880, when I was established in business for myself in Laurence Pountney Lane (my first office), my commissionaire came in to me with a card bearing the name, "Baron Da Costa Ricci," and accordingly Baron Da Costa Ricci came in. "Good morning, Mr. van de Linde," said he, "it's some years since we first met—in "1858, I think, some 22 years ago. I am very glad to "see you here in business for yourself. I hope you are "getting on all right." "Oh, thank you, Baron. I "have got good backers in my City and West End "bankers, who have secured me several important "audits, including that of four Indian State Railways." "Oh," he said, "I know all about that, and that's why "I have come to see you. As you are a recognised "authority on railways, my Government want you to "undertake for them the audit of the Royal Trans-"African Railway, which I hope you will see your way "to do. It is a simple affair, but we have to have an "official auditor to satisfy the debenture-holders." Of course, I gladly accepted, and I said: "It is very good "of you, Baron, to have thought of me, but what gave "you the idea?" "Well, my dear friend, when in

"1858 I was a young man to whom every penny was "of importance, you very kindly added 15s. a week to "my income, getting me over many a difficulty, so now "I want to repay you if I can." I thanked him warmly, telling him that that was not the usual course adopted, for people, when they got on in the world, were rather apt to forget their earlier struggling days, and I therefore thought it reflected very much to his credit that he was such a noble exception to this rule. We have kept on the audit ever since; owing, however, to the revolution in Portugal, the word "Royal" has had to be dropped, and the railway is now called "The Trans-African Railway Company," the secretary, Mr. Thomas Castelli, being the son of the original secretary, and thus our relations both with father and son have ever been of the most friendly nature.

Mr. Bellamy was a keen fisherman, in fact, that was his one and only hobby; after a successful day's fishing he generally brought me up the next morning some delicious fresh fish caught overnight. He lived with his wife and daughter in a flat at Westminster, often inviting me over there to dinner, when he made me a present of a selection of his best songs, then extremely popular, and all the rage, in fact.

At the end of three months' time Mr. Da Costa Ricci's prognostication proved true, so he informed Mr. Bellamy that he felt I was now fitted to undertake the duties of Portuguese translator to his railway; Mr. Bellamy reported this to his board. There were present on that occasion the Chairman (Mr. Robert Benson), Mr. Wm. Gladstone, Mr. Greenfield (a stockbroker), and the Hon. S. P. Vereker (afterwards Lord Gort), formerly treasurer of the company in Brazil, and therefore a polished Portuguese scholar. It was arranged that the three candidates (the two youngsters and myself) should be examined by Mr. Greenfield and the Hon. S. P. Vereker, some ten days afterwards, at the offices of the company. It was Mr. Gladstone who purposely suggested this postponement of ten days, and for the following reason. When the board were breaking up, he stopped both these gentlemen as they were going out, and button-holeing them said: "Look here, Vereker and Greenfield, I want "you both to come up to dine at my house. This is "Friday; will next Monday suit you? We dine at 7.30." Having a great regard for Mr. Gladstone, they both accepted. When they had left the office, Mr. Gladstone turned round to Mr. Bellamy and said: "Bellamy, I want you to come too." So, of course, Mr. Bellamy accepted. The next morning Mrs. Gladstone called upon my mother and invited her and myself to dinner to meet these gentlemen, saying that she would send for us in her carriage, which would also take us back. So the fateful dinner accordingly took place on the following Monday evening, and those sitting down to it were Mr. and Mrs. William Gladstone, the Hon. S. P. Vereker, Mr. Greenfield, Mr. W. H. Bellamy, Mr. William Gladstone, Junr. (Mr. Gladstone's eldest son and partner), my mother, and myself—eight in all. The dinner went off with flying colours. Mr. Gladstone showed my mother every attention, while Mrs. Gladstone was extremely affable and friendly towards both Mr. Vereker and Mr. Greenfield. When the examination came off a week later, the two youngsters were nowhere, and with flying colours I was at once unanimously appointed on a very liberal scale of so much a folio for my translations, with the present of a bonus of £40 to cover my out-of-pocket expenses. Considering that I had only paid Mr. Da Costa Ricci for thirteen weeks at the rate of 15s. a week, besides one week, say 2s., to the original master, my out-of-pocket expenses did not even come to £10, so that I cleared a full £30 over the transaction, which came in very seasonably towards paying for our summer holiday in 1859, when my mother, my sister, and myself were invited over to spend a month at Velp near Arnheim, in Guelderland, at the estate recently purchased by Mr. Klein, just back with an immense fortune from Java. We gladly accepted this invitation; it all fitted in all right, as my two brothers were then at school at Bourbourg at my uncle's—Ferdinand Monteuuis—my mother's brother.

The property adjoining Mr. Klein's was occupied by the Duc et Duchesse de Chambord, the legitimate heirs to the French throne as belonging to the Bourbon, the elder branch of the French royal family, in contradistinction to the Orleans younger race, the last representative of which was Louis Phillipe, then a refugee at the English Court and living, through Queen Victoria's bounty, at Claremont, in Surrey. When the revolution of 1848 took place, Louis Napoleon assuming the reins of office, Louis Phillipe and his family hurriedly fled from France, he assuming the name of "Smith," and posing as an English schoolmaster. When in 1871, after the Franco-German war, Napoleon III, with the Empress Eugénie and the Prince Imperial, took refuge in England, Queen Victoria also befriended them, notwithstanding the remonstrances of Louis Phillipe, but Queen Victoria simply ignored him, giving him clearly to understand that he had better mind his own business, and not meddle with what did not concern him. The French Royalist party invariably called the Duc de Chambord "Henri V," recognising him as King of France "*de jure*" if he were not so "*de facto*." After the fall of Napoleon III and the establishment of the French Republic with Thiers as its first President, followed by General Macmahon, the latter, a thorough Royalist, actually paved the way for the return of the French Royal Family to the throne of France, the said throne being offered to the Duc de Chambord under the title of "Henri V," but the whole thing fell through owing to the obstinacy of the Duc, who absolutely declined to give up the white flag of France for the Republican tricolour.

The Duc et Duchesse de Chambord, having no children of their own, took a great fancy to my sister and myself, and often invited us over to their grounds to tea. We were both thorough French scholars, and my mother a perfect French lady, so we all got on very well together. Our royal hosts were always very courteous to my dear mother, and she in return, being a true French Royalist, entertained the greatest respect for them. I may mention in this connection that, during the wars of Napoleon I, my mother's father was a wealthy landed proprietor in the north of France, but all his fortune suddenly collapsed because Napoleon I commandeered his farm, stock, horses, cattle, fodder, and everything else his army could lay their hands upon, he being paid in exchange by "*assignats,*" which proved to be absolutely valueless. These "*assignats*" certainly gave my grandfather the right to a small property at Mayence on the Rhine, but being an out-and-out Frenchman, hating the Germans, he very soon sold the property for a mere song, after which—having had a good education—he set up at Bourbourg in the Pas-de-Calais as a schoolmaster, where he had a very great success.

Early in the year 1860, after I had been about fifteen months at the Pernambuco Railway, Mr. Robert Benson called me into Mr. Bellamy's room, when he made me the following proposal.

His firm were the London agents of the Illinois Central Railway, Mr. Robert Saville managing that department for Messrs. Robert Benson & Co. Mr. Saville had just arranged to go into partnership with a gentleman as "Robert Saville & Co., Australian Merchants," so Mr. Benson, knowing that I was thoroughly up in transfer and railway work, offered me the post at an enhanced salary, allowing me at the same time to retain my translatorship at the Pernambuco Railway. I accordingly accepted the new appointment with many thanks. Mr. William Gladstone, when he heard of it, was very much hurt, giving Mr. Robert Benson a bit of his mind by telling him that he had been poaching on his preserves, as he (Mr. William Gladstone) had intended taking me into his own office. However, it was too late to alter now, so I went to Messrs. Robert Benson & Co., whose office then was 62 Gresham House, on the ground floor, while the Pernambuco Railway was 199 Gresham House, on the third floor. The partners in the firm were Mr. Robert Benson, Mr.

Pascoe Charles Glyn, and Mr. William Ferguson, and they all three at once took a liking to me, often inviting me to their respective houses. In fact, very soon after I got to my office, Mr. Glyn invited me first to stay at his house in Eton Square, and later on at his country seat in Tunbridge Wells, where I had a very pleasant week with him, his wife, and children. I may mention that, many years afterwards, his grandson entered my office and was with me for some time until he went abroad, just the same as Cecil Gladstone—Mr. Gladstone's son—had also entered my office previously. I managed the Illinois Central Railway London agency for exactly a year until 1861, when Mr. Glyn, who had great influence with Mr. Robert Benson, suggested to him that my talents were being frittered away at the Illinois Central Railway, and that I should take up the management of their Produce Department, a much more important branch of the house. Mr. Benson gave his consent, and my old friend Robert Armour Gutteridge, the transfer clerk of the Pernambuco Railway, was appointed to take my place at the Illinois Central Railway, Barnes and Harris of the Accountancy Department between them undertaking the transfer work. Their duties then were not onerous, for by that time the railway was built and equipped, so that the accounts from Brazil had been brought down to the simplest nature.

Mr. Robert Benson and his brother William (the father of the present actor) both belonged to the Society of Friends, though as a rule, except when conversing with strict Quakers, they avoided using the recognised "Thee" and "Thou" singular, but used the plural "You" instead. One of their rich Quaker friends died, leaving an enormous fortune, the income of which during her lifetime went to his widow, and at her death the whole of the colossal corpus reverted to his fifteen nephews and nieces. Mr. Robert Benson and his brother William were appointed executors and trustees, Mr. Robert Benson taking over the sole charge of the accounts, which were kept in the office. He at once sent for me and suggested that he and I should manage the estate between us "during office hours," and that the books and vouchers should all be kept in a tin box with duplicate keys, one for himself and the other for me. It was further arranged that during the continuance of the trust I was to receive a handsome yearly honorarium; that on the death of the testator's widow I was to assist in winding-up her separate estate, but without further remuneration. All this suited me exactly, and I gladly fell in with all Mr. Benson's wishes on the subject, so we got on splendidly together, for he trusted me implicitly, and I always took care that his confidence in me should not be shaken; which indeed it never was, I am thankful to be able to say.

He was a thoroughly practical methodical man, very prompt in all his actions—his favourite expression, when he wanted anything done promptly, and that was invariably the case, being, "van de Linde, I want this done immediately, if not sooner," and I took care to follow out implicitly all his requirements. He was a past master in bookkeeping and the keeping of accounts, while I was per contra a thorough ignoramus. However, under his able, clear, and patient tuition, I soon mastered what we had in hand, so that by the time the trust was finally closed I was thoroughly *au fait* with it all. The trust lasted some three or four years, when we had to prepare the final accounts for submission to the Court. This we succeeded in doing to the thorough satisfaction of the Chancery Judge to whom these accounts were presented and at once passed by him without one single query being raised. When the two trustees (Mr. Robert and Mr. William Benson) came before him to be relieved of their duties (voluntarily rendered by them without stint of any kind) the Judge shook them both warmly by the hand and congratulated them upon placing before the Court the clearest and best set of accounts he had ever seen. Mr. Robert Benson very kindly passed this compliment on to me, adding: " You see, van de Linde, we did not do so very badly, after all." The fifteen nephews and nieces who shared the corpus of the estate between them very warmly endorsed all that the Judge had said, giving practical expression to their satisfaction by making me (with Mr. Benson's full consent) a very handsome pecuniary gift in addition to my regular remuneration. I fancy this spontaneous generous act on the part of these beneficiaries quite pleased Mr. Benson, as a crowning proof that we had discharged our duties both thoroughly and efficiently; it certainly pleased me, and I went home that night with a light heart and gladsome countenance; so " All's well that ends well," as the saying is.

The valuable experience I thus gained in the accounts of executors and trustees stood me in very great stead years after when I started for myself as a professional accountant, for that class of business became a very important branch of my office, and is so still. In former days it was the solicitors who came in for the bulk of it, but, for the last thirty years and more, we Chartered Accountants have come in for our full share of it.

We had in our office a wild Irishman named O'Grady, who was very suspicious, always locking up his desk and keeping the key on his bunch safe in his trousers' pocket. However, one day Mr. Benson called him away suddenly, not giving him time to lock his desk or take his keys. As soon as he had left the office on Mr. Benson's errand, our insurance man, Cowan (a canny Scotchman), who owed him a grudge, went and borrowed of our office messenger Jackson (an old soldier) a duplicate key, locking up O'Grady's bunch inside his desk and returning Jackson the duplicate key. When O'Grady got back he searched high and low for his keys, which were not to be found, so he sent for a locksmith to pick the lock of his desk, for we never let on about the duplicate key. When his desk was open there were his keys sure enough safe inside. "Well," said O'Grady, "I must have locked them up by accident," but how this was managed beats my comprehension. O'Grady was very fond of raspberry vinegar, a bottle of which he kept on the floor by his side. One day Cowan and another choice spirit got hold of this bottle while O'Grady was at his lunch, drank half the bottle and filled it up with red ink. When O'Grady came back to have a drink, he thought it tasted funny, so he took the bottle round to the people he had bought it off and made such a loud disturbance over it that, to get rid of him, they gave him another full bottle free of charge; so Paddy scored after all, and ever after that he kept the bottle locked up in his desk in order to avoid any possible misadventures in the future, for he somehow suspected that our friend Cowan was at the bottom of it.

Our messenger, John Jackson, was, as I said above, an old soldier. When he was in the army he was drum-major, so he always declared that "he was the right-hand man of the British army," as indeed he was in one sense. We all of us had a great regard for Jackson; he and I were great pals. His younger brother was also in our office, as his deputy, but quite a different man; but we liked him all the same, he was always so willing and obliging. I remember once saying to Jackson: "Now then, run, Jackson, for Mr. Benson is in a hurry." "Sir," said he, drawing himself up to his full height, "did you ever know the British soldier to run? Never; "and I am not going to begin doing so," and he marched away in a most dignified manner. But, although he may noι actually have run, he did Mr. Benson's errand very quickly, being back again with the answer in a very short time.

I became of age on 9 May 1861, when Mr. Glyn, with the concurrence of his two other partners, entrusted me with the procuration of the House, an honour I vastly appreciated, and held continuously till the middle of 1875, when soon after the lamented death of Mr. Robert Benson there was a dissolution of partnership, when I entered upon the accountancy career which has been my continuous profession ever since, and of which I am indeed fully proud, for I assert without fear or favour that it is indeed an honourable one.

The manager of our Marine Insurance Department was a Scotchman named Cowan; his father was Lord

Cowan, a Scotch Judge, but about the time that his friend, our second partner, Mr. William Ferguson, retired from the London firm to take up an active part in the Liverpool one (Cropper, Ferguson & Co.), Cowan also left and went back to Scotland. His place in our office was taken by a young fellow who came to us direct from Lloyd's, but as he was not much of a success, I was asked to add this branch of the business to that of the Produce, and in which I was given all necessary clerical assistance, training the fellows under me thoroughly and to my entire satisfaction. This system of combining under one responsible supervision the two important departments of Produce and Marine Insurance (with its collateral Fire Insurance), answered admirably, for I was thus able to see that all the Produce in which the firm was interested (either directly or indirectly) was at once properly covered by Marine Insurance, and on safe arrival in this country by Fire Insurance also. Thus from 1862 onwards began my very close connection with Marine Insurance, both with the London companies and "Lloyd's" over the Royal Exchange. This close connection went on uninterruptedly from 1862 to 1875, when it was temporarily severed for a couple of years, to be actively resumed again in the autumn of 1877, when, at the request of the Liverpool as well as the London Marine Insurance Companies, as also of Lloyd's, I went out to the West Indies to settle for them an important Marine Insurance case, and another one for a leading London bank; both of which I brought to a successful termination, returning home in the autumn of 1878. Soon after, my firm were appointed auditors to the Committee of Lloyd's, and very soon afterwards to Lloyd's Register of British and Foreign Shipping, both of which important appointments (with their various ramifications) we still hold to the present day.

My time at the office was always pretty well filled up. If I had any marine risks to cover, which I generally had, I would go round and show them soon after 10.30 a.m. to the various companies and the underwriters at Lloyd's, and so get them covered as soon as possible. This being done, I would proceed to our various brokers in Mincing Lane and arrange with them as to selling any produce we happened to have on hand. This produce would either be advertised and put up for sale by public auction at the sale rooms in Mincing Lane or at the Baltic, according to the particular class of the produce in question, or else offered for private sale, as the case might be. At 1 o'clock sharp I generally either lunched at the refreshment department of the Mincing Lane Sale Rooms, or else up in "the Captains' Room" at Lloyd's, according to whom I more particularly wanted to talk with quietly at either place—in the one case a produce broker, and in the other a marine underwriter.

Having done my morning's work and had my lunch, I would then return to the office to put in hand there what I had managed in the morning, and to see if anything fresh had come in meanwhile necessitating my having to go out again; and so I generally found something to fully occupy me until about 5 o'clock, when I went home after what I hoped was always a profitable day's work.

I remember that awful catastrophe just off Dungeness, the collision and sinking of the "Northfleet" (an emigrant ship outward bound to Australia) by the Spanish ship "Murillo," which, hoping to get away unnoticed, did not wait to help rescue her unfortunate victims (a very large death roll indeed), but scuttled off as fast as she could—keeping out of British waters for many years. But she had been found out and her movements quietly but carefully watched. So one day, when she thought that all danger of discovery was safely over, she quietly reappeared in British waters, when she was at once seized by the authorities and duly adjudicated upon.

I remember I was up at Lloyd's the morning after the disaster, and was talking to my friend Leonard Wakefield, when a telegraph boy handed him a message, which on opening he found to be from the late Queen Victoria expressing deepest sympathy and asking for the latest news, which Wakefield of course at once sent off to Her Majesty. He then had the telegram placed in a prominent position on the notice board for the information of members generally.

In connection with Lloyd's, I well remember the fight between Tom Sayers and Heenan. My friend Jim Anning was Tom Sayers' backer, and the next day after the fight he took his protegé round to the Baltic, to Mincing Lane, and to Lloyd's. I rather fancy that he took him on to the Stock Exchange also. At all these places our plucky British hero was welcomed with loud applause, and a substantial purse was collected for him. I was up in the Room when Jim Anning brought him up, and had the privilege of contributing my modest mite to the purse that one of the leading Lloyd's Committeemen took round. Sayers had a great ovation, and business for the time being was entirely suspended.

The underwriters at Lloyd's have ever enjoyed, and deservedly so, an exceptionally high character for honourable and straightforward dealing; for instance, when they have even not been legally responsible they have proved to be most liberal; this fact has been clearly established, not on one, but on repeated occasions, and has been the subject of unqualified commendation both before Parliamentary Committees and the full House of Commons. In fact, it was there publicly stated (*inter alia*) that the underwriters were disputing a point of law when the assured were unable to produce a certain voucher, and without which they could not possibly hope to succeed.

The assured were unable to produce the voucher, but when the underwriters found that the issue of the action depended upon this they declared that though the verdict was actually in their favour they would rather be cheated and pay the loss, amounting to some thousands of pounds, and they did so. Underwriters, too, have not hesitated to pay a loss where the merchant had made a serious mistake; for example, insuring *ship* instead of *goods*, and *vice versa*. Ships have been known to be in good faith insured from one place when they actually sailed from another place, and even under such circumstances losses arising thereout have been paid, though clearly *not* covered by the policy. Unfortunately, however, so many gross and heavy frauds have been practised upon underwriters that they need to be careful to guard against such attempted and systematic impositions, but if once they are satisfied as to *bona fides* they have always been known to act in a most liberal and fair spirit. All the foregoing is matter of history, and forms part of the Records of the House of Commons. I, too, can personally testify that some fifty years ago, when the "Tenasserim" was suddenly lost shortly after leaving Liverpool at the end of December 1865, I discovered that the open slip I had taken out for the firm of merchants, in whose office I then was, was inadvertently short by some hundreds of pounds; but on this coming to the knowledge of the underwriters they immediately increased their lines *pro rata* and so completed the risk. That very afternoon they signed a policy for the full amount, and that day week they punctually handed to me their respective cheques in payment of the total loss. I can never forget the courteous and kindly manner in which they thus graciously got me out of a serious difficulty, for, remember, I was only a clerk at the time. I have just been reminded of two recent similar acts of liberality on their part, more striking still though, for in these two latter cases the underwriters settled total losses on two policies that through oversight did not even exist—one of them, too, was for a large amount, some £15,000.

In the institution of lifeboats, Lloyd's took an initiative leading part, giving the same a practical reality by the unanimous decision of the members to encourage by liberal and effective aid the building of lifeboats, and this was actively kept up at Lloyd's until the thing was taken in hand in 1824 by the National Lifeboat Institution.

It was Lloyd's, also, who established the Patriotic Fund. The idea originated with Sir Francis Baring, M.P., and Mr. John Julius Angerstein in the early part of 1803, springing directly from the important events that were then happening, resulting in the declaration of war with France on 18 May 1803. Two months later, on 20 July 1803, there was held at Lloyd's, on the first floor of the Royal Exchange, under the presidency of Alderman Sir Brook Watson, the then chairman of Lloyd's, a general meeting of its members more largely attended than any on record, when the institution of the Patriotic Fund was decided upon by a unanimous vote. The country at large took up the matter with great enthusiasm, and generous contributions flowed in from all sides; the total amount collected by the committee during the first six years ending July 1809 amounted to £424,832. At the conclusion of peace their labours came to an end, but the accounts were not closed till 1826, when it was found that the total amount received by the Patriotic Fund from the commencement was £629,823 14s. 1d.

I have stated above that the original accounts of the Patriotic Fund were not closed until the year 1826. In connection with the Boer war they were reopened, and once more under the auspices of Lloyd's. At the commencement of the present century, being up in the "Room" (the name by which Lloyd's is generally known, just as the Stock Exchange is known as "The House"), my old friend Leonard Wakefield, one of the Committee, called me and took me up to Mr. Herbert de Rougemont, the chairman of Lloyd's Patriotic Fund. These two gentlemen informed me that it was the general wish of the Committee that my firm should accept the appointment of Professional Auditors to the Fund. I at once said we should be very happy to become Honorary Auditors to the Fund, but that we could not think of accepting any fee or remuneration of any kind, as we wished our services to be purely voluntary. Upon these gentlemen demurring, I thought it well to remind them that my connection with Lloyd's dated as far back as 1862; that the whole of the Committee were old personal friends of mine, rendering their valuable services in an absolutely voluntary capacity, and that I very humbly but decidedly claimed to come in on the same footing. They then saw and appreciated the force of my argument, there and then acquiescing in my request.

So I at once set to work on my new duties, devoting quite a week of my own time to restarting the accounts and putting everything on a proper businesslike footing. I then handed over the details of the work to a competent clerk in our office, maintaining, however, throughout, the personal supervision of everything.

Towards the end of July 1909, returning late from a country audit, I decided to dine at the City Carlton (my) Club in St. Swithin's Lane. As soon as the hall porter saw me he said he had a large wooden case for me. On asking him to open the case I found that it contained a massive solid silver salver, bearing the following inscription engraved in the centre of it:—

Presented to Gérard van de Linde, Esq., by the Trustees of Lloyd's Patriotic Fund in grateful appreciation of the Services of his Firm as Honorary Auditors, 1900 *to* 1909.

HERBERT DE ROUGEMONT,

21*st July* 1909. *Chairman.*

The Committee at the same time presented my nephew and partner, Freddie van de Linde, with a very handsome silver cigarette box, which he values very highly.

Accompanying the gift to me of the silver salver was a very flattering letter of thanks, signed by Mr. Herbert de Rougemont, as chairman, which I have had suitably framed. It now hangs in a very conspicuous place in my library, and I am naturally very proud of this graceful recognition on the part of of the Committee for our voluntary services. Needless to say we are still honorary auditors of this noble Fund, and I am hoping that a portion of the present Prince of Wales' Fund will be handed over to the Committee of Lloyd's Patriotic Fund to deal with in the same efficient manner as they have administered this Fund ever since they took it up again in 1900.

Lloyd's medal for the Preservation of Life at Sea is also always highly prized by the brave recipient of this honour.

These are just a few of the instances that have caused Lloyd's name to be respected, honoured, and (I think I may add) loved in every part of the globe.

I might fill a volume were I to attempt recounting a tithe even of their noble self-denying acts. A visit to Lloyd's is indeed well worth paying. The genial secretary, Admiral Inglefield, will, I venture to think, gladly grant visitors this favour, and if it does not happen to be Committee Day, to allow them to inspect the valuable relics and treasures carefully arranged in due order in the Committee Room, not forgetting the celebrated "Lutine Bell," with its very interesting historical reminiscences.

The following good-natured skit, which I reproduce from my *Biography of a Lloyd's Policy,* will, I am sure, prove of general interest to my readers. The names are all *bona fide* ones, and the bulk of them still exist. Very many of them I got to know very well, and to make them *nolens volens* underwrite my risks for me—good, bad, or indifferent. I am thankful to say that they were not losers in the long run; on the contrary, it was as a rule my pleasing duty to hand them periodically a substantial cheque in settlement of their underwriting account with the firm. The skit in question is headed:—

"A Literal, Critical and Poetical Transcript from Lloyd's," and reads thus:—

"A *Black* and a *White,* with a *Brown* and a *Green,*
And also a *Grey* at Lloyd's room may be seen;
With *Parson* and *Clark,* then a *Bishop* and *Pryor,*
And *Waters,* how strange, adding fuel to the fire.
While, at the same time, 'twill sure pass belief,
There's a *Winter,* a *Garland, Furze, Budd,* and a *Leaf.*
With *Freshfield,* and *Greenhill, Lovegrove* and a *Dale,*
Though there's never a breeze, there's always a *Gale:*
No music is there though a *Whistler* and *Harper*.
There's a *Blunt* and a *Sharp,* many flats, but no sharper.
There's a *Daniell,* a *Samuel,* a *Sampson,* an *Abell*—
The first and the last write at the same table.
Then there's *Virtue* and *Faith* there, with *Wylie* and *Rasch,*
Disagreeing elsewhere, yet at Lloyd's never clash;
There's a *Long* and a *Short, Small, Little,* and *Fatt,*
With one *Robert Dewar,* who ne'er wears his hat.
No drinking goes on though there's *Porter* and *Sack,*
Lots of Scotchmen there are beginning with *Mac*—
McDonald to wit, *McIntosh* and *McGhie,*
McFarquhar, McKenzie, McAndrew, Mackie.

Though no tradesmen or shopmen are found, yet herewith,
Come a *Taylor*, a *Saddler*, a *Paynter*, a *Smyth* ;
Also *Butler* and *Chapman*, with *Baker* and *Glover*,
Come up to Lloyd's room their bad risks to cover.
Fox, *Shepherd*, *Hart*, *Buck*, likewise come every day,
And though many an ass there is only one *Bray*.
There's a *Mill* and a *Miller A-dam* and a *Poole*,
A *Constable*, *Sheriff*, a *Law*, and a *Rule*,
There's a *Newmann*, a *Niemann*, a *Redman*, a *Pitman*,
But to rhyme with the last there is no other fit man ;
These, with *Young*, *Cheap*, and *Lent*, *Luckie*, *Hastie*, and *Slow*
With dear *Mr. Allnutt*, *Allfrey*, and *Auldjo*.
Are all the queer names that at Lloyd's I can show.

About the year 1862 witnessed the commencement of hostilities in America between the "Federals" in the North, and the "Confederates" in the South, and generally known known as "The Confederate War."

Our intimate connection with the Illinois Central Railway naturally led us all at the office to closely watch the course of events with the very deepest interest.

I remember when the first letters from the other side, after the declaration, came over to our office, we were asked to excuse all shortcomings, for so many of their officials had gone to the front, among others Ackerman, the secretary; Burnside, the treasurer, who became "Admiral Burnside"; Sherman (of Duncan, Sherman & Co.), a director, who became General Sherman, and many others. A partner of the firm of one of our American correspondents was also reported to us as having gone to the front, and that was Grant, afterwards General Grant, and subsequently President of the United States of America. It was Grant who pursued the war to the bitter end, and brought it eventually to a termination, but at what a sacrifice of human life. He simply had an absolute disregard for human life, so, knowing that the North *numerically* outnumbered the South, he just pitted one army against another until both were wiped out. He then repeated the operation *de novo* until the Confederates were practically annihilated, and the remnant sued for terms at any price, and they got them too.

I shall never forget the stirring incident known as "The 'Trent' affair," when two Confederate agents (Slidell and Mason) were forcibly removed from "The Trent," a Royal Mail steamer, by officers of a Federal man-of-war, and taken off as prisoners. The sensation universally roused in England by this unwarrantable outrage was simply terrific. As regards Slidell and Mason they were only the second and minor consideration, the paramount one being that the honour of the British Flag had been violated and outraged. The Government, backed by the whole nation, sternly demanded instant reparation by the two agents being at once set at liberty and unreservedly given up, failing which England would at once recognise the South (the Confederates) and declare war against the North (the Federals). For days the question of peace and war hung tremblingly in the balance, and America made no secret of the fact that, if England declared war, America would repudiate all her pecuniary obligations.

Consequent upon this threat very large quantities of American securities were hurriedly transferred from English to Dutch names, when at the very darkest and gloomiest moment the North (Federals) caved in and surrendered the two men, thus saving the situation. As a matter of fact, Lord Palmerston (with an enormous backing behind him) was all for recognising the South (Confederates); and in this he had the support of the French nation, as well as that of the English nation.

At the close of the Confederate War and when peace had been declared, Jefferson Davis, the first and only Confederate President, came over to this country, and while in London paid a visit at our office to Mr. Robert Benson, who, with his usual natural grace, received his guest courteously, but I hardly fancy took very kindly to him. I was called in on some point, and at Mr. Benson's suggestion Jefferson Davis asked me a question which I was able to answer satisfactorily. He spoke with the usual American nasal twang, and was an ideal type of a typical Yankee, with his narrow lantern jaw, hollow cheeks, his straight black hair, clean shaven face, with the exception of a long narrow pointed "goatee" on his chin in true Yankee fashion. He reminded me very much of Dickens' American counterparts as so graphically portrayed in his inimitable "Martin Chuzzlewit," in connection with "Eden," which I am credibly informed stood for the "Freelands" of the Illinois Central Railway in its early struggling days, which it has long since got over, and is now a thoroughly flourishing concern—its $100 stock standing at $110, when in the struggling early days it stood as low as $60 (that is to say, at 40 per cent. discount). Richard Cobden was a large holder of this stock, and not infrequently came round to our office to consult Mr. Benson about it, when Mr. Benson invariably handed him over to me. I wonder, if Cobden had been living now, whether he would have still been a Free Trader! I rather fancy not.

Shortly after the conclusion of the Confederate War, matters soon settled down again to their former normal condition. The South forgot their grievances and were reconciled to the North, the whole country, North and South, becoming once again "The United States," not only in name but in solid reality as well. Business relations were again resumed, and a great demand set in to purchase iron rails from this country, and to ship them to the States. The firm in Gresham House having good business agents over there, soon secured the lion's share of these purchasing orders. We accordingly purchased these rails, mostly from the Welsh manufacturers, but occasionally also from a firm of ironmasters on the north-east coast. Their rails, however, were not looked upon with much favour, for although being hard (a good quality *per se*), they were at the same time brittle and apt to break. On the other hand the Welsh rails, though somewhat softer, were more malleable, and therefore more easily handled. This new branch of our business devolved upon me, as also the chartering of suitable ships. The "template" pattern was invariably of two kinds, viz. the 50 lb. (to the yard) Erie pattern, and the 56 lb. (to the yard) Pennsylvania Fish Plate pattern, and we invariably purchased these rails in parcels of 1,000 tons, and their multiples. The principal ports of destination were New York, Brooklyn, or Jersey City for the North, and Galveston for the South.

Galveston had a nasty unsafe bar outside her harbour, so I had to choose a vessel of a light draught, say 450 tons register, giving her a maximum of 600 tons of rails to carry, chartering, when available, a ship owned by William Yeo, of Bideford, a trustworthy, reliable ship-owner in great favour with the underwriters. But on one occasion, not being able to secure one of Yeo's handy vessels, I had to be content with chartering an American one, the "Neversink," of 450 tons register, giving her 600 tons, and her destination was Galveston. The underwriters always charged a higher rate of premium for Galveston than for New York, &c., the rate of insurance varying for both ports according to the season of the year. I, however, never had any difficulty as to this, for I knew my underwriters personally, both at the marine companies, as well as up at Lloyd's, so we invariably fixed the rate of insurance ("premium of insurance") between us to our mutual satisfaction, this being the case with the "Neversink." She got in her cargo all right, starting for Galveston in due course. But just as she got outside Galveston Bar, she struck a sunken reef, went down bodily, and became a total wreck. I immediately went up to the Room, and the underwriters at once agreed to pay 90 per cent. of the sum insured on account, there being reasonable hopes that the remaining 10 per cent. would be recovered out of the salvage, and in a week's time (to the day) they handed me their respective cheques for the 90 per cent. on account. Meanwhile I had asked for their instructions as to the salvage arrangements, and they gave me the stereotyped answer: "Act as if you were uninsured." I understood what they meant, and so we at once telegraphed our agents at Galveston to make the best terms possible, wiring them to me before finally closing. The very next day we got their reply, worded as follows: "Salvage charges 50 per cent. ('Rail for rail') on all cargo recovered; no cure, no pay." As I was satisfied that these were reasonable and, to us, advantageous terms, I did not wait to notify the underwriters in the Room, but we at once telegraphed our agents at Galveston accepting and confirming the offer, begging them to proceed at once with the salvage, which they accordingly did. By the earliest available mail from their side we received their letter confirming everything, and adding that in accordance with the 50 per cent. ("Rail for Rail") salvage charge, as the railway company were sadly in want of all the rails they could get, they had arranged with the salvors to buy their 50 per cent. ("Rail for Rail") at a reasonable rate, paying them in hard cash and sending off at once the whole portion of the cargo thus salved to the railway company, who were only too glad to get them, paying the full contract price for the delivery, as the sea water, if anything, had improved rather than deteriorated the rails. While the salvors were about it they unwittingly came across another cargo of rails of exactly the same pattern out of a ship adjoining the "Neversink." This they recovered, and the whole of the two cargoes, 1,200 (not 600) tons in all, were thus salved and despatched to the railway company, nobody outside being one bit the wiser. As we had purchased of the salvors their own half on very moderate terms, but better than they would have obtained in the usual course, and with which they were perfectly satisfied, I was actually able to return the underwriters the 90 per cent. they had paid us on account, and even then we secured a fair margin of profit on the transaction. This was the one and only loss I had ever to claim on shipments of rails from our underwriters; and even then I firmly believe that had we chartered one of Yeo's vessels, with a careful captain, instead of the "Neversink," our cargo would never have sunk, but, as it turned out, it was all for the best, and everyone was satisfied.

Mr. Pascoe Glyn's elder brother having died in 1864, he took his place at Glyn's Banking House, 67 Lombard Street, becoming their leading partner until the day of his death. When he left us, Mr. Robert Benson was joined by Mr. Robert James Wigram and Mr. Richard Henry Glyn (Mr. Pascoe's cousin), the title of the firm still remaining Robert Benson & Co. They were both nice, genial men, with whom I got on all right. Soon afterwards we moved our offices from 62 Gresham House to 10 King's Arms Yard, where we had the first and all the upper floors. It was a decided improvement. I had a large corner of the office all to myself, with my special table; at my right was an extra door leading into the partners' room, and at my back was a long, high table, where I had my lieutenants always handy by me at my beck and call, everything being thus arranged very comfortably. The partners lunched upstairs on the second floor, whilst the staff were provided with lunch, at the firm's expense, on the third floor; and Jackson (who was unmarried), occupied the remaining rooms on the third floor, with the exception of the staff luncheon room, being thus always on the spot and readily available.

I had plenty to occupy myself, as usual, with at our new offices, which were very handy both for Lloyd's, the various Marine Insurance Companies, and Mincing Lane, where I was always very welcome, making personal friends of the underwriters up in the Room, who, when I started in business in 1877, became important clients.

The produce brokers in Mincing Lane, although not giving me actual business, were also useful to me in many ways. It sometimes happened that, in the course of my business, technical points cropped up, when I could always rely upon their help to solve my difficulty, so putting me straight with my clients.

The intelligent reader will doubtless remember that the year 1866 was a more or less disastrous one for the credit of the mercantile community generally, for it was in 1866 (and, if I remember aright, on Ascension Day, when the Bank of England directors did not meet till after they had attended church service) that the house of Overend & Gurney, without any previous note of warning, suddenly suspended payment, bringing down with them in their failure many an unfortunate, innocent merchant and trader, for their paper was considered as good as a Bank of England note, and was held at home and abroad to a fabulous amount. The only fortunate being who unwittingly profited by their downfall was my old friend, Pat Nickalls, a young but rising stock-jobber. His elder brother, Tom Nickalls, was well known on the Stock Exchange as "The Erie King," because for many years he had practically controlled that speculative but favourite market known as the Erie Market.

The day before the suspension of Overend & Gurney their shares stood at a fabulous premium, while the very next day they went down to an equally fabulous discount, sustaining, as a Yankee friend of mine aptly termed it, "a perpendicular fall."

Well, then, on this very day previous, my friend Pat Nickalls, in the ordinary course of business, sold to a broker a large parcel of Overend & Gurney shares, hoping to buy them back during the course of the day at such a price as, with the turn of the market, would leave him a fair margin of profit. Not a bit of it, the shares kept on steadily rising all that day with no sellers, and nothing but buyers on the market. Poor Pat went home, as he afterwards told me, in a terrible state of mind, fearing that he, through that one perfectly legitimate transaction, was practically an irretrievably ruined man. Next morning he went to the City in a dazed condition, when just fancy his amazement at learning that the doors of the well-known house of Overend & Gurney were closed once and for all, never to reopen again. The shares, which all the previous day had been rising to a fabulous premium, at once dropped to an equally fabulous discount. Before going home that afternoon he bought back those shares at practically his own price, realising a handsome profit on the transaction. From that time everything prospered with him, for he was looked upon as one of the lucky ones, and everyone knows that nothing succeeds like success, and that was his fortunate experience. When in 1870 I went to live at Lyndhurst, Bexley Heath, he was living not far off at Little Danson, and we became firm friends. Twenty years after, when I moved in 1890 to Glebe Knoll, Bromley, he moved about the same time to Chislehurst, was knighted, and became Sir Paterson Nickalls.

CHAPTER III.

Some Literary and Dramatic Memories: With an Excursion to France.

My father was a very great admirer of the late Charles Dickens, and simply devoured his works as soon as ever they came out. The one that at the time created the greatest sensation was "Pickwick." It was brought out in twenty monthly numbers, published at 1s. each. The first number appeared in April 1836 and the last number in November 1837, but June 1837 was dropped out, and, therefore, to make up for it, November 1837 was published as a double number —Nos. 19 and 20. My father had just come over to England at the time, and told me that as soon as ever these numbers appeared they were simply snatched up at once, and as each number was finished the readers gave a sigh of despair; waiting for the following month to come when they would get their further number. "Sketches by Boz" was the first work Dickens ever published under the above pseudonym of "Boz," and I am told that the reason he chose this name was because it was an abbreviation of Moses, the pet name of his youngest brother, whose real name was Moses, in recognition of "The Vicar of Wakefield." "Moses," when pronounced by anyone with a cold in his head, became "Boses," the abbreviation of which was "Boz." My father told me that this pseudonym was kept inviolate for some time, and as the book was a great favourite with the general reading public, they kept constantly asking, "I wonder who the Dickens is Boz?" little knowing that they were spotting his real name. "Sketches by Boz" first appeared in the old "Monthly Magazine," as also in "The Evening Chronicle." The sketches were collected and published in two volumes in 1837, illustrated by George Cruickshank. In 1839 the two series were issued together in one volume, again illustrated by George Cruickshank. It was my great privilege to hear Charles Dickens read, and on that memorable occasion he read to us "The Boots at the Holly Tree Inn" and "The Tuggs at Ramsgate." It was indeed a thrilling occasion, intensified by watching the rapt attention of the audience—a very large one, too.

In the early days when we lived in Cromwell House, Highgate, I heard the original George Grossmith (the father of the first actor of that name) give a reading at the Highgate Literary and Scientific Institution, choosing for his subject the trial scene of "Bardell v. Pickwick," and that, too, I very much enjoyed.

When I lived at Bexley Heath, and again at Bromley, I often used to explore the Dickens country. I remember once taking the train to Rochester and visiting the alms-houses there called the "Watts' Charity," immortalised in Dickens's Christmas number, "The Seven Poor Travellers." I know the inn well where the supper came from. From Rochester I walked on to Gad's Hill—the residence of Charles Dickens, and then on to Gravesend, where I had a late lunch at the Clarendon Hotel, and then walked back to Bexley Heath by way of Dartford.

Another of my favourite jaunts was to take the North Kent train from Bexley to Rochester, and from there to walk through Lord Darnley's splendid park—" Mereworth "—to Cobham, visiting at Cobham the quaint old colony of almshouses there, and at the back of the same the monuments to the memory of the Darnley family, the Lords of the Manor of Cobham. After that, I went to the " Leather Bottel," and sat in the special parlour, in Dickens's chair. While lunch was preparing, I went outside and saw the site where stood the original wonderful stone which " Pickwick " discovered with great glee. This walk through Lord Darnley's estate and the village of Cobham to the " Leather Bottel " is graphically described by Dickens in " Pickwick," when he, Winkle, and Snodgrass visited their friend Tupman, whom they expected to find in the depths of despair, and did find eating a very good lunch. I got to be very friendly with the landlord of the " Leather Bottel," and when I told him that I was a personal friend of Sir Sydney Waterlow's, instead of giving me the ordinary visitors' book, he at once brought me out the special visitors' book given to him by Sir Sydney H. Waterlow himself, and I afterwards inscribed my name in this sacred book whenever I went there. From the " Leather Bottel " I took a nice walk down the hill on the left to Sole Street Station, where I took the London, Chatham and Dover train back to Bromley Station, when I lived there; but previously, when I lived at Bexley Heath, I had to hire a trap to drive me from Cobham to Gravesend. I have mentioned previously that, taking my cue from " David Copperfield," I had every reason to suppose that Charles Dickens knew his Highgate well. When

I was staying at Yarmouth I visited at Gorleston "Peggoty's" old tenement, a flat-bottomed boat turned upside down. When staying at Broadstairs I also visited Bleak House, connected with "David Copperfield," and also Canterbury. Another of my favourite jaunts was to go to Chigwell in Essex, immortalised by Charles Dickens in "Barnaby Rudge." I was living then at the time at Tottenham, so it was an easy walk there through lovely country.

Dickens, when so graphically describing the old Maypole Inn at Chigwell, had evidently in his mind its exact counterpart, the King's Head, then flourishing in those days, and from 1780 up to the present day; the old hostelry still exists in all its glory at the present time, and is frequently called "Dickens." Chigwell is an old-world place, well deserving a pilgrimage. I used to take the early morning train on a Friday to the Forest Hotel—have a coach drive in the morning, lunch at the hotel, another coach drive in the afternoon, sleep at the hotel, and do the same thing the following day. In this way I got in four coach drives, and thoroughly investigated a lot of the country which Dickens describes in "Barnaby Rudge."

My parents were very fond both of the legitimate drama and of music of all kinds, including opera. Whenever they went to any of these entertainments they invariably took me with them. An old friend of ours, Mrs. Frost, wife of the Rev. George Frost, of Kensington, was the ground landlady of Sadler's Wells Theatre, having, in her own right, the permanent use of the large stage box on the first tier, which she was always pleased to lend us. Whenever we went, my mother generally wrote a day or two beforehand to Mr. Samuel Phelps, the lessee, and suggested the plays we would like to see, among others the following:—Shakespeare's "As you like it," "The Tempest," and "The Merchant of Venice," all got up in high-class style. Phelps always acceded to her wishes, putting on the playbill, "By Special Request," and bowing to my mother, who was sitting in front in the stage box.

I think "As you like it" a most beautiful pastoral play. I was rather amused with the way Mr. Marston, Phelps' colleague, used to mouth his part. You could always know he was coming on the stage, because he began talking in the wings before he came on. Notwithstanding this, he was a good actor. The play of "As you like it" commends itself to me by being so full of well-known quotations, such as:—"All the world's a stage, and all the men and women merely players," also "A fool, a fool, I met a fool," recited by the melancholy Jacques, finishing up with "Motley's the only wear."

"The Tempest" was another beautiful play, where Miss Fanny Josephs as Ariel sings in Act V, Scene 1, this lovely melody:—

"Where the bee sucks, there suck I,
"In a cowslip's bell I lie;
"There I couch when owls do cry.
"On the bat's back I do fly,
"After summer merrily:
"Merrily, merrily, shall I live now
"Under the blossom that hangs on the bough."

Miss Josephs had a sweet voice, and was a bright little actress, thoroughly well trained by Phelps (who always saw that both actors and actresses alike did themselves and him justice), so that her part of "Ariel" suited her exactly, and she gained in it a well deserved success; being so real and simple, it all came to her quite naturally, and without the slightest effort whatever. Mr. Phelps' leading actress was Miss Helen Faucit, who afterwards became Lady Martin.

"The Merchant of Venice" was a masterly play, in which Phelps, as "Shylock," surpassed himself. I cannot now remember who took the part of "Portia," but whoever it was did it effectively. The beauty of Shakespeare's plays is that they invariably combine light comedy with tragedy; that is at it should be.

Another piece that we much enjoyed was a little comedietta entitled "The First Night," in which Phelps took the parts of the Frenchman, the leader of the orchestra, and the father of the heroine. It was all simply splendid; Phelps made an idealistic Frenchman, his gesticulations being perfect. Many years afterwards the piece was revived at "His Majesty's Theatre" by Sir Herbert Beerbohm Tree, he, too, entering into the full spirit of this bright little gem of a play.

We were also fond of the little theatre called the "Strand," for which our friend, Mr. Clarkington, the eminent photographer of Regent Street, often got us passes. The manageress was Miss Ada Swanborough; she took the leading part, but the great star was Miss Marie Wilton, now Lady Bancroft. She and Miss Saunders were just grand in burlesque. I remember one or two of these—"Kenilworth," for instance, where they both came on as young swells, and Marie Wilton, with a lackadaisical voice, said :

" I so very seedy am,
" I'll take a pot of dimidiam and dimidiam." (Half-and-half.)

The part of Amy Robsart was taken by Miss Ada Swanborough, who wore for the occasion an enormous crinoline, which saved her life; for when the trap-door incident occurred, and she was supposed to be killed by being pushed down below, one of the actors rushed on to the stage, joyfully shouting:

" Saved, saved, saved, for the last grand scene,
" Her feet went through, but not her crinoline."

The part of good Queen Bess, who was got up magnificently, was taken by Clarke, a stalwart male actor in queenly attire. Queen Bess was supposed to have come to Tilbury Fort on a penny steamer, landing there in great state, and shouting out in a stentorian voice: " Ease her, stop her, turn her astarn." The effect was indeed ludicrous. Another piece that we much enjoyed was the burlesque of " The Maid and the Magpie," where Clarke took the part of the drunken father, heavily roped, and thus brought before the magistrate. He had not yet got over his drinking bout, so the magistrate said to him: " Prisoner, you are tipsy!" " No, your honour, only rather tight," was the prisoner's hiccupy reply. Another theatre we used to visit was the Adelphi, with Wright, Paul Bedford, and Madame Celeste in " The Green Bushes." Madame Celeste took the part of Miami. I shall never forget Paul Bedford's voice in " I believe you, my boy "; it was rich in Irish brogue. We also loved seeing Charles Matthews (one of the most polished actors of the day) with Madame Vestris, his wife. Charles Matthews was splendid in impecunious parts, one of his best being " Lend me 5s."

He was the father of the present Sir Charles Matthews, K.C.

We heard Toole when he first came out, with Dillon and Miss Mellon, in "Belphégor," the part of "Belphégor" being taken by Dillon, while Toole, who played the big drum, took the part of the clown. I shall never forget his calling out to the audience, "Alive, alive, alive-O!" But his particular piece, to my mind, was "Ici on parle francais." It was most amusing to hear him in the part of the landlord of the apartments, bearding one of his trying French lodgers by saying to him, "I vill tell ze Lord Mayor of you." To which the Frenchman replied: "Pouf! for ze Lord Mayor, I vill blow his nose for him," meaning he would hit him on the nose, then throwing his boots out of the door, shout out: "Clean my duc de Vellingtons, garçon."

Buckstone and Compton, of the Haymarket, were, of course, inimitable in "Box and Cox," and so were dear old Mr. and Mrs. Keely, their favourite piece being "Good for Nothing." But the actor whom I think appealed to me the most was Robson, of the "Olympic." He was a comedian of the highest order, and would have been the same as a tragedian, were it not that his being short of stature was a disadvantage. However, occasionally he launched out into real tragedy, and then he was simply grand. His celebrated piece for this was "The Porter's Knot," a most pathetic drama; but he was also very good in light comedy. I remember him very well in "Boots at the Swan," where two maiden ladies, interviewing him, questioned him about his experiences. He began: "Ladies, when I was a little child, only so high, I was seized by gypsies." "Oh," said the ladies, "how very interesting." Robson went on: "who stripped me." "Oh, how shocking!" exclaimed the spinsters. "But remember, ladies, I was only so high!" and they forgave him.

Another of his favourite parts was in the burlesque of "Mazeppa," where he was supposed to be bound on to the back of a wild horse and so thrust into the desert. The wild horse was really a wooden rocking-horse from the Lowther Arcade; Robson, as "Mazeppa," saying in a tragic voice: "Bring forth the fiery untamed steed from the wilds of Lowther Arcadia." He was then strapped on to the rocking-horse, and pulled back off the stage by ropes. It had a very ludicrous effect.

But I had other amusements in these early days, and not the least were my somewhat frequent opportunities of foreign travel. On a certain Monday morning in the summer of 1862, my sister and myself boarded the South Eastern Railway steamer at Dover, and in due course arrived at Calais. My old friend, Monsieur Dessein, was expecting us, and after an excellent *déjeuner* (lunch) at his celebrated hotel, having kindly secured for us the coupé, holding the three of us very comfortably, he saw us off safely by the diligence to Bourbourg (18 miles off), where we stayed a couple of full days with cousin Benjamin Vandenbroucque. Tuesday morning (the day after our arrival) Benjamin took us over in his waggonette to his seaside residence at Gravelines, an easy drive of four miles from Bourbourg, where he gave us an excellent *déjeuner,* which we all thoroughly enjoyed. The next day (Wednesday) we spent with my other cousin, Ferdinand Monteuuis, and his genial family, who received us with open arms, Benjamin and his wife being, of course, of our party.

On the following morning (Thursday) they, having already secured for us the coupé again, all saw us off in the diligence to Dunkerque, an easy eleven miles, where we arrived in good time for early lunch at the house of my cousin Isidore Monteuuis, with whom we stayed till the following Saturday morning. While at Dunkerque (or Dunkirk in English) I revisited my old friend the swimming master, who, after making me say once more " Vive l'Empereur," pitched me head foremost into deep water, and when he saw me come up all right, like a cork on the top of the water, he said to me: " Tiens, mon ami, tu nages très bien maintenant et n'as plus besoin de leçons, adieu et au revoir." We much enjoyed our short visit to Dunkirk. They were so truly kind, just like they were at Bourbourg.

On the following Saturday morning we took the early diligence from Dunkirk straight away for Calais, just stopping to change horses at Bourbourg, where our cousins, the Monteuuis and the Vandenbroucques, met us with many osculatory greetings. We were fortunate in again securing the coupé, arriving in good time at Calais, a distance of 29 miles from Dunkirk. The diligence put us down at Calais at the Hotel Dessein, where Mr. Dessein was on the look out for us with a nice appetising *déjeuner,* which we partook of with great gusto, thoroughly enjoying it, for our 29-miles diligence drive had given us a splendid appetite, fully bearing out the Latin proverb: *Fames condimentum optimum.*

After lunch we drove off in a one-horse carriage of Mr. Dessein's (not a market cart this time) to Guines, a short easy drive, where we arrived early that afternoon, being received by Uncle l'Abbé with open arms and renewed osculatory demonstrations all round, in which my cousin Eugène Monteuuis joined. He had been staying at Boulogne at the house of his brother Auguste; hearing we were expected at Guines, he had come over with a pressing invitation from his brother and his wife that, on leaving Guines for Boulogne, we should make Mr. and Mrs. Auguste's house our headquarters. So it was arranged accordingly. Uncle l'Abbé kindly invited Eugène to be one of our party, but out of regard to Monsieur le Curé's aged and only servant (Marie), Eugène and I slept at the hotel, my sister occupying the state spare bedroom known as "La chambre à coucher de Monseigneur l'Eveque," the Bishop occupying it whenever he came to stay with my uncle. My uncle reminded both Eugène and myself that we were to take all our meals with them *en famille,* and only, therefore, to order two bedrooms: nothing more.

We spent a happy time at Guines, regretting only that our time was so short. The next morning (Sunday), after delicious café au lait, roll, and farm fresh butter, while uncle and Eugène went to mass at my uncle's church adjoining, I took my two ladies to the Bois de Guines and thence to the Champ du Drap d'Or (The Field of the Cloth of Gold), where our English king, Henry VIII, met Francis I of France, at a grand tournament and military sports, duly recorded by the heralds of the day and handed down by the historians with due pomp and ceremony.

Having thus feasted our eyes and memories of the past with all the ancient chivalry thereto attaching, we brought our thoughts back again to the more prosaic times of the then present day (1862). So having bid *au revoir* to Le Champ du Drap d'Or we wended our way to the canal, and, watching the barges lazily wending their way to Guines, we followed them, thoroughly enjoying the novel scene. These barges are sometimes towed by a horse or a mule, but more generally by a couple of men holding a pole between them at the end of the barge's rope. This reminds me of the story of the man on a walking tour with a knapsack at his back; he had tramped along for some distance when, feeling a bit tired, he sat down to rest a bit before starting off again. Just then he saw a barge coming along towed by two men as above indicated. "By Jove, the very thing," said he. "I say, my good fellows, what will you charge to take me to Guines" (some six miles off). "Well," answered the boss, who was a bit of a wag in his way, "if you get on board the barge as a regular "passenger the charge will be three francs, but if you "help us tow the barge, turn and turn about, it will only "be one franc." "All right," said our hero, "I'm on," so throwing his knapsack into the barge he caught hold of the pole and helped to tow the barge the whole way to Guines, leaving the other two to share the "turn and turn about between them." When he got to his destination he once more shouldered his knapsack, at the same time tendering the boss the one franc agreed upon between them. But the boss, though a bit of a wag, was also honest in his way, so he told our friend to put the one franc back in his purse and go in with them to drink a "choppe" (tankard of brown beer) at their expense. He accepted their offer, and had the "choppe," wishing them "*au revoir*" and so they parted good friends.

On our way back to my uncle's we met an old Highgate schoolfellow, Thoumin, the son of Dr. Thoumin, the local medico, who at once recognised both my sister and myself. We walked back together, he shook hands with my uncle, whom he knew well, and then invited us to supper at his father's, appealing to my uncle for his permission. My uncle immediately gave his willing consent, for he knew Dr. Thoumin, and so felt sure that it would be all right; we consequently accepted the invitation and spent a pleasant time with my old schoolmate, for we had lots to talk about. In this way the time passed quickly when it came to wish them good-night and return to Uncle l'Abbé's, where I left my sister, and then Eugène and I went together to our hotel, soon getting in between the sheets and sleeping the sleep of the just.

Next morning (Monday), waking thoroughly refreshed after our good night's rest, Eugène and I were both up betimes and trotted off merrily to the "Presbytère," to rejoin Uncle l'Abbé and my sister for "café au lait complet." We were met at the front door by Marie with her usual smiling face, who ushered us into uncle's private sanctum and not into the big "*salon,*" which for the moment we could not make out. But the mystery was soon solved; and after the usual French osculatory greeting we sat down to our first breakfast, and then Uncle l'Abbé told us of the pleasant surprise he had in store for us, and why we were breakfasting in his small sanctum instead of in the big salon.

He began by asking us how long we could stop; could we stop a fortnight? We shook our heads gloomily—then a week at any rate? We again shook our heads sadly, explaining that we were due home that very Monday week, and that the longest we could stay was the following Wednesday morning. Uncle l'Abbé smiled resignedly, and said: "Well, you are not like one of "my neighbouring vicaires (curates), who only recently "left me. He came to stop a week, but at the end of "the week, as we both got on so well together, I invited "him to stay another week, which he did. At the end "of that week I renewed my invitation for another week, "but with tears in his eyes he said he had already stayed "a full fortnight, and must go back home. On my "asking him what was his hurry, he replied that he "always made a point of changing his shirt, and putting "on a clean one, once a fortnight."

My uncle then added that, as we could on this occasion only make a very short stay, he had arranged for a clerical dinner for that very day at 12 o'clock, to which he had invited the Bishop, the Grand Vicaire, and all his clergy from the adjoining parishes, as also the Mayor and "*adjoint*"; he added that we were all lunching together in the adjoining salon, where half-a-dozen neighbourly females of his parish were helping Marie lay the cloth and prepare the dinner—which indeed was a wonderful repast. Uncle had written out the menu—an elaborate, I might almost say an endless one, for we sat down at 12 o'clock sharp, and only rose from the table at 6 p.m., when the Bishop, clergy, and all the guests, ourselves included, rose to attend vespers in uncle's church.

Our first dish was "Jambon de York provenant de Guines" ("York ham coming from Guines"), which Marie cut up at the sideboard, handing a plate to each guest, doing the same with a magnificent salmon.

But when it came to the leg of mutton, Uncle l'Abbé told Marie to put the joint before him as he would carve it, which he did, leaving only a very small portion on the bone. As he carved the slices he placed them neatly on a large dish, which he told Marie to hand round for the guests to help themselves, which she proceeded to do. But, unfortunately, she began with a raw-boned vicaire, who calmly took the whole dish, and, thinking of the York ham and the salmon, fancied that that was his portion, to the dismay of the other guests, who saw nothing but a meagre mutton-bone in front of them. But my uncle at once rose to the occasion; turning to the "vicaire" (curate), he said to him: "I hope Monsieur le Vicaire you have what you fancy?" His reply was: "Thank you, Monsieur le Curé (vicar), I should like a little more fat, if you please." My uncle cut the fat off the bone and put it on a plate, which Marie handed to him. He accepted it with a "*merci*" (thank you), and quietly finished the dish. Fortunately, by that time, Marie had put before my uncle a huge turkey ("Dindon provenant de Bourbourg"), a gift from cousin Benjamin Vandenbroucque, who always made a point of sending us one every Christmas to St. John's Park. In the same way, the salmon was a gift of my two cousins, Auguste and Eugène Monteuuis. Confidence being once more restored, my uncle carved the turkey, putting the slices on a big dish, which Marie handed round, but this time beginning with "Monseigneur l'Eveque" (the Bishop) and ending with the "vicaire," who helped himself pretty freely, leaving, however, a little on the dish, as he saw my uncle was not yet helped. The next course was new potatoes—"Pommes de terre" or "Patates" (their local name). The Bishop thoroughly enjoyed them, and, being in a genial mood, he turned to the "vicaire" and said to him: "Try some of these patates, Monsieur le Vicaire, they are excellent." The laconic reply was: "Merci, "Monseigneur, I never eat them; they are only fit for "pigs." For a moment dead silence, until the Bishop, (a real good genial sort of man) relieved the situation by smiling pleasantly as if it were an excellent joke. My uncle joined in; we all took up the running, so that in the end the "vicaire" really thought that he had distinguished himself. Sweets of various kinds followed the solids, and then the banquet finished up with delicious café noir, but without either cigars or cigarettes, so Eugene and I quietly slipped back into the sanctum, whither Marie brought us our coffee, and enjoyed our whiff without anyone being a bit the wiser. We managed to slip back into the salon just as a general move was being made to adjourn for vespers in my uncle's church. The Bishop officiated, and after vespers the guests all dispersed, leaving my uncle alone with us four.

The next day (Tuesday) we were all the guests of Monsieur le Maire and of Monsieur l'Adjoint, to a banquet given by these two gentlemen (both batchelors) in our honour. It was all very well in its way, but not a patch on the one of the previous day. However, perhaps that was all the better for us, keeping up the

Latin motto of "*Mens sana in corpore sano*" (a sound mind in a sound body). A cobbler had this Latin motto stuck up prominently over his shop front. But his rival, who had only recently set up shop opposite, thought he would improve upon the first motto, and so stuck up over his own shop front in huge gold letters: "Men's and women's sana in corpore sano," to the amusement of all intelligent passers-by, who thought it was a good joke on the part of the second and rival cobbler.

All things in time come to an end, especially pleasant things, so early the next morning Eugène and I chartered a carriage and pair between us, and after our "café au lait complet," we wished dear Uncle l'Abbé a hearty good-bye (more osculatory demonstrations all round of a very tender nature, in which dear old Marie insisted upon having her fair share). We arrived at Marquise in excellent time for 12 o'clock *déjeuner à la fourchette,* the guests of our cousins the Sauvagets. Marquise was the birthplace of my dear mother, but after the death of her father and mother (my grandparents), there were no Monteuuis left, so the family was represented by cousins —the Sauvagets, the Boningues, and the Brouttas.

We finished that afternoon in a pilgrimage to the cemetery to visit the family vault of the Monteuuis (really *de Monteuuis*) though at the time of the French Revolution in 1789, my ancestors dropped the prefix "*de*," which the family never resumed. The last occupants of the family vault were my grandfather, my grandmother, and my uncle and aunt, Monsieur et Madame Henri Monteuuis, whom we all three lovingly remembered. Having paid our respects to the memory of these dear ones, we went back to 6 o'clock dinner at the Sauvagets. Afternoon tea was then unknown in France. If you wanted tea you had to buy it by the ounce, like senna, at the chemist's. My mother used to tell us children the thrilling adventures of Madame Gibou and her wonderful tea. Her nephew, just back from China, had given her an ounce of China tea. The old lady put it into a saucepan of boiling water for over an hour. She then drained the water away and poured the tea-leaves on to a dish, seasoning them lavishly with pepper, salt, mace, ginger, and other spices. Then she began eating it, thinking she had a delicious treat before her, and was going thoroughly to enjoy it. But the first mouthful undeceived her; she turned pale, and so just threw the whole of the precious contents into the fire. When the nephew visited his aunt (from whom he had pecuniary expectations), she rated him soundly, ordering him out of the house, and telling him never to venture into her presence again. So the poor fellow lost his inheritance : he was his aunt's sole living relative, for when the old lady died it was found that she had left all her money to a lunatic asylum.

We journeyed from Marquise to make an exploration of Boulogne, a very interesting city, especially the Haute Ville, with the ramparts all round. The difference between the Haute Ville and the Basse Ville is that the Haute Ville is very old-fashioned, and is mostly inhabited by old French families (all very proper, but dull and slow), whereas the Basse Ville is up to date and full of life.

We first went along the Jetée de l'Est (1,950 feet long), on the Boulogne side, having on our way a look at the lifeboat alongside, designed, built, and presented to the town by my cousin, Edouard de Poilly, a rising naval architect. On this jetty, or pier, is a celebrated restaurant, where one gets shell-fish of all kinds, including oysters. We then rambled along the beach, where there is excellent safe bathing on the hard sands, free of all shingle, and on our way back just looked in at the Casino, overlooking the sands, then along the sea-road as far as the column, 190 feet high and finished in 1841, to commemorate the intended invasion of England (1801-4) by Napoleon I, whose bronze statue is on the top. The invasion, as it happens, never came off, but the column still remains. It stands on a level plain, a base for military manœuvres. We then got back into the town, visited the market place (a busy scene), the parish church, and then up to the Haute Ville, walking round the ramparts, a splendid promenade, to the Cathedral of Notre Dame, which we just looked into to admire the picture of the Virgin and Child. The Haute Ville includes the chateau where Louis Napoleon (afterwards Napoleon III) was confined in 1840. Boulogne was formerly a noted gambling town, and contains two streets, originally called "Rue de l'Ecu" (I cannot recall its present name), and "Rue tant perd tant paie" ("Whatever you lose you must pay"), since altered to "Rue de l'Amiral Bruix." Boulogne contains, besides, two other streets with strange appellations, "Rue Ecoute s'il pleut" ("Listen if it rains"), and "Rue des Religieuses Anglaises" ("English Nuns"). I believe there are, or were, other similar ones, but I cannot now recall them to mind. On our way back to Auguste's, we just looked in at the "Fish Market," a wonderful institution, where in those days the celebrated Caroline was the moving spirit. When, therefore, any fishermen's procession took place in the town, she headed that of the fishwives, by whom she was looked upon as their queen, and obeyed accordingly. My mother, aunt, and she were great friends; they always called her "Caroline," which pleased her.

The three-and-a-half-days we spent at Boulogne passed away quickly, as we filled up every minute of our time there. On the Friday morning we hired a waggonette and pair and went over to Etaples. It is a pleasant 17 miles from Boulogne, through the lovely Bois de Boulogne, but not at all resembling the one of the same name in Paris. This one was picturesque in the extreme, and until recent years abounded in wild boar, which the more adventurous Boulonnais and English visitors delighted in hunting, but they have since disappeared. We ordered lunch at the only decent inn, and then visited the parish church, Eugéne and I finishing up with a sea bath, but we had to be sharp over it, for the tide rises and falls very quickly. We, however, managed all right. We enjoyed our primitive lunch, the roast mutton savouring very strongly of garlic ("*ail*"), which we rather liked. After lunch we drove back to Boulogne in time for five o'clock tea; had a rest before dinner; going to bed early, for the long drive of 34 miles had made us sleepy. Next morning (Saturday), after our *petit déjeuner,* we started in the waggonette and pair for Ambleteuse (an easy drive of five miles), taking our lunch with us. As we were in excellent time, and while lunch was preparing, some of us boarded the flat-bottomed row-boat; rowing out a bit and anchoring fore and aft, we began fishing for cod.

We were very successful, soon catching about six, which we brought back with us. As they were rather varied in size, we picked out the smallest and cooked them for our lunch; they were simply delicious. The others we took back with us to Boulogne. Having lunched leisurely and rested awhile to aid digestion, we started back again, and got to Boulogne, getting in in comfortable time for tea. After tea we went for a stroll in the town to buy chocolate and dressed fisher-folk dolls (male and female) to take back home with us, getting back in good time for dinner. I should mention that, going to Ambleteuse, we passed the village of Wimille, a corruption for "Windmill," just as Sangatte (another village in the neighbourhood) is a corruption for "Sandgate," two English names dating back before the time of Queen Mary, when the whole district was in the hands of the English.

We spent a quiet peaceful week-end at Boulogne. Our steamer, one of the General Steam Navigation Company's line, left for London at 1 o'clock on the Monday morning, so, having already booked our berths, we went on board soon after 10 o'clock, getting comfortably to sleep before we started, waking the next morning in smooth water, and being well able to enjoy the regulation breakfast of those days, which meant boiled and fried fish, eggs and bacon, chops and steaks, rolls, toast and butter, with tea and coffee, all for the moderate price of 2s. a head.

We soon got to Gravesend, where the Custom House officers came on board; they knew my sister and myself of old. I showed them the chocolate and fisherfolk dolls, which they passed at once. In a couple of hours afterwards we arrived off London Bridge, soon after 10 a.m., chartered a four-wheeler, and an hour afterwards arrived at 11 St. John's Park, where my dear mother received us *a bras ouverts*. So came a very pleasant holiday to a pleasant end.

CHAPTER IV.

INDIA FIFTY YEARS AGO.—I.

ONE morning early in the November of 1866, I was sitting at my office table, when the partners' door opened, and all three of them being present, the junior partner (Mr. Richard Glyn) asked me whether I would care to go out for them to India in about a fortnight or three weeks' time. I at once told him I would give him a definite answer the next morning, after consulting with my wife. My wife, seeing the great advantage it would probably be to me, stifled her own conjugal feelings, and agreed with me that I ought to accept the offer.

So the following morning I told the partners that I was quite ready to go, and suggested taking the P. & O. steamer "*Poonah,*" due to leave Marseilles for Bombay the following month, Wednesday, 5 December, thus giving me just time, with none to spare, to make the necessary arrangements. They at once fell in with my suggestion, so that very morning I went round to the P. & O. to book my passage, managing to secure a first-class cabin to myself as far as Alexandria, where we were to leave the steamer and take the train (for it was before the days of the Suez Canal) from Alexandria to Suez, there catching the "*Delhi*" on to Bombay, by which steamer I was also fortunate in securing a cabin to myself; and here let me say I have always managed to get a cabin to myself on all the various lines by which I have travelled. I then went round to the various shops to secure my necessary outfit, with a large Bullock trunk to pack it all up in, began to make my various private and business arrangements, and on the 1st December following set out on my journey across France to catch the "*Poonah*" at Marseilles, whence we departed for Alexandria, where we arrived on December 12th. Here began my Oriental journey proper, and what now follows is mainly taken from a diary which I kept, during the time it lasted.

Our long railway journey from Alexandria to Suez was full of wonder and interest. We were first attracted to cotton fields in full bloom (Egyptian cotton is of good quality and highly prized). The white bloom of the cotton plant is very beautiful. Our train, which certainly does not hurry itself, and for which we are not sorry, gives us ample time to notice things as we glide along: for instance, natives with their string of camels, all in single file, have a decided Old Testament ring about them; they reminded us of the old Patriarchs—Abraham, Isaac, and Jacob. Then we pass a cluster of date palms, and an Egyptian, clad in his gorgeous bright blue costume, up one of these trees gathering the fruit.

Further on we see a plantation of orange trees bending down with the weight of the ripe fruit they bear in such luxuriance. Then fig trees, acacias, castor-oil trees, apricot trees—but the most wonderful tree of all is the pagoda tree, with its magnificent luxuriant bloom; and then the banyan tree, the twigs of which bend down to the ground and strike root, so that a collection of banyan trees, with its shoots firmly planted, very soon constitutes a well-nigh impregnable forest: the whole scene of vegetation being crowned by a field of fine white cabbages and winter onions.

From the windows of our train we notice a high straight obelisk called "Pompey's Pillar," and then catch sight of an Egyptian ploughing with a buffalo and a camel yoked together to the plough—a very common occurrence, as it appears, in Egypt. We then pass what at first sight appears to be a collection of large mole hills, but in reality an Egyptian village of mud huts, built close together, with just an opening for the door, the fowls and goats making of these huts their regular habitations in common with their masters. After that come minaret towers, with a mosque where the Egyptians perform their devotions, shouting out in their vernacular, "*There is only one God! Allah is his name, and Mohammed is his prophet,*" and then we pass a Mohammedan burial ground. The graves remind one of large-sized bird traps (*à la* four bricks), the whole smelling abominably. The Egyptian sanitary arrangements are surely of a very low order. The Egyptian windmills are certainly a natural curiosity; they are square buildings, squat and flat at the top, with the sails on the top instead of at the side. At 12.50 p.m. we reach the river Nile, and our railway runs alongside it for some considerable distance. Its banks are generally flat and muddy.

At 3.54 (Egyptian time) I catch sight of the Pyramids and am soon passing near them. The base of each covers 12 acres of ground; they are beyond description in their simple appearance, combined with the marvels attaching to their wonderful history. And now we approach Cairo, a grand old city with its mosques, minarets, and palaces. Being built on the slope of a hill its manifold attractions stand out in bold relief. The cyprus trees are fine. We pass two or three European mansions with walled gardens, very refreshing after those villages of mud huts. This morning we were in Europe, while this evening we are in Africa (what a contrast); and soon we expect to be steaming away on the Red Sea. And now we reach Cairo itself, where we change into other carriages and are soon off again, leaving vegetation behind us, and are now in the desert, one vast expanse of sand. The sun sets in all its glory, and after that we suddenly drift into darkness, for there is no twilight in the East. We pass peculiar square mounds—graves in the desert, the graves of those who died going through it. In the remote ages this desert was fertile, for we come upon remains of what is now a fossil forest. The gradual disappearance of water and all moisture must have brought the place to its present state of desolation, resulting in sand and nothing but sand, which invades our eyes, nostrils, and mouth, so we close our carriage windows to keep it out as much as possible. The attendant lights the carriage lamps, and, having nothing better to do, we start eating oranges, which are very refreshing and give real relief to our parched throats.

At some more than usually dirty station, swarming with Egyptians, we stop to lunch. These dirty Egyptians are, most of them, totally blind—the remaining few only having one eye—an awful sight, caused by flies that, attracted by the powerful stench of the

Egyptians, flock in swarms upon their eyes, the lazy, dirty Egyptians thus attacked being in fact too indolent to brush them off, thus losing their eyesight: a ghastly sight indeed, the victims without eyes looking like so many skeletons. Our lunch (and, as it turned out, dinner combined) costs us 5s. a head, with 2s. extra for beer. It is a lunch indeed! A lean scraggy fowl divided up into the smallest possible portions composes our first course; this is followed by tough buffalo, and called "*Bœuf à la mode,*" with capers. Our solitary vegetables consist of peas in butter (actually quite good and appetising). Then rank Dutch cheese, followed by rotten stewed prunes and oranges, the whole having to be bolted in just a quarter of an hour, and no more.

After you have eaten the first mouthful of your first course the attendants come round to collect the money, clamouring for "Bachsheesh" (a tip). This is to be our only meal until we board the "*Delhi*" at 11.30 that night. Out of sheer desperation we seize hold of the oranges and make off with them; six oranges fall to my share. The attendants smile at our innocence, for outside the room are shoals of boys selling six oranges for one penny, others selling dirty rings of bread strung on their filthy arms with slabs of cheese to match; whilst girls are selling water out of curious porous pitchers, and men selling water in goats' skins.

We see little of Suez, where we join the "*Delhi,*" and thence we submit ourselves to the heat of the Red Sea. Life passes lazily until we land at Aden one fine night, when the moon is at its full and shining brightly, so that we can see everything clearly before us. The first thing that strikes us is the barren, mountainous look of the place, relieved here and there with a few white bungalows belonging to the English (officers and merchants). The road is nothing but sand; had we landed at daytime, the glare would have been simply impossible. At once we wend our way to the post office, where I, having charge of the passengers' letters, after getting them stamped, post them. This business over, we take a stroll on to the bazaar, looking at the things for sale. I have never in my life seen such a heterogeneous lot—things of all kinds. I invest in a pith mushroom-shaped solar topee, after which we all go to the Prince of Wales Hotel, where we have supper. It is a miserable place, reminding one of the worst public-house taproom in England. We have coffee, which is so vile that we have to leave it; then we order Aden oysters, having to wait while they smash them open with stones. The oysters are not so bad, but there is little of them. We then have Allsopp's bottled beer, sardines (all musty), with crabs, both putrid and hot (they have only just been boiled). The waiter finishes up by bringing us a horrid mixture which he calls Irish stew, together with chops, which we cannot touch. The cigars are worse, and this is all we get for our 5s. supper. After supper, we sit outside to watch our fellow passengers racing on Arab steeds; at last they turn their horses' heads and start for the cantonments some four miles off; they dare not go into the interior, for, as sure as fate, they would be speared by an Arab. The ship's doctor, two other passengers, with myself, start off in the direction they are going for a walk, for we find it a luxury to stretch our legs. We go as far as the half-way house, there sitting down; a Mohammedan comes up wanting us to buy lemonade. We shut him up by telling him that it is against his creed to sell anything after sunset. We then turn back; on one side of us are high rocks, on the other the seashore—the whole place being black with coal.

We arrive in the magnificent harbour of Bombay late one evening, and I am thinking of remaining on board the "*Delhi*" for the night, and am getting the steward to make up a bed somewhere on deck, when a letter is placed in my hands. It is written in perfect English, and is from the manager of the Bombay Dockyard (a Parsee, whose family from father to son have for generations held this post; in fact, ever since the dockyard was moved from Surat to Bombay), saying that at the request of his cousins, an important firm of Parsee merchants and our correspondents in Bombay, the dockyard steam launch is alongside the "*Delhi*" to take me and my luggage ashore. Of course, this alters all my preconceived plans of remaining on board till the next morning; so, having wished everyone a hurried good-bye, with no end of engagements to see them again during the next few days at tiffin, afternoon, and dinner galore, I bid adieu to the good ship "*Delhi,*" step into the steam launch, and we are off for our three mile run to the Apollo Bunder (the P. and O. landing stage). I find there a letter (written again in perfect English) from the Parsee merchants, saying that their mail phaeton, pair of horses, and coachman are at my disposal during the whole of my stay in Bombay; that the coachman has orders to take me and my luggage to the Adelphi Hotel, where they have ordered me a bedroom, and that next morning the coachman will await my convenience to drive me to their office in Parsee Bazaar Street. We are not long arriving at our destination, where I sit down to write a "*chit*" (note) to my Parsee friends, saying I hope to call on them in the morning about 11; this I give to my coachman to hand to his master, telling him to call for me at 10 a.m. In taking it he salaams humbly, and is off, leaving me alone in all my glory. I look in at my bedroom, and, although it is really all right, containing a large bed surrounded by mosquito curtains, which I simply loathe, somehow I do not fancy it, so I tell the hotel servant, who fortunately speaks English in a fashion, to move my bed without any curtains on to my verandah. Being thoroughly tired out, I am soon fast asleep, sleeping soundly till 6.30 the following morning, when I awake, feeling very seedy and in great pain. No wonder! the mosquitoes have just been feasting on my unprotected face, which is just one round mass—nose, cheeks, and eyes on one common level, except that the eyes are well-nigh bunged up, so that I can only with the greatest difficulty use them. They have also viciously attacked my wrists and ankles—very vulnerable points, as I find out to my cost. However, it is no use crying over spilt milk, so I make the best of a bad bargain. The hotel servant brings me a cup of delicious tea with a Huntley & Palmer's dry biscuit. I then sponge my face with rather a strong solution of liquid ammonia which he brings me. I find almost instant relief, so get into bed again, telling him to wake me at 8.30 a.m. sharp, with a hot bath in the largest bath the hotel possesses. He says he quite understands, so I now turn over for a good sleep, trying to forget my woes, which, after all, are not so bad—they might indeed be much worse, and even then endurable. At 8.30 a.m. the hotel servant tells me my hot bath is ready in my dressing-room, so I get up to sample it. Horror of horrors! it is the very smallest hip bath I ever came across. I sit down in it, soap myself, and just manage with the greatest difficulty to sponge myself with the hot water at the bottom of it, but it is a tight fit. Then, thinking I have had about enough of it, I attempt to get out. Not a bit of it: when I rise, the bath rises with me, and I aimlessly wander about the room with it at my stern, like a mail coat of armour, all the while the water runs down along the floor, emptying the bath. Then by an almost superhuman effort, I manage to free myself, the bath dropping with a heavy thud on the floor. The hotel servant, hearing the noise, rushes up to know the cause of it, and then I let him have it. He leaves my bedroom a sadder but a wiser man. Soon after, he re-enters the room to know how soon I shall be ready for breakfast, and what would I fancy. Before I can order breakfast, and just as I have finished dressing, Captain Lidbetter comes in, and hurries me away in his buggy to his bungalow close by, where he gives me a glorious breakfast, finishing up with a splendid cigar, all thoroughly enjoyable. We get back to the Adelphi Hotel, where he dismisses his buggy, bids me pack my kit, which I do, not knowing what is coming next. He orders me to pay my bill, which I do most obediently. It is now 10 a.m., my trap drives up, the coachman loads up my luggage, and we all three drive to the Byculla Hotel close by. Here Lidbetter secures me a splendidly cool bedroom with verandah, and a roomy bathroom with a huge full length bath in it, hot and cold water laid on *ad lib.* "Now," says Lidbetter, "this is more like "it. You will be comfortable here; at that wretched "Adelphi you would have simply hated yourself."

So we set to with a will, Lidbetter helping me unpack and stow away my things in my roomy cupboards and drawers, getting everything shipshape. We then get into my trap and are driven to Parsee Bazaar Street to call upon our Parsee friends, for Lidbetter knows them well, doing business with them. He introduces me, and I thank them for all their kindness to me. They take me into an adjoining room, which they say is at my sole disposal. I thank them, accepting their kind offer, but at the same time reminding them that Messrs. Hutchison, Dods & Co., our Bombay agents, are expecting me, and that I am more or less in their hands, so we leave it an open question. I wish them good-bye for the time being, driving with Lidbetter to the office of Messrs. Hutchison, Dods & Co. close by. He introduces me to Mr. John S. Dods and to Mr. Grendon Tippett, the manager, and then leaves me, saying he will fetch me at 7 p.m. to take me to dinner. Dods then dismisses my coachman, telling him to call for me at 2.30 p.m. at the Bombay Club. Dods and Tippet then explain that it is mail day, and that I have till 1 p.m. to write my letters, while they finish theirs. Dods shows me a room that he had had fitted up for me: I like the idea of having that second room in Parsee Bazaar Street, so I send round to my Parsee friends a "*chit*" to expect me soon after 2.30 that afternoon. At 1 p.m., having finished our correspondence, Dods drives me in his mail phaeton to the Bombay Club; Tippet following in his buggy, which he drives, his native standing behind, holding on by two straps. They stand me an excellent lunch, *inter alia,* "Pickled cutlets," with all sorts of good things, finishing up with curried prawns and Bombay duck. Then a Cavite Manila cheroot, with real good proper Mocha coffee. Dods proposes and Tippet seconds me, thus I am at once made a member of the Bombay Club. They tell me I need not worry to go to a tobacconist's for my cigars, that the Club can supply all I need; so to begin with I invest in a box of Manila Cavite cheroots, also five Trichinopoli cheroots and five Pondicherry cigars to sample at my leisure. They then explain to me that on the following Saturday morning they are off up country for a week's shoot, it being then the Christmas holidays; that all English offices are doing the same, but that the native offices keep open the whole time. So that is why Dods approved of my having the Parsee Bazaar Street room to fall back upon, adding, however, that during that time I cannot possibly do any business. They offer to take me up country with them; but I thank them, saying I want to look round a bit to get acclimatised. They approve of this. Dods then invites me up to dine with Langley, Tippett, and himself at their bungalow on Malabar Hill to-morrow (Friday), and to stay the night. He will fetch me at my hotel and drive me there with my bag, so that I shall not need my trap, but that on the following Saturday morning my coachman had better be round there at 6.30 to see them all three off, and then drive me back to the Byculla Hotel. Of course, I accept like a shot, and, my trap being there, Dods gives my coachman in Hindustani full instructions about it all. He then drives me on to Parsee Bazaar Street, where I tell my native friends of all these various arrangements, and they, too, tell me that during these coming holidays there will be no work done either among the Europeans or at the Courts. All this settled, I tell my coachman to drive like mad to the office of Messrs. Hearne, Cleveland & Peile, the Government solicitors. I am just in time to catch Mr. Charles Peile, for he, too, is off at 3 p.m. up country for a big shoot. I leave with him my letter of introduction and certain papers. He calls his half-caste Portuguese clerk and hands them to him, telling him to have everything ready for me when I come there again after the holidays. We then bid each other good-bye, and I am driven off to the Agra and Masterman Bank, the manager of which is Mr. W. H. Peile, another brother, to whom I present my letter of introduction. He says: "It is all right; my brother "James and his wife are in the next room expecting "you; come in." They are very glad to see me, and James suggests that, as we have a good hour before tea, we drive up at once to the Byculla Club, where he will propose me; adding, we are sure to find a member there to second me, so that, all being well, I can move in to the Club from the Byculla Hotel close by the first thing the following Saturday morning, provided, of course, that I am not "blackballed" in the meantime. At the Club, where my Peile is on the committee, we find another committee-man, so these two propose and second me in due form. They introduce me to three or four other important members, who very kindly back my nomination papers, all assuring me that by Saturday (the day after to-morrow) I shall have become a "pucker" member of the Club. They then introduce me to the secretary, who confirms their assurance that it will be all right. Then thanking them, Peile and I drive back to the Bank, where we have afternoon tea, which we thoroughly enjoy. *My* Mr. Peile does not smoke, but his brother William does, so we each sample one of my Cavites (No. 2 size), which we find excellent. William says I can have the free use of a room at the Bank whenever I want, so that I can write letters quietly or do anything else I wish. Lidbetter had already offered me a room in his office, so that between the lot I have now four rooms at my disposal, "*embarras de choix*," but very useful at a pinch, so I thankfully accept his kind offer.

We all four sit chatting away, making various very jolly plans for the next few days, it being arranged that, as soon as I am comfortably installed at the Byculla Club, I will call round at Government House to leave there for Sir Bartle Frere my letter of introduction and my visiting card with my club address, the proper thing to do. I then wish them good-bye, getting back to the hotel in ample time for a good long warm bath, which I thoroughly enjoy, and am rigged out all right when Captain Lidbetter calls for me to drive me out in his buggy to his bungalow at Breach Candy, where I find his chum, Captain Dixon, waiting for us; and we all sit down quietly to dinner, spending a jolly evening all together till 10 o'clock, when my man comes round and drives me back to my hotel, and I am not sorry to get in between the sheets for a comfortable night's rest. I have discarded all idea of mosquito curtains; the ferocious vampires had their fill of my blood last night and this morning, so that now, having nothing to suck, they do not molest me. One thing, too, my room at the Byculla Hotel is much cooler and cleaner than the one I had at the Adelphi, and that makes all the difference in the world.

Next morning, Friday, 28 December 1866, after breakfast, I drive into the Fort with my bag, leaving it at Dods' office. He gets Tippet to take me round to "Walters," where I invest in a tall silk hat, paying 15 rupees, or 30s., and have a dozen thin white cotton jackets for dinner. The "*pucker*" thing to do when you go to any dinner is for your boy (body servant) to take one of these jackets with him, and according to circumstances you take off your dress coat and put on one of these jackets, but if there are ladies present it is usual to keep on the dress coat, unless it happens to be just a quiet family party, when it is quite the proper thing to wear the white jacket. It all depends; so by doing what I see the other fellows do, I can always keep all right and up to proper regulation form, for here in Bombay the rules of etiquette are very strict indeed.

I then go round to see the Peiles at the Bank, who invite me to tiffin, but I have to refuse, as I am lunching with Flanagan (an old London chum) at the Bombay Club. Look up Gladding, who proposes an excursion to-morrow (Saturday) to Elephanta, picnic there, dining with him afterwards at his bungalow. After tiffin we all (Dods and Tippet included) watch a Parsee wedding procession, a gorgeous display of colour. Having feasted our eyes on this festive scene, Dods drives me out to his bungalow at Malabar Hill in his mail phaeton, Tippet promising to come on later, in time for dinner. The drive along the Esplanade and Marine Lines is very beautiful. Between us and the sea is "Rotten Row," the favourite ride for Bombay equestrians, and always well patronised. The sea breeze is refreshing, and the whole thing invigorating. I very much enjoy the drive until we come to the native town between the Fort and Malabar Hill; it is rather dirty and malodorous, but we soon get out of it on to the Malabar Road, by Back Bay, where the "Back Bay Reclamation Company, Limited," pretty nigh ruined the half of Bombay the previous year (1865). A pleasant half hour's drive brings us to our destination. The bungalow is delightfully situated on a hill, standing in its own walled in "compound" (garden), with plenty of shade from the date, cocoanut, palm, cotton, and other trees growing luxuriantly round it. In front we get a grand view of the sea. Tippet and Langley come in just in time for dinner, where, for the first time, I wear my white linen jacket, which I find comfortably cool and light. After dinner we adjourn upstairs to the verandah to smoke and drink coffee, spending a pleasant evening till 11 o'clock, when the boy brings in "*pegs*" (sodas and brandy); we all take a modest quencher and then retire to roost.

Saturday morning, 29 December, we are awakened at 5 with a cup of tea. We then have our respective "tubs," and after a hasty breakfast we drive away in our respective traps to the Bombay and Baroda Railway Station, arriving there at 6.45 a.m., in good time for the three gallant sportsmen to catch their 7 a.m. train up country. They have each brought with them their "boy" apiece, their beds, and a tent, with provisions (both solid and liquid) to last them the week. They had already reserved their large roomy first-class compartment, and soon settle down comfortably. Everybody seems to be going up-country for the holidays. The third-class carriages, with a second tier of seats, one above the other, are literally packed. I alight from their compartment just in time, wish them good-bye—they are off to enjoy their well-earned holiday, while I, in a somewhat pensive mood, am driven to the Byculla Hotel, where I pay my bill and pack up my kit, which is taken over to the Byculla Club close by, where I find I have been duly elected an honorary member, so that I can enter into possession at once. I find that at present there is no bedroom vacant, so am given a large roomy tent all to myself, where I am soon comfortably installed with all my belongings. I have a jolly bath, dressing in fresh cool clothes, followed by breakfast. After which I drive into the Fort, call on the Peiles to let them know I am all right, then I go round to Government House, leaving there my letter of introduction, together with my visiting card, on which I have had engraved my address: "Byculla Club." I go round to Gladding's, but find that we cannot manage Elephanta to-day, as the tide does not suit, for we could not get back till past 10 p.m., so we play the organ (a hand one), and then have tiffin in his comfortable quarters. We loaf about till 4 p.m., when we have tea, and then go for a drive on the sea front, where I meet the Peiles, also driving. Mrs. Peile gives me a jolly good wigging for daring to show up at that fashionable hour, in the most fashionable part of Bombay, in an Ellwood grey felt helmet. I tell her I am very sorry, that I have a tall silk hat which I only bought yesterday on purpose to put on for these functions. "Then why ever did you not put it on "to-day, pray may I ask; never do it again, or I will "cut you dead," she says. I explain that we were really going to Elephanta, &c. &c., and manage to pacify her. To get out of the gadding crowd, we drive on to Calabar Hill and Point, to call on some fellows there. We find them in, chaffing one of their guests most unmercifully. It appears that this fellow (" Smith " we will call him, so as not to give him away, for he is a real good sort), lives out at Tannah, on the Bombay and Baroda Railway, on which he has a first-class season ticket. His rule is to get home to late dinner, and yesterday he left Bombay with that intention. The compartment he got into was empty, so as soon as the train started he quietly dozed off (having no one to talk to). He slept right on till the train got to its destination, never waking even when it started back, and so he went on undisturbed, the train meanwhile continuing the even tenor of its way until suddenly he woke about 5 a.m., the train having been brought to a standstill about two hours previously, and shunted in the depôt just outside Bombay Station. Just then it started again, backed into the station, and was off once more, arriving at Tannah a little before 6 a.m., where he alighted, and walked home, to find his wife in an awful way, but she soon quieted down on seeing him once more safe and sound, got him a cup of refreshing tea, after which he had a cold bath, feeling once more all right again. He soon pegged away at a hearty breakfast, for he had had nothing to eat since yesterday's tiffin.

"Smith," who is our bill broker, invites me down to dine and sleep at his place at Tannah the first day I happen to have free; that is in about a week's time, when I was able to go, very much enjoying my visit. We then drive back to Gladding's bungalow to 7 p.m. dinner, which I enjoy. I then ask him to let me off at 9 p.m., as I want to get back to the Club in good time, having several things to see to. When I get back to my tent I find a man waiting for me with a letter from Macnee, inviting me to dine at his place on Monday evening, and recommending the bearer as my "boy" (personal servant) at rupees 15 (30s. a month); so I engage him, arranging for him to sleep in a small servant's tent close to mine.

Next morning, Sunday, 30 December 1866, he gets out my things, prepares my bath, and I dress. After breakfast I look about me till 10.30 a.m., when I tell my coachman to drive me to church, but he does not understand me, nor does any native whom I ask. At last I meet an Englishman coming out of the Club, so I ask him what is the Hindustani for "Go to church." His answer startles me, for he says very seriously, "Go to the devil." The man understands and drives me at once to Byculla Church. On getting back to the Club after service, I find that "*Dawal,*" pronounced "Devil," is the Hindustani for church.

It has rather a strange effect to see the punkahs swinging over our heads in church; they are connected to long ropes which men pull outside. But it is drowsy work, so they sometimes drop off to sleep. The punkahs at once stop, and the congregation follow suit by dropping off to sleep also, like the "*punkah wallahs.*"

After service, Kavanagh and I drive up to Sands' bungalow at Breach Candy, to pay our respects to a bride and bridegroom. Mrs. Hamilton (then Miss Crutwell) came out with Mr. Sands on the "*Delhi.*" They all receive us very warmly, Mr. Sands insisting on our staying to tiffin, which we do. I ought to have attended the wedding, for which I had an invitation, but shirked it at the last moment, sending a wedding present with my excuses instead. She cuts me off a large piece of wedding cake, giving it me with the favour that I ought to have worn. They had intended going by the 2.30 p.m. train up country, but find there is no such train on Sunday, so they have to put off their departure till next morning. We have an early tea, and then Kavanagh and I drive back to the Club, Kavanagh going on to Government House. I dress for dinner, and sit outside the porch of the Club awaiting Flanagan's arrival. He soon comes up in his brougham, and we are driven round to his bungalow at Breach Candy. Flanagan is a bachelor, chumming with Mr. and Mrs. Green and their children. I find I know Green, for in the old Highgate days I was always coming across him. Before dinner we take a stroll along Breach Candy, as far as the bungalow of my friend Mr. (now Sir) Andrew Scoble. We don't dine till 8, waiting for Mrs. Macfarlane, who has gone to evening service at the Cathedral. Mrs. Macfarlane drives up quite punctually, so we all sit down to dinner in good time. My "boy" waits on me at dinner, where, by the kind permission of the ladies, we gentlemen all wear our white cotton jackets. My "boy" had left at 10 p.m., and as there was no carriage to take me back, Flanagan very kindly puts me up for the night, providing me with sleeping apparel, making me, in fact, quite comfortable.

Monday morning, 31 December, I am up at 6 o'clock, and after a cup of tea, with bananas, I have a tub, putting on my dress clothes. After breakfast we decide upon taking a steamer to Oola, spending the day there. It is one of the islands in the harbour, so we pack up any quantity of provisions, stow them all in Green's mail phaeton, and we all four drive off to our destination, stopping, however, at the Byculla Club, where I get out and change my clothes. We start off again for Carnac Bunder, where we just manage to catch a steamer for Oola. By taking four first-class return tickets we have the whole of the quarter-deck to ourselves, while the second and third-class seats are quite crammed with natives. The scenery we pass is simply grand. We see the Ghautz mountains, with Poonah and Matheran beyond (both of which sanatoria I visited later on). We reach Oola at 1 p.m., where a special boat takes us with our provisions on the island, where we have tiffin *al fresco* all to ourselves. Tiffin over, we rejoin our steamer, which has been specially awaiting our convenience, for no one else but ourselves got off. The steamer turns round, landing us at Carnac Bunder about 4.30 p.m. Charter a buggy, which drives me to Macnee's office just as he was about giving me up.

However, being an old London pal, he is very nice about it.

His brougham is at his office, but we prefer walking the first part of the way along Rotten Row, the Esplanade, Marine Lines Circus, and cricket ground, when we get in and are driven up to his bungalow on Camballa Hill, where we dine comfortably together, and I go back to my club in a buggy.

Macnee sending me on that Portuguese half-caste, whom I engage as my "boy," reminds me of a testimonial James Braithwaite Peile showed me, written by an Englishman for his late servant, who, not being able to read, was very proud of it. It runs thus:—

> "*The bearer, Fernandez Sousa, my late boy, is the cleverest*
> "*scoundrel out; all the time he was with me he robbed me*
> "*right and left—but then he never let anyone else rob me, so*
> "*that I can thoroughly recommend him. I am only parting*
> "*with him as I am going home for good.—English signature.*"

Marvellous to relate that, with that testimonial, Fernandez Sousa at once got another billet. Peile was telling me that the way these native servants rob their English masters is very dodgy; it is mostly in English clothes, especially thick ones. When supervising the wardrobe they put these away in a bottom drawer, later on in a remote cupboard, and so on until they disappear altogether.

Next morning, 1 January 1867, I have my hair cut in my tent by the club native barber; he charges me half a rupee (1s.), so I pull out my Bullock trunk from under my bed, get out my Ellwood helmet, which contains socks, pocket-handkerchiefs, also a bag of

English gold and silver of the value of about £120. I take out 1s., and put everything back in the Bullock trunk. I should mention that the compound is full of native workmen, but no thought of anything wrong occurs to me.

It is New Year's Day, and I stay to tea with the three Peiles, and then Mrs. Peile drives me on to hear the band, as I have my tall silk hat on. Mr. W. J. Peile invites me to tiffin and dinner the following day. He has some Trust Accounts he wants to show me and get my advice about. Of course I accept, appreciating the compliment he pays me.

Gladding dines with me at the Club. On going to bed in my tent that night I pull out my Bullock trunk from under my bed and take out my helmet to get out a pair of socks to keep the mosquitoes from my ankles. I put the helmet and, as I think, its contents back, lock up the trunk, stowing it back again under my bed, and then I discover that the bag of money has rolled on to the floor. It is such a labour lugging out that trunk and unlocking it that I just put the bag under my pillow, with my gold watch and chain, also my white shirt, containing rather valuable studs and sleeve links. For a wonder I sleep that night under mosquito curtains, quite an unusual thing for me to do. Somehow I have a presentiment of something wrong, as on going to bed I find my "boy" talking with the "*Ramousi*" (watchman), and I don't like it.

Wednesday, 2 January 1867.—I am awakened in the middle of the night by a nasty smell, which I find comes from my oil lamp snuffing out, and then leaving me in total darkness. I call out "Boy!" and he comes with a lighted candle. The first thing he says is: "Master, your trunk is gone." I look under my bed, and sure enough it is gone, with all my jewellery in it; but under my pillow I find my bag of gold, watch chain, and white shirt all right. I hastily dress, pack up my kit, which I have taken from my tent, and go into the Club itself. Captain Nasmyth is in his room, and hearing the noise asks what it all means. I explain to him. He at once says: "Put all your kit in here, van de Linde, it will be quite safe," and I do so. The Club head steward comes along with six or seven Sepoys; we each have a lighted candle, protected by a glass shade, and thus equipped we all start in Indian file to reconnoitre. We begin with my tent, where we find at the back a large hole where an entrance has been forced. We go through, and are soon in the open plain. "Look out for snakes, that's all." We go along for five minutes (not more) when we hear a shout; we rush up to find my Bullock trunk forced open, with its varied contents scattered on the ground. I miss, however, my Ellwood helmet with five pairs of socks and six pocket handkerchiefs. I find my flat Russian leather jewel case lying closed on the ground, with all its contents there safe. They had evidently taken it for a Prayer Book. Everything is put back into the trunk; we march back to my tent, where I get into bed and am soon fast asleep, the seven Sepoys keeping guard all round. At 8 a.m. I am awakened by the inspector of police, who asks me to count all my linen, &c., in my trunk, to know what is missing, and I tell him of the missing helmet containing the five pairs of socks and six pocket handkerchiefs, also my comb and brushes in the leather case. The Sepoys ask for backsheesh, which the inspector advises me to refuse, and he sends them about their business. I go back to the Club to breakfast; the head steward comes in to say how sorry they all are, but that the Club will make up for whatever I have lost, and that meanwhile he has got me an upstairs bedroom with verandah, bathroom, and lavatory all complete, with drawers and cupboards where I can lock up everything and so feel perfectly safe and happy. On the whole I think I have scored all round. The head steward has all my linen (which had got very much crumpled and soiled in the melée) thoroughly washed and put back in my room that very afternoon, and for which I pay rupees 2½ (5s.). I go to the Byculla Hotel and have a chat with Captain le Mesurier, who strongly advises my putting my "boy" into "*choki*" (prison) "*ek dum*" there and then. Captain Nasmyth at the Club advises the same thing. I hire a buggy and drive into the Fort, where I call upon Macnee at his office. He says he is sure my boy is innocent, but that of course I must please myself. I then go on to the Bank, where I see the Peiles; they quite coincide with what Captain Nasmyth and Captain le Mesurier advise about choki, or at any rate instant dismissal. I adopt the latter course; so, after tiffin, Mr. James Braithwaite Peile and I drive in my trap to the Club. We interview the secretary, who sends for my "boy." I give him the sack, Peile and the Club secretary telling him he is very fortunate that it is not "*choki*," which they both tell him he richly deserves. He takes his dismissal very meekly. I really fancy he is relieved that it is not "*choki*" after all. The Club secretary then tells me he has exactly the "boy" for me. He sends for him; I like his appearance, and so does Peile, so I engage him at once at 20 rupees (or £2) a month, which I think reasonable. Peile says we won't dress for dinner, but that my new "boy" had better be round with my white jacket to wait on me. He can then go back with me after dinner to my Club, sitting in front with my coachman.

I find two letters awaiting me: one is from Mrs. Scoble, inviting me to dine with her husband (a member of the Bombay Council) and herself the following Sunday evening at 8 o'clock at their bungalow at Breach Candy. The other is from Mrs. Arthur, who writes at the request of her brother and sister-in-law, Sir Bartle and Lady Frere, inviting me to breakfast with them "*en famille*" the following Monday morning at 9 at Government House, where we shall be a quiet family party of Sir Bartle and Lady Frere and their two daughters, Colonel and Mrs. Arthur and their two daughters. I pass both letters on to Mr. Peile, who says: "van de Linde, I congratulate you, but please don't cut us quite with all your aristocratic friends." I say: "No fear, Mr. Peile, I never cut my old friends. I know better than to be such a fool." And then I tell him the story of the celebrated author who is invited to afternoon tea at a fashionable lady's house in Mayfair. When he gets there he is shown into the drawing-room, and, while he is waiting for his hostess to appear, he sees three of his works *uncut* lying on the table. Just then the hostess appears, when he says to her, pointing to the three books : " I am glad to make your acquaint-" ance, Mrs. Nouveau Riche; I see you do not cut your " old friends." This tickles Mr. Peile, who advises me to write at once accepting both invitations, which I do. We then drive back to the Bank, where I spend the rest of the afternoon with W. H. Peile on his Trust Accounts, Mrs. Peile very kindly sending us in our tea. In this way we get through comfortably before dinner. W. H. Peile asks me what he owes me. I tell him, " Ask me another." Of course, I am only too pleased to have been of use.

Next day, Thursday, 3 January 1867, I again lunch at the Bank with the Peiles; I then call in on Walters to order the thinnest possible dark blue serge coat and waistcoat, socks, pocket-handkerchiefs, and a dark grey cloth helmet, comb and brushes in leather case, for which they give me two receipted bills—one for the coat and waistcoat, the other for the various things I had lost in the raid. I pass the latter on to the Club secretary, who at once hands me cash in repayment.

The next morning I call at Messrs. Hutchison, Dods & Co.; they are all back, so I set to work in real earnest, and am glad to do so. Have tiffin with them at the Bombay Club, driving back to the Byculla Club to dinner. During that morning I also call upon my solicitors, asking for Charles Peile. He has just gone into Court on a big Government case, so I see his Portuguese half-caste clerk—the wretched chap has not even touched one of the papers referring to my case. I talk to him quite seriously; he promises to have everything ready for me that day week. When I go that day week I find he has again done nothing, so I regularly go for him, call him a few choice names in the Anglo-Saxon vernacular, and insist on seeing Mr. Charles Peile at once. I am shown into his office, and unburden my grievances. He is very apologetic, and says it will never occur again, as now that he has finished and won his Government case, he will in future attend to me personally. Just then his partner, Mr. Hearne, comes in, smiling all over. "I say, Mr. van de Linde, what-"ever have you done to our poor unfortunate clerk to "upset him so. He has just been in to me, begging "me to bind him over to keep the peace, lest he might "strike you." Mr. Charles Peile explains everything to his partner, who says: "This is really too good. "Justice Westhrop, who has your case in hand, is "dining with me to-night; I want you and Peile to "join us. The Judge enjoys a joke, and Peile, con-"sidering you have just won your case in his Court, "you can afford to tell him, even though it is against "yourself." So we both accept, and spend a very pleasant evening, the learned Judge quite entering into the spirit of the joke, which he enjoys immensely.

Needless to add, my legal business goes on swimmingly after that, so that when I appear before Justice Westhrop in his official capacity, he gives me every attention and compliments me upon having put my facts so clearly before him.

On Saturday morning, 5 January, after early tea and my bath, I start off with my "boy" for Girgaum to breakfast with Captain Lidbetter. He is upstairs in his verandah, finishing his Guzeratte lesson. He introduces me to his "moonshee" (native teacher), advising me to take lessons of him—not a bad idea, so I accept. It is arranged that the "moonshee" is to come round to the Club twice a week (Wednesdays and Saturdays) at 5 a.m. to give me an hour's lesson. I give my "boy" strict instructions to wake me in time, which he always does in the following vernacular: "Sahib, "sahib, panch buggee hai Moonshee hai" ("Sir, sir, it is five o'clock, the Moonshee is there"). So I tumble out of bed and join my moonshee in the verandah in my pyjamas. He gets me on splendidly; I learn a lot, and now, after over 38 years, still remember a great deal, so that when I go over to Camberley to see my old Calcutta friend, Mr. R. A. Lyall, we generally get to spouting Guzeratti together. We breakfast, and chat away till 10.30 a.m., when I dismiss my "boy" and Lidbetter drives me in his buggy to the Fort, to Hutchison & Dods' office there, where, with the exception of tiffin at the Bombay Club, I work away steadily till 5 p.m., when we have a cup of tea and then stroll on to Dods' bungalow on Malabar Hill, where he invites me to dinner, lending me a white jacket. He also puts me up for the night, with his usual hospitality.

Next morning (Sunday) Dods' "boy" brings me a cup of tea. I then go upstairs and find Dods and Langley just going for a ride, and Tippet for a walk with his dog "Pegs." He takes me part of the way as far as the native town, where I hire a buggy, in which I am driven to the Club, where I have my bath and breakfast. I then stroll to the Byculla Church with my thickly-lined green silk umbrella, as the sun is intensely hot and I don't want to catch a sunstroke.

Coming out of church I meet Colonel and Mrs. Arthur; she introduces me to her husband, and they both say how glad they are that I can go to breakfast next morning at Government House. The Hon. Mr. Parsons is with them; they go back in their brougham, while Mr. Parsons kindly drives me in his buggy to the Club, saying it is not safe for me to walk in the sun. Hearing that I am breakfasting at Government House next morning, he kindly promises to call for me at the Club and leave me there. At tiffin my "boy" brings me a big letter which reads as follows:—

"*The Harbour and Pilotage Board requests the honour of Mr*
"*Gérard van de Linde's presence at the laying of the Foundation*
"*Stone of the Lighthouse on Kennery Island by His Excellency*
"*Sir Henry Bartle Edward Frere, G.C.S.I. and K.C.B., Governor*
"*of Bombay, on Saturday, the 19th instant.*

"*Henry Morland, Lieut. (late I.N.), Secretary.*

"*Bombay,* 5 *January* 1867.

"*An early answer is requested.—P.T.O.*"

"*Programme for the* 19*th day of January* 1867.

"*Harbour Board and guests to leave Apollo Bunder*	10.30 *a.m.*
"*His Excellency the Governor, Staff, &c.* *do.*	11 0 ,,
"*His Excellency to arrive at Kennery Island at*	1 *to* 1.15 *p.m.*
"*Corner stone to be laid at*	1.15 *to* 2.0 ,,
"*Lunch on the Island at*	2.30 ,,
"*To leave the Island about*	5.0 ,,
"*Carriages to be ordered at the Apollo Pier about*	6.30 ,,

I of course accept the invitation at once. My coachman drives me to the Scobles', taking my "boy" on the box; but no white jacket this time—full war paint, swallow-tails, all regulation and pucker. The Scobles treat me like an old friend, Mr. Andrew Scoble shaking me cordially by the hand, reminding me that he and my father were warm friends, and that he also knew dear old Dr. Thomas Hodgkin. I tell him of his death at Jaffa, 6 April 1866; he had not heard of it. The dinner passes off very pleasantly. I drive back to my Club and am soon fast asleep in my very comfortable diggings.

Next morning (Monday) I have my early tea and then go for a stroll, get back to my bath, and dress, wearing my black silk hat for this special occasion. Mr. Parsons calls for me in good time and drives me to Government House. Mrs. Arthur very kindly introduces me to Sir Bartle and Lady Frere and their two daughters. They are all most kind and genial, saying that they are soon giving a State ball at Government House, for which I shall receive a card of invitation. Sir Bartle Frere asks me whether I have received the invitation for the Kennery Island function. I tell him I have; he says he is glad to hear it, because he had given Morland a hint to send me one, so he hopes to see me there. I thank him and say I am afraid there will be no ladies present. He says no, unfortunately; they had tried to arrange it, but found it would not do. I tell Sir Bartle Frere how I had once seen his niece, Miss Arthur, gracefully bound over a barrier at a Paris station, and how we followed her example, all of us just catching our train, which, if we had missed, would have meant missing our steamer as well. He replies: "Oh, yes; "I heard something about it, Mr. van de Linde, but I "hardly think you would call my niece a 'bounder' "all the same; at least I hope not." We all laugh at this joke on the part of His Excellency. Soon after, the party breaks up. I thank them, and then drive back to Dods' office, where I work away till tiffin time, when we all three adjourn to the Bombay Club to tiffin, where I meet my old "Delhi" passenger, Frazer Hore. He was dining last evening with me at the Scobles', and is always very friendly. He is on the Committee of the Bombay Club, and tells the secretary and coffee-room steward to look after me, which they do.

My old Cromwell House schoolfellow, Robert Lee, is in the office of Smith, Fleming & Co.; he has given me a letter of introduction to their Bombay house, William Nicholls & Co., who occupy palatial offices in Elphinstone Circus. They have the whole house—"*Godowns*" (warehouses) on the ground floor; their offices on the first floor; dining, drawing, and smoking-rooms on the second floor, with bedrooms above for the whole of their European (not native) staff. So I go round and show my letter, seeing Mitchell and Macaulay, who receive me very kindly. I remind Macaulay that, when I was a kiddie, my mother and I sat behind his uncle, Lord Macaulay, in a warehouse in St. Paul's Churchyard, to see the Lord Mayor's Show. Just then Hamilton Maxwell, one of the partners, comes out and I am introduced to him. He invites me to dine upstairs that evening, as they have a bit of a function on, with a sing-song afterwards, offering to put me up for the night; so I accept. Maxwell has a splendid steam yacht; he is getting up a party next week for a picnic to the island of Elephanta to see the celebrated caves there, and invites me to join him. This will be a splendid way of doing this trip, for, being an experienced skipper, he has seen that the tides serve all right for the day of our excursion. After tiffin, Tippet takes me for a stroll along the esplanade by the seashore, where we get a grand view of Malabar Hill. I then meet my trap coming to fetch me, and am driven to the Club, where I dress and pack my bag, with white jacket inside, taking my "boy" with me, who sits outside with the coachman, and getting in good time to Elphinstone Circus. At any dinner, whether large or small, one always takes one's "boy" with one. The "boy" stands behind his master's chair, and waits upon him. Every guest just orders whatever drinks he fancies, so that it is quite a usual thing to see the following put upon the table:—"*Simkin*" (champagne)—"*Simkin cup*"; Claret—Claret Cup; Moselle—Moselle Cup; Beer—Beer Mug (we have over here splendid Bass's ale in cask, and bottled by Stone); Cyder—Cyder Cup; Soda and brandy (strange to say, no one ever drank whisky); Sherry, but no Port, &c. &c. Mitchell overtakes me on horseback and rides alongside of me. He tells me the reason he is a bit late is that he has been rigging an Englishman out in decent clothes, and is giving him a free pass home in one of their vessels. It appears that this fellow for the last two years has been travelling all through Central India (out of sheer bravado, being dared to do it) alone, in native attire, but he was obliged to get away from the natives, fearing that they might poison him this very day, which happens to be one of their special religious festivals.

We have a very pleasant dinner, everything going off A1. My sleeping accommodation is excellent. I also enjoy my morning tea and tub. My trap comes round, and Mitchell takes me to see their sawmills and timber swamp, an immense space of land all utilised. I am introduced to the manager, Mr. Mackenzie, who takes us into his private office to show me various kinds of wood, as, for instance, American pine, Australian hard woods, blue gum, Java mahogany, New Zealand Kaurie pine, Norwegian red pine, Baltic timber, Borneo memenbang, Penang kapor, Singapore tempenez, Daru, cedar, oak, rose teak, mountain ash, Deccan teak, Malabar teak, Rangoon teak, English poplar and birch, finishing up with ebony. His desk is of highly polished teak, and is very fine indeed. We then go over the timber factory.

It is 8 a.m., and they have just started. The panorama from outside is grand; we stand on high ground and see Mazagon, Elephanta Island, Matheran, and the Ghautz Mountains. Bombay Harbour is full of large ships, with two or three of William Nicholls & Co.'s steam barges to bring in the timber; this is also floated and brought in on rafts. The heap of sawdust is tremendous, all of different colours, reminding one of the sand formation of Alum Bay in the Isle of Wight. The machinery inside is simply stupendous, especially the "Goliath Travelling Crane," used for unloading ships. They think nothing of cutting up timber of 90 feet length and weighing in the piece 15 tons. The planing machine, at one stroke, planes both sides of the board, while at the same time grooving and bevelling the edges. The travelling bench, too, is very effective. We watch the tenoning and mortising machines, the grooving machine, saw sharpening machine, machine for boring holes in iron clamps, &c. We admire in the carpenter's shop the tables, chairs, window frames, doors, railings, and cabinets, all made on the premises, mostly out of hard teak, very solid and durable. We drive back to Elphinstone Circus just in time for 9 o'clock breakfast, which we indeed enjoy. On my way to Dods' office I am horrified at meeting a leper. The man's face and body are devoid of all natural colour. Work away at the office till two, when I lunch at the Club with Flanagan. Call on Macnee, and find him very sympathetic about my having had to "sack" his nominee. This is a great relief to me. Then follows a legal consultation with Charles Peile at his office, which lasts from 3 to 5 p.m., and is fraught with excellent results.

The consultation over to our mutual satisfaction, my trap takes me back to the Club round by the hard sea sands, where I am amused by watching the Parsees playing cricket with a *soft* ball; there are at least thirty of them. Dressed up in their pyjamas and cotton gowns they are just like so many overgrown schoolboys. The bowler runs at least some fifty yards before delivering his ball, to give it an impetus, and even then it only rolls miserably slowly along; the batter scoops frightfully, strikes a fierce blow as he thinks, the ball hits me on the chest, but being *soft* it does not hurt in the least. I then watch the horsemen on Rotten Row, galloping as if their very existence depended upon it. I fight shy of the bandstand, not being got up in regulation rig. I dine at the Bombay Club at 7 p.m., drinking iced Moselle Cup. It is delicious. After dinner I sit out in the verandah in front, and smoke my first Trichinopoli cheroot—very strong but excellent. I thoroughly enjoy it. At 9.30 p.m. my trap fetches me, and I am driven up to the Byculla Club.

CHAPTER V.

INDIA FIFTY YEARS AGO.—II.

THE foregoing is a pretty fair sample of my daily routine life in Bombay, so I will now pass on rapidly, only noting by the way anything that strikes me as being of especial interest.

I pay a visit to the dockyard, and see the master-builder there. His name is Jamsetjee Dhungeebhoy Wadia—a splendid fellow, speaking English perfectly. He shows me all over the dockyard, including a small yacht he is constructing for the Gaekwar of Baroda. It is worked by a paddle and a screw, which are turned by the hand, no steam being used.

Just as I am leaving, my Parsee friend the dockmaster brings out a flat despatch box made of solid teak, with the following inscription inside:—"*This box is made* "*out of the stern piece of the late Honourable Com-* "*pany's steam vessel 'Hugh Lindsay,' the first built* "*in Bombay or India. She was built in the Bombay* "*Dockyard in the year* 1828, *and wrecked off Bassadore* "*in* 1865." This he very kindly presents to me. It is very capacious inside, fitted with a Bramah lock with inset brass handle on the top. I find it most useful; it occupies an honoured place on my library table, the admiration and envy of all beholders.

The history of the dockyard is unique. In 1735 the ancestor of the present dockyard master and master builder, Lowjee Nassawanjee Wadia, came over from

K 2

Surat and founded this Government dockyard, was made master-builder, and ever since that date the appointment has been in the Wadia family, descending regularly from father to son. The salary is rupees 700 a month, or rupees 8,400 a year—that is, £840 a year—besides perquisites, but so honest have these Wadias been that not one of them died rich. The following is the chronological list of these master-builders, from the commencement to the present day (1867).

1735 to 1774—Lowjee Nassawanjee Wadia.
1774 to 1793—Manockjee Wadia and Bomanjee Wadia, jointly
1793 to 1805—Namjee Wadia and Jamsetjee Wadia ,,
1805 to 1821—Jamsetjee Wadia and Nowronjee Wadia ,,
1821 to 1844—Nowronjee Wadia and Cursetjee Wadia ,,
1844 to 1857—Cursetjee Wadia and Jehanjeer Wadia ,,
1857 to 1862—Jehanjeer Wadia and Hirjeebhoy Merwanjee Wadia, jointly.
1862 to 1865—Jehanjeer Wadia and Jamsetjee Dhunjeebhoy Wadia, jointly.
1865 onwards—Jamsetjee Dhunjeebhoy Wadia and Rustomjee Wadia, jointly.

These docks are well worth a visit. I am shown over the "*Penguin*," a Government gunboat that has had several brushes with slavers on the coast of Africa. The "*Penguin*" has captured several slavers, many of the freed slaves being now able-bodied seamen on the "*Penguin*." The captain has earned £380 prize money, and each of the officers £150. We then visit the "*Duleep Singh*," a Liverpool trader that has just come over with 488 troops. The "mascot" on board is a pet monkey. We go over the ship, and see the men's quarters (the 488, I mean). At the further end is the "prison," and the irons, only used if a man happens to be refractory. We visit one or two other ships and then wish the master-builder and his friends good-bye, thanking them for all they have shown us.

Saturday, 19 January 1867, is a memorable day for me. I drive down to the dockyard, where I meet the master-builder. We both go together to the Apollo Bunder, where the dockyard cutter takes us to the "*Camel*" steamer, bound for Kennery. Under the kind tutelage of my friend Jamsetjee Dhumjeebhoy Wadia, the dockyard master-builder, I feel I am all right. He introduces me to Lieutenant Henry Morland, the secretary, also to Captain Stuart, of "*The Tweed,*" besides several other notabilities (too numerous to mention). We arrive at Kennery Island at 12.30 a.m. The place looks glorious. The island, a stronghold in former days of the old Mahratta chiefs (really pirates), is well fortified. To-day it is all decked out with gay bunting, flags, and festoons; tents pitched for commissariat purposes, and a splendid arch with bold letters "WELCOME" greets us. We land and ascend sundry rough, rugged stone steps some 400 feet high, to the summit of the island, the site of the proposed lighthouse, the foundation stone of which is to-day being laid by His Excellency the Governor of Bombay, Sir Henry Bartle Edward Frere, G.C.S.I. and K.C.B. His Excellency lands, greeted by a salute of 17 guns. The procession forms, and all ascend the summit. The engineer fills up the hole in the bottom stone with a bottle containing a full set of coins of the day, a copy of the *Times of India* and of the *Bombay Gazette*; he fills up the hole with oil, upon which comes the brass plate with the following inscription :—

> "*This stone of the Kennery Lighthouse, erected by the*
> "*Bombay Harbour and Pilotage Board, was laid by His*
> "*Excellency Sir Henry Bartle Edward Frere, G.C.S.I. and*
> "*K.C.B., on the 19th day of January 1867 and in the 29th*
> "*year of the reign of Victoria, of the United Kingdom of*
> "*Great Britain and Ireland, Queen.*"

and then the top corner stone carefully poised, ready for His Excellency, who soon comes up. We all take off our hats; he begs us put them on again. I am splendidly placed, standing about six feet from His Excellency, and command a capital view all round.

The proceedings commence by the Commissioner of Customs and President of the Harbour Board, Mr. A. D. Robertson, reading a long address, all about the island, the pirates, the lighting and defences; to which His Excellency replies in an elaborate speech, eloquently delivered, after which the Rev. Mr. Fletcher offers up a fervent prayer that the Almighty will abundantly bless to-day's great work, inaugurated for the general good of humanity of all nationalities and creeds. His Excellency then takes the silver trowel, daubing the mortar well over the surface before him; the stone then gradually descends, is fixed permanently into its place, and with square, level, and mallet the Governor completes the ceremony with the following solemn emphasis :— "*I declare this corner stone of the Kennery Lighthouse* "*to be well and truly laid, and may the blessing of God* "*Almighty, the Father, Son, and Holy Ghost rest upon* "*this work, which is for the benefit of His creatures,*" to which we all respond "AMEN." The band strikes up "*God Save the Queen,*" all hats are raised, we give three lusty cheers, and the ceremony is over. The silver trowel which figures so prominently in to-day's proceedings was specially manufactured by the mechanics at the Mint with suitable inscriptions on each side.

We wend our way down the hill, soon finding ourselves comfortably seated in the cool refreshment tent, where the catering is done from the Bombay Club by a local contractor, who provides for 300 guests at an all-round sum of 5,000 rupees (over £500). We all say he has made a good thing out of his contract. But everything is of first-rate quality, with no stint anywhere, so everyone is perfectly happy and satisfied all round. A salute of 17 guns signifies the successful laying of the stone. His Excellency joins us, and we all settle down to enjoy our hearty meal. Simkin flows like water, any unoccupied interval being enlivened by pulling crackers and letting off detonating squibs. I sit between the master-builder and the chief engineer; opposite me is Mr. Dossabhoy Framjee, the third magistrate in the Police Court. Upon this occasion the Parsees sit at table with the Europeans, but had Sir Jamsetjee Jejeebhoy been present they would have had a separate table to themselves. The Hindoo guests stand by, looking on; their creed forbids them to eat with us. Besides, this is their sacred month, during which they may not eat from sunrise to sunset.

We indulge in several speeches, enlivened by the band striking up "*God save the Queen,*" "*God bless the Prince and Princess of Wales*"; following these, two loyal toasts proposed by the chairman, His

Excellency the Governor. Mr. A. D. Robertson then proposes the health of Sir Bartle Frere, to which His Excellency responds in a sparkling speech. More toasts, and then His Excellency (accompanied by his staff) rises, leaves the table, and goes on board his steamer the "*May Frere*" (his elder daughter's name); we give three lusty cheers, and a final salute of 17 more guns is fired off, in honour of their departure.

I generally have a stroll before breakfast along the lovely Malabar Hill, which leads eventually to Malabar Point, the marine residence of His Excellency the Governor. He has told me that I can always look in and stroll along the grounds, whether he is there or not.

One morning, without telling my chums anything about it, I start off for Malabar Point, passing on my way the Walkeswar, the sacred village of the Hindus. I find the road crowded with carriages of all descriptions, and cannot make out what brings so many Hindus out here at this early hour of the morning. I meet an Englishman, who informs me, it being the first day of the new moon, all the Hindus in Bombay have come out this morning to the sacred village to perform "*Poojah*" (their religious ceremony); he recommends me to go in for a look round, but to keep my thick stick with me, for I might be the only European there, and the Hindus, when worked up to religious frenzy, might try to molest me if they saw me unarmed.

Before going in, I stroll along to Malabar Point, leaving my card at Government House. His Excellency is up at Poonah to-day, but I readily get leave to explore, and am well repaid for my pains. The view around is simply splenid. I go out upon the rocks, wending my way back to the western side so as to be out of the sun; all of a sudden my attention is arrested by seeing a procession of some 20,000 Hindus in all sorts of gay colours thronging the shore, and coming towards me. I stand by and watch the whole throng come within about 100 yards of me, when they all stop to undress. When they throw themselves into the sea, much to my alarm, for I fancy they are all going to commit suicide, but this is only a part of their sacred rite. They stand about in the water for some time, and then come out again, looking like an army of savages, for they are everyone of them black, male and female. They then dry themselves, put on new garments, never before worn, of very gorgeous colours. The sun shining on them has a grand effect, while all sorts of musical instruments are being played. The noise is simply deafening.

With my thick stick in my hand I summon up courage to penetrate into the sacred village of Walkeswar. They look daggers at me, but I do not care. The dogs, wretched creatures, prowl about, as if they would like to devour me. I enter the very heart of the village. The throng is immense. I have to elbow my way through. Luckily, the people having just washed and put on clean clothes, the stench is not so bad as it would otherwise have been.

Now another sight arrests my attention, and that is a large tank about 100 feet square, full of water, with steps leading down to it, which forms the centre of the village. This tank is literally full of Hindus, men, women, and children, washing themselves in it, while at the same time purifying their garments. The water is holy, so the people drink it; they will still have to drink it, notwithstanding these ablutions, until the next rains in June. I am pestered on all sides by religious beggars, fellows with their faces covered with white, the very holiest of the Hindus, of the highest caste. These men reach this exalted position by the amount of torture they inflict upon themselves. They lie down on the ground, beginning by hitting themselves unmercifully, then their wives set to work to beat them, which the good ladies, for the salvation of their husbands' souls, do with a will indeed. All this time these beggars keep uttering frightful yells, the awed spectators look on, showering small coin into their vessel. The mendicants then strew the ground with hard rice, on which they roll themselves, sore as they are already by the beating they have just been having from their wives. But the climax is to follow. Had I not seen it with mine own eyes I would never have believed it.

A rush is made to a tree, the sacred tree of the place. A trapeze hangs from the branch, under which a slow fire of wood is burning. The most devout and holiest of these men submits to have his legs tied to the trapeze, from which he hangs down and is swung backwards and forwards by another man over this slow fire. The torture must be agonising. I can see the blood run down the veins of the back of this man. He does not utter a sound, and there he goes on swinging for half an hour. The sight is too sickening for me to see this man's face, which is actually roasting. I turn away in disgust unconcealed, to the rage of the spectators, who would have gone for me, but fortunately just at that moment, our office "*schroff*" (native banker) turns up miraculously, takes my arm, and leads me back in safety to my bungalow.

I think I would like to jot down here a list of our bungalow establishment, which consists of the following domestics:—

1 "*Hamaal*" (makes beds, cleans basins, dusts chairs).
1 "*Musdaal*" (washes plates and dishes, trims lamps).
1 "*Matra*" (empties slops).
1 "*Matrane*" (his wife to help him).
1 "*Cook*" (attends to cooking the food).
1 "*Cook's mate*" (rolls out the curry, chops up the meat).
1 "*Mollie*" (the gardener).
1 "*Bheestie*" (the water carrier).
1 "*Dhobie*" (who washes our linen).
1 "*Punkawallah*" (who pulls the Punka, creating a draught).
1 "*Garrywallah*" to each of us (coachman).
1 "*Gorrywallah*" (stable boy).
1 "*Shikari*" (huntsman and beater of game).
1 "*Cootawallah*" (attends to our dogs).
1 "*Butler*" (sees to housekeeping, attending the market to purchase all our provisions).
1 "*Coolie*" (to carry the provisions from market).
1 "*Boy*" to each of us (sees to our clothes and waits on us at table under the butler's orders).
1 "*Barber*" (to cut our hair and shave us).

Their wages come to between £350 and £400 a year. We find them all absolutely essential, we could not do with one servant less; rather different to our English domestic arrangements.

I soon find that sharing a bungalow comes far more expensive than living at the Club; however, it is far jollier.

This day, Saturday, 23 February 1867, is a red-letter day with me; it marks the first time that I have ever travelled on an Indian railroad. We leave Bombay, entering the Mofussil by crossing the viaduct from Bombay to Salsett. Here we come upon a beautiful view, as we pass along the Elphinstone Land and Reclamation Company's works, the native boats sailing under the viaduct, all very quaintly picturesque. From Salsett we come upon the mainland, with a grand view of Elephanta and Trombay Islands This mainland is quite different from the island on which stands the city of Bombay; the first sight of it interests both Hutchison and myself immensely. We pass along the side of the Ghautz Mountains, getting splendid views the whole way. The vegetation growing up the mountain side is both diversified and luxuriant. As we proceed we gradually lose sight of the palm-trees, their place being supplied by the wild fig, the teak, and many other trees.

All along our journey my three companions amuse their weak brains by endeavouring to play practical jokes upon me, but they do not quite manage it, for I generally end by selling them all round.

At 5 p.m. we reach our destination—Narel. A crowd of coolies seize our luggage, marching up the hill with it, accompanied by our "boys," who also share it with the coolies. They have a nine-mile tramp before them, so they have their work well cut out. We find a collection of *Tats* (native horses) waiting to take us up the hill. They have been sent down by Pinto. We each choose one and start for Matheran, 3,500 feet above the level of the sea. We are now at the foot of it, and shall have to creep along the mountain ridge for nine miles, until we reach the top. The road up to Matheran is just one narrow zigzag path, along which we go galloping in *pucker* style.

If our *Tats* stumbled we should probably be pitched over the ravine, which would be the end of us. Unfortunately, the horse that I have chosen is not so fleet as the others. Hutchison has the fastest one, so that every now and then I am left behind in the gallops, but I generally manage to catch them up when they begin to trot.

It is altogether a delightful scene. The Ghautz Mountains up above, with the deep ravines and plains at our feet. form a marvellous contrast. The vegetation is luxuriant. We come upon a great number of wild orchids, which we determine to gather on our way back. As we proceed we disturb a whole army of monkeys and baboons, who rattle down the trees, making a grand noise, chattering away all the time. In the course of our ride we come upon a snake's trail. It is quite fresh, for the reptile has only just got out of our way. The parrots are flying over our heads, rivalling the monkeys with their chatter. The birds are singing; the trees and flowers exhale a delicious aromatic fragrance. The flowers are all gorgeous in colour, the tints of the different foliages are magnificent in their variety. At one moment, from one aspect, all the leaves on the trees are brown, appearing as if they were withered, just as if the season were late autumn. A sudden turn in the road brings us upon the mangoes, luxuriant in their fresh foliage of early spring. We then come upon some trees in full flower and fruit, reminding us of the summer. Then we see the leafless tree, bringing to our recollection winter in all its bleakness. But the sun has set above; darkness will soon overtake us, in fact, before we can possibly reach our destination. Every moment we expect to hear the tiger's roar, for we have now entered the thick Indian jungle, having just passed the toll-gate of civilisation, where we paid the toll of 2 pice each, that is to say, three farthings apiece, so now we really must hurry on to our destination.

We have already wound round the mountain I do not know how many times, passing by the places of rock where the water pours down in torrents during the monsoon.

Now and again we have watched our "boys" and the coolies wending their long weary way on foot below, carrying our kit between them. At length we reach the summit, commanding a grand prospect all round, but we have no time to spare now, as we have still two-and-a-half miles to go. It is already 6.15 p.m. Darkness overtakes us, so we decide to gallop through the jungle straight till we reach Pinto's, not stopping till we get to his hospitable threshold. We all set off like mad. I am, as usual, again last, and the dust from the other *Tats* nearly stifles me. However, I keep up with them as long as ever I can, but eventually lose sight of the last man (Tippet). However, they have told me it is straight ahead, so I go blindly forward, trusting to Providence. I go on all right for the first mile and a half, when I suddenly come to a fork of two roads. Whichever shall I take? For the life of me I do not know, so I leave it to my *Tat* to choose. We soon come upon some lights. I am hoping it is Pinto's. Alas! a delusion and a snare. I have lost my way, and am come upon unknown habitations. I shout out "Pinto's." One of the men rushes forward, leads my *Tat* on to a narrow path in the jungle; he then points me to go on, which I do, but all of a sudden my *Tat* shies, refusing to move. I find there is a snake in his path; this makes my *Tat* turn round three or four times, during which I fancy I am going to be thrown every minute. However, I just manage to keep my seat and start off all right. For a change I now come upon three roads, making me fear that now I am really lost—lost in an Indian jungle—pitch dark, with all sorts of wild beasts, including tigers, cheetahs, and snakes! In this dilemma I again let my *Tat* have his own way. By and by, when I have quite made up my mind that I shall have to wander all night disconsolately through the forest, I come upon a bungalow. Hurrah! It is Pinto's at last, but where are the other three, I should like to know? It is now seven o'clock, and not one of them has turned up yet. However, as they are three, they can take care of themselves, so I have a refreshing peg, a good wash, and settle down to read *Pickwick,* which I find lying on the bungalow table. At about half-past seven they all three turn up, looking frightfully worried. They have long since missed me, quite giving me up for lost. When they first missed me, they turned back until they came upon our "boys" and coolies, whom they asked whether they had seen anything of me. No such luck. So they set to scouring the country, at the same time sending the coolies to look after me, right and left. Finally they decide to go on to Pinto's to hold there a council of war. I fiendishly have a good laugh at them now that all danger is past, chaffing them unmercifully at having got in first after all with my slow *Tat*. We all four of us, however, are relieved that things have thus ended all right.

One morning, Hutchison and I set out for a brisk walk to the Parsee Towers of Silence. We see the huge gridiron upon which the dead bodies are laid to the mercies of the fowls of the air. We are not allowed into the enclosure; not even Parsees are allowed admission, save the priests alone. All round the enclosure are palm trees, the boughs of which are crowded with large kites and other foul birds of prey, who gorge upon the dead bodies and putrid remains. The Parsees look upon them as being sacred birds. The ground all round the enclosure is strewn with human bones of every description. We now come upon some native habitations where the men, women, children, and animals are all huddled together, reminding one of the huts I saw in later years at Connemara on the west coast of Ireland, though there is this difference—here the young girls go about in a comparative state of nature, their sole attire being a ring in their nose, armlet, and toe rings. Some of the more prosperous ones also wear bangles; these are all of pure gold. This is the fashion among the natives, thus to hoard their wealth. Unfortunately, however, it sometimes happens that these unfortunate children are murdered for the sake of the wealth they carry about with them on their person.

Wednesday, 6 March 1867.—After breakfast Tippet drives me round to see a cotton press. It is called The Fort Press, where cotton, under its powerful agency, is reduced to about a tenth part of its capacity, thereby affecting a great saving in freight, which is reckoned by cubic measurement and not by weight. The process is thus : A large car is filled with loose cotton, its weight representing a bale; this loose cotton is bundled into the receptacle of the press, with a piece of cloth placed top and bottom. The cotton when pressed, before the two sides are put on, looks splendidly even. When the two sides are put on, the bale is lashed round and round with stout rope. The bale is then sent down a trap-door on to the lower floor, where women sew on the two ends compactly; the bale is then branded "Fort Press," and carried away to make room for the next one.

On another occasion, in company with Salmon, an official friend, I pay a state visit to the Ranee of Angrias Colaba (the native queen). She is the widow of the late King Angrias, Rajah of the district, but since the quelling of the Mutiny, ten years ago, his strongholds were seized and dismantled. Being now dead, his widow is the sole relict of his former glory. She resides at Alibagh. She is expecting us, so when we ride up to the great courtyard of the palace the retainers give us a native cheer with a salaam to welcome us. We dismount, enter the palace, ascend to the royal apartments, preceded by ushers until we come into the Ranee's presence. I speak literally, for though she is not in our presence, sitting in the shade behind a screen, while we, who are in the light, cannot see her, she sees us all right. This is called being in "*purdah*" (concealed). There are seats for us on which we sit down, making our salaam. The Ranee greets us; the Prime Minister sits opposite us, treating us with profound respect. Salmon keeps up a grand conversation in Mahratta with the Ranee. She asks him a lot about me, which he tells her. We now prepare to leave, but the ceremony is not yet over. The Chamberlain signs to the attendants to prepare for two guests. In a few minutes they come in laden with gifts from the Ranee—a chaplet of roses for each of us, which we put on our arm or wrist; two bouquets fastened to a stick. The Chamberlain sprinkles them with rose-water and our handkerchiefs with otto of roses, after which "*pan sopari*" (betel nut and condiments) is brought in. This we just touch, the remainder we give to the attendants as "*largesse.*" We salaam to the Ranee, and retire amidst shouts of "Salaam" raised in our honour. The ceremony is now indeed over. We ride round the village of Worsoolee to visit a tank which is being constructed under Salmon's directions. It is a jolly ride of two miles. We pass a gorgeous Hindu temple on our way, with lots of bamboo trees, the first I have seen in India.

Tuesday, 9 April 1867.—Salmon beguiles me. Instead of going back to Bombay we start at noon for a visit to the famous Caves of Elephanta. We disembark and have tiffin in one of the caves. Elephanta was formerly the great island for Hindu worship. The caves where we have our tiffin are on the top of the hill. We have some distance to climb up solid square steps right up to the top. These solid steps, 10 feet wide, were constructed by the Gaekwar of Baroda and at his expense. Arrived at the top we are met by the sergeant in charge, who salaams us and then takes us to the best place where we can have our tiffin. These caves are certainly wonderful—huge caves carved out of the solid rock—the interior of each like an immense hall. The pillars supporting the roof have been carved out of the solid rock; nothing has been added, it is all in one piece. At the end and round the sides are sculptures of gods and goddesses, also carved out of the solid rock, while round the large cave are small caves containing various altars. "Elephanta" is so named because when the Portuguese took it, some 400 years ago, the principal cave contained a large elephant of pure gold with diamond eyes. Here it is that we see the worst kind of ancient idolatry—the "Linga worship"—the worship of the creative principle. The grand figure of Vishnu, the goddess with three heads, is before us, a masterpiece of sculpture, as also the figure of the god and goddess, the junction of Siva and Vishnu, all in one piece, with four arms and only one breast. Under one of the side caves is a spring of pure icy cold water.

Saturday, 11 May 1867.—Hutchison and I a few days ago had received a card of invitation from Mr. Dinshaw Manockjee Petit to a Nautch party this evening at 9.30 at his bungalow on Malabar Hill, close to ours, which we had accepted. We turn up about 10 p.m. The whole place is brilliantly lighted up; the compound and terraces are swarming with Parsee guests and relatives, who are waiting there to welcome the marriage procession of the bridegrooms coming to fetch their respective brides. We walk on a little, and soon we hear music and shouting; we approach the two bungalows of the bridegrooms, which are opposite each other. The two processions join and come towards us. First come the two bands; one plays "Bonnie Dundee," the other "I'm off to Charlestown"—the one regardless of the other, so that the effect is somewhat incongruous. Then follow the priests, all clad in white; after them the bridegrooms with their male friends—these are also all dressed in white like the priests, except that they wear oilcloth turban hats. After this come the ladies, richly attired in many coloured silks of gorgeous tints, followed by the children. The first part of the procession, comprising the priests and men all in white, is very plain; but the second part, with the women and children, is very picturesquely effective. Behind the lot come the friends who are not of the Parsee caste, such as Hindus, &c. Then follow a number of carriages with people inside. Everyone carries in his hand a bouquet of white orange blossoms, with a pink rose in the middle. Men follow behind with baskets of cocoanuts to present to the Hindu guests, whose religion precludes them feasting with their Parsee friends. The festivity this evening is a repetition of what has been going on for some days to celebrate the wedding of our host's two daughters. The first wedding came off this evening at 7 o'clock, the second wedding comes off at midnight. The bridegrooms are Dadabhoy Hormusjee Cama (nephew of Muncherjee Hormusjee Cama), who marries the elder daughter, and Merwanjee Panday (son of Merwanjee Framjee Panday), who marries the younger one. The bungalow, the largest in Bombay, is one blaze of light. Mr. Dinshaw Manockjee Petit is there with some twenty relatives to welcome us. We enter the saloon—another blaze of light. It is already crowded with guests. Mr. Mody, on seeing me, comes forward insisting on my taking his seat. At one end of the saloon are the three musicians, playing, on their peculiar instruments, Indian airs, while the Nautch girls are standing ready to begin. After singing a mournful melody they gradually turn it into an enlivening one, and then they start dancing. It is just a sort of sailing along gracefully, no pirouetting nor throwing heels or legs about—just a dreamy, sleepy, voluptuous dance. Their movements throughout are slow and lethargic. They wear bangles on their ankles, which make a monotonous sound as they dance, or rather glide along. At 11 p.m. refreshments are handed round. We ramble about the place. Old Dinshaw is evidently proud of his bungalow, as also of the whole affair, which is a great success. He takes us all over the place, upstairs, downstairs, and in my lady's chamber, where one or two Parsee ladies are lying asleep on a couch. We wish to retire, but he insists on taking us right through everywhere, telling us he was his own architect, and planned everything himself. Dinshaw then takes us into the refreshment room, where a big spread is laid out for his European friends, while in an adjoining room the Parsee guests are regaling themselves.

We surround Dinshaw and drink his health in bumpers of champagne, singing "For he's a jolly good fellow." This pleases the old boy immensely. He makes us taste some of his famous mangoes, fresh cut out of his compound; they are simply delicious. The mango is such a rich, luscious, juicy fruit that the proper way to enjoy it is in a warm bath, with a tray across to hold the divine fruit. A self-playing piano is discoursing sweet music; it cost Rupees 15,000, or £1,500 sterling—a noble instrument. First it plays Indian airs, then English airs, such as "Home, Sweet Home," "The last Rose of Summer," &c. &c. Then the Nautch girls begin dancing again, and then we have "The Scotch Bagpipes." It is close upon midnight; the second wedding is about to take place at Mr. Cama's bungalow. We are each presented with a bridal bouquet and a bottle of otto of roses, and then we retire with much salaaming and handshaking. We pass Cama's bungalow, and are invited in to witness the marriage ceremony. When it is too late, we find that we two are the only Europeans present. However, it is all right; Hutchison and I are given the seats of honour, and put quite at our ease by our hospitable host. Mr. Cama is a meek, unassuming man—the exact type of a high-class Parsee—he is enormously wealthy. When he came over to London a few years ago he procured a letter of introduction to the Bank of England, where he rather astonished the clerk there by quietly filling up his paying-in slip for £100,000 sterling with which to open his banking account. Fans are handed round and more refreshments—iced cream pudding; Neapolitan, strawberry, and pineapple ices; iced simkin—everything of the very best. We ask Cama how long this will last before the wedding ceremony begins. He says:

"Perhaps till 3; perhaps till 5 o'clock in the morning." This is enough for us; we make a bolt.

I attended the Mohurrum in Bombay last Wednesday, 15 May 1867. The word signifies that it is sacred and defended by the law from an age long anterior even to that in which Mohammed appeared on the scene. There were formerly four months in the year—namely, "Mohurrum," "Rajeb," "Dhu'lkaada," and "Dhu'l-kajja"—which were regarded by the Arabs as sacred, during which time they were not permitted to carry on warfare. So strictly was this theory carried into practice that all through the duration of these four months respectively the men took the heads from their spears, while at the same time they laid aside their bows and arrows.

Although the Mohurrum is observed by both factions of Mohammedans—that is to say, the "Sunis" and the "Shias"—the practice of the two is widely different; for although they profess one creed, they are bitterly opposed the one to the other, so that the Mohurrum, their great joint festival, is observed by these two factions in diametrically opposite ways.

Among the "Shias" it is observed as a season of profound mourning, for it was on the tenth of the month that their hero, "Hussein," was slain under circumstances which give him the position of a martyr. On the other hand, the "Sunis" keep the day as one of rejoicing and not of sorrow. It would appear that the Shias (separatists) are followers of Ali, an ancestor of Hussein: they carry out the custom of exhibiting the "tabuts" or "taziyas," representing the tomb of their martyred Hussein; while the Sunis also adopt them, but in pure mockery. Throughout the whole of the Mohammedan area the Mohurrum is observed as an ordinance of the Koran, but it is in India alone that the custom of carrying about the "tabuts" prevails. On some of these occasions disturbances, not infrequently ending in bloodshed, arise from the bigotry of the adherents of the rival factions, so that at home it is always pleasant intelligence to read that the Mohurrum has passed off without disturbance. I may mention that the death of Hussein happened over twelve hundred years ago, thus separating from that period the followers of Mohammed into these two factions—the Sunis, who are zealous in the cause of Ayesha, Omar, Osman, and Abutekr; while the Shias execrate the memories of the last-named three, and only in a less degree that of Ayesha herself. The Shias have come in time to regard Ali as more than mortal. The Mohammedan year is a lunar one, while ours is a solar one. The tenth day of the Mohurrum occurs, therefore, at various periods of our calendar. The owners of the finest armour lend their glittering helmets and burnished coats of mail to the warriors who join in the procession. Carpenters work for nothing, constructing the tiers of seats for the audience, while soldiers come forward quickly to represent the contending hosts. If by any chance a man be killed during the performance of the "tazeeah," it is considered that his soul goes directly to the regions of eternal bliss. If anything should go wrong during the performance, it would be considered a sign of the displeasure of the Almighty.

On the morning of the tenth day of Mohurrum, Wednesday, 15th May 1867, the great festival took place. We were there to see it. To the most of us the striking feature was a figure borne on a bier, representing the body of Hussein, covered with blood, while hovering over the body was a white dove. Deep sobs exhibit the emotion of the people, old and young being alike affected. Walking round and round the ring of the mourners are groups who form circles of a dozen or twenty men. bending down to the ground, beating their bare breasts, and uttering cries of "Wah! wah! Hussein." The sound produced by this violent beating of bare breasts is peculiar, and although the whole assembly do the like, the harmony is wonderfully preserved. After this portion of the ceremony, the devotees become much exhausted. Rose-water is thrown over their heads and their faces. From the violence of the penance, the skin of the breasts of many has become so inflamed that a pink tinge is visible even through the dusky natural hue. The ceremony concluded by further representations on the part of the natives. I am happy be able to say that the police arrangements for the preservation of the peace in Bombay during the whole of the Mohurrum of 1867 were admirably carried out. Each "tabut," when in the street, had so many police sepoys attached to it, while the fellows who appeared dressed as tigers—their main object being frolic—had to pay something for a licence. The "tabut" days are not altogether confined to the Sunis, for many of the low-caste Hindus are to be seen on these days assisting to carry the "tabuts," vying with the Mohammedans in noisy gesticulation.

Of course, the great fear throughout this great festival is lest the two processions of the Sunis and Shias should come into conflict. By the careful arrangements of the police this has been this year avoided, so that everything has passed of quite quietly.

Sunday, 30 June 1867.—After chota hazree we all three visit the Government Commissariat compound to visit the elephants. To do this we have to go through the native bazaar, a much cleaner one than at Bombay. The youngsters—male and female—go rambling about in nature's garb, showing off their aldermanic proportions, brought about by the quantity of rice they eat, which their mothers are just now grinding up for them. We meet a few camels laden with packs. When we reach the Government Commissariat compound we come upon 150 camels and 40 elephants being fed.

The elephants (huge monsters) stand all in a line, with heavy iron chains round their immense legs attached to strong iron stakes. They are indeed powerful brutes; each elephant has his "*mahout*" (keeper) squatting at the animal's side. Their legs are like huge rocks; they have fine tusks, the tips have been sawn off and brass caps put upon them. This is for the sake of safety; it also prevents the tusks from splitting. In a shed close by are the two patriarchs. They are ferocious monsters, having already killed several natives, so that now every precaution has to be taken with them. To this end they are bound in chains, as it were, hand and foot. The most remarkable feature about the elephant is his immensely broad powerful forehead; with this and his equally powerful head he does all his work, pushing with his head, while at the same time bringing all the power of his immense frame to bear; he cannot draw a bit. His eyes are very small, but they look very knowing. His ears are in shreds, for it is by the ear that he is led; his mahout sticks an iron hook in the animal's ear, making him go to the right or the left. The elephant is never harnessed, his mahout guides him entirely by the iron hook in the beast's ear.

The camels, on the other hand, are quite docile, looking more like ostriches than like animals; their long necks with their sagacious heads make them look quite handsome. They are very sure-footed, but to a novice the motion on their back is anything but pleasant; it is apt to bring on a feeling of nausea akin to sea-sickness. The regular riders adapt themselves to the swing of the animal, moving their bodies to suit the camel's motion. Each saddle is in compartments; the man rides in the middle, while a pack is put in front of him, with another pack behind him. The riders wear stirrups, leading the camel by a rope running through his nostrils; it is made fast at each end, so that the man has only to pull to the right or to the left, just as in ordinary driving. Youngsters are busy at work gathering the camels' dung; it is very valuable, being used for incense.

The Gold Mohur or Pagoda tree is a worthy emblem of the east. It is in its branches that the minas, the parrots, and the humming-birds take up their abode. Driving back to the bungalow we first meet a native with two armadilloes—animals all over scales, useful for killing ants and other vermin in a bungalow.

Another native comes along with a huge cobra snake that he has just caught, after the reptile had gorged a fowl whole, which is still in his throat, giving him a bloated appearance; his fangs have not been removed, so he is an ugly customer, but the native is a snake charmer and keeps him in subjection. A snake is quickly disabled, for, as soon as he rises to dart, a small switch brought down round his neck will at once break the spinal cord of even the biggest, which at once drops down helpless. The snake charmer is followed by a man with some twenty monkeys for sale, while another has a lot of parrots all tied by their legs to a long string. Then come a troop of donkeys, heavily laden with tiles, then a herd of goats with their long shaggy beards; after that come a string of camels—a regular menagerie, in fact. We come upon a magnificent banyan tree, where we sit down to rest. This tree is always sending down fresh fibres from the branches: these fibres take root and shoot up to the branches, which again drop down fresh fibres. These all strike root, become fresh trunks of trees, and so whole forests spring up, so to say, from one tree. Between Delhi and Agra there is a famous banyan tree, under which a whole regiment of artillery can encamp. There are also fine specimens at Ahmedabad. This tree is regarded as sacred by the Hindus, who build round its main trunk a flat brick platform. This main trunk is painted red and yellow, and is supposed to contain a Hindu god.

We rest on the platform, where we witness a curious scene. Two Hindu women walk round and round the tree, while a *fakeer* (a Hindu priest) sits by with a large basket of mangoes beside him. As the women pass by, he gives each a mango, which they drop into another basket. The ceremony goes on until the one basket is emptied and the other is filled. By the tree is the image of the god, painted red, with the "*linga*" stone by its side, together with the jar of sacred "*ghi*" (butter) and oil, a "*lotah*" (brass vessel) of water, and a cocoanut. The ceremony is for one of two purposes: either that the women are barren, and are thus trying to propitiate their god to make them fruitful, or else they are doing sacrifice for a safe deliverance. We get back to the bungalow at 9.30 a.m., after four hours' hard walking.

That afternoon Hirjeebhoy drives Hutchison and me to visit the jail. It covers an immense area; the gaunt grim walls look most imposing. The platform on which the scaffolding for hanging is fixed is always standing over the western entrance. We enter by the eastern entrance. We first come upon a large square yard where the convicts are kept. There are about 50 of them; they are seated on a wooden platform picking oakum. Some of them are English sailors serving a short term for refusing to work out their agreement on board ship. Conspicuous among the others is a fine handsome-looking young fellow who is in for three years for forgery. While the other prisoners appear to look upon the whole thing as a huge joke, and making fun of it, this young fellow sits silently aloof from the rest. He evidently feels his degradation, which is enhanced when he catches sight of us, so, not wishing to wound his feelings any further, we hurry away to another spot. He appreciates our action, and bows gracefully as we disappear out of his sight.

The old hands do not have much difficulty in picking their oakum. Although the rope that is given them in pieces of a foot long is thoroughly sodden with tar, they untwist the principal hanks and then beat the ends against the stones. This loosens the fibre, which very soon comes apart. They use their toes as well as their fingers. They put a big hank between their big toe and the one next to it, and then with their two hands they quickly unravel it, and then they take up another hank, dealing with it in the same way. We then visit the various workshops; here caste prejudices are strictly observed, so that the prisoners have allotted to them tasks which do not clash with their religion. We first pay a visit to the Basket factory and to the Carpenter's shop, which are both under one shed under the female ward, which is above them. A young half-caste ("*chi chi*") carpenter is making a splendidly strong big chest out of hard teak—the jailor says it is for him—the finish is excellent. The man works as much with his toes as with his hands, to steady what he is at work upon, whether planing or cutting out with a chisel. The basket-makers are not less expert; they work away with a will and energy which is quite remarkable. They all seem to be as happy as the day is long. The whole place is neat and clean. We next visit the Cocoanut-matting department. The first stage here is to watch the junk being made up into rope, and then the several lines (the width of the required mat) being stretched on the loom side by side, and passed over a roller; these are for the *length*. A lot of natives are twining rope on shuttles; these are for the cross lines for the *width*. As the cocoanut fibre is too knotty and hard for the alternate lines to drop into their places by means of a frame, two men, one on each side, pick out the alternate lines with their fingers. When they have got them all they throw the shuttle through, thus making a cross line, which they tighten with a flat piece of wood. They then begin again, taking up this time the other alternate lines; it is hard work for the fingers, though. Two men between them can only make three yards of matting in a day. The matting is excellent. It is on the floor of this workshop that the English convicts sleep; their bedding is lashed to one of the walls. The opposite wall has a number of doors leading into small cells where the natives sleep, three or four in a cell. These are locked up at night. The ventilation everywhere is very good. Should an English convict prove refractory he is put into one of these cells, either alone or with another English prisoner. We now come to the Weaving department, where we watch the various processes. The space here is cramped, and the light is not good. Prison cloth, used for trouserings, is made here. In the hot season most of the Englishmen in Bombay wear this material, which is made up into trousers by their "*durzees*"—native tailors. The pattern is always the same—a uniform square.

We now come to the Towel department. These towels are very strong; they are eagerly bought up, being quite cheap. The long bath towels fetch 12 rupees a dozen—that is, 2s. apiece.

The jailor regrets he cannot show us the working of the treadmill; it is out of order owing to the two swing balls at the top having got out of the perpendicular.

They are now being put straight again, ready for use in a day or two.

The jailor tells us the prisoners suffer intensely from prickly heat while having a tread at the mill, but that at home it is hardly any punishment at all; here it is a very severe punishment. We visit the condemned cells, where four murderers were confined this last spring awaiting their execution. They were hanged for murdering, in the native town, two "marwarries" (money dealers).

These condemned cells are also used for refractory prisoners, who go in generally for 56 hours. There is one in now—a young Hindu—he is crouched up in a corner, a pitiable object; he will be let out to-night. He is in for three years, having committed an accumulation of villainies. The jailor shows us the prison celebrity; he has just had his bath—a fine stalwart "sedi" (a liberated African slave), who amused himself a short time ago by rushing about the streets of Bombay brandishing a knife, with which he stabbed every sepoy (native policeman) he came across. He actually killed seven in this way, before he was captured. He is in for life; why he was not hanged out and out is a mystery. The "sedi" comes out of his bathroom, chatting and grinning as if he never were so happy in his life. He salaams to us in right regal fashion. An effectual punishment for refractory convicts is to put their feet in the stocks. There are plenty of these stocks about, but just now they are all empty—an hour ago they were in full play. We pass the celebrated prison tank; its water is far famed, being excellent.

Prisoners thrive on it. A Parsee came in thin and haggard; after three months in jail he came out plump and rosy cheeked. But with the recovery of his liberty he lost his good looks, soon becoming as thin and haggard as ever. His mother used to say, with tears in her eyes: "Ah, my poor son, he misses the good "water of Mazagon Jail; he will never be well until he "goes back again." Sure enough, he was in jail once more the very next day for some trifling offence, and very soon recovered his good looks.

The prison fare is good: the natives live on curry, rice, and water; the Europeans on curry, rice, beef, vegetables, gruel, and bread ("skilly" and "toke"), with the same excellent water, alternated with Vehar Lake water, the supply for Bombay. The place is exceedingly healthy, the hospital well-nigh empty, nothing much the matter with the invalids, who are mostly shamming through laziness; no fever, no cholera—the natives are far better here than in their own dwellings in the native town. The debtors' section is the merriest-looking place out; they consider it a huge joke living there at the expense of their creditors, who have to contribute so much a day for their support. If the creditor any one day fails to pay this money, the debtor at once becomes a free man. He is also free after two years' imprisonment, at the same time becoming free of his debt—that is, for any one individual debt for which he has been confined; so, if his creditors care, they can keep him in for an indefinite period, by only proceeding against him for one debt at a time. In this way five of his creditors could keep him in "choki" for ten years. There is an old native here—he owes rupees 40,000, or £4,000 sterling. He has been in prison twenty months; in another four months he will be a free man, having done his creditors out of those rupees 40,000! I say to him: "Why don't you pay up like an honourable man and come out of jail?" The old sinner coolly replies: "Why should I? I am "comfortable here. I could not make rupees 40,000 "outside in four months. Besides which, so long as "I am here, my creditors cannot attach my property." He is known to be actually worth three lacs, or £30,000 sterling. The English law here is far too lenient to natives. In their own native Courts justice is far more severe and efficient, so that a creditor stands a chance; here he has none. The debtor simply bosses the show all round.

The licence that is allowed in the debtors' side of the prison is astounding. They have Nautches as often as they like, they live on the fat of the land, for the money which they withhold from their creditors procures them all that they want. The other day was this old sinner's birthday; he gave a great entertainment to which he invited twenty of his friends outside as his guests. All of a sudden I find I have no "dibs" (rupees) about me, nor has Hutchison either. So I ask Hirjeebhoy to lend me 5 rupees. He says: "I have "not got them about me, but I will borrow them from "a man here who owes me a lac (£10,000)." Sure enough, he does, and with this I tip our jailor, thus borrowed from the debtor. Fancy in England borrowing 10s. from a man who owes you £10,000.

We wish the debtor good-bye, tell him he is an old sinner, and that he may never expect to see those

5 rupees again, to which he laughingly replies: "Oh, "that's all right; I'll lend you five more on the same "terms if you like," and he actually offers them me with the most barefaced effrontery.

On my way home from Bombay (where, needless to say, I left many of the kindest friends I have ever made) I took advantage of our halt at Suez to take a stroll through that outpost of the East. Suez is truly oriental, so that my walk is a very picturesque one. I come across any number of Arabs, camels, and veiled women, all permeated with languid sleepiness—all work is suspended from 11 a.m. till 3 p.m., during which time everyone has his meals, followed by a siesta. The air is peculiarly dry. I meet Major Pearse, who accompanies me the rest of the way. We pass by several Salt Pans, when suddenly we come upon the Fresh Water Canal, which reminds me exactly of the River Lea from Tottenham onwards. Locks and tow path on each side of the Canal—in fact, everything complete. The Canal is studded with barges and boats of all descriptions, just like being at home again. The Major rather thinks of staying on a while, as to go up as far as Ismalia in a boat he will have to pay 130 francs (£5 4s.); from there he will get a steamer the remainder of the way for a few francs. The Salt Water Canal is not near completion yet, it is supposed to be open for traffic in the summer of 1869. My old Boulogne friend, Monsieur Voisin, is the head engineer out here. Ferdinand Lesseps has most implicit confidence in him, he is just now at Ismalia, so I shall not see him, but I give Pearse a note (no longer a "chit") for him, as I am sure he will gladly show him around everywhere.

The thermometer is up to 90 in the shade, but being a dry, not a moist, concentrated heat we stand it without inconvenience. Having seen as much as we can in our limited time we return to Suez. On our way to the entrance of the city we come to a venerable old archway, where we rest awhile, sheltered from the sun's rays by a stone projection. Here we find a seller of freshly gathered dates. They hang in great clusters from boughs of the date palms—we have our fill of them, they are simply deliciously fresh, hard, and acid. We make our lunch off them, bestowing 6d. on the vendor, which makes him supremely happy. Opposite us, and still under our archway, is a Greek shop. The owner comes out with a huge stone porous jar (a "cooja") of deliciously cold water, which he pours out for us in two large tumblers; it tastes like nectar. He then rolls up two cigarettes of Turkish tobacco, licking the edges, which he politely offers us, but which we gracefully decline. Sitting under this archway we catch two or three real glimpses of Oriental life. Camels in single file carrying huge packs, each having its own driver; buffaloes, with skins full of water; females with long black garments descending from their nose down to their toes, just leaving two black eyes full of fire visible—their nose is adorned with a covering of brass rings. We pass two or three mosques and minarets, and then make straight for the bazaar, a thoroughly Eastern one; the road through is narrow, and the upper stories of the houses overhanging on each side meet within a foot of each other. We come upon quaint bits of architecture with glorious Moorish interiors. Up one avenue we notice a castellated wall with a turret projecting, from the window sill of which leans a fair damsel in flowing garments of pure deep blue; the effect is indeed striking. On each side the dealers are exposing their wares; they are a wild nondescript lot with a great deal of the vagrant Arab about them. They look rather eagerly at my gold watch and chain with the hanging Indian gold coins, also at Pearse's money bag; but we are alive to their tricks, so we give them a wide berth. We enter a shop to buy a map of the Canal, which I have still by me; the owner presses each of us to buy a revolver, assuring us that only two days ago twelve men were murdered; we have presence of mind to refuse, but, deeming that discretion is the better part of valour, we wend our way back to the Suez Hotel. And here, at Suez, my Oriental experiences came to an end. I journeyed home by way of Marseilles and Paris, and on Monday morning, November 4th 1867, was once more in the familiar office in King's Arms Yard, to meet with a warm reception from my three principals, who complimented me on the success of my mission, and at the same time on the healthiness of my looks.

CHAPTER VI.

Business in Two Continents.

WHEN I returned from India in 1867 I saw the Emperor Napoleon III and the Empress Eugénie in all their glory at the Paris Exhibition; and one day I went to Versailles, and was in the private rooms of the Trianon when all of a sudden we saw the door shut, and, on asking why, were told that the Empress of the French with the Queen of Holland (whom I knew) were visiting the State apartments, so that no one else was allowed in, but those who were in were allowed to remain. The Empress (then at the height of her beauty) invited the Queen of Holland to play on the harpsichord originally used by Marie Antoinette, and the Queen did so. I was rather amused at the old Colonel in charge of the Trianon saying to me in a loud whisper, and pointing to his dirty white gloves :—"*Pas de chance avec mes vieux gants, sans le temps de les changer.*" I smiled, and consoled him by telling him that, if he kept in the background, his gloves would not be noticed, as indeed they were not.

The summer of 1870 was barely over when the Franco-German war broke out, where the Prince Imperial had his baptism of fire. Years after (in 1884) I visited the battlefields and came across the "*Lulu Stein*" (Louis Stone), which the Germans had put in irony to mark the spot where the Prince stood. The war ended with the surrender, at Sedan, of the French Emperor, who was taken prisoner by the Germans to Berlin. The Empress Eugénie, with the Prince Imperial, came over to England, being installed at Camden House, Chislehurst, on 10 December 1870, where the Emperor Napoleon III joined them early in the following year, 1871.

The summer after that, when I was living at Bexley Heath, we invited the Imperial party to come over to our local flower show, held that year at Danson Park. The Emperor graciously accepted, but the Empress and the Prince Imperial were previously engaged at Woolwich, so were unable to be present. I was deputed to receive the Emperor, which I did, showing him all over; but what a sad contrast to the dapper, bright, well-dressed Emperor I had seen at the Paris Exhibition in 1867! He had grown stout, shaggy, and looked very ill, as indeed the poor man was. But all the same he took great interest in the exhibits, thanking me very warmly as he left. We, of course, spoke French together the whole time. He died at Camden House on 9 January 1873, and was buried in the little Roman Catholic Chapel at Chislehurst on 15 January 1873. There was an enormous concourse of mourners at the funeral, myself among the rest; it was a most touching, impressive occasion.

The Prince Imperial went later on to Zululand, where he was killed on 1 June 1879. The funeral took place at the chapel at Chislehurst on 12 July 1879. It was a military funeral, a long procession all the way from Woolwich to Chislehurst. I also attended that funeral.

The following year (1880) the Empress Eugénie left Chislehurst, settling down at Farnborough, where she built a mausoleum, to which the remains of her husband and son were removed, and reburied there. Our late Queen Victoria also erected a recumbent monument to the memory of the Prince Imperial. I have seen them both; they are very beautiful, each of them in exquisite taste.

In the spring of 1875 Mr. Robert Benson, my old friend and master ever since 1858, died suddenly; his death altered my career very materially, for in the summer of that year a dissolution of the firm took place. My many friends took this opportunity of strongly recommending me to try fresh fields and pastures new, going out of their way to offer me lucrative appointments at home and abroad. After mature consideration, and with their full concurrence, I entered the office of a leading firm of accountants as manager, with a private room, one of their country and continental departments being placed under my sole control. One of the first matters I thus took up was at Birmingham, where I stayed seven weeks at the "Queen's Hotel." The old Earl of Dudley was staying at the hotel at the time, so I got to know him, for after dinner we sat at the same table at the end of the dining room writing our letters. The Earl always had by him four silver candlesticks, each containing thick wax candles; he very kindly shared the light with me upon these occasions. I generally spent the week-ends in the neighbourhood, unless I had to come home for any special reason; this was not often. In this way I visited Kenilworth,

Warwick, Stratford-on-Avon, Leamington, and Malvern, staying there at the North Malvern Hotel, situated on high ground with a grand view all round.

After a good lunch, when I tasted perry for the first time, I explored the Great Herefordshire Beacon and the Great Worcestershire Beacon, and I did the same the next morning before breakfast, rising through the clouds and mist into bright sunshine overhead; all of a sudden the clouds and mist rolled away, giving me an uninterrupted view of the plain below. It was, indeed, a wonderful sight.

While transacting this business in Birmingham, I suddenly found out, just before Christmas, that my clients held French patents, with a small temporary workshop at St. Denis, four miles from Paris, but that, if they did not start working there before the end of the year, the patents would lapse. I made this discovery on a Wednesday afternoon, I immediately rushed off home to Bexley Heath, packed my bag, had a hurried meal, and caught the night mail for Paris, arriving there the next morning, Thursday, and putting up at the Hotel Continental. I swallowed a cup of tea, and drove to a leading French lawyer, whom I found at home drinking his café au lait in his dressing gown. I handed him all the papers, with full particulars, arranging to meet him at 10 a.m. at the Law Courts, which I did. I there made the requisite depositions before the Judge, who granted me at once the desired permit. Armed with this document we at once took a victoria to St. Denis, where we were expected, for I had taken the precaution to write to the foreman from London the afternoon previous to my contemplated call on him.

Consequently, when we arrived, I found the furnace thoroughly heated, with the irons in the fire. One of these was taken out red hot, and with a strong hammer and chisel I struck a blow, severing a piece off to the required length. I repeated this operation with two other lengths, so that I had in all three pieces. The foreman and the lawyer were witnesses to what I had done. The three pieces were properly cooled and taken by us back to Paris, the foreman accompanying us; we all three first had lunch together at the Hotel Continental. We then adjourned to the office of the lawyer, who drew up the necessary documents for me to sign, the lawyer and the foreman witnessing the same. We then took everything to the Judge, including the three pieces of hammered iron, practically converted into steel by the morning's process; the Judge duly attested the three documents, attaching his official seal to each: one we lodged in the archives of the Court with a piece of the converted steel; one the lawyer gave to the foreman, also with a piece of the converted steel; while the third (with the piece of converted steel) I took back with me to London.

Everything was completed by 5 o'clock that afternoon; the lawyer and the foreman dined with me at 6 p.m., when I settled up accounts between us, everything being all satisfactorily completed in time for me to catch the night mail back to London. Soon after the turn of the year (in 1876) my clients sold the works in Birmingham, and at St. Denis, at a remunerative price, so that all this ended to the full satisfaction of all parties concerned.

That very summer of 1876 I found I had to proceed to Cartagena, on the south-eastern coast of Spain in the province of Murcia, to attend a lengthy arbitration. I enjoyed it all very much; I had my old 1858 Foreign Office passport visaed by the French and Spanish Consuls in London. The route I took going out was by mail train, London, via Paris, direct to Marseilles, where I caught the French Oran (African) mail steamer, which stopped at Cartagena. I put up there at the Fonda Francesca, where I stayed just one month, bathing every morning in the Mediterranean Sea. The sea trip from Marseilles to Cartagena was simply delightful; it was just like being on a private steam yacht, for we had very few passengers on board. I lived on deck the whole time, morning, noon, and night. The meals were served there under a nice cool awning; they were very light and tasty. I also managed my sea bath every day, so I had all I needed.

The arbitration was one of the most peculiar functions I had ever witnessed. On arriving at Cartagena I presented my letter of introduction to the British Consul, asking him to introduce me to the very best Spanish lawyer in Cartagena, which he did, taking me round himself. It appears that he was the only lawyer in Cartagena, and was already secured by the other side. "Whatever shall I do?" I exclaimed in despair. "Oh, it is quite simple," said the Spanish lawyer; "I will act for both sides as arbitrator, on condition "that our friend the British Consul kindly gives me "the benefit of his assistance from time to time as I "require it." This arrangement, though a novel one, worked admirably throughout, leading to excellent practical results. The Spanish lawyer was the soul of honour, absolutely impartial, while at the same time, with all his wits about him, he never missed a point. He and the British Consul (very old friends) worked together in full harmony. But it was essentially very slow work; we began the arbitration every afternoon at 5 o'clock, all of us (including the arbitrator) sitting on cane-bottomed chairs *outside* the lawyer's office in the open street; at 7 p.m. we had finished for the day. When a moot point arose the lawyer calmly rolled three cigarettes, deliberately smoking them one after another while he considered the matter; he then either gave his ruling, or, if he was not yet satisfied, he uttered the magic word "*Mañana*" (to-morrow), passing on meanwhile to the next point before him.

As I had absolutely nothing whatever to do from 7 p.m. to 5 p.m. the following day, Sundays and Saints' Days (their name is "legion"), the British Consul took pity on me. He had a splendid steam yacht and a light hooded gig, with a fast trotting cob, and with these took me for splendid excursions all along the coast in his steam yacht, and inland in his gig. In this way we scoured the country—north, south, east, and west—for miles. The province of Murcia is essentially Moorish, abounding in old Moorish remains, most interesting. The British Consul was a bit of an antiquary, so that he was able to explain everything to me. Cartagena is a strongly fortified city, it is one of the principal naval harbours of Spain; the arsenal is an important one. The ruins of the cathedral are interesting. Murcia, the capital, about forty miles inland and which I visited by rail, is far more interesting; it is beautifully situated on the river Segura, and is replete with reminiscences of former Moorish days. It contains a fine cathedral of the fourteenth century, with interesting chapels; one of the charms of the city are the ancient balconied houses, they are quaintly picturesque. The inhabitants are justly proud of their grand old city of Murcia.

The Spanish wines procurable in Barcelona were execrable—the red wine heavy, thick, and generally sour; the white wine very dry and bilious. My usual beverage was French or Italian Vermouth, heavily diluted with Vichy water. The food was not bad. The standard native dish, Olla Podrida, I quite got to like, and do so still. All things in due time come to an end, so that by the time I had been out a month the arbitrator delivered his award, which, strange to say, pleased both sides. I know that I was thoroughly satisfied, as was also my client when I got back to London and saw him about it. Unfortunately there was no steamer available for me to return by, so I took the mail train to Madrid, arriving there at 5 a.m., and as I could not get on again till that night, I booked a sleeper, and then put up for the day at the Hotel de Paris (a wretchedly low-pitched place, but the only one of its kind then; now, however, superseded by the Hotels Ritz and Ingles, both decided improvements on the old out of date Paris). Having the whole day before me, I first had a bath, change of clothes, and café au lait complet, after which I took a victoria to the Puerta del Sol, a large piazza (open place) in the centre of the city, where Madrid life is seen in all its pristine glory; from there I visited the Palacio Real, the imposing Royal Palace, a large square building on a great height above the River Manzanares. The state rooms, notably the Salon de Embajadéres (Ambassadors' or Throne Room), are richly decorated. I also visited the Real Capilla (Chapel Royal), where I was shown a fragment of the Crown of Thorns and a nail from the Cross; after that I visited the Museo del Prado, where I saw the collection of pictures, which is classed with the first in Europe. It contains about 2,000 masterpieces—the Spanish school predominating with grand representations by Velasques, Murillo, Riba, and others; these are mostly in the long chamber, Galleria Principal. The Italian and Flemish masters are also well to the front.

After adjusting a few pressing matters in London on my return home, I was deputed by the Judge in Chambers of the High Court of Chancery to proceed, by the first train the next day, to Barnsley, to take the management of a colliery in that district on behalf of the ground landlord, who was seeking to re-enter in possession on account of his rent being overdue. It was in consequence of this that the Court of Chancery had appointed a receiver to take over the property meanwhile, the Court approving of my acting as local manager to keep the colliery at work as a going concern; this was all important in the common interests of all parties. On arrival at Barnsley I put up at the Queen's Hotel, exactly opposite the railway station. The next morning I was at 9 o'clock at the local bank presenting to the manager my authority, duly signed by the Judge, to take over the account; the manager at once transferred the balance to my name. This being satisfactorily arranged, I instructed the bank manager to honour no further cheques on the old account without my written authority. But I made an exception in favour of the employees of the colliery, explaining to the bank manager that, as I was taking over the property as a going concern, it was only right that all outstanding salaries and wages should be duly met, and he at once saw the force of what I said, telling me at the same time that this action on my part removed a great weight from his mind. He further stated that he felt sure I should not be a loser by this, for he would take care to let the office staff know that I had done it quite spontaneously, and without any outside pressure whatever.

Finding that there was a train starting shortly for Silkstone, my destination, I took it, and in the course of thirty minutes I reached the colliery, presented my credentials, and was there and then duly recognised by all concerned. The first thing I did was to call the whole of the staff, as also the pit's manager, into my private office, where I told them what steps I had taken to protect their salaries and wages; I at the same time advised them all to clear their cheques that very day, so that after that I might start fair with a clean sheet; they all thanked me, losing no time in profiting by my advice.

I only stayed a day or two at the Queen's Hotel, Barnsley; but while there I dined with a friend at the King's Head Hotel, where he gave me a Barnsley Chop

—a wonderful meal of three chops rolled into one; most delicious. From Barnsley I moved to the Stanhope Arms Hotel, Cawthorne, in the heart of lovely country, with free entry to the grounds of Cannon Hall, belonging to Mr. Stanhope, the lord of the manor. It was within a very easy walk of my colliery, so that I was able to go back comfortably every day to lunch, instead of taking in sandwiches, which I loathe. Finding that my stay at the colliery was likely to be a prolonged one, I went up home one Saturday morning for the week end, returning with my wife, children, and nursery governess on the Monday morning to Cawthorne. But we only stayed a week there when I took them back to the Queen's Hotel, Barnsley, where they made us very comfortable. We stayed on there some weeks, until the strike at the various collieries in the district (my own included) took place. I was then strongly urged to send my family home. Not a bit of it: I hired a furnished cottage at Silkstone itself, in the very heart of the fray, and we all moved in there the next day; an excellent move on our part, for the miners, seeing that we trusted them implicitly, loyally reciprocated the confidence we had reposed in them. We thus became fast friends all through the strike. My wife and children visited them at their cottages, so further winning their hearts. In this way, by a little skilful manœuvring, we were able to help each other materially: in this way more especially—the strike only affected the men working under the surface; all the *top* coal (that is, coal cropping up to the surface) was free. Now the colliery happened to have one or two seams thus fortunately placed, notably a good thick seam of very valuable cannel coal, fetching a top price in the market, and very easily won. We kept on, therefore, a good lot of miners winning this coal, consequently the weekly wages bill, for which I had to drive into Barnsley every Friday afternoon, was a tolerably heavy one after all. Saturday was always an off-day at the colliery. The miners kept splendid fox-terriers, with which they had sporting ratting contests on Saturdays at Barnsley. In order to keep their dogs in good condition they fed them on legs of mutton, while they and their families simply "clemmed" (starved), living on bread and potatoes. My wife and children often took good hot joints to these poor cottagers; they were well repaid by seeing their happy smiling faces, for they loyally ate these dinners, as we intended they should. As soon as the strike at the colliery had become an assured fact, I at once gave orders to bring up all the pit ponies. I was at the pit's mouth when they came up. Most, if not all, of them, although in excellent condition, were quite blind, having either been born down below, or else sent down when quite young. When the colliers saw the ponies come up it set them thinking, as they knew then that, acting in the best interests of all concerned, I had made all arrangements to provide for every contingency, and was leaving nothing to chance. Another precaution I took at the same time was to have the colliery continuously pumped, thus keeping the water well down and preventing any fear of flooding. This again gave the miners further food for careful reflection, and it was thus all to the good.

Soon after this, having now had two years' experience at accountancy, I decided (with the full concurrence of my chiefs) to start in business for myself; which I did on 1 May 1877, opening my offices at 12 Laurence Pountney Lane, Cannon Street. My first bit of business was for my old friend, Sir Sydney H. Waterlow. It was a confidential matter, which I managed to carry out to the full satisfaction of himself and his partners. Sir Sydney sent me a substantial cheque by way of honorarium, together with a very flattering letter of thanks, which he authorised me to use whenever I thought it might come in serviceable, as indeed it did. I received many congratulatory letters acknowledging receipt of my circular. All my correspondents seemed pleased that I had seen my way to start for myself; they all thought it was the right thing to do, and wished me every success. Among these was my old friend the Earl of Devon, of Powderham Castle, Exeter, who, later on, was able to influence good business in my way.

My old master and friend, the Honourable Pascoe Charles Glyn, lost no time in taking me in hand. He introduced me to his partners at the bank, and before very long they had all sent me business; in fact, one of them called on me at my office two days after, asking me to accompany him there and then to an office where he wished me to investigate a matter for him. Mr. Glyn also introduced me to the solicitors of the bank, who, a few days after, sent for me at 11 a.m. to take up a matter on which I had to report by 11.30 the next morning. I at once set to work, and was at it all that day and night, taking my work home with me, and finishing at 6 o'clock the following morning. I had taken out everything on half sheets of foolscap, written in copying ink; these I took to the office, press-copied, and was at the solicitor's office by 11 a.m. I found him in consultation with the solicitor on the other side. They both studied my report carefully in my presence; the opposition solicitor declared it to be a masterpiece in every respect, and that he should not only recommend his clients to adopt *in toto*, but get them to instruct him to request me to carry out its provisions in due course, which I did to the satisfaction of all concerned.

Quite recently I showed my partners the press copy of this report of mine; they all three unanimously declared that it was simply splendid, but they could not for the life of them make out how I had managed to do it so thoroughly in such a limited time. My answer to that was, that my heart was in the work. And here let me say that in our business the power of concentration is everything. So that, while I am occupied on any particular matter, I invariably concentrate the whole of my thoughts and energies upon it, to the exclusion of all else. My partners and staff do the same. So that is why we are able to turn out work of which we are not ashamed, for, in addition to the power of concentration we bring to our work, we take care at the same time that it should be thorough in every detail.

Another good friend of mine was my neighbour, Mr. G. A. Tucker, the manager of the Union Bank of London. We always travelled up together in the same train; he took a great interest in my progress, gave me excellent advice, following it up from time to time by putting good business in my way, besides recommending me to others. The deputy chairman of the bank was my old friend Sir Sydney H. Waterlow, so between the two I was in excellent hands. But my great support and sheet anchor was my old Highgate friend, Mr. Robert John Lodge, the manager of the Marine Insurance Company, of which Sir Charles Henry Mills (afterwards Lord Hillingdon) was a director. He advised me to go and see the Hon. Pascoe Charles Glyn at the bank, and get him to introduce me to Mr. Price, the manager of the Ocean Marine Insurance Company, of which Mr. Glyn was a director. Mr. Glyn at once took me round to the office of the Ocean Marine, and then, in consultation with Mr. Price, told me that the Marine Offices and Lloyd's had a big lawsuit on in Havana, which they wished me to take up. They had first thought of employing Mr. Underdown, the eminent Q.C., who was the great authority on Spanish law, but they all felt that, with my intimate knowledge of marine insurance, extending over many years, I was, after all, their man. Mr. Glyn then gave me two bits of practical advice—one was "Point de zèle, mon ami" ("no zeal, my friend"), I think it was an expression of Talleyrand; the other was, that I was never to take up second-rate or shoddy business; because, if I did, they would get to hear of it, and have to drop me there and then. Mr. Glyn and Mr. Price then both told me to put myself unreservedly in the hands of Mr. Robert J. Lodge, as he had the entire conduct of the whole thing. Mr. Lodge sent me on to my old friend Mr. Rose at the Commercial Union Assurance Company, as also my equally old friend, Mr. Tozer, of the Universal Marine Insurance Company. Both these gentlemen coached me up pretty thoroughly, and then sent me up to Lloyd's to see the leading underwriters there (all old friends of mine also, as it happened). Mr. Lodge then introduced me to Mr. William Walton, the solicitor who had the conduct of the case, both for the Insurance Companies as also for Lloyd's. Mr. Walton took me round to Mr. Rucker, the underwriter of the London Assurance Corporation, and the chairman of the Salvage Association; they sent for the secretary, Mr. Gordon, and after consultation together it was arranged that everything would be ready for me to start in about six weeks' time, and that, meanwhile, Mr. Walton would arrange with the various offices where my life was insured, to turn my present policies into "Whole World Policies," he, Mr. Walton, on behalf of his clients, paying them the difference. We then arranged a cypher code between us on my suggestion.

The fact is I am rather an expert at cypher codes, having already started two, one for India, and the other for Canada and the United States of America. I was mentioning the fact one day lunching up at Lloyd's, when a man said: "Oh, I see you telegraph "a man 'Genesis,' which means 'I am in difficulties'; "to which the reply comes back, 'Exodus,' 'I have "bolted.'"

Some few years after, I was deputed by a foreign bank to compile them a cypher code. For this I chose short Latin words thus—"*amo,*" "*amas,*" "*amat,*" with annexes "*ne*" and "*ve,*" reading "*amatne*" and "*amatve,*" and so on. I had to procure the permission of the telegraph authorities for these two annexes "*ne*" and "*ve,*" but, after seeing them and explaining everything, they gave it all right.

Reverting for one moment to marine insurance: I think it may be interesting to state that in the very early days of the eighteenth century, and possibly even in the closing years of the seventeenth century, Lloyd's held the sole monopoly for marine insurance—until 24 June 1720, when charters of incorporation were granted as a monopoly to the first two marine insurance companies, "The London Assurance Corporation" and "The Royal Exchange Assurance Corporation"; while at the same time the underwriters at Lloyd's still held their own, remaining as strong and as powerful as ever. On 24 June 1824 the above companies' monopoly was repealed, and the Alliance Marine Assurance Company, with a capital of £5,000,000 and Mr. Nathan Rothschild as chairman, was started. A few months later the Indemnity Mutual Assurance Company came into existence, followed in 1836 by the Marine Insurance Company, and in 1859 by the Ocean Marine Insurance Company. In 1860 the Universal Marine Insurance Company and two others were started, followed on 1 January 1863 by the Commercial Union Assurance Company and another marine insurance company. In 1864 seven more new companies came into existence, but five of them soon became defunct, and subsequent to 1864 upwards of twenty more were started, of which at least two-thirds perished very soon after their untimely birth. But the marine insurance companies whose names are given above, as also Lloyd's, are all going strong, and the inauguration on 1 July 1884 of the Institute of London Underwriters has fostered and promoted an "*entente cordiale*" between the various marine insurance companies and Lloyd's, with whom, as friendly, honourable competitors, they act on all matters of common and general interest in harmonious concert. Their interests on vital points are identical, and all concerned (as above) know it, too, and act accordingly.

On leaving Mr. Walton that day I ran across an old acquaintance, who thus accosted me: "I have been "looking for you, Mr. van de Linde; I want you to "help me promote a company, of which you will be "auditor." To which I replied: "Thanks, but my "business is to wind up and not to promote com-"panies." To which he replied: "Well, then, I have "the very thing for you. You promote and audit my "company this year, and next year you wind it up." I gave the scoundrel a scathing sneer, and left him without a word. I went back to the "Marine" to tell Mr. Lodge that all was arranged for me to start in about five weeks' time, to which he replied: "Capital, Master van de Linde" (he always addressed me thus). "Now "go home, pack up your bag and start by first train "to-morrow morning for Stoke-upon-Trent, ask there "for my brother Oliver, he lives at Longport, and is "expecting you."

So the next morning I caught a very early train to Stoke, getting there about 12.30 p.m. On asking the station-master where I was likely to find Mr. Oliver Lodge, he replied: "Why, there he is, just getting into "his trap, run after him and catch him; the porter "will carry your bag for you."

Mr. Oliver Lodge (the image of his brother Robert) was immensely tickled at my thus stopping him. He expected me by a later train. "Jump up," he said; "here, give me your bag"; and together we rattled away to Hanley. It was market day there, so we had lunch at the market ordinary, and a very good lunch it was, too. After lunch and a smoke, Mr. Lodge drove me to his house at Longport, a magnificent mansion, standing in its own lovely grounds, with a regular farmyard attached. The story goes that when he set up his poultry run he bought 25 hens and 25 cocks. Next morning there was only *one* cock left; Master Chanticleer had killed the other 24. Mr. Lodge, in his innocence, thought he would give each hen a mate, but, as it turned out, this evidently was not to be the case. The 25 hens were all right, going quite strong.

The time I spent with my kind friends Mr. and Mrs. Oliver Lodge at Longport was both useful and interesting. I found their books and accounts in excellent order, and by introducing one or two little additions I placed their system on a practical, firm foundation; this system has never once been varied, it is still in existence in all its pristine simplicity, so that when my firm go down there every six months for the half-yearly audit, they find everything ready and in order.

While I was down at Longport Mr. Lodge took me for some splendid drives; we went all over Trentham, besides visiting Copelands, Mintons, and other notable far-famed potteries, where everything of interest was explained to me. It was a case of open sesame everywhere, for my friend and host was a *persona grata* wherever he went.

About the beginning of December 1877, everything being ready for me, and having been duly furnished with the proper credentials, letters of credit, with plenty of ready cash to go on with, I settled up everything in London and at home, taking, the following morning, an early train to Liverpool, putting up at the North Western Hotel, Lime Street, there. After that I called on the agents (Messrs. Ismay, Imrie & Co.) of the White Star Line to engage my passage in the "*Celtic*" (3,000 tons), leaving for New York the next day. These gentlemen knew all about me, having been expecting me. They apologised that they could now only give me a four-berth state cabin to myself; they had kept an eight berth one open until that very morning, but, as they had not heard from me, they had just let it. I told them the four-berth cabin would do all right; I found it was just splendid. I then looked up my old Bombay friend Henry Grendon Tippet, whose office was close by; he forcibly took possession of me, rushed back in a cab to the hotel, seized my hand-bag, saying we would call in the morning for my heavy luggage, and off we went to his charming country place at West Kirby on the River Dee and Cheshire coast, close to Hoylake. There I was introduced to Mrs. Tippet, and we spent a delightful time together talking of olden days.

Next morning, after a leisurely breakfast, Tippet took me back to Liverpool; we called at the office of the White Star Line to ascertain finally about the "*Celtic*" leaving, when we were told that the tender would be alongside the landing-stage at 12 (noon). This gave us ample time to get back to the hotel, secure my letters, charter a four-wheeler for my luggage, and get to the landing stage; Tippet sticking to me all the time like the good old pal of former days. He accompanied me to the "*Celtic*," admired my state room, and after a friendly " peg " together he was off again for the shore; he was the last person to get on board the tender. The "*Celtic*" immediately weighed anchor, and was off: at the same time the tender steamed away, so Tippet and I were able to wave our caps once more as a parting salute; after that we went down to lunch, an excellent repast, both recherché and simple, all thoroughly appetising. After leaving Queenstown, where we picked up the mails, our journey was very rough; in fact, we were just at the fag-end of a storm which had been raging for the past fortnight, and in which the American man-of-war "*Huron*" had been wrecked off Cape Hatteras. We were only allowed on deck at odd intervals, and then only in charge of a sailor, for the decks were icy cold, covered with hoar frost which made them very slippery, added to which the steamer rolled and pitched like anything. At meals we had to have the fiddles fastened to the tables, but it was only the hardy ones who came to table; the bulk of the passengers were moaning in their berths, too ill for anything, they had to be strapped securely to prevent them pitching clean out. During the whole time I was on board I never missed a single meal, nor my daily hot sea bath either.

At last we sighted land and were anchored at early morning in smooth water at Sandy Hook, with Staten Island facing us on our left, and Long Island directly opposite us, and to our right. While we waited here in quarantine the sailors amused themselves by fishing; they were rewarded by catching a monster shark, which they flopped upon the deck, keeping him a safe prisoner by lines encircling the brute. My word, did he not dance a bit, showing his huge jaws with heavy teeth. At last one of the sailors, approaching him cautiously, managed to break his spine with a hatchet; after that he was done for. After breakfast the Custom House officers came on board with the sanitary authorities. The doctors passed us all without a single exception, so we had a clean bill of health. The Custom House officers did the same with our luggage, for we had nothing dutiable to declare. We drew up the anchor, steamed away, and were soon alongside the battery at New York, where I chartered a hackney coach and pair, which took me and my luggage to the Fifth Avenue Hotel. For this the jarvey charged me three dollars, or 12s., pretty stiff for a 30 minutes' drive. At the hotel I secured a room, and then, on the advice of the hall porter, I took a tram, which landed me at the offices of the company running steamers to Havana. I there learnt that the next steamer was not leaving for four days; knowing who I was, for the Waltons had written out to them about me, they very kindly gave me a large state cabin to myself, and took charge of my heavy luggage, which they promised to put on board in my cabin for me. I then went back to the hotel, where I had lunch—oysters plain, stewed, fried, and scolloped, also baked clams (simply delicious), followed by canvas back duck. At table everybody drank plain water, so I did the same. After dinner every one of them made a rush to the bar clamouring for Bourbon whisky, which they tossed off neat; I did *not* do the same.

I inquired of my friendly hall porter at what time the first train left for Montreal. He told me the mail train left New York Depôt at 9 p.m., and was in quite early the next morning at Montreal. My brother Arthur lived at Montreal, so I proceeded to the famous Canadian city that very night and spent two delightful days with him and his family, after which I sped back to New York and set out on my journey to Havana by the s.s. "*Niagara.*"

We took a little less than four days doing the journey from New York to Havana, for soon after breakfast on the fourth morning we entered the harbour, anchoring opposite Morro Castle. On landing we were greeted by the Consul-General, Mr. George Augustus Cowper, and the Vice-Consul, Mr. Lionel A. Carden (afterwards Sir Lionel A. Carden). With their kind assistance I was not long in getting my luggage cleared at the Custom House. My passport was then demanded of me, and I had to give it up; a stamp of 10 pesetas was affixed at the back, for which I had to pay 10 pesetas in gold (8s.). I only got it back on leaving the Island the following summer, when another stamp, this time of 20 pesetas, was affixed, and for which I had to pay gold again (16s.).

Mr. Cowper told me that, it being the Christmas holidays, the Courts of Justice were closed till after 6 January (Epiphany), reopening 7 January 1878, but that he would take me on to my bankers, Messrs. J. Demestre & Co., which he did. Old José Demestre received me courteously, and when I showed him my letter of credit, he put his finger to his eye, turned down the lid, and said: "*Yo la ha visto.*" I thought he meant, "Do you see any green in my eye?" but what he really said was: "Yes, I have seen it." He asked me whether I wanted any money at present, explaining to me that the gold (*Oro*) dollar was worth 4s., whereas the paper (*Papel*) one was only worth 1s. 8d.; that is, a gold dollar was worth two and a half paper ones, owing to the Cuban insurrection still raging in the Island. I arranged to take paper money for the present, as this was in current use, while gold was only needed for payments into Court. We then went over to interview Mr. José Antonio Fesser (Lloyd's agent) at his office. He, too, received me warmly, placing a private room in his office at my disposal, as did also the Consul-General. Mr. Fesser told me that he was bringing up to me that afternoon the "*Dossier*" of legal papers belonging to the suit, which the Court officials had lent him for my inspection during the holidays.

Mr. Cowper then said that, for the present, I had better be his guest at his country seat at Marianao; that he had sent on my luggage to the station, whither he would walk to catch the usual lunch train. In India I would have driven, but here in Havana, owing to the climate being a moist and not a dry heat, everybody was able to walk about all day long with impunity.

It was a short pleasant journey. Mr. Cowper's house, a bungalow with one storey above, was agreeably situated in a large garden, full of plantains or bananas hanging in heavy clusters. These were all green at present, and the clusters were so cut from the trees; they then ripened in the dark, and after about three or four days were ready to eat.

Mrs. Cowper and her family gave me a hearty welcome. My bedroom (with a verandah in front) on the first floor was deliciously cool and pleasant.

After lunch Mr. Fesser came with the "*Dossier*" of legal documents: as these were all in Spanish, the British Consul sent round for a Spanish lawyer living close by, who spoke American English passably. We gave him the "*Dossier*" to take with him, to report to me later on, which he did; so that after the holidays, when the Courts reopened, I had thoroughly mastered them.

After tea Mr. Cowper took me round to the bungalow of his friends Mr. Upman and Mr. Bock (the rival wholesale tobacco merchants), who lived quite harmoniously together. Each of these gentlemen presented me with a box of their choicest cigars, telling me that when I had smoked them, if I liked them, I could have as many more at the same price, on condition that Mr. Cowper and I came round of an evening for a cup of coffee and friendly smoke together. Mr. Cowper kindly relieved me of my diffidence by saying that we should, of course, be only too happy to do so. We accordingly went round that very evening to their hospitable bungalow. All this, as I told them, did so remind me of my old Bombay days.

My stay during the Christmas holidays with the Cowpers was very enjoyable; but when the Courts reopened I felt it would be better for me to be more on the spot. So by Mr. Cowper's advice I took a good bedroom on the first floor at the Hotel Pasage, quite a new one in the heart of the city, where I was taken on inclusive terms at seven dollars, or 28s. a day, where I was very comfortable. I missed my excellent cigars of Mr. Upman and Mr. Bock, but I generally spent Sunday out with the Cowpers, when we always went in to our friends' bungalow next door for our customary cigar and black coffee.

Later on Mr. Fesser took me round to Partagas Factory, when I ordered a box of "Regalia de la Reina," as also another one of "Patagas Brevas," both excellent, with a delicious aroma. Since then I have always smoked that brand, and from choice the "Brevas." I am still smoking them at the present day, though it is now forty years since I made my first acquaintance with them.

Mr. Fesser and I generally attended the Courts together to watch our case. It was in good hands, for my leading counsel was the son of the President of the High Court. But the delays seemed to me endless. I thought we should never get through the preliminaries, with the short sittings, the constant holidays, and a heap of other things keeping us back.

At the Court everybody smoked cigars, from the Judge right down to the usher. One morning I was in Court with Mr. Cowper and Mr. Fesser, who both were smoking, while I was not. All of a sudden the Judge raised his hand to stop the proceedings, while he sent round the usher with his cigar case for me to take one of his lordship's, which I did. We both bowed affably, when the proceedings recommenced. But it was a villainous cigar. I could not smoke it, so Mr. Fesser, noticing my aversion, quietly gave me one of his excellent ones, hiding the Judge's till we got outside, when I gave it to a beggar, who gladly accepted it. This beggar was the licensed crossing-sweeper outside the

Courts. Whenever the old sinner saw me coming along he deliberately put out his cigar, that he might relight it again from my cigar. But I found that his rank cigar tainted my good one, so one day I gave him a lighted match instead; this, it appears, was a mortal insult, he looked daggers at me as he threw the lighted match away; but it had the desired effect, for he never troubled me again. I was, and am still, partial to smoking "green cigars," but they must be absolutely "green." I used to go into Partagas to order 200 or 300 cigars at a time; while I waited they rolled me up six or seven absolutely "green" (they were delicious), sending on the remainder to my hotel. When I went home I invested in these cigars to the value of £40, carriage and duty free; these Partagas kindly had delivered to my own house in England, to await my return.

My Indian experience had shown me the urgency of taking regular exercise: out in Havana I had no horse to ride, so I used to get up early in the morning, drink a cup of black coffee (not tea), and then start off for a long walk, scouring the neighbourhood all round for miles. I would get back to the hotel wet to the skin, but a hot bath, with clean dry clothes, put me all right. After dressing leisurely, to keep the perspiration from starting, I had a comfortable late breakfast, which did for lunch as well, and then walked either to the office of Mr. Cowper or Mr. Fesser, as occasion required. Lionel Carden (the British Vice-Consul) and I got to be fast friends, and are so still. I have received from him, as Sir Lionel A. Carden, the British Plenipotentiary in Mexico, most interesting letters. He is an absolutely fearless man, of whom we are all proud. He has now retired on his pension and is living, with Lady Carden, in South Kensington, where I recently spent an afternoon with them both; we had a very pleasant time together talking of the olden days of 1877-1878, now over 37 years ago. Sir Lionel was just as cheery as ever, but I deeply regret to say that since I began writing this book my old friend has passed away.

Soon after my arrival I spent a pleasant week-end at Matanzas on the north coast, just a little east of Havana.

I now had further opportunity of seeing the country, for I spent that Easter of 1878 with Zulueta (or, to give him his title, "The Marquis of Alava," but he was generally addressed as "Zulueta") on his sugar estates. We were escorted by a guard of 50 soldiers, increased when we arrived at our destination to 100, for the Cuban insurrection, although on the wane, was still going pretty strong, as a last final dying effort. I tasted there for lunch, for the first time, "Octopus" (Devil fish). It was delicious, rather expensive though, as it cost 8s. the pound, but all the food there was first rate. I spent a very enjoyable time, but my visit had a most tragic ending. The Monday morning Zulueta and I were leaving for Havana I had the special train to take me with my luggage to the railway junction, while Zulueta started on horseback to meet me at the junction. When I got to the station I found everything in confusion, everybody running to and fro shouting out "Poor Zulueta"; on getting to the waiting-room I found my friend reclining on a couch with his head bandaged. It appears that, in riding to the junction, his horse stumbled, pitching him over his head. We got him back to Havana in a reserved compartment and drove him to his house that Easter Monday afternoon.

He appeared to be going on to slow recovery till the Friday midday, when, contrary to his doctor's, his wife's, and his son's urgent advice, he insisted on having the mail letters brought to his bedside for his perusal and signature. All went well till he reached the very last letter, the wording of which he did not approve; he dashed his pen across the letter, but the effort overcame him, for in a moment he sank back, dying on the spot.

The next afternoon (Saturday) we buried him in the cathedral. The Archbishop of Havana conducted the funeral, with all the local clergy following in procession, accompanied by the Governor-General, all Judges of the High Court and other officials, followed by Consul Cowper, Vice-Consul Carden, and myself.

We all first met in the mortuary chapel ("Chapelle Ardente") in the house itself; on the table of the anteroom was a huge salver of enormous cigars, to which everybody helped himself, including the Archbishop, Cowper, and Carden. I was the only one who followed who did not smoke.

As we approached the cathedral the procession suddenly stopped, marking time; this was to enable the Archbishop (a slow smoker) to finish his cigar before entering the sacred edifice.

Soon afterwards the Cuban insurrection was quelled, while at the same time the Queen of Spain (Mercedes, first cousin and first wife of the King of Spain, the father of the present King by his second wife, an Austrian princess) suddenly died at Madrid. The news, however, was *officially* suppressed for a whole week, so as not to interfere with the peace festivities; it was felt that it would have been dangerous to have suppressed them, so they were allowed to go on.

They commenced on a Sunday. The main feature of interest centred in the various processions illustrating the costumes of the inhabitants of the various Spanish Provinces; these were most effective. The whole finished up on the Saturday afternoon with a bull fight, but I drew the line there, and although I had received a special card of invitation from the Governor-General himself, I politely refused. His Excellency was furious until I got Mr. Fesser to explain to him that I refused through no want of courtesy, but that I felt I could not possibly be present, the whole thing being repugnant to my feelings.

That Saturday night the peace festivities came to an end, and the following morning the funeral rites began in all due solemnity. Everyone of note, including the Governor-General, the Judges, and other officials, attended the service in the cathedral, where, attended by Mr. Fesser, I also was present.

Having by the middle of July 1878 won my two law suits (one for the Marine Underwriters, and the other for the bank), as there was nothing further to detain me in Havana I looked about for a steamer to take me back to New York. I was fortunate in securing an outside deck cabin in "*The City of Benares,*" due to leave on a Wednesday, about the end of the month. Unfortunately, on the Sunday afternoon previous, sitting out in the sun in Consul Cowper's garden at Marianao, I contracted a slight attack of yellow fever. The doctor who attended me happened to be the doctor of "*The City of Benares,*" so I was all right; he nursed me most patiently at The Hotel Pasage, smuggling me on board the steamer at the last moment, and carefully attending to me the whole way, until I reached New York. Fortunately Cowper and Carden were both at the Custom House to see me off, and release my passport by paying 20 dollars for the fresh adhesive stamp on it. When we got to New York my (the ship's) doctor gave the authorities a clean bill of health, keeping me well in the background all the time. After the steamer's inspection was finally concluded the doctor had me smuggled ashore and put into a hackney coach, while he cleared my luggage. Just as I was lying back in the coach one of the steamer's passengers looked in and, seeing me, said: "I guess, stranger, what you want is a masked pill." Perhaps he was right.

The doctor then kindly took me to the Fifth Avenue Hotel, put me to bed, making arrangements for my starting that night in a sleeper for Montreal, and telegraphing my brother Arthur to meet me the following morning at the station, to take me to his own house, at the same time telling him to have a doctor to attend to me.

All the time I was on board my sole nourishment was weak tea and dry toast. But the doctor thought I might now venture on chicken broth, to be followed later on by mutton broth and beef tea. He wrote the Montreal doctor full instructions as to my case, saw me off in the train, giving me, the last thing, another basin of chicken broth. The doctor was simply my guardian angel, for, under God's good providence, he saved my life. When it came to remunerating him, he absolutely refused to accept a cent more than his bare fee.

I got to Montreal the next morning feeling wonderfully refreshed, after a good night's rest. The doctor and my brother Arthur were both at the station to meet me. I gave the former his colleague's letter, which he quite understood.

I was driven back by them both to my brother's house, where, after another basin of chicken broth, I was put to bed for a week, living on liquid food the whole time. I was very anxious to catch the Allan steamer "*Sarmatian*" home, leaving for Liverpool that day week. Thanks to the doctor's skilful treatment I was able to manage this, securing an excellent large roomy cabin of four berths all to myself. The "*Sarmatian*" had recently brought over the Duke and Duchess (Princess Louise) of Argyll—the Duke being the new Viceroy of Canada. All the arrangements on board were simply splendid; I revelled especially in the Scotch broth, the very thing I needed. The "*Sarmatian*" took the northerly course, by the Straits of Belle Isle and Rimouski, where the final mails were put on board. We sighted a few icebergs, giving them, however, a wide berth. We had a pleasant uneventful run, putting in at Londonderry, on the north-east coast of Ireland, where we discharged our mails, and then, steaming back into the open past Lough Foyle, we skirted Port Rush and the Giant's Causeway; the water here was so deep that we were able to keep quite close in shore, thus getting a splendid view of the Giant's Causeway, with its wonderful steps leading right down from the top to the very water's edge. The next afternoon we steamed majestically into the River Mersey, anchored, and were taken in the steam tender to the landing-stage at Liverpool. There I was met by Tippet ("dear old Gren"), to whom I had wired from Londonderry. He wanted to take me back to his house at West Kirby, but I told him I did not feel up to it; so he took me on to the North Western Hotel, Lime Street, got me a good room, and spent the rest of the day with me. Next morning he was back at the hotel, and saw me safe off in a reserved compartment for Euston, which I reached quite comfortably, getting back home to Bexley Heath early that afternoon. Next morning I called on Mr. Walton at his office; he was very glad to see me, referring me to Mr. Robert J. Lodge. This gentleman received me most warmly, telling me he had been deputed by the various Marine Insurance Companies and Underwriters at Lloyd's to settle my remuneration; which he did there and then, the same being on a very liberal scale, but he said they all felt I deserved it. Mr. Lodge also handed me a splendid testimonial, signed by the Chairman of the Salvage Association, thanking me for what I had done. I then went to the Foreign Bank, where I had an equally cordial reception from the general manager, who handed me a handsome cheque for my fee, together with a flattering letter of thanks.

I told Mr. Lodge that, by the doctor's orders, my wife was taking me the next day to North Wales for a month's thorough change. Of this he quite approved, telling me to forget all about business, and not to return till I felt thoroughly well again; for, when I felt up to it, they had lots of good business for me to take up. I then went round to see the Hon. Pascoe Charles Glyn, at the bank. Now that I had a substantial cash credit at my own bank, I asked him whether I might transfer my account to his. This pleased him. I did it at once, and Mr. Glyn himself countersigned opposite my name.

CHAPTER VII.

Wales, Ireland, France.

IN order to re-establish my health, my wife and I now set off for a holiday in North Wales, breaking our journey at Chester, a most interesting old Roman city on the elevated bank of the River Dee. The wall surrounding the city makes an agreeable walk of two miles. But the streets known as *The Rows* constitute the chief charm of the city. The carriage way of the streets is excavated several feet below the original level; on each side are ranges of shops, while upon the roofs are walking ways with other shops; many of the largest, most attractive ones in the city above, forming a covering, are the upper apartments. Thus are formed continuous lines of covered galleries, which make a sheltered promenade. While perambulating these *Rows* one should observe several remarkable old timber buildings, with elaborately carved gables, still in excellent preservation, notably in Watergate, Bridgegate, and Northgate Streets. We just had time to visit the various interesting old places, while at the same time having a hurried peep at the Cathedral and the Castle.

I soon picked up wonderfully. Three days after reaching Bangor I was climbing Snowdon from the Llanberris side all by myself, without even a guide or a boy to show me the way. I did thoroughly enjoy it, especially the rest and lunch at the top, which is 3,571 feet above the sea level.

In addition to climbing Snowdon from Llanberris, I also ascended the mountain from Capel Curig, a distance of six miles from Bettwys-y-coed, when we were staying there. This is a far more difficult climb. The morning I made the ascent it was blowing a gale, so I was thankful to drop into the hollow at the summit, where I was sheltered from the wind, a great relief. I lunched at the summit, and, when I was ready to return, the wind had quite dropped, making the descent an easy one.

Having thoroughly well exhausted Bangor and its environs we moved on to Penmaenmawr; on the sea coast at the back there is a mountain of the same name, but only 1,000 feet high. I used to climb up one side and come down the other side very easily, but worth doing all the same. I took a sea bath regularly wherever I got the opportunity; I found it both refreshing and invigorating.

At our apartments at Penmaenmawr we got to know a nice couple and their son. My wife took short, easy excursions with the lady, while I joined her husband and her son in more lengthy ones.

One afternoon after lunch we three started for a long walk on the heights, hoping to get to Aber, have tea there, returning to Penmaenmawr in time for dinner. But unfortunately we never got to Aber, nor back in time for dinner, for by following a water course continuously we lost our way irretrievably.

Darkness overtook us, we got off the beaten track wandering helplessly along. At last I shouted "Saved! I smell bacon frying"; and sure enough I was right, for just then we came across a cottage. We knocked at the door; the good wife, who was just having supper with her husband, told us we were miles away from Aber, right among the slate quarries of Bethesda. They had just finished supper, so their boy took us to the inn at Bethesda, where they gave us eggs and bacon for supper, and two comfortable bedrooms, in which we slept soundly. The next morning, after a hearty breakfast (again of eggs and bacon), we started back for Penmaenmawr, on our way passing the slate quarries, among which we had wandered the previous evening, coming across several ominous unprotected pits, into which, had we fallen, we should have been killed on the spot; a most providential escape indeed.

From Bethesda we worked our way back to Aber, a distance of some four miles (which we overshot the previous afternoon). Aber is a delightful little village at the entrance of a romantic glen and beautiful waterfall (Rhayadr Mawr), which time, on this occasion, did not permit us to explore; though we did so the next day, five of us (the two families) picknicking there in the wooded glen. After that, we wended our way (2½ miles onward) to Llanfairfechan, coming to the Pass of Penmaenmawr, a huge rock presenting towards the sea a rugged well-nigh perpendicular front 1,553 feet above sea level; we negotiated this pass. At the entrance we found a small public-house, with a signboard on which was the following couplet by Dean Swift:—

> *" Before you venture hence to pass,*
> *" Take a good refreshing glass."*

which we accordingly did.

At the extremity of the pass we found another "pub"; on the sign-board we read the following couplet, also by Dean Swift:—

"Now you're over take another,
"Your drooping spirits to recover."

We accordingly took "another," reaching soon afterwards our comfortable apartments, where we found our respective wives very glad to welcome us once more safely back.

From Penmaenmawr we moved on to Conway, putting up at the Castle Hotel, visiting from there the celebrated Conway Castle, a fine old ruin, built in 1284 by our King Edward I to command The Pass of Penmaenmawr, in its day one of the most magnificent fortresses of Great Britain, for, as Pennant describes it, "one more beautiful never arose." The Conway Suspension Bridge, built by Telford in the years 1822 to 1826 (the same engineer who constructed the Menai Bridge), is also a grand structure.

From Conway we made a day's excursion to Llandudno, visiting The Great Orme's Head as also The Little Orme's Head, along a lovely carriage drive.

Leaving Conway, we stayed a few days at the Royal Oak Hotel, Bettwys-y-coed, an ideal place. The old sign-board, still kept at the hotel as an heirloom, was painted by the late Mr. David Cox, the celebrated Royal Academician.

"Bettws," as it is pronounced and called for short, is a favourite haunt of the angler, as well as the artist. The views around present features of quiet lovely grandeur, in which river, cataract, woodland,

and mountain commingle alternately. My favourite jaunt was to the Conway Falls. The view up the adjacent valley is one of the sweetest pictures upon which the eye can rest. Other favourite spots are the Fairy Glen and Pandy Mill, Rhayadr-y-Wennol ("The spout, or the foaming cataract of the Swallow"), about two miles from the village, but they well repay a visit.

Another day's excursion this time was starting, after breakfast, along the vale of the Lledr up to Dolwyddelan Castle, a wonderful wild-looking old fortress, a distance of five miles skirting the beautiful little mountain river, and then on to the foot of Moel Siabod, where we had a picnic lunch and rested awhile. My wife then got out her work and waited for me while I climbed Moel Siabod, a mountain 2,878 feet above sea level, from the top of which I got a grand prospect all round; arriving at the foot of the mountain I rejoined my wife, and on our way back we unearthed a little inn, where we had delicious tea with cream, thin bread and butter, and a new laid egg apiece; we thoroughly enjoyed our meal, and, in a little under the two hours, were back at the hotel in time for dinner.

From Bettws-y-coed we went on to Harlech, staying the week end there at the Castle Hotel, facing Harlech Castle, a grand historical old fortress dating back from the time of our English King Edward I.

From Harlech we went on to Barmouth, putting up for the night there at the Lion Hotel. Barmouth is a fashionable watering seaside place at the mouth of the river Maw, so I got a delicious sea bath there on the splendid sands, swimming in deep water to The Friars' Island, at the back.

The next morning we both secured seats on the top of the coach to Dolgelly (pronounced "Dolgethly"), a continued series of lovely pictures all the way, skirting the river Mawddach. Arrived at our destination, we engaged apartments at Brynbella, where we were most comfortable. After lunch I looked in at the Lion Hotel, where I had in the smoking room a cup of the hotel black coffe (not bad), with my own cigar. I casually opened the visitors' book, where I read, to my amusement :—

> "*If ever you go to Dolgelly*" (pronounced "*Dolgethly*")
> "*Don't stop at the Lion Hotel,*
> "*For there's nothing to put in your bethly*" (with two l's),
> "*And no one to answer the bell.*"

The whole thing is a pure libel; everything is all right at the Lion Hotel, so the landlord and his guests enjoy the rhyme hugely.

I enjoyed climbing Cader Idris, 3,100 feet above sea level; this sublime elevation, for abrupt tremendous precipices as well as for varied extensive views, far surpasses Snowdon, and, in fact, any other Welsh mountain. I lunched as usual at the summit, and then descended by The Foxes' Path, a rather difficult feat, for the whole way down was loose rubble; so I just stuck my heels into it, putting my head well back, and, with my stick to steady me, I slid down the whole way without an effort of any kind. I did this quite alone, without the assistance of any guide; in fact, I never had one for any of my excursions in Wales.

The waterfalls around Dolgelly are simply grand. Our first visit was to The Torrent Walk; we spent a delightful morning doing it thoroughly, for it formed one of the most remarkably delightful scenes we came across. To visit The Fall of the Cain we had to hire a carriage, for it is eight miles from the town, but well worth the expense and the journey there and back.

The Fall of the Cain comprises three separate falls—(*a*) Rhayadr Dû, a double fall of sixty feet; (*b*) Pistyll-y-Mawddach (the spout of the Mawddach); (*c*) Pistyll-y-Cain, the highest and finest of the three.

We had lunch at the Oakley Arms Inn, Tynygroes, on our way back, close to the Falls, which we especially enjoyed out in the open, with grand scenery all around.

Other fine excursions were: (*a*) Llyn Tringorainen (the pool of the three pebbles), a small lake by the roadside; these three pebbles are said to be three grains which the giant Idris threw out of his shoe, as they troubled him in walking.

(*b*) Llyn Tal-y-Lllyn, a noble sheet of water following on to the "little pool."

(*c*) Abergwynant Woods, situated on the south side of the estuary below Penmaenpool, distant some three miles from Dolgelly. These woods are intersected by walks with lovely peeps every now and again of the estuary, as also of the surrounding country.

We regretfully bade adieu to Dolgelly, returning home by rail along the Lake of Bala, stopping the night at the Lion Hotel, Shrewsbury; continuing our journey from there on the Great Western Railway most comfortably, for the broad gauge was then in force all over the line.

In due course we arrived home, after a most delightful holiday, which did us both all the good in the world; in fact, when I got back to the City everyone was struck by my changed appearance—I was quite another man, set up again, and ready for any amount of good, solid, hard work: sure proof that North Wales is an ideal country for those whose health needs lasting restoration.

The Monday after my return home I was back again at my office by 9 a.m., with any amount of work from my kind friends and clients, Messrs. Glyn, Mills, Currie & Co., Messrs. Coutts & Co., Mr. Lodge, the Salvage Association, and Lloyd's; between them all I found plenty to occupy me fully, so that I soon had to take a couple of clerks, followed soon after by my engaging other clerks.

The Marine Insurance offices got me to take up several matters for them abroad. Among others to release a new ship at Madeira, which had been abandoned by the captain and crew as leaky; a false alarm, for she floated all right and was picked up by a small schooner of 250 tons and taken in to Madeira. I had to hurry off to Nantes, where the owner of the 250 tonner lived, to release my vessel of 2,000 tons—ship, cargo, and freight valued at £50,000. Armed with a bankers' letter of credit for that amount, I released her by depositing the bail (£50,000) with the Court at Nantes; the upshot was that the owners (and consequently the underwriters) of the 2,000 tonner had to pay one-third salvage money of the total value. This cost them some £17,000, rather a heavy amount to pay for the captain's cowardice and want of common sense. Another case I took charge of was in connection with the underwriters versus a firm of foreign shipowners. I discovered by a mere fluke that there had been concealment on the part of the owners, and so I saved the underwriters from paying this unjust claim.

I managed one or two other similar cases, but then found out that I must, for the time being at all events, give up this class of business, as my constant absences abroad clashed with my home work; my underwriting friends saw my point and gave me a freer hand for the future.

Just then an old Highgate friend called upon me to start his accounts on a more up-to-date basis, and I did; but it was a tough job, for up to the present he had kept his Cash Book in cypher, thus: *Cumberland*, each letter standing in its order for "1, 2, 3, 4, 5, 6, 7, 8, 9, 0," respectively. The first thing I did was to have a fresh Cash Book started from the date of the previous quarter with plain figures, superseding the cypher letters as above. Even then, however, I was not yet out of the wood, for the books had been kept so far by single entry, a barbarous, antiquated system. However, I soon started them on the proper basis of double entry. But all this took time; my client Mr. P., however, was very patient through it all, and used to cheer me up by saying: "It is all right, van de Linde, take your time over it, and remember the four P.'s." On asking him what he meant by "the four P's," he said: "Patience, Perseverance, Pluck, and Piety." I took his advice, and by so doing accomplished my object to his and my entire satisfaction.

My old Bexley Heath friend, Mr. Alfred Bean, and my old underwriting friend, Dick Jones, were respectively chairman and deputy chairman of the Bexley Heath Railway, then in course of construction under the auspices of the South Eastern Railway Company, of which I was appointed auditor, a post I held until the railway was completed, when the South Eastern Railway bought up the line. I was at the opening ceremony, a very interesting one. We first had lunch at the Charing Cross Hotel, Sir Myles Fenton presiding, after which a special train conveyed us all over the line, stopping at each station, where we got out to inspect everything; our final station was when we returned back again direct to Charing Cross, where this pleasant function ended.

Although I had had to give up for the time being the continental work for the marine offices and Lloyd's underwriters, I still kept in close touch with them, so that I was not long in being appointed Auditor to the Committee of Lloyd's, and its Trust Funds.

Later on this was followed by my being appointed Auditor to Lloyd's Register of British and Foreign Shipping. These two appointments, I am proud to say, my firm still hold.

As arranged when I left Montreal in 1878, my brother Arthur returned home the following year (1879) and entered my office as my manager. He was a great help to me in many ways; his second son (Henry Arthur) was born in that year. Both he and his elder brother (Frederick Gérard) are, with Mr. Walter Frederick Wiseman, my present partners; for their father, my brother Arthur, died a few years after his return to England, while I had the further misfortune of losing my own two dear sons : Gérard Caspar van de Linde on 7 November 1889, at the age of 25 (he was originally buried at Bexley Heath Cemetery), and Sidney Cooper van de Linde, 28 March 1896, aged 26. These two dear boys were both of them my partners until the day of their death. They were universally beloved and respected by all who knew them. They are both now buried in my family grave at Bromley, Kent, for when my elder son died, in 1889, we removed from Bexley Heath to Bromley. When dear Sidney died, in 1896, he was buried in Bromley Cemetery; where shortly after, by the written sanction of Sir Matthew Whyte Ridley, the then Home Secretary, the body of my dear son Caspar was removed from Bexley Heath to Bromley Cemetery.

Having now got my office staff into good working order under the management of my brother Arthur, I had more time to myself, and so was able once more to take up Continental work on behalf of the Marine Insurance Companies, as also the Underwriters at Lloyd's.

On one of these occasions I found myself at Rotterdam, and while I had my room at the Weimar Hotel, I used as a rule to have my lunch and dinner with my clients' correspondent there, a cheery Dutchman of the good old school. Thus we had lunch at 12 (noon), consisting of slices of thin bread and butter, cheese sliced very thin in the middle, with thin slices of gingerbread on the top, a regular three-decker arrangement. This frugal meal was washed down with hot coffee and milk. His office was on the ground floor of his dwelling-house, so the lunch barely took up a quarter of an hour's time, when we got to work again down below.

At 4 p.m. the office was closed for two hours for dinner, work being once more resumed down below at 6 p.m. till any hour onwards.

I kicked at this primitive way of transacting business, telling my friend very pointedly that I would stand it for this one visit only; but that when I came over again the next time I should lunch at my hotel at 1 o'clock, go back to work till 7 p.m., returning then to the hotel for dinner and bed.

My phlegmatic friend smiled pleasantly, saying he would try on my return to accommodate his office hours to meet my wishes; which sure enough he did, for on my second visit we went on working down below till 1 p.m., when he took me upstairs to a proper lunch, with black coffee and a cigar to follow. We then worked on till 6 p.m., when he took me out for a good hour's drive, returning in time for 7.30 dinner at his house upstairs.

He told me that, after I had left the last time, he had freely mentioned my views to his colleagues on the Exchange, and had converted them all to my way of conducting business properly. They all thought them not only excellent, but quite feasible, so, accordingly, they fixed the office hours in future to be from 9 a.m. to 7 p.m., with an hour's break in the middle of the day for lunch. I was told that this new arrangement worked all right, and that the clerks were especially pleased, and venerated my memory as "Saint Gerrit" (my father's Christian name was "Gerrit"), not "Saint Lubbock." I was gratified to be of some use to my fellow labourers, to ease in some slight measure the daily routine of necessary work.

On 11 May 1880 the Institute of Chartered Accountants in England and Wales was established by Royal Charter. All accountants who had been in continuous practice for five years prior to that date were at once admitted as Fellows, while those who had been in continuous practice for three years (myself among the number) were similarly admitted as Associates. I was away at the time, but on my return in July I at once sent in my written application, my sponsors thereon being Mr. Bertram Wodehouse Currie (of Messrs. Glyn, Mills, Currie & Co.), Mr. Charles Frederick Murray (of Messrs. Murray, Hutchins, Stirling & Co.), Mr. G. A. Tucker (manager Union Bank of London), Mr. Edward Cooper (my brother-in-law), and my old Highgate friend, Mr. George Ladbury, on the Council of the Institute.

My application came before the Council at their next meeting on 4 August 1880, when I was at once elected an Associate (A.C.A.) of the Institute, with liberty to have two articled pupils; my first articled pupil was my elder son, Gérard Caspar.

In the spring of 1882, having been in practice as an accountant for five years, I applied to be admitted a Fellow to the Institute of Chartered Accountants in

England and Wales, my paper on this occasion being endorsed by the Honourable Pascoe Charles Glyn, Mr. G. A. Tucker (both bankers), Mr. F. C. Murray (solicitor), and Mr. George Ladbury (on the Council). At the very next meeting of the Council, on 3 May 1882, I was duly elected a Fellow (F.C.A.) of the Institute, and have been so ever since.

On mentioning this to a very old friend and firm client, he congratulated me warmly, saying at the same time that my election was most opportune, for he wanted me to accompany him the following Monday evening (8 May 1882) to Dublin, to help him in investigating a business there in which his wife had an interest. We accordingly started, arriving in Dublin the following morning (Tuesday), and putting up at the Shelbourne Hotel, exactly facing Stephen's Green, the gift of Mr. Guiness, the brewer, who paid all the expenses of laying it out.

We found Dublin in the throes of consternation, for the previous Saturday (6 May 1882) Lord Frederick Cavendish (the brother of the late Duke of Devonshire), who had only arrived that very morning to take up his duties as Secretary of State for Ireland, had, with Mr. Thomas H. Burke (the Under Secretary), been foully assassinated by Fenians in the Phœnix Park, on their way from the Vice-Regal Lodge to the Castle. A cross on the greensward marks the spot where the outrage took place, and which we visited after office hours that very afternoon, on the outside of a jaunting car, at the same time having a look at the celebrated Strawberry Beds, just then bursting out into bloom.

My friend also took me over by train to Bray, where we had a peep at Bray Head, and another drive outside a jaunting car to "the Dargle," the Powerscourt Waterfall, and the Vartry supply of water for the city of Dublin. On another occasion he took me over St. Patrick's Cathedral (of which Swift was Dean until he died, in 1745). The Cathedral was in recent years thoroughly restored by the late Sir Benjamin Lee Guinness, Bart., at a cost of £140,000; while Sir Arthur E. Guinness (afterwards Lord Ardelaun) laid out, at his own cost, the beautiful pleasure ground, consisting of 33 acres, now known as Stephen's Green.

Later on my friend took me over to Dalkey, a lovely spot, famous for its Dublin Bay herrings and prawns, the size of small lobsters—most delicious. Dalkey is on Dublin Bay, which compares very favourably with the Bay of Naples; in fact, a terrace overlooking the bay is called "Sorrento." We dined with mutual friends at Dalkey. Before dinner we climbed up Killiney Hill, half-way on to Bray, and Bray Head.

Our visit to Dublin was quite satisfactory, and it was mutually agreed that I should go over there twice a year to audit the accounts.

The office was in Bride Street. On our way there and back from our hotel we passed an isolated house with a garden, surrounded by a high wall. In this garden was a shed with a green roof. We often wondered what it meant, little dreaming at the time that it belonged to Councillor Carey, the Fenian and prime conspirator in the Phœnix Park murders.

All this came out at the trial, when Carey turned Queen's evidence. The man who drove the murderers back from the Park in his four-wheeler was nicknamed "Skin the Goat," and, after the murder, four-wheelers were at a discount, and were selling at any price, the drivers objecting to be called "Skin the Goat."

One morning, soon after the trial and conviction of the murderers, I was driving in the Phœnix Park, and on my way back I passed Kilmainham Jail, with the black flag flying, a token that the murderers had just been executed inside the prison walls.

That autumn, when I went to Dublin for the half-yearly audit, I took one of my clerks, Cecil Harvey, with me. We took the steamer which started on a Sunday from St. Katharine's Dock, calling on the Monday, first at Portsmouth, and the same afternoon at Southampton, where we joined her, spending the week-end (Saturday to Monday) with my cousin Auguste Monteuuis at his palatial residence there.

Our next stop was Plymouth, then Falmouth, where we arrived in the afternoon, and only started again the next morning; this gave us time to go ashore to have tea and dinner at the Pendennis Castle Hotel. Our final stop was Dublin; we skirted the coast all the way from the south of Ireland, keeping so close in shore that we had an excellent view of the country, all the way up the River Liffey, to North Wall, Dublin, where we landed, driving straight away to the Shelbourne Hotel, St. Stephen's Green.

The next morning, on calling in at Bride Street, we found that they were hardly ready for us, so, after putting in a good hard day's work on preliminaries, we decided to return in a week's time, when all would be quite finished, and ready for us to go on with to completion.

So the next morning we started by an early train for Bray, putting up at the Bray Head Hotel, which we made our headquarters. We spent the time before lunch in climbing Bray Head, a bold headland jutting out to sea, and commanding magnificent views all round. We descended by the old side to Greystones and Delgany, returning by the Glen of the Downs, an ideal spot for a picnic. After an excellent lunch we called on the Earl of Meath at Kilruddery, a friend and client of mine (as he is so still). His Lordship was in, and very kindly showed us all over his magnificent demesne, with the old Roman theatre still intact on the fresh green sward; he then took us through his extensive grounds. He owns the half of two mountains, which both come right down on each side of where we were standing; the one is Bray Head, while the other is "The Little Sugar Loaf."

The next morning, after breakfast, we chartered an outside jaunting car for the day, to explore the beauties of the Wicklow Mountains; we confined our observations that day to Glendalough (a lovely lake), and the Seven Churches adjoining, lunching and having afternoon tea at the Royal Hotel, a small comfortable inn charmingly situated on the borders of the lake, where we might have had bedrooms, but we preferred returning to our Bray Head Hotel to sleep; it was more comfortable, besides being preferable in more ways than one.

Glendalough and the Seven Churches adjoining this beautiful lake are replete with reminiscences of St. Kevin, the patron saint of the whole district. Our guide, a thorough Paddy, who had evidently kissed the Blarney Stone (the preliminary to drawing the long bow in an artistic way), was full of them. He pointed out to us a huge stone, with finger marks, as also a shallow round hollow, both clearly imprinted upon it. St. Kevin was once seated upon this stone, with his left hand touching it, while his right elbow rested upon the stone, and his right hand was outstretched: he was meditating. A pigeon alighted upon his right hand, laying therein three eggs in three consecutive days. St. Kevin sat the whole three weeks motionless upon that stone, while the pigeon hatched off her eggs in his right hand. Hence the two indentations—the one with his finger marks, and the other with the hollow, where his elbow reclined upon the stone.

St. Kevin's Bed, a rough hollow space hewn out of the solid rock, very steep and sloping down at an angle, on the extreme edge of Glendalough, was where the Saint slept. I was hauled in bodily by the guide, who placed me in the bed; but it was a perilous task, for had he made the slightest slip we should both of us have been pitched headlong into the lake below. I certainly preferred my own bed at the Bray Head Hotel—for one thing it was not so angular.

The guide also told us the romantic story of how the fair damsel "Kathleen, with eyes of unholy blue," tried to tempt St. Kevin with her winning devices, but failed. St. Anthony's temptations were evidently nothing to those of St. Kevin; they had to take a back seat, in fact.

After lunch we visited the Seven Churches, venerable ruins of ancient days, with their tall, narrow, round towers, of uniform width, reminding one of shot towers. The guide had many stories about these, too numerous to record here. We then had afternoon tea at the Royal Hotel, where we had had lunch; we then drove back in our jaunting car to our Bray Head Hotel, in good time for a comfortable wash, brush up, and change before our 7.30 p.m. dinner.

Next morning, after breakfast, we went to Shillelagh, a celebrated village, where the blackthorn is grown from which is fashioned Paddy's favourite weapon of defence, the shillelagh. When our then Prince of Wales (afterwards King Edward VII) visited this village soon afterwards, he purchased one of these murderous weapons, paying Paddy one golden English sovereign for it, at the same time giving him a hearty shake of the hand. After the Prince had gone, Paddy spat upon his hand for luck, swearing that he would never wash it again. Doubtless, being a good Catholic, he solemnly kept that vow. In the same way, when the Prince landed off the steamer at Kingstown, he bought a copy of the *Irish Times* from Davey, the paper vendor, giving him one English sovereign in payment, and also shaking his hand, much to Davey's delight. Davey is a well-known celebrity at Kingstown, he always comes over once a year to attend our "Derby" on Epsom Downs, and he came over in 1915 and 1916, just as usual, although no Derby was run. Alighting from the train after a pleasant run of 50 miles from Bray, past Greystones, Wicklow, Glengary, Rathdrum, Avoca, and Wooden Bridge, we thoroughly explored the renowned village of Shillelagh, absolutely refusing to buy one of its murderous namesakes. We then hired a jaunting car, which drove us 17 miles to the Wooden Bridge Hotel at Wooden Bridge, where we had an excellent lunch, which we thoroughly enjoyed. After lunch we strolled on to The Meeting of the Waters, a romantic spot at the junction of the rivers, immortalised by Tom Moore.

Immediately after lunch we took our train back from Bray to Westland Row, Dublin, passing on our way Killiney, Dalkey, Kingstown, and Blackrock, driving back to our old comfortable quarters at the Shelbourne Hotel. After a wash and a change we took an outside car to Howth, some 9 miles away along the sea coast to the north of Dublin. We climbed the Hill of Howth, getting from the summit grand views of the coast and country around. We then hurriedly visited The Collegiate Church (of the twelfth century), the College (of the sixteenth century), and the Castle.

We finished up with tea at the Claremont Hotel, and were then driven back to the Shelbourne Hotel.

The next morning found us both hard at work at Bride Street, where we found everything ready for us. We got through our work very comfortably without a hitch, so that we were able to catch the bi-weekly steamer back from North Wall, Dublin, calling at Falmouth, Plymouth, Southampton, and Portsmouth, going straight on by her to the St. Katharine's Dock, where we landed. While our steamer was discharging and taking in cargo (including a fresh supply of coals), we had tea at the Pendennis Castle Hotel, Falmouth, and a prowl round the town; "The Old Curiosity Shop" there is well worth a visit. We preferred not to go ashore, either at Plymouth or at Portsmouth—but we had time to look up my cousin Auguste Monteuuis in Southampton, having lunch with him and his wife—seeing all we wished to see from the steamer's deck; for, not taking in coals at either of these two ports, we were able to do so with comfort, without getting grimed with dirt.

In the late autumn (bordering upon winter) of that year, by the advice of dear old doctor Joseph Kidd, I took my wife and daughter to Biarritz, on the south-west coast of France, putting up at La Maison Nartus, on the Atalaye. This house is a favourite resort of English officers, but we were most fortunate in just securing the very last suite of comfortable apartments on the first floor, with an equally comfortable dining-room on the ground floor, where we had lunch and dinner, while we had our first breakfast in our drawing-room upstairs on the first floor, in fact, forming part of our suite of apartments.

The Atalaye is a noble promontory jutting out to sea, it is crowned by a ruined old castle, surrounded by a picturesque chaos of rocks (La Chinaougue). On one side is the small fishing harbour, while on the other, reached by a tunnel 82 yards in length, is a harbour of refuge, the half ruined pier of which affords a fine view of the Spanish mountains near the mouth of the Bidassoa: from the tunnel a road descends to the Port Vieux, a narrow, perfectly safe creek between the rocks; here stands the bathing establishment for persons who are weakly, or unaccustomed to the sea. Farther on is another beach, La Côte des Basques, where the waves, with nothing to arrest them, attain extraordinary force. There is a third bathing establishment here, where, on the second Sunday in September, the Basques resort in vast numbers, bathing all together—a very curious sight.

But the first and principal bathing establishment is on La Grande Plage, built in Moorish style, with a terrace which always presents a scene of great animation; the fine sandy beach makes a safe, pleasant bathing place, the force of the waves being broken by a barrier of rock. The elegant Russian church stands opposite the former Villa Eugénie, erected by the late Emperor Napoleon III for the Empress, his wife, but converted in 1894 into the Hotel du Palais.

It may not be generally known that twelve crops of hay (one a month) are quite usual in Biarritz and its neighbourhood.

On rising in the morning I used to go to the market to buy absolutely fresh shrimps, just caught, and, being boiled while I waited, these made an excellent relish to our first breakfast. When we had our cycles we thought nothing of cycling by Hendaye, along the River Bidassoa, to L'Ile des faisans, or de la Conférence, upon which island conferences between sovereigns and ambassadors of France and Spain have frequently taken place.

We stayed at La Maison Nartus again the following autumn-winter; but after that (the house being already full) we migrated to the Hotel d'Angleterre, kept by Madame Campagne and her son, who made us so exceedingly comfortable that we always stayed there the following years we went to Biarritz. Once when we were staying at the Hotel d'Angleterre Leopold II, the late King of the Belgians, was also stopping there with his private secretary; he had no ostensible suite of any kind in his entourage, but he was closely watched and safely guarded at every step and on every occasion by private detectives in plain clothes, who followed him wherever he went. He was a great walker, detesting carriage exercise. Thus, on his way out to Biarritz, he suddenly took it into his head to alight at Bayonne, walking from there (that time quite alone) to Biarritz, leaving his private secretary to look after the luggage. When the train arrived at Biarritz the Prefect had sent his state carriage to take the King to the hotel, but there was no King to take up; while the private secretary quietly stepped into the hotel omnibus, seeing that the luggage was put upon the top.

In the same way, on returning from Biarritz, the King would insist upon walking to the station, a distance of about two miles. He was late in leaving the hotel, so that he kept the train waiting a good half-hour for His Majesty, who calmly and leisurely walked up, taking his seat in the train without hurrying himself one bit.

We had meanwhile chartered a carriage to the station to see the King off; he recognised us and gave us a friendly nod as the train glided off.

We met His Majesty later on at Cimiez, above Nice: he was staying there at the Excelsior Hotel Regina, while we were at the Grand Hotel Cimiez, where our late Queen Victoria wintered in 1895-1896. King Leopold always walked down to Nice, and up again to Cimiez, never by any chance taking the tram, which started from his hotel.

From Biarritz it was always our custom to take delightful excursions, which I well remember. One morning, immediately after our early breakfast, we started in a coach and four. I sat with the driver. At St. Jean de Luz we alighted, leaving our coach, four horses, and driver there to pick us up on our return, and taking a narrower coach, also driven by four horses. I sat with the driver as before; he was a bright young fellow, absolutely devoid of all fear. From St. Jean de Luz we drove along "la route Nationale" till we reached the French frontier at Hendaye; there we branched off to the left, skirting the River Bidassoa till we came to Béhobie, where we alighted at the French custom house, while the officials took note of our horses and coach, giving us a certificate, for which they charged five centimes (one halfpenny). We then crossed the river over to Béhobia (spelt this time with an "*a*" instead of an "*e*") in Spain: there the Spanish custom house officials went through the same formalities, giving us also a certificate, for which they charged ten pesetas ("*Oro*," or 8s. in English money). This contribution is supposed to be used for keeping up the roads, but, as a matter of fact, they were in a disgracefully primitive state, so there it was that our troubles began, as we once more skirted the River

Bidassoa (but this time on the Spanish side) until we reached Vera, a very primitive village, with an even more primitive inn, where we partook of an equally primitive lunch consisting of thick Spanish soup with broad beans, flavoured with garlic; sausages warmed up, also flavoured with garlic; coarse cheese, butter and bread: the whole washed down with the wine of the country (a heavy red wine), which we drank diluted with plenty of cold water, finishing up with café au lait for the ladies, but café noir for the gentlemen. Our party consisted of the Baron de Gemaux, his sister and his daughter, a young Frenchman with his tutor, my wife, my daughter, and myself; four ladies and four gentlemen, making eight in all. Although the food was primitive, and somewhat coarse, it went down all right; for, as the Latin writer pertinently declares, "*Fames condimentum optimum.*" We had to stay at Vera two hours to rest the horses, but we spent the time agreeably in exploring this primitive village with its quaint old church.

Our return journey seemed even more perilous than the previous one, the four ladies kept up a continuous shriek, while the abbé kept crossing himself, offering us at the same time plenary absolution. Eventually we arrived safely at Hendaye, where we turned to the right, getting once more on to "la route Nationale," and driving to St. Jean de Luz, where we changed into our larger, more roomy coach. We tipped our venturesome Jehu handsomely, making his eyes sparkle with joy. Just as we were starting again he took me on one side to ask me how I thought he had got on, to which (all danger being now over) I gave him an encouraging reply : he said he was glad, for it was the first time he had ever driven four-in-hand; in fact, he had only up till then driven the hotel omnibus to the railway station and back. I gave him an extra tip, telling him at the same time not to mention this episode to any of my party, or there would be ructions.

Another of our favourite drives was to Cambo, the abode of Rostand, the celebrated dramatist, author of *Cyrano de Bergerac*. I saw this play acted in Paris at *Le Theatre de la Porte St. Martin* (Sarah Bernhardt's theatre, in which she acted with Coquelin, who took the title rôle. It was indeed a great treat to see and hear these two great actors play together, for both Coquelin and Sarah Bernhardt were simply inimitable). Cambo is a picturesque village situated on the right bank of the River Nive (Haut Cambo) and partly in the valley (Bas Cambo). We had a delicious lunch at the Hotel Angleterre, but before lunch I had a hot sulphur iron bath in the establishment close by, and, after the bath, drinking the same mineral water. A great gathering of Basques annually takes place there on St. John's Eve (23 June), when each tries to drink the greatest possible amount of water whilst the clock is striking twelve (midnight), in order to insure his well-being until the following anniversary.

The drive to Cambo and back was very enjoyable. I also went there alone by steamer from Bayonne, along the River Nive; the steamer giving me ample time for another hot mineral bath, followed by lunch. Of the two excursions, I think I preferred the river one to that by road, although that also was very fine.

On another occasion we took a carriage after lunch to Bayonne, an interesting old city, formerly Spanish, but now French. It was here that the late Queen Victoria stayed when she first visited these parts; the cathedral dates from 1140, and was rebuilt after a fire in 1213. The citadel, built by Vauban in 1674-1679, is considered one of his best works. It has never been taken, and over the entrance is the inscription, "*Nunquam polluta.*" From there we visited the English Cemeteries (for there are two of them), where are buried English officers and soldiers who fell at the unsuccessful siege of 1814. After that we went on the pier, where the River Adour runs into the sea, and then strolled on to the hard sands, finishing up with afternoon tea at the Café du Grand Balcon, and then driving back to our hotel. On another occasion we drove, after lunch (ten miles each way), to St. Jean de Luz, where we had afternoon tea at the Hotel d'Angleterre, splendidly situated on the beach.

But our big excursion was by very early train to San Sebastian, in Spain, getting out at Hendaye, where we were rowed across the River Bidassoa to Fuentarabia, a decayed interesting old town, which has not only a picturesque but also a thoroughly Spanish appearance, with very narrow streets dating from the tenth century. The houses are large buildings with coats of arms and balconies of iron work, bearing witness to the bygone prosperity of the town. The population, of Basque origin, is extremly interesting. The castle, almost in ruins, greatly took our fancy; it was for sale, the price asked being 100,000 pesetas (something under £4,000) with a title of nobility reverting to the purchaser. We visited the old church, highly decorated with that lavish, luxuriant extravagance characteristic of Spanish churches.

We then were rowed back to Hendaye, where we took our train on to San Sebastian, getting there in good time for lunch at the Grand Hotel Escurial.

After lunch we visited the place, an important seaport, delightfully situated as a fashionable seaside resort, very much patronised by the Royal family of Spain, Magdalena Palace being their summer residence. The Cathedral (dating from 1078) is considered to be the most important example of early Romanesque architecture in Spain. But what struck us most were the graves of English officers and soldiers, hewn out of the solid rock on the cliffs overlooking the sea: these graves were in an excellent state of preservation, being well kept up; they certainly well deserve a pilgrimage to their hallowed shrine. We returned to tea at the hotel, catching our train back to Irun (Spanish), and Hendaye (French), where we changed from a Spanish into a French train, the gauges between the two countries being different. This is certainly a very great drawback to the train to Madrid and Lisbon, for all passengers are compelled to change trains at Hendaye.

One afternoon, walking back from Bayonne to Biarritz, we came across some Basques playing the national game of Pelota. This game is really a Spanish one. I saw it once played at Barcelona, but the Basques, who, though French, are in close touch with the Spaniards, also play it with great effect. It is a game requiring a steady eye, combined with great skill and strength: when played effectually (as it was on both these occasions) it is a most interesting game, with always a crowd of ardent sympathisers to watch and applaud any fine stroke displaying extra skill and strength.

Another favourite jaunt of mine was on foot inland behind St. Jean de Luz on the way to the Rhune Mountain (2,950 feet, which I did not ascend) by Ascain in the valley of the Nivelle; all this is historical ground connected with Wellington and the Peninsular War of 1813-1814. La Croix blanche, marking the site of a great battle, stands on an eminence dominating the whole district, and from which I had a grand view all round. Some of the old fortifications still remain: though now in ruins, they are an interesting memento of former years.

We sometimes varied our visits to Biarritz by spending the first part at Biarritz, and from there going on to Pau for a week, stopping at the Hotel Gassion, grandly situated on an eminence on the Boulevard du Midi, commanding a magnificent panorama of the Valley of the Gave, and of the whole range of the Pyrenees, with the stream the Gave du Pau at the base. We crossed the Gave by a bridge, walking on to Jurançon on our right, noted for its famous Jurançon wine. The castle on the right of the Boulevard du Midi was the residence of Antoine de Bourbon of France and his wife Jeanne d'Albret, under whom and their son, afterwards Henry IV of France, the zenith of prosperity was reached.

Jeanne d'Albret was no ordinary woman, she possessed "*l'âme entière aux choses viriles,*" so was able to sing a Béarnaise song while giving birth to her son, in order, as his father said, that he might be "*ni pleurer, ni rechigné.*" Antoine, the father, on his part, carried off the infant to rub his lips with a clove of garlic, and to give him a taste of the local Jurançon red wine. While at the castle we saw the cradle of the royal infant; it is made of a large tortoise shell. It is shown on the second floor of the museum attached to the castle, consisting of the ground floor, the first floor, and the second floor, replete with priceless treasures of works of art of all descriptions, including Gobelins tapestries, tables of Syrenean marble, and of mosaics composed of porphyry and Swedish agate, presented by Bernadotte, the first king of Sweden, who was born at Pau in 1764; he lived till 1844 (four years after I was born). Another gift of Bernadotte is a table with a slab of Swedish rose-porphyry. The museum contains fine historical and other paintings, cabinets, Venetian glass, Sevres vases, &c. &c. Pau possesses also a municipal museum containing masterpieces by Ary Scheffer, Deveria, Rubens, Jorduens, Teniers, Vernet, and other celebrated artists.

We enjoyed some grand drives at Pau, scouring the country around for miles in every direction, and from there we once took the train to Argeles, putting up at the Hotel de France, kept by Monsieur et Madame Peyrafitte, who made us most comfortable; they had two splendid dogs, whom I christened "Huz" and "Buz": they were my constant companions in all my excursions. On one occasion a savage dog rushed out at me, but, before he had a chance, both "Huz" and "Buz" went for him, all but killing the brute. The master came out, humbly apologising, and thrashed the dog so soundly that he never offended again.

Argeles is a delightful place for excursions, the most interesting one being to Lourdes, about 15 miles off. I spent two long days there, driving from Argeles in a victoria of the hotel, which I commandeered for our private use: the first day I went alone, the second day my ladies accompanied me. On the first occasion I got there just as a Belgian pilgrimage with twelve long trains had arrived, so that in the evening I joined in the procession, but, unfortunately, I was the only one present without a lighted candle.

Everything was conducted in a most orderly manner: there was no begging nor collecting of any kind, simply boxes put up in convenient corners, where people could give or not as they felt inclined. I cannot now remember at what hotel I had lunch and dinner, but I know it was the same hotel at which Emile Zola stopped a week, when he wrote his celebrated work, *Lourdes,* containing seven chapters, that is to say, one chapter a day. It is a faithfully graphic description of the place, with its various surroundings.

The second visit I paid there was with my ladies, who were most interested in all they saw. We lunched and had tea at the same hotel, returning to Argeles in time for 7.30 p.m. dinner. The first pilgrimage was of quite recent date, viz. 1858. Bernadette Soubirous, the heroine, died in a convent in 1880: the authorities at Lourdes treated her very badly, literally driving her out of Lourdes, although it was through her means that the present celebrity of the town is due.

On another occasion, taking the morning, we visited Cauterets, lunching at the Grand Hotel d'Angleterre, a celebrated place for the various sulphate and alkaline waters, while others contain sulphur and sodium, all supplied by 24 springs. The springs have a temperature of 131 degrees Fahrenheit, but at the "buvette" of the establishment it is only 115, while at the "buvette" beside the spring it is 129 degrees.

We returned to Cauterets after lunch, sleeping the night there and taking, the next morning, a victoria to drive us on to Gavarnie, where we left my wife at the Hotel des Voyageurs, while my daughter and I each took a donkey at 2 francs apiece to ride on to La Cirque de Gavarnie to visit this superb amphitheatre; the head of its area is 5,380 feet above sea level, enclosed by limestone mountains rising in three stages to the height of 6,900, 8,5co, and 9,000 feet respectively. The slopes between each successive stage are covered with perpetual snow and glaciers, forming 13 cascades, of which two never dry up. The principal fall is La Cascade de Gavarnie, 1,385 feet in height, the highest in Europe, except one in Norway (the Dugerfos), which is only 100 feet higher; when there is plenty of water it forms one single fall, but in summer it descends in two leaps of 958 and 427 feet respectively, making in all 1,385 feet, as mentioned above. That winter, when we visited it, the water was entirely frozen, forming innumerable icicles of great length; these, all glittering in the sun, looked singularly beautiful. We regained our hotel at Gavarnie, where a splendid lunch awaited us; this we thoroughly enjoyed, and then wended our way back by carriage to Cauterets, whence we took our train on to Argeles.

In the same way we visited, by the little mountain train, Luz, walking thence to St. Sauveur, half a mile beyond Luz. Both of these places are noted for their sulphur baths, which are in great repute. There is a fine public promenade at St. Sauveur (Le Jardin Anglais) sloping steeply down the stream, crossing a bridge (Le Pont Napoléon) 220 feet long (with a span of 150 feet) at a height of 212 feet, thus gaining the road back to Luz, where we had lunch at l'Hotel de l'Univers. After lunch we visited Les Thermes (the bathing establishment), the Church of the Templars (dating from the twelfth century), as also the museum of antiquities in the tower of the Templars church. We then strolled on to visit the picturesque ruins of Le Chateau Sancte Marie, situated on a hill, getting there and back in an hour to Luz, where we had afternoon tea before taking our small mountain train back to Argeles.

Our last excursion from Argeles was to Barèges, 4,040 feet above sea level, a village of one long street running up the left bank of the River Bastau, also noted for its warm baths, which are impregnated with sulphate of soda, and are the most powerful in the Pyrenees. La Promenade Horizontale makes a grand walk leading up to La forêt de Barèges.

Avalanches and the rush of waters from the neighbouring mountains constitute the two special dangers of the place: masses of snow of more than 100,000 cubic feet being thus hurled upon the village. When we visited Barèges that early spring it had just been overwhelmed by a terrific avalanche, leaving the village one mass of ruins and desolation. We managed to partake of a hasty lunch at l'Hotel de l'Europe; after which we were only too glad to hurry out of the place, taking our train back to Argeles, where we felt ourselves once again safely out of danger.

After leaving Argeles (which we did with very great regret, for it is an ideal spot, and which we visited again on two occasions) we wended our way by train, via Lourdes and Tarbes, to Bagnères de Bigorre, putting up at Le Grand Hotel de Paris, where we were made most comfortable. I frequented the baths regularly, finishing up with a drink at La Buvette. The place has ten separate bathing establishments: the two principal ones belonging to the town are Les Thermes (where I went) and Les Néothermes, the other eight being private ones.

La Promenade makes a nice shady walk. It is bounded by the River Adour, which falls into the sea at Bayonne, and is spanned by a bridge.

From Bagnères de Bigorre we took the train via Tarbes and Montréjeau to Bagnères de Luchon, putting up at Le Grand Hotel. Luchon is a bright, charming place with 48 sulphur springs of mineral waters, mostly all containing sulphate of sodium. I enjoyed my baths here very much, with a drink of the waters at La Buvette. In front of the baths stretches the fine Promenade des Quinconces, where we attended the morning concerts from 10 to 11 o'clock, paying 20 centimes (2d.) each for our chairs; in the evening the concerts are held at the Grand Casino, a handsome building in a park of nine acres.

We visited the waterfalls of Juzet and Montauban, both within a couple of miles of the town, as also the ruined tower of Castelviel (signifying Castle Old), of the fourteenth century, two miles up the valley, standing on an isolated hill 2,530 feet above sea level. Luchon is 2,065 feet above sea level, so, after all, it was an easy climb of only 465 feet to the summit of Castelviel, whence we got grand views all around. With Luchon we finished, for the time being, our peregrinations in the Pyrenees, where we had spent enjoyably interesting times, doing every place we visited thoroughly, as is our wont so to do.

CHAPTER VIII.

HOLLAND, GERMANY, BAVARIA, BOHEMIA, SAXONY, SWITZERLAND, PARIS.

JUST about this time I was appointed, at the unanimous request of the creditors, official liquidator to the Western Insurance Company, Limited, one of the most disgraceful swindles I ever came across. The shareholders, as well as the directors, were all men of straw, the capital was mostly fictitious, the actual cash arising out of premiums received by the company. However I had, in my friend Mr. Evelyn William Powles (an old Lloyd's man), an excellent manager to my Marine Insurance Department, and he, in conjunction with my son Caspar, set to work to cope with this Augean stable. One afternoon they came to me with the startling news that they had just succeeded in unearthing two gigantic frauds. In going through the various claims, settled and paid, they came across two of a very suspicious nature. Each of the two policies, upon which the respective claims were indorsed and settled, was issued to the same man, Perossi, the chairman of the company. There were no shipping documents to substantiate either of these two claims, for each policy (a gambling, speculative one) had, inserted in the body of it, the clause "Policy proof of interest" ("P. P. I.," for short). It was the managing director who had signed both these policies, and later on had endorsed upon each, the settled claims running into several thousand pounds sterling. On examining closely Policy A it was found that the embossed Government stamp upon it bore a date later than that on which the ship in question was posted in "The Room" (Lloyd's) as a total loss. The embossed stamp upon Policy B was all right in respect of date, but on inquiry at Lloyd's it turned out that the ship was no loss at all, but a safe arrival, without any damage or claim whatever attaching to her. I immediately brought these facts to the solicitors in the liquidation, who at once passed them on to counsel (the leading expert in such matters). Counsel's opinion came back that very afternoon, that both were undoubtedly clear cases of fraud which could be readily proved. Armed with this legal authority I lost no time in calling upon the Public Prosecutor, to whom I explained the whole matter. He at once grasped the situation. Both Perossi (the chairman) and the managing director were arrested for fraud. Their trial took place at the assizes at Plymouth, where my son and Mr. Powles went down to give evidence: this was found to be so conclusively clear that the jury, without leaving the box, returned a verdict of "Guilty" against both prisoners. Perossi got seven years' penal servitude, and the managing director two years, the Judge complimenting both my witnesses upon their able testimony. The Plymouth daily papers, too, were loud in our praise.

This brings me to the summer of 1884, when Caspar hinted to me that a trip abroad would not come amiss—it would clear away the cobwebs in his brain. So I interviewed my friend Mr. Robert John Lodge, of the "Marine," before whom I put the facts of our recent trial and Caspar's wonderful mastery of the whole case, which pleased him so much that I felt bold to ask: "I "suppose, Mr. Lodge, you don't happen by any chance "to have a P. & O. steamer stranded on the Rhine?" (of course, an absolutely impossible thing, as I very well knew, and he too knew that I knew). So he replied very gravely: "No, friend van de Linde, I don't "happen to have any such casualty calling for your "intervention, but the most excellent Theophilus" (his son and my private solicitor) "is just now stranded on "behalf of clients with a wretched colliery in Bohemia, "for which he wants you to go out to investigate and "report upon the same. If you decide to take it up, "be sure to take Caspar with you. Now get along "with you, and go at once to see 'Tophy,' who is "expecting you"; so I at once went and interviewed "the most excellent Theophilus." We at once settled everything there and then, to our mutual satisfaction, both Lodge *père et fils* telling us not to hurry, but to take our time and make it a bit of a holiday, for it was an important matter involving a large sum of money, so that it carried with it a good fee, in addition to liberal out-of-pocket expenses.

On the very Friday (15 August 1884) of that week Caspar and I left Liverpool Street by the 5.30 p.m. train, reaching Parkeston Quay, Harwich, at 7.30 a.m., putting our kit (each a small Gladstone and a knapsack —I believe in travelling light) on board our steamer, "*The Claud Hamilton,*" had a comfortable dinner ashore, leaving at 10 p.m. for Rotterdam. The next morning (after a smooth passage) we were up at 6 o'clock, had tea and a biscuit on deck, sighting, at about 7 a.m., the coast of Holland, the Custom House officers boarding us at the Brielle, a little way up the River Maas. These gentlemen were very civil, at once passing our luggage, for everything we had with us was absolutely clean; but they are at once down upon any passengers carrying dirty linen; rather hard upon our friends "the Teutons," who are somewhat weak in this respect. We reached the "Boompjes," Rotterdam, at 8.30 a.m., deposited our luggage at the railway station close by, and then went on to the Victoria Hotel, kept by my old friend John Tyssen, formerly purser on the "*Batavier*" steamer. Mr. Tyssen gave us a rattling good breakfast, consisting of a grilled sole, done to a turn, a fillet steak with fried potatoes and onions, an "omelette aux fines herbes," "Edamer" (Dutch) cheese, and fruit, washed down with Rhine wine and German seltzer, followed by an excellent cup of black coffee. Unfortunately, I had forgotten to bring my cigars with me, so I invested in a Rotterdam one; this was enough for me, it simply put me off my smoke for at least three months, for it took me all that time to get the taste of cabbage, not only out of my mouth, but also out of my system generally. Caspar, on the contrary, rather enjoyed this kind of smoke, which apparently agreed with him. After our *déjeuner à la fourchette* we strolled about the city, which had very much changed since I first visited it in 1848 and the early fifties, well over 30 years previously. We caught the 10.41 a.m. train for the Hague, passing through Schiedam and Delft. Arrived at the Hague, we deposited our kit at the Rhein station, and then looked about this gem of a city. We then took the steam tram to Scheveningen, where we bathed in the sea (" *Bains mixtes* "), much to Caspar's horror; after that we partook of a snack in the way of light refreshment, and then looked about a bit, when we took a horse tram round the town and back to the Hague, a lovely drive all along the Avenues. We dined at the buffet of the railway station, whence we caught our express train to Cologne, passing through Gouda (noted for its cheese), Arnheim, in Guelderland, whose motto is: " *Hoog van moed, klein van goed, een zwaard in de hand, is't wapen van Gelderland.*" " Great in courage, " poor in goods, sword in hand, such is the motto of " Guelderland "). At Emmerich, the Prussian frontier, where our luggage was examined, we changed carriages, and then via Dusseldorf to Cologne, putting up at the Hotel St. Paul, where, after a good supper, we turned in, sleeping the sleep of the just.

We were up the next morning (Sunday, 17 August) at 6.30. Went about the city charmed with everything we saw and attended early Mass at the cathedral, crossed the bridge to Deutz and then back to our hotel to breakfast, catching the 9 a.m. express train to Bonn, putting up at the Royal Hotel on the River Rhine, commanding charming views of the " Seven Mountains " and the surrounding country. At 10 a.m. we had a swim in the Rhine Baths; although enclosed, the stream runs very swiftly, so that we were quickly carried from one end of the long bath to the other. As we could not swim against the stream we simply walked back on the platform at the side. We then strolled round the city till 1 o'clock, when we returned to the hotel to lunch, and afterwards took the steamer across to Königswinter, a charming place, where we found the omnibus which took us to the Drachenfels Railway, whence we reached the top of the mountain, a tremendous ascent. At the summit we had a magnificent view all around. We then partook of refreshment at the "Restauration" close by, after which we walked down admiring the vineyards along the sides of the hills. The steamer back was pretty crowded, and half-an-hour late in starting. However, we got back all right to our hotel, where our dinner-supper consisted of raw herrings, raw ham (both A1), cutlets, and Rhine wine. The next morning (Monday 18th), after a bath in the Rhine, a peep at the University, and breakfast, we caught the steamer "*Wilhelm Kaiser und Konig*" from Bonn right away to Biebrich, the station for Wiesbaden; a lovely trip indeed, undoubtedly well-known to all my intelligent readers, so I will not weary them with describing its many beauties. At Wiesbaden we put up at the Hotel du Rhin, where they made us very comfortable. The next morning (Tuesday 19 August) we indulged in a hot mineral bath before breakfast. After breakfast we climbed the Neroberg (a mountain with a fine view); after lunch we caught the 3.15 p.m. train to Frankfort on the Main, putting up at the Westenhalle Hotel. We visited this interesting old city, strolled into the Palace Garden, where we heard a very fine concert. We then dined at our hotel at 6.30 p.m. After dinner we went off to the Zoological Gardens, where there was another concert going on (with two bands this time). We had our coffee there out in the open, listening to the music, while Caspar smoked serenely.

Next morning (Wednesday, 20 August) we had an early swim in the River Main, breakfasted at 7.30 a.m., catching the 8.15 a.m. train to Heidelberg, reaching there at 10.15 a.m. We drove straight up the hill to the Schloss Hotel, where they gave us two lovely bedrooms commanding fine views. We visited the castle, and the celebrated Heidelberg Tun, holding 49,000 gallons of wine. It was built in 1725, and had been filled three times since that date. The next morning (Thursday, 21 August) we strolled all over Heidelberg, finishing up with a bath in the River Neckar. We then hired a boat, intending to row to the "Philosopher's Walk"; but the current was too swift, so we gave up our boat and walked to Wolfsbrunnen, where there is a trout pond. We bought some fresh trout, just caught, took it back to our hotel, where we made a trout lunch off our purchase. We then climbed the Molkenkur and the Konigstuhl Mountains, forming part of the Schwartzwald (Black Forest) range.

Next morning (Friday, 22 August) we caught the early train for Heilbronn. Heilbronn is delightfully situated on the River Neckar, and is reckoned to be one of the most interesting towns in Wurtemberg. After visiting its many curious monuments we had lunch at the railway station (where we had left our kit meanwhile), and then resumed our railway journey to Nurnberg, putting up at the Wurttemberger Hof, close to the station—a splendid hotel, which I have ever since frequented, my last visit there being in the spring of 1914.

We arrived at our hotel at 5.45 p.m., and, after a refreshing warm bath, we took the landlord's tip and dined at a restaurant in 8 Spital Strasse. The proprietor, Herr Hans Trenheit, pointed out to us a lady seated at an adjoining table who was a Bavarian princess, dining there quite simply like ourselves. This is the celebrated restaurant of Nurnberg; it is quite a small place, but the cooking is excellent. The next morning we took a carriage right round the walls of Nurnberg—a most interesting drive. We then visited the St. Lorenz Kirche, erected during the years 1283 to 1477; the Jewish synagogue; the Frauen Kirche, erected in 1355-1361, with a curious sixteenth century clock; and the Sebald Kirche—all very beautiful, especially the first. The celebrated fountain known as the Schone Brunnen (beautiful fountain, or spring), erected in 1385 to 1396, particularly took our fancy, and no wonder, for it is one of the most beautiful Gothic fountains in existence. We had an early lunch at 12.30 p.m., and then visited the Germanic National Museum (situated in an old Carthusian monastery), containing priceless treasures of antiquities, sculpture, paintings, and military objects. We then had a swim in the baths, tea, and, later on, supper at 9 o'clock, consisting of sausages, sauer kraut, black bread, and Rhine wine.

Next morning (Sunday, 24 August) we went to morning service, after which we caught the 12.15 p.m. train to Teplitz, lunching in the train. Our luggage was examined at Egar, the Austrian frontier. We reached Teplitz at 9 p.m., putting up at the Post Hotel in the Langasse Strasse.

Next morning (Monday, 25 August) we went to the Curgarten, drinking the waters to the strains of sweet music. At 11 o'clock we went to the Schlossgarten, where we heard fresh music. We very much enjoyed the light Pilsener beer at lunch. I believe it is made of rice. After lunch we had coffee at a Restauration, and, later on, a hot mineral bath in the Kaiserbad. We then went to another concert in the Curgarten, and after that we paid a visit to the Electric Exhibition. While we supped in the Curgarten a famous military band gave us a very fine selection of good music. After that, we heard the same band play—this time we heard it through the telephone.

Next morning (Tuesday, 26 August) we were up at 3.30, catching the 4.45 a.m. train to Krupa. As the crow flies it is about twenty miles from Teplitz, but it took us five hours to get there—"The Lightning Express" with a vengeance! At Krupa, our business friends met us and drove us to Saax, where they gave us an excellent breakfast, and from there drove us to Hredl, which we reached at 10.30 a.m. Our friends took us all over the property, really belonging to the clients of "the most excellent Theophilus." After lunch I went down the coal mine—a most primitive affair. I got into a basket, and was let down very gently by a rope, keeping one leg out the whole time to steady myself so as to prevent the basket catching a rough angle of the shaft; had it done so, the basket would have turned turtle, pitching me head over heels to the bottom. As it was, I negotiated the whole thing very comfortably, while Caspar went on a shooting expedition, coming back loaded with birds.

The next morning I went down the mine again, where the mining engineer joined me (one at a time, the basket would not hold two). He explained to me various technicalities connected with the mine, all of which I took due note; Caspar all the time shooting again, bringing down a brace of partridges, which we had for supper. They were excellent. The next morning he shot three larks and a hare—all before breakfast.

On Friday, 29 August, we left Hredl for Prague, putting up at the Hotel Blue Star (Blauer Stern Hotel); we just managed a bath in the River Moldau before lunching at the Café Montag. After lunch we visited the celebrated Hradschin, and from there to the Hradschiner Platz and the Imperial Palace, dating from the fourteenth century. On 23 May 1618 two of its councillors—Martinitz and Slawata—were hurled from a window of the Council Chamber, thus bringing about the Thirty Years' War. We then visited the Church of St. Stephen and the Cathedral (Dom) of St. Veit (St. Vitus), founded in 1344, which, though still incomplete, is considered to be the finest church in Bohemia. In its chapels are paintings, sculpture, and elaborate altars, with a silver shrine of St. John Nepomue, the patron saint of Bohemia, in whose memory is held on 16 May the great annual pilgrimage held on the very spot where he was thrown into the river on 16 May 1383. The royal monument is in the nave of the "Dom" erected over the graves of the Kings of Bohemia. To the east of the "Dom" is the ancient church of St. George, of the tenth century.

In the evening we crossed over to the Sophien Insel, where we had supper out of doors, listening to the band. Next morning (Saturday, 30 August) we took the 7.34 a.m. train to Dresden, reaching there about

1 o'clock. Our luggage was examined on the way at Bodenbach, where we lunched. At Dresden we stopped at the Hotel Bellevue, standing in a unique position on the River Elbe, facing the Royal Palace, the Opera House, the Cathedral, and the Picture Gallery. The Konigliche Schloss (Royal Palace) contains the world-renowned Grunes Gewolbe (the Green Vault), replete with priceless collections of curiosities, jewels, enamels, crystals, coins, medals, ivories, and other works of art. Dresden, the capital of the kingdom of Saxony, simply teems with wonderful art galleries, notably, among others, the Zwinger, the Johanneum, the Konigliche Porzellanniederlage (Royal Dresden Porcelain China Depôt), the Japamsche Palais, the Albertinum, the Kunst-Gewerbe Museum, and the Aula, once the banquetting room of the Bruhl Palace, with its painted ceilings, gilt doors, &c. We visited most of these museums, as also the Roman Catholic Hof Kirche and the Sophienhof Kirche, which is the Protestant Hof Kirche. No wonder that Dresden has always been one of the most frequented cities in Germany, with spacious residences on all sides, constituting the English and the American quarters. We managed a bath in the River Elbe, drove to the Grosse Garden, returning by the Zoological Gardens. In the evening we dined out in the open on the Bruhl Terrace, where we heard very good music.

On the Sunday (31 August) we attended the English Church, had *table d'hôte* at 1 p.m., and after our coffee (and Caspar his cigar) we drove to the railway station, catching the 4.20 p.m. train to Wehlen, thus commencing our tour through Saxon Switzerland (Säxische

Schweitz). We put up at the Freyer's Hotel, and then had a bath in the River Elbe, returned to the hotel, where we ordered supper, and then took a grand walk to the Bären Stein, a famous hill on the opposite side of the river and commanding a very beautiful view. We enjoyed our supper, which was excellent; besides, we had earned it.

The next morning (Monday, 1 September), after a river bath and breakfast, we despatched our knapsacks on to Schandau (having already sent on our two Gladstone bags from Dresden back to our hotel, the Blauer Stern, at Prague); we then went to the Wehler Grund and on to the Uttewalder Grund, one of the finest rocky gorges in Saxon Switzerland. It is a dry deep one, with the sides so lofty and close together that some parts are never reached by the sun's rays. Then on through the Felsenthor to the Bastei, a precipitous rock (640 feet high) on the opposite side of the River Elbe. When we reached its summit we commanded the very finest point in the Saxon Switzerland, the view being simply entrancingly beautiful. Then down to the Amstelgrund, where we stopped for lunch out in the open by the waterfall, which, however, was not then in action—the fact being that the landlord just waited to see what we ordered to drink. When we told him to bring us a large bottle of good red Rhine wine, he did so, and at once half turned on the tap, removing at the same time a wooden board, thus setting the waterfall running. By and by he replaced the board, which at once stopped the water flowing. But Caspar was one too many for him, for he sprang forward and once more removed the board, putting it by his side, while at the same time turning the tap full on, thus giving us a splendid waterfall. But just then the landlord came up, and with tears in his eyes begged for the board once more, declaring that if he did not at once turn off the water, the supply would cease for the remainder of the season. As by that time we were ready to start off, we paid our bill, and gave him the craved-for permission, at which he beamed once more, while he wished us a hearty "Nach wieder sehen" ("good-bye," or in French, "au revoir").

We then wended our way to Hockstein, a rock 360 feet high (1,040 feet above the sea), which we climbed, thus gaining a good view of the little town of Hohnstein, and then, descending through the Wolfsschlucht, we reached Polenzthal, a cool refreshing place, with the inevitable "Restauration," which, however, we did not patronise, but pushed on to Brand, 905 feet high, commanding fine views north, south, east, and west. At Brand we had intended taking a carriage to Schandau, but there was none to be had, so we simply tramped it, arriving at our destination at 6.15 p.m., putting up at the Damschiff Hotel, where we ordered dinner, having a swim in the River Elbe while it was being got ready for us.

Next morning (Tuesday, 2 September) we had another swim in the river, while His Majesty the King of Saxony looked on approvingly. After breakfast we started for the smaller waterfall, getting there at 11 a.m. After refreshing ourselves, we got two horses and rode on to the greater waterfall, where we alighted. We then ascended the Kuhstall (1,246 feet), an archway of rock twenty feet high, where, after climbing 83 steps, we reached the summit, and were repaid by the grand view all around. After that we descended by a narrow gorge in the rock, meeting our horses on the other side. We then made for the Kleine Winterberg, where we met an old woman from whom we bought deliciously ripe blackberries, with sugar. We then rode up a very steep ascent to the Grosse Winterberg (1,824 feet); the tower on the summit was very imposing. We had lunch up there, and then walked down to the Prebischthor (1,226 feet), an imposing natural rocky arch, far more imposing than the one at Kuhstall. From the summit we got the grandest view of the whole of Saxon Switzerland.

Here we refreshed ourselves with an excellent bottle of wine, diluted with natural mineral water. This very harmless drink was most refreshing. We then descended to Herrnskretschen, on the River Elbe, whence we were ferried across to Schonau, where we had hoped to find a carriage to drive us up to the Schneeberg (Snow Mountain); but we had no such luck, so we just plodded steadily on, having supper at a Gasthof, consisting of sausages, hard-boiled eggs, black bread, and beer. After resting awhile, a man came up, who offered to act as our guide and porter up to the Schneeberg, so we started off at 9 p.m., he carrying our two knapsacks, and as it was a lovely night we tramped along merrily, arriving at 10.30 p.m. at our destination, the Schneeberg, altitude 2,372 feet—the highest of the Bohemian sandstone hills. Our landlord was expecting us, so that we were soon comfortably between the sheets and sound asleep.

Next morning (Wednesday, 3 September 1884) we were called at 4.30, swallowed a cup of hot café au lait, munching a biscuit with it, and then climbed to the top of the tower (114 feet high), whence we saw the sun rise in all its glory, at the same time admiring the magnificent panorama from our splendid vantage ground. After that we turned in again, and had a good long sleep till 8.30 a.m., when we got up, dressed, ate a hearty breakfast at 9 o'clock, starting at 10.15 down to Bodenbach, a girl with a basket of eggs on her head acting as guide and carrying our knapsacks, one in each hand, right down to our hotel (the Post). We had a delightful swim in the River Elbe, then a good lunch at the hotel, catching the 3.10 p.m. train for Prague, reaching there about 8.30 p.m., supping comfortably at our hotel (the Blauer Stern), and then went to bed and to sleep.

Next morning (Thursday, 4 September 1884) we visited the city, getting back to 1 o'clock lunch, where the works manager and the mining engineer, having come over from Hredl, joined us. We spent the whole afternoon together, going over the various details for my report to London. After which we went to the Palm Garden to dine, while the band played, and then to bed.

Our two business friends stayed the night with us, and the following morning, on revising our work of the previous afternoon, we found we still required some further particulars to complete everything, so they returned that afternoon to Hredl to procure what we needed. It was a good week before I got everything to my satisfaction, and when I did I completed my report, and sent it off to London with all the papers, thus getting everything completely off my hands. At the same time we sent off home our knapsacks carefully packed with purchases we had made; thus travelling light, with only our small Gladstone each—quite enough.

The week we had to wait at Prague we employed very enjoyably in taking daily excursions all around, doing everything very thoroughly to our heart's content. On Friday (12 September 1884) we dined at 6 p.m., starting at 7.30 p.m. for the West Bahnhof, to catch our train for Munich. We secured a compartment to ourselves, sleeping comfortably till 3 o'clock the next morning, when we reached Fürth, where our luggage was examined, for we had bid good-bye to Bohemia and Austria, being now in Bavaria.

We slept on comfortably in our reserved railway compartment till 8 a.m., when we changed into the express train from Berlin, which took us to Munich, and which we reached that Saturday morning (13 September) at 10 o'clock, driving straight to the Four Seasons Hotel, where we had a delicious warm bath, and then a good solid breakfast, washed down with the celebrated Munich beer. We hired a guide, who took us to the National Museum, and were deeply impressed with the priceless treasures it contains. We then visited the Hof Theatre, the largest in Europe; from the roof we had a splendid view of the snow-capped mountains. We then visited various palaces and gardens; after which we took a carriage to the Gate of Victory, from there to the New Pinakothek, and then on to the Old Pinakothek—both wonderful pictures galleries, containing works of practically all the old and the new masters.

From there we drove to the Basilica, with its 64 marble columns. After that our carriage took us to the gigantic bronze figure of a woman, entitled "Bavaria." We mount in the interior and sit in the young lady's head, using her eyes to look out of. We finished our drive by visiting the English Garden. Munich is a city replete with interest, well repaying a prolonged stay there. I have repeatedly visited it since, always finding fresh beauties to attract me on each successive occasion that I go there. We then had an early dinner at our hotel, catching the 8.10 p.m. train for Lindau. We again secured a compartment to ourselves, sleeping comfortably till 3.30 a.m. (Sunday morning, 14 September 1884), and arriving at 3.47 a.m. at Lindau, driving to the Hotel Helvetia, where we went to bed for a couple of hours, getting up at 6 a.m. to café au lait complet, and catching the 7.25 a.m. steamer across Lake Constance (the Bodensee) to Rorschach, which we reached at 8.30 a.m. The scenery crossing the Lake was grand, the snow-capped mountains glistening in the sun (a wonderful sight). On arrival we had a second breakfast, and then took the train to St. Gallen, 9½ miles off, during which the train ascends 850 feet. St. Gallen is a pretty town. We went to the French Protestant Church, and after the service we looked in at the German Roman Catholic Church. It may be interesting to note that the banks of Lake Constance belong to five different countries—namely, Bavaria, Wurtemberg, Baden, Switzerland, and Austria; all which five I know quite thoroughly, having often visited each of them at various times and intervals, both on business and for pleasure.

We put up at the Steigner Hotel at St. Gallen, climbing the Rosenberg (2,470 feet altitude). St. Gallen being 2,208 feet high it was not much of a climb, but we got a good view from the top; after which we climbed the Freudenberg (2,910 feet high), getting from the top a grand view of snow-capped Sentis (9,000 feet high), and which, by an optical illusion, appeared to be quite close.

The next morning (Monday, 15 September 1884) we caught the 8.10 train to Rorschach, sending our two Gladstones on to Zurich whilst we went on to Constance, and (after a bath in the Lake) taking the steamer to Schaffhausen, walking thence (1½ miles) to Neuhausen, whence we saw "the Falls of the Rhine." We first went through the village over the bridge *above* the Falls; we then took a roomy row-boat right *under* the Falls, getting up on to a rock. The effect was gorgèous, the sun through the foaming silvery spray, going up like smoke, formed several rainbows. We were then rowed over to the other side, under the Castle, to the Fichetz. The spray there came right over us, but, having the boatman's mackintoshes on, we did not get wet.

After visiting the Castle we walked a mile on to Dachsen, lunching at the Hotel Witzig, and then catching the 5.55 p.m. train, reaching Zurich (Hotel Bauer au lac) at 8.10 p.m. The first part of the railway journey, as far as Winterthur, was very interesting, giving us good views of the Rhine. Arrived at Zurich, we went on to the Palm Garden to tea and music combined.

The next day (Tuesday, 16 September) we bathed in the Lake, caught the 8.10 a.m. steamer right up the Lake of Zurich to Rapperswil (a distance of 22½ miles), which we reached at 10.15 a.m., where we ordered *déjeuner à la fourchette* at the Hotel du Lac, visiting the Castle containing the black marble column with the Polish eagle (commemorating the commencement of the hundred years' struggle of the Poles for independence), the Polish National Museum, and finally the monument standing between three different cantons. After our *déjeuner* we caught the 11.28 a.m. steamer back, soon, however, changing into another steamer which hugged the other side of the Lake. We got back soon after 2 p.m., visited the town, including the Botanical Gardens, the Polytechnic, the Picture Gallery, the Haute Promenade, the Cathedral; then a swim in the Lake (most refreshing).

Next morning (Wednesday, 17 September) we first sent our kit on to the steamer's office at Arth, on the Lake of Zug, and then caught the 7.30 a.m. train up the Uetliberg mountain (2,865 feet in altitude, Zurich being 1,345 feet), reaching the summit in half-an-hour, where we had breakfast with a Zurich friend at the Hotel Pension Uetliberg, who kindly walked with us all the way along the ridge till we came to the Albis Hoch wacht; a delightful excursion of three hours, ascending and descending on the Albis range, chiefly through a charming shady wood. At Albis we all three branched off down to Zug, which we reached at 2 p.m. Bidding good-bye to our kind Zurich friend, we had a bath and a swim in the Lake of Zug. (This bathing establishment shortly afterwards suddenly collapsed, everything being pitched helter-skelter into the Lake.) We then looked around the place till 3.30 p.m., when we caught the steamer to Arth, lunching on board. At Arth we picked up our kit and caught the 5.2 p.m. train up the Rigi—a grand ride, the gradient being on an average 1′ in 5′: a pretty steep one, I guess; we had to hang on by our eyelids. We reached the summit, the Rigi Kulm, 5,905 feet in altitude, just as the sun was setting—a grand sight. We put up at the Rigi Kulm Hotel, dining at table d'hôte at 7 o'clock.

The next morning (Thursday, 18 September) we were awakened at 5 o'clock by the blowing of a horn to get up to see the sun rise. It was frightfully cold; we had to dress by candle-light, arriving on the scaffolding (arrayed each of us in hotel mackintoshes) at 5.30 a.m. When the sun began to rise the boys yodelled for miles round, and the horn was blown again. We left the hotel in time to catch the 6.30 a.m. train down to Vitznau, where we had breakfast, and, sending on our kit to Lucerne, we caught the 8.40 a.m. steamer to Tell's Platte, where we took a row-boat to Tell's Chapel, containing four pictures representing the history of William Tell. From there we walked on to Fluelen, where we bathed in the Lake of Lucerne ("Le lac des quatre Cantons" in French, "Vierwald Stätter see" in German; both of which mean, in English, "The Lake of the Four Cantons," namely, Uri, Schwyz, Unterwalden, and Lucerne), unsurpassed in Switzerland in magnificence of scenery so intimately associated with the traditions as graphically described by Schiller in his "William Tell"; Schiller's Stone standing on the bank facing Tell's Chapel. After our swim in the Lake we looked over the old ruined castle of Rudenz and the church. We then lunched at the Hotel Tell, catching the 1.40 p.m. steamer back to Lucerne, passing the chalet where the three confederates—namely, Werney Stauffacher, Erny an der Halden, and Walter Fürst—stood on the night of 7 November 1307, with thirty-three other patriots from the cantons of Uri, Schwyz, and Unterwalden, when they all solemnly swore to drive out their hated oppressors. We reached Lucerne at 4.30 p.m., where we picked up our kit, driving in the hotel omnibus to the Schweizer Hof, by far the best hotel in the whole of Switzerland, and quite reasonable. We always go there. We visited the town, including the celebrated Lion of Lucerne, executed in 1821 to the memory of 26 officers and 760 soldiers of the Swiss Guard, who fell in defending the Tuileries on 10 August 1792. The dying lion (28 feet in length) reclining in a grotto, transfixed by a broken lance, while sheltering the Bourbon Lily with its paw, is hewn out of the natural sandstone by Thorwaldsen. The chapel adjoining contains the escutcheons of the officers, with the inscription, "Invictis pax" ("Peace to the unconquered"). We then visited the Glacier Garden, containing 32 "pot-holes," "glacier mills," or giant cauldrons discovered in 1872, and connected by means of steps and bridges. We then crossed the River Reuss by the three celebrated bridges, the one called "The Dance of Death," from paintings on the ceilings by Holbein, being the most remarkable of the three. We then visited the Hof Kirche (the Cathedral), where we listened to an organ recital depicting a thunderstorm, while a real thunderstorm was raging the whole time, and forming a very grand coincidence. The organist then gave us "Rock of Ages," which he played in five different ways. After our 7.30 p.m. table d'hôte dinner we adjourned to the garden outside to listen to a concert.

The next morning (Friday, 19 September 1884) we again crossed two of the bridges, and went up the Gutsch (1,720 feet, Lucerne being 1,437) by special train, for being pressed for time we could not wait for the regular one. We climbed the summit (1,920 feet), where we had a drink at the Hotel Pension Gutsch, while we enjoyed the views all around us. At Lucerne we caught the 10 a.m. steamer, reaching Alpnach at 11.40 a.m., where we took the diligence over the Brunig Pass. By paying extra we secured two outside top seats. We arrived at Sarnen at 12 (noon), where, having a quarter of an hour to wait, we partook of a hasty lunch. Later on, at 1 o'clock, we came to the Sarner See (1,530 feet), a lake four miles long, well stocked with fish. At Sachseln (1,598 feet) we came to the church (built in 1663), containing, among other relics, the bones of St. Nikolaus. We reached Lungern (2,475 feet) at 3.30 p.m., where, having to wait an hour, we had a table d'hôte lunch at the Lion d'or Hotel. We really did not need it, but were quailed into doing so by a fierce-looking termagant, a veritable vixen (female fox), dressed in an appalling native costume, wearing her stays outside, the front being at the back, and *vice versa*. We ordered coffee for two, but she only brought one cup, saying that Caspar looked much too young to take it. When, however, she saw Caspar smoking a villainous long black Swiss cigar, she relented and brought him the coffee. We then started again on a diligence with five horses—the country was simply lovely—through a mountain pass, reaching the Brunig Pass at 5.30 p.m. Thence reaching Meyringen in time for late table d'hôte dinner.

The next morning we started on foot for Grindenwald, and were accompanied by a guide who also acted as porter, carrying our kit. On our way we visited the Reichenbach Falls, where we saw a magnificent rainbow formed by the water dashing down. We then passed the Rosenlani glacier, with heavy snow on all the surrounding hills. We reached Scheideck at about 12 (noon), where we had lunch, and then ascended the great Scheideck (6,430 feet high). We went on the Scheideck Glacier, but it was a bit risky, owing to the many avalanches falling from the precipices above. We afterwards went up to the Grindenwald Glacier, entering some 50 yards inside through a passage 10 feet by 5 cut out of the solid rock. The blue colour of the ice was splendid, but the weather bitterly cold. We had a grand view of the Wetterhorn (12,165 feet high); it seemed quite close, but was, in fact, some distance off. Along the Scheideck Pass the chalets are reckoned to be the finest in Switzerland. We reached Grindewald at 6 p.m., where we had tea, and by driving very fast reached the Grand Hotel Victoria, at Interlaken, at 8 p.m., where, after a change, we dined.

The next morning we breakfasted early, and then walked to Ringgenberg, attending the service there, after which we visited the ruined castle and strolled along the Brienser See, on which Ringgenberg is situated. We bought a beautiful inlaid wood mosaic table and two chairs carved with edelweiss; they were sent home, and they all three still adorn our front hall, being very much admired.

After a primitive lunch we strolled back to Interlaken. From the hotel there is a magnificent view of the Jungfrau (13,671 feet high), with her dazzling shroud of eternal snow. After tea on the verandah outside the hotel we strolled along the village of Interlaken, getting back to 6.30 p.m. table d'hôte dinner.

The next morning, after an early first breakfast, we started at 7.30 a.m. in a carriage and pair for Lauterbrunnen, 10 miles off. We there took a guide, who walked us up the Wengern Alp—a very steep ascent of two hours—which we reached at 11.30 a.m., but it was very cloudy, so we got no view, but saw a grand avalanche which, falling, sounded like thunder.

We then went on to the Little Scheideck, reaching it at 12.30, just in time for a good lunch, which we thoroughly enjoyed. We then went down, seeing three or four avalanches. The sun came out, giving us a good view of Murren, with its three mountains opposite—the Eiger, the Möuch, and the Jungfrau. We reached Lauterbrunnen at 5.15 p.m., where we took a carriage back to our hotel at Interlaken in time for 7.30 p.m. table d'hôte dinner.

The next morning we started at 8 o'clock in a carriage and pair to Kandersteg in pouring rain, which, however, passed off, so that when we arrived at Frutigen at 1.30, where we lunched at the Hotel Bellevue, it was quite fine. After lunch we resumed our drive, stopping at the Blauer See (Blue Lake), 2,950 feet high, where we alighted and were rowed across. The lake is picturesquely embosomed in woods, and remarkable for its intense blue colour. We had tea on the terrace overlooking the Lake, and then resumed our seats, reaching Kandersteg at 7 p.m., stopping at the Bär Hotel, where we had a comfortable dinner. The next morning we started at 7 o'clock for the Gemmi Pass, an interesting up-hill walk of four hours, ascending the summit—the Daube (7,553 feet high). We then descended the Gemmi Pass, most interesting and startling, for the path was just 5 feet wide. We soon reached the brink of an almost perpendicular rocky wall, 1,660 feet high. The windings down the pass are hewn out of the solid rock, resembling a spiral staircase, the upper parts at places actually projecting beyond the lower. The steepest parts and most sudden corners are protected by parapets. The descent on horseback is now prohibited, a marble cross commemorating an accident to a lady rider, who was thrown headlong down the precipice. We reached the Baths of Leuk at 1 p.m., and were very interested in watching the bathers. We then lunched at the Hotel des Alpes. After lunch we took a carriage and pair to Leuk, crossed the Rhone, and caught the train to Martigny, stopping at the Hotel Clerc, where we dined at 8 p.m., and stayed the night; but not to sleep, for we were voraciously attacked by mosquitoes. Next morning our eyes were practically closed, being so much swollen.

We left at 8 a.m. in a carriage and pair, accompanied by two American ladies (Mrs. and Miss Griffin), from Chicago. On our way we passed the beautiful Gorges of the Durnant, and had a grand view of the Bernese Oberland. We rested our horses at Salvan, and then went on to Finhaut (or Fins-hauts), 4,060 feet, where we lunched at the Hotel des Alpes. We then resumed our carriage along the Tête Noire Pass—which is very fine—and had a grand view of the Trient Glacier. We stopped at Argentière, where a guide took us over the Argentière Glacier. We alighted at Chamonix at the Hotel Couttet, where we dined with the Griffins at 7.30 p.m. table d'hôte, with a lovely fire, which was most acceptable. Next morning we started at 7 o'clock with Miss Griffin for Montanvert, 2½ hours from Chamonix. We had some refreshment at Montanvert, and then crossed the Mer de Glace, accompanied by a guide and a man to cut steps for us, for we were surrounded by hills of ice—most wonderful. The crossing took us about 1½ hours, when we walked along the Mauvais Pass. It certainly deserves its name, for it was certainly anything but easy, and right on the side of a steep precipice. We then went on to the Chapeau, after which we descended the valley and had a good square meal at the Mer de Glace Hotel.

Miss Griffin's mule had rejoined her at the Chapeau, so we three then ascended the Flegère, a three hours' climb. At the top there was a good telescope, through which we followed the ascent of Mont Blanc, seeing everything quite distinctly. After refreshment we went down again to the Hotel Couttet, where we met Mr., Mrs., and Miss Merriam, of Springfield, Massachusetts, who were visiting Mrs. Griffin.

We much enjoyed our excellent dinner over a good fire.

We left Chamonix Saturday, 27 September, 1884, at 7 a.m. in the diligence for Geneva, accompanied by the Griffins and the Merriams. It was raining when we started, but soon cleared up, and became a splendid day. During our 54 miles' drive we changed horses six times, and had either five or six horses, according to the roads.

When we reached Geneva we bade our American friends good-bye, calling at the Hotel Metropole for tea and letters, and then took a carriage to the steamboat pier for Lausanne, where we took the funiculaire up to the town, dining at the Hotel Gibbon, and catching the 8.40 p.m. train for Paris.

We reached Paris the next morning at 7.30, and drove to the Hotel Lille et d'Albion, where we had a warm bath and cup of tea. We then rested till it was time to attend the English church. After the service we walked round the Place de la Concorde, through the Tuileries and Palais Royal. We lunched at 12.30 p.m., on oysters, fillet de bœuf, cheese, and claret. We then drove to the Bois de Boulogne, past the Emperor's Farm, Sir Richard Wallace's house, and a castle built for Charles X for a wager in nine days, as many days as there had been Kings of the name of Charles preceding Charles X. We had a peep at Fort Valerien, passed the race-course, alighted at the Arch de Triomphe, and walked back to our hotel through the Champs Elysées, the Tuileries, and the Rue de Rivoli, dining at our hotel; and after that had a short stroll before going to bed.

The next morning we were up early, and, immediately after breakfast, we engaged one of the hotel guides to show us round Paris. We went along the Avenue de l'Opera, admiring the imposing façade of the Grand Opera House and the various boulevards. Being Monday (cleaning day), we could not visit the Galleries, so we walked round the Louvre, seeing the door through which the Empress Eugénie escaped from the Communists. We were much struck with the imposing shops in the Palais Royal, where I bought some Sevres china, which was packed up and sent home for me. We then visited the Palais de Justice, the former Palace of King Louis IX ("Saint Louis"), admiring its lovely frescoes, where he and his mother, "la Reine Blanche," are depicted releasing prisoners, administering justice under an oak tree, inaugurating the Crusades, and other interesting episodes. We then visited La Sainte Chapelle. It is very lovely. Our guide pointed out to us the barred window through which Louis XI performed his devotions. After that the Cathedral of Notre Dame, where the Prince Imperial was baptised in great pomp. We were shown the treasures and the memorials of the three Archbishops who had been assassinated, the first on the boulevards, the second while officiating at the altar, and the third in cold blood by the Communists.

While the horrors were still upon us the guide took us to the Morgue, but having already seen the dissecting room at St. George's Hospital, we were more or less acclimatised. Then, in order to soothe our nerves, he took us round Le Jardin des Plantes and the Zoological Gardens, then on to the Column of La Bastille, the site of the old prison of that name, destroyed by the Republicans in 1793, but the Column itself was only built in 1830.

We then had lunch at a Bouillon Duval, doing justice to it; oysters, trotters, artichokes, "light and elegant," as the Yankees would say.

After lunch we visited the Church of St. Paul, erected by St. Louis in the thirteenth century. Then a drive through the Quartier Latin (the students' sanctum), the Palace and Jardin des Luxemburg, Les Invalides, with the magnificent tomb of the first Napoleon, made out of a single block of porphyry marble, a present from Alexander the Great; we admired the flags, trophies of great battles fought by Napoleon, and where we read his request as follows:—"*Je désire que mes cendres reposent sur les bords de la Seine, au milieu de ce peuple français que j'ai tant aimé.*"

Two niches are left vacant. They were intended for Napoleon III and the Empress Eugénie.

The others are filled up by Jerome Napoleon ("le petit Roi de Rome," son of Napoleon I, and called "Napoleon II"), Marshal Turenne Vauban (the Engineer), Marshal of France, who gave the plans for the fortification of Paris, &c. &c. Then down to the Champ de Mars, where were held the exhibitions of 1867 (which I visited on my return from India) and of 1878 (which I did not visit, being at the time in the West Indies). Then on to the Trocadero, where we ascended the Tower by the lift, gaining a splendid view of Paris; then a visit to the Aquarium, the Madeleine, and a drive to the Buttes de Chaumont, a lovely park built over what was before one of the worst slums of Paris. Our Jehu then drove us to the cemetery of Père la Chaise, where we saw the tombs of Héloise and Abelard, Rossini, Fould, Rachel, Ledu Rollin, Aubert Rousseau, Claparède, and others. After that we were driven back to our hotel by the new statue of the Republic, built in 1883, and the Place de la République.

We noticed on all the buildings the motto of the Communists, "Liberté, Egalité, et Fraternité."

We dined at the Hotel Continental, and then went to the Hippodrome, where we saw some good horsemanship. Paris lighted up looked very fine.

The next morning (Tuesday, 30 September 1864), after an early breakfast, we went over the Church of Saint Rock. The following day there was to be a bicentenary service to commemorate the death of Pierre Corneille, 1 October 1684.

We saw the monument of Le Notre, the gardener who designed the gardens at Versailles. We then admired the fourteen stations of the Cross, which are very fine.

After that we took the coach, "personally conducted," to Versailles, through the Bois de Boulogne, on to St. Cloud, where we got down and walked through the Palace, a heap of ruins; the grounds are very fine. We saw the house where Gambetta died and the one where Napoleon I disarmed the 500, declaring himself the First Consul. The building is now used for storing firewood.

On reaching Versailles we stopped at the house where Ferdinand de Lesseps, of Suez Canal fame, was born. We then visited the building containing the State carriages, all connected with the former grandeur of the first and third Napoleons, one alone costing 1,000,000 francs (£40,000), only used twice. We then went over the Grand Trianon, built by Louis XIV (Le Grand Monarque) in 1683 for Madame de Maintenon, and then the various rooms, including the bedroom of Napoleon I, and were shown the finest cameo in the world (1700 B.C.) and a malachite vase (a present from Alexander I of

Russia to Napoleon I), also Queen Victoria's apartments, prepared for her by Napoleon III, but only occupied by her half an hour. We enjoyed our lunch at the Hotel de la Chasse. We then visited the reception room of Louis XIII, with the names of all the great heroes of that day, inscribed "*a toutes les gloires de la France*"; Marie Antoinette's reception room, with Sevres clock and candelabra; the bedroom of Louis XIV (the bed valued at 100,000 francs, £4,000); the Tapis Vert, where the bridegroom, blindfolded, had to walk across the carpet, and if he got off it every one was allowed to kiss the bride; then the Hall of Mercury, where Louis XIV lay in state; the Hall of Hercules, with the painted ceiling, the largest in the world; the Royal Chapel, the finest church outside Paris, with Louis XIV pew; the paintings by Horace Vernes and other great artists, including the portrait of Rothschild as Shylock the Jew. We then visited the Galleries de l'Europe of 1792; the Hall of Peace, where Jules Favre and Bismarck signed the Treaty of Peace after the Franco-German war; the Salon des Glaces, where the Empress Eugénie gave a ball in honour of Queen Victoria; the private apartments of Marie Antoinette, whence she made her escape and her Swiss guards were killed, in commemoration of which the Lion of Lucerne was sculptured.

We drove back from Versailles to Paris, making a collection on the road for our coachman, who drove us fast and very well. We dined at our hotel, returning by night boat via Dieppe and Newhaven; got to London soon after 12, where I conducted that very day an important audit.

CHAPTER IX.

NORMANDY, BRITTANY.

A COUPLE of years afterwards I went on a walking tour through Normandy with a knapsack on my back, accompanied by a young friend who prided himself on his walking powers.

We travelled by night via Newhaven and Dieppe, which we reached the following morning. We had a smooth passage across, so were able to enjoy our short night's rest.

Arrived at Dieppe, we went to a good hotel, where we had a hot bath and a splendid breakfast ("Déjeuner à la fourchette), which we much enjoyed, and, being a good square meal, we felt that it ought to last us till we got to Rouen, where we hoped to dine and sleep.

So we shouldered our knapsacks and started on our tramp from Dieppe for Rouen, a distance of 38 English miles.

We stopped occasionally on the way to quench our thirst with a jug of draught raw cyder, which we found most refreshing.

But about three o'clock that afternoon, finding that we had still a long way to reach our destination, we thought we would try and get a lift if possible.

Just then a market cart passed us. We hailed the driver, who told us that he was going to Rouen, and as there was plenty of room for both of us he kindly agreed to drive us there, naming a ridiculously low sum for his fare. So we at once jumped up, and much enjoyed the drive after our long tramp, so that when we reached Rouen we felt quite refreshed. We put up at the Grand Hotel d'Angleterre, a first-class house, pleasantly situated on the Quay, where we had a late dinner and bed. Rouen is an unique city, and quite took our fancy. The next morning we started visiting " la Catedrale de Notre Dame," an imposing Gothic pile ranging from 1270 to the sixteenth century. Richard Coeur de Lion died in Rouen in 1199. His heart is buried below the choir; his coffin, with other relics, is shown in the Treasury. But the church that impressed us the most was that of Saint Ouen (fourteenth century). It is a beautiful Gothic edifice, larger than the cathedral, both in length, breadth, and height. The museum contains a fine collection of paintings by old and modern masters, also some very good sculpture. By the side of "le vieux marche" stands "la Rue Jeanne d'Arc," where Joan of Arc (recently canonized) was in 1431 burnt as a witch. Close by stands La Grosse Horloge, a gigantic clock, reminding me of the one at Strassbourg, only larger. In the afternoon we took a delightful trip by steamer on the River Seine to Elbœuf and back. Returning to our hotel, my friend, who gloried in his upright military bearing, began humming the German national hymn, " *Wacht am Rhein* " (" The Watch on the Rhine "). This was too much for the police, who simply hated anything connected with Germany, so a gendarme marched him off to La Gendarmerie, where I followed. Had he apologised in the slightest all would have been well. Not a bit of it; he was just simply proud of what he had done, so he was at once taken to the hotel by a gendarme, who stood over him while he packed his knapsack, and then conducted him to the railway station and put him in charge of the guard, with strict orders to see him on board the Dieppe steamer starting that night for Newhaven.

I was all right with the police, to whom I showed my Foreign Office passport, and, speaking French like a native, they readily accepted my explanation, the officer telling me that they had really acted in my friend's best interests in sending him back home. They firmly believed he was a German until I proved to them that he was English.

The next day I tramped to Lisieux, putting up at the Hotel de France. It is one of the most attractive of the old-world towns in France, full of picturesque bits, with its many old houses. The Gothic cathedral of the twelfth century has a noble facade. Thomas à Becket found refuge at the Priory of St. Ouen le Pice, close to the town. The next morning I had a long tramp (with a lift nearing the end) to Caen, which is 30 miles from Lisieux. I put up at the Hotel de France. Caen is a place of special interest for English visitors. It is full of memories of William the Conqueror and of his wife Matilda, who both died at Caen. The empty tomb of William is before the high altar of "l'Eglise de l'abbaye aux hommes," erected by William, but his remains were thrown out twice during popular disturbances in 1562 and 1793, since which latter date they have never been replaced.

His wife, "La Reine Matilde," in 1066 founded "l'abbaye aux dames," where she died and was buried. Her remains have never been disturbed. There are several old churches, all most interesting. At dinner that evening they served me up tripe as one of the dishes, "tripes à la mode de Caen." It was very appetising, with a flavour of garlic (ail), which I rather like.

When I was travelling the previous year in Guernsey and Jersey I came across a quaint ceremony connected with Rollo, a Norwegian chieftain who in the year 912 was ceded by Charles the Simple, King of France, the province of Normandy, of which he became its first Duke. Rollo was a wise Christian governor, the people regarding his laws and justice with sacred obedience; thus, in the case of encroachment, invasion of property, or of any act of oppression the aggrieved party called upon the name of Rollo three times and repeated the words, "*Ha-Ro, à l'aide, mon Prince,*" which was an appeal to Rollo for succour. This appeal is held to be so sacred that the aggressor at once desists, and leaves the matter to be settled by a court of law. This "*clameur de Haro*" had a remarkable illustration 170 years after the death of Rollo, on the occasion of the funeral of William the Conqueror. It appears that in order to build the great Abbey at Caen, where the King intended his own tomb to be placed, he had caused several houses to be pulled down to enlarge the area, among them one for which the owner had not been paid for his loss. The son of the owner, observing that the grave of the Conqueror was being prepared in the very ground formerly belonging to his father, fearlessly came into the assembly, and in the name of Rollo forbade them to go on, making use of these words: "The ground wherein you are going to lay this man is mine, and I affirm that none may in justice bury their dead in ground belonging to another. I therefore appeal to Rollo, the founder and father of our nation, who, though dead, lives in his laws, to right my cause." This courageous appeal, made in the presence of the deceased monarch's own son, had at once the desired effect. The man's claim was recognised and satisfied, upon which he withdrew his opposition, and the body of the King was laid in the grave. While at Caen I verified the fact, of which I had already been told the details when travelling in Jersey the previous year, where trials in this peculiar form of appeal are still frequently brought before the Royal Court of Justice. The prosecution is carried on by the Crown, and the losing party (whether plaintiff or defendant) pays a small fine to the sovereign, because the sacred name of Rollo is not to be carelessly invoked.

From Caen I tramped on to Bayeux, putting up at the Hotel Luxembourg. It contains the Gothic twelfth century Cathedral of Notre Dame, which I carefully inspected both inside and outside, as it is all very fine. But the attraction of the place is the famous Bayeux Tapestry, which is shown in the small museum. The tapestry represents the invasion of England in 1066 by William the Conqueror. It is 230 feet long and 18 inches wide. Queen Matilda, the wife of William I, is supposed to have worked it. From there I tramped on to Saint Lo, where I saw the Imperial stables of the late Emperor Napoleon III, who had taken a great pride in them down to the time of the Franco-German war in 1870. After lunch I tramped on to Coutances (Hotel de France). Its graceful, magnificent cathedral of the thirteenth century is one of the most beautiful churches in France; it is a perfect museum of architectural detail, its Gothic dome or lantern being absolutely unique.

From there I tramped, the next morning, on to Granville, where I had a good lunch, continuing then on to Avranches (Hotel de France). Henry II.'s stone (the site of the cathedral before 1790), is where the King did penance for the murder of Thomas à Becket. From there I tramped, the next morning, to Dol, which contains a beautiful Gothic cathedral. I got a guide there, who rowed me over to Mont Saint Michel, a facsimile of Saint Michael's Mount opposite Marazion in Cornwall. The man rowed me back to Dol, where I lunched at the Grand Hotel. I then tramped on to Saint Malo, from where I took the night steamer back to Southampton, and thence by train from Waterloo back to my home at Lyndhurst, Bexley Heath, Kent, having had a most enjoyable holiday in spite of the very unfortunate contretemps at the outset connected with my young friend, who was a bit of a madcap after all.

CHAPTER X.

Continental Business Round Trip.—I.

JUST about this time (1888 onwards) I was asked to take up important work on the Continent in connection with various industries, with agencies in this country. This necessitated my having frequently to go abroad under very pleasant auspices, for my Continental clients always treated me as one of their personal friends. I have still a very fine porcelain fruit dish, given to me by one of them, which I value very highly.

I stayed at the various hotels where my work lay, except that in the Jura and Vosges Mountains, there being no hotels, I was invariably invited to the houses of the three respective clients (two in the Jura and one in the Vosges).

I wrote to the clients in the Jura in English, announcing my approaching visit. One of the partners spoke English and translated it to the other, who did not. The latter took my letter home with him to lunch to show his wife.

She looked at it and, seeing it was in English, she returned it to her husband, saying: "You know very well, Léon, that I do not understand English," to which he replied, "No, my dear, but you understand character by the handwriting; please tell me what you think of the character of the writer of this letter." After studying my letter carefully, she returned the letter to her husband, saying, "I like that handwriting; it is quite straightforward. You can trust Mr. van de Linde. Write and say we shall be very happy to receive him here for as long as he can stay."

This was in 1888 at Morvillars, where we at once became great friends, and I have been there ever since once a year in the summer. In the spring I go to the partner's house at Beaucourt. This gentleman once cured me of a very severe attack of influenza, and that so quietly, patiently and efficaciously that I quite enjoyed being nursed by him and his kind wife. I soon got well.

My third French client in this particular industry (M. Paul ——) lives at Plancher les Mines in the Vosges. They all three, in the olden days, used to drive me about from one place to the other, but in recent years it has always been in their magnificent automobiles, in which my nephew Henry (who always accompanies me) and I have had glorious runs, often of 100 miles in a day, stopping at delightful inns by the side of trout streams, where the delicious small blue trout is fresh caught—a very great luxury indeed.

M. Paul —— was and is still Mayor of Plancher les Mines, as his ancestors had been for time immemorial before him. When I first knew him in 1888 he had been married a few months, so, when I visited him again the following spring, he was the proud father of a bouncing boy Henri, who some years ago was for a year in our office, and is now a cavalry officer in a French regiment serving at the front, as are also his two younger brothers, Georges and Albert, all three splendid fellows.

When the proud father brought me his boy I said to him : "*Monsieur Paul, vous êtes maintenant Père et Mère* (*Maire*) *en meme temps,*" which means, " Mr. Paul, you are now Father and Mother (Mayor) at the same time," a joke I made up on the spur of the moment, which we all thoroughly enjoyed. Kindly note that it is my private property, and that all rights are reserved, so please do not attempt to poach.

In a previous part of these Reminiscences and in connection with my two business visits to Rotterdam, I mention that I received the Dutch soubriquet of "St. Gerrit." Later on I received the French one of "St. Gérard."

It was on the occasion of one of my visits to Beaucourt where, just then, I was off my smoke for the time being, so when I declined the fragrant Havana cigar that my Beaucourt friend offered me he at once dubbed me "Saint Gérard." This was too much for my self-denial; I accepted the fragrant weed, smoked it and enjoyed it, but by so doing I lost my saintship, which, after all, was perhaps just as well.

CHAPTER XI.

CONTINENTAL BUSINESS TRIP, II.—LE DUC DE BROGLIE.

PREVIOUS to my taking up this special Continental industry in 1888, and which (until the commencement of the war last August, 1914) I continued to manage, I also, on the kind introduction of two London bankers, undertook, in 1886 onward, another important Continental industry, also having ramifications in this country. The leading spirit was the late Duc de Broglie, formerly French Ambassador at the Court of St. James. This nobleman was the President of the St. Gobain Company, founded more than 200 years previously by the celebrated Vauban, under Royal auspices. It is a curious fact that, following in the steps of our own and other Royal families, Monsieur le Duc de Broglie was, although not of Royal descent, a Duke, while his son was a Prince, under the title of Monsieur le Prince de Broglie.

In the early summer of 1888 (the year of the Paris Exhibition) I received a friendly letter from the Duke telling me that he purposed in the month of July giving a banquet to his English, German, Belgian, and French colleagues, bringing up, he hoped, the number of guests to about 40, and to make a success of this important function he asked for my friendly co-operation to act as honorary secretary on his behalf, an honour I was only too proud to undertake. I accordingly sent him out a list, with full names and addresses, of all the guests. They numbered exactly 40, so that was all right. This list the Duke adopted *in toto,* himself issuing all the invitations. Needless to say, everyone accepted. I had already seen to that when compiling my list.

The banquet was held at Le Restaurant Helder, in "la rue de Helder," and was a very choice function.

The Duke presided at the head of the table, while I, as his vice, faced him at the foot. After drinking the loyal toasts the President proposed my health as follows:—"*Messieurs, nous buvons à la santé de notre Secrétaire honoraire, le baudet, Monsieur Gérard van de Linde, qui supporte tous nos fardeaux, mais n'est pas un âne,*" which, translated into English, reads: "Gentlemen, we drink to the health of our Honorary Secretary, the donkey, Mr. Gérard van de Linde, who bears all our burdens, but is not an ass." Vociferous continued applause. It was the first time in my life that I ever felt really bashful, but I certainly did so upon this memorable occasion.

The Duke then paid me an unprecedented compliment. The Company's works were situated at St. Gobain and at Chauny, and they were jealously chary of admitting strangers; in fact, when I first took up this business the London manager (Monsieur de Grand Ry) warned me never to ask to go there. But on this momentous evening the Duke called the Paris manager (Monsieur Albert Biver) up and told him he particularly wanted me to be invited to spend that week end down at both places—and I went. I had the time of my life down at St. Gobain with the Paris manager and his brother, the works manager (Monsieur Hector Biver).

By special direction of the Duke, the Royal (afterwards the Imperial) State apartments were allotted to me. I occupied the State rooms sacred to the use of the Kings and Queens of France, and afterwards of Napoleon III and the Empress Eugénie, while our own late Queen Victoria also occupied upon one occasion these State apartments.

That Saturday evening, after a splendid dinner, a great surprise was opened out to me. My two hosts conducted me down into the grounds, where flowed a tranquil river; we all three got into a gondola, and were rowed by two gondoliers on this river, which very soon ran underground for a distance of some two or three miles. Our gondola, and the two sides of this underground river, were brilliantly illuminated with bright lamps, interspersed with Chinese lanterns, the whole producing a most brilliant effect, nothing more nor less than fairyland.

The next day we had a long drive to the other works at Chauny, where we partook of a very choice lunch. It was a perfect day, and I thoroughly enjoyed the lovely day through glorious country. On our way I was taken over le Chateau de Chauny, a venerable old pile replete with historical reminiscences.

The next day we returned to Paris, when Mr. Biver took me to the top of the Eiffel Tower, where he entertained me to lunch as a parting act of hospitality on his part. This Tower is 984 feet high; it is situated on the Champ de Mars, and is the loftiest tower in the whole world.

One summer, while I was in Paris upon business, I was introduced to Monsieur Georges Petit, the celebrated print engraver, who asked me to undertake a matter for him, which I did. On paying me my fee he made me a present of some celebrated engravings, among others the following:—"*L'Angélus*" (with four others), by J. F. MILLET; "*Solitude,*" by CH. DAUBIGNY; "*Ville d'Avry,*" by C. COROT; "*Les Enfants de Charles I,*" by VAN DYCK; "*La Confidence,*" by E. MEISSONIER; and "*1814,*" by the same artist. This last picture represents Napoleon I on horseback at the head of a regiment of cavalry, riding through the snow.

I had always imagined that it represented Napoleon's celebrated retreat from Moscow, and was, therefore, very much surprised when I read in the daily newspapers of July, 1915, that this retreat took place in 1812. On 26 July 1915 I accordingly wrote the following letter, which appeared in *The Globe* of 28 July 1915:—

MOSCOW.

SIR,—I have seen in the recent daily papers references to Napoleon's retreat from Moscow as happening in 1812, whereas I have a print of Meissonier's celebrated historical picture fixing the date as 1814. I wonder which is right?

Your obedient servant,

GÉRARD VAN DE LINDE.

Reigate Hill, 26 July 1915.

*** The French entered Moscow on September 14, 1812, and evacuated it in the following month.—THE EDITOR.

On 30 July 1915 *The Globe* published the following explanatory letter from Mr. Frank Birdwood, bearing date 28 July 1915:—

MOSCOW, 1812.

SIR,—Mr. Gérard van de Linde has been misled by the gloss which certain publishers put on the title of Meissonier's picture. Because it portrays Napoleon marching through the snow and apparently in retreat, they have sometimes thought fit to label it with a sub-title, "The Retreat from Moscow." As a fact, the sole title of this "celebrated historical picture" is a date which fixes what the canvas represents, the retreat of Napoleon on Paris, a retreat which I believe military critics regard as his greatest feat at arms.

To-day Meissonier's work is of interest, not because it brings before us the annihilation of the Grand Army, but because it recalls a series of rearguard actions fought step by step along the lines of the German raid last August into France. I would weary your readers with no historic parallel, but perhaps it may hearten some to be reminded that as Chalons touched the high-water mark of German success, so a good many centuries back it was at that city that the first Attila met his Marathon.

I beg to remain, Sir, your obedient servant,

FRANK BIRDWOOD.

Ealing, W., July 28, 1915.

This correspondence, of course, settles the matter, but I still am under the impression that very many share my preconceived idea that this picture represented Napoleon's retreat from Moscow, and there I leave the matter once and for all.

On 7 November, 1889, we had the great grief to lose our dear son Gérard Caspar, who died on that day at "Lyndhurst," Bexley Heath. After the funeral we all four (my wife, son Sidney, daughter Ethel, and I) went that same afternoon on a visit to our dear friends, Mrs. and Miss Hitchcock, at Danbury, in Essex, and from there took a furnished house ("Claremont") in Bromley, Kent, whence we moved into "Glebe Knoll," Beckenham Lane, Bromley, Kent, where we stayed close upon twenty years, until we went to our present quarters, "Beech Hill House," Reigate Hill, Surrey.

In the year 1890 Baldwin Sydney Harvey came to my office, and when my remaining son Sidney Cooper had passed his final examination Sidney became my partner and Harvey was his first articled pupil, and was himself admitted as an Associate of the Institute of Chartered Accountants on 2 February 1898.

When, soon after Easter of that year, Baldwin, at the personal request of the late Lord Hillingdon, entered the banking house of Glyn, Mills, Currie & Co. as assistant secretary to his father (on 10 March, 1905), he succeeded him as secretary, an honoured post he has ever since maintained, to the satisfaction of all concerned.

CHAPTER XII.

MR. A. S. HARVEY'S HOLIDAY TRIPS ABROAD WITH US.

MY relations with Mr. Alfred Spalding Harvey, and, in fact, with all his family, were ever of the closest. Mr. Harvey always gave me a warm welcome to his house at The Grove, Highgate, where I spent many a happy week end, while I was never so pleased as when he felt free to come over to us for a couple of days or so. On these occasions we had some splendid outings, taking cycling rides together. We also spent many a happy summer holiday together with our respective families at Murren, Pontresina (the Kronenhof and Bellavista), (5,915 feet), and The Riffelalp (Hotel Riffelalp, 7,307 feet). Mr. Harvey (like all hard workers) thoroughly enjoyed his well-earned holiday. He at once threw off all business worries, and entered fully into the delights of his new surroundings. He was an intrepid mountaineer—thought nothing of a long tramp over the Diavolezza Pass (9,767 feet high), to accomplish which he made an exceedingly early start before daybreak to the Bernina Houses (5 miles from Pontresina), soon after which the climb began. His great object in making this early start was to get on to the snow while it was still hard, for as soon as the sun's rays began to melt it the walking became both difficult and somewhat dangerous. This excursion, which easily ran into 12 hours on the stretch, was a little beyond me, but I enjoyed walking with him up to the Muottas Muraigl (8,270 feet), to the Schafberg

(8,965 feet high), to Piz Languard (10,715 feet high), and to the Muottas da Pontresina. We also thoroughly enjoyed a day on the Roseg Glacier and on the Morteratsch Glacier. We generally took our lunch with us, consisting of sandwiches and hard-boiled eggs.

A pleasant afternoon's walk was to the Meierei, a charming outdoor restaurant on the borders of the Lake of Saint Moritz, where we had afternoon tea, with delicious cakes, while we listened to the band play. We once or twice drove round Samaden, Saint Moritz (with its lake or sea), Camfer (with its lake), Silva Plana (with its lake), on to Silz Maria (with its lake of "Sils"), or Maloga (5,943 feet high), lunching at the Hotel Maloga Kulm, where I had previously stayed a couple of days. After lunch we strolled to la Promenade des Artistes close by, to which we came across several Glacier Mills (or caldrons), some very large (the largest is 20 feet across and 35 feet deep), worn into the solid rock by the action of the Forno Glacier, which once covered the whole of the Upper Engadine Lake district. Before returning we peeped down the Maloya Pass, with its winding road leading into Italy. I have driven down this pass; it is the easiest of them all, for I have done all these passes at different times—the Albula, the Brenner, the Brunig, the Julier, the Simplon, the Bernina, and the Fluela, over and under, the St. Gothard (over and under). But the most remarkable of all, and which I have done three times, is the celebrated Stelvio Pass, approached on the Swiss side by the New Baths of Bounio, with a most comfortable hotel, where I spent a couple of very enjoyable days. The summit of the Stelvio Pass is 9,055 feet, the highest carriage drive in

Europe. At the summit a column is fixed in a heap of stones marking the boundary of three different countries, namely, Switzerland, Italy, and the Tyrol (Austria). The road down on the other side skirts the Ortler Spiz (12,800 feet high), and the lovely Monte Cristallo, the virgin white snow in the bright sunshine forming a dazzling sight. I have also crossed some passes over the Pyrenees, the Jura, and the Vosges Mountains, all of them most interesting and enjoyable. We returned to Pontresina the same way as we came in the morning, stopping for tea at the Wildermann Hotel, situated on the lovely Lake of Silva Plana, 5,958 feet high. There was some talk of canalising these four lakes (Saint Moritz, Camfer, Silva Plana, and Silz) and running steamers on them right away from Saint Moritz to Maloga, but, so far as I can make out, it has been mere talk and nothing more. Another long afternoon drive of 19 miles there and back was to the Heuthal, a lovely valley abounding with edelweiss, on to the Alp Grüne, whence we got a grand view down into Italy. Afternoon tea and a rest at the Bernina Hospice, after which back by the same way to the hotel, passing the Bernina Houses (6,720 feet high), where commences the ascent of the Diavolezza Route. It may interest my readers to know that I rear edelweiss from seed of my own sowing on my Alpine rock Swiss garden. I have several plants in full bloom, the flowers quite equalling, if not surpassing, both in size and colour, those I used to gather in the Heuthal and other Swiss rocky heights.

Our two respective families (Harvey and van de Linde), recruited by Mr. and Mrs. R. T. Jones, T. P. O'Connor, M.P. (a grand acquisition), and Ernest Ford, formed a happy, congenial party at the Hotel Riffelalp, on the Riffelalp (7,307 feet high), under the able guidance of Dean Lefroy, of Norwich. The Dean knew every inch of the place all around, going there regularly yearly for many years past, and dying there, being buried in the churchyard adjoining the English church erected there under his auspices. Overnight, after dinner, he would arrange the excursions for the next day. One of the best was over the Monte Rosa Glacier, an enormous expanse of ice. At the commencement of the season the Dean planted bottles all along the route; these acted as signposts, for no one ever dreamt of removing them or in any way interfering with anything connected with the dear old Dean. The guides simply worshipped him, for he was always most kind and thoughtful in procuring them pecuniary aid where he felt it was needed. On one occasion he raised as much as £400 sterling for the widow and orphans of a local guide who had perished on the Matterhorn. Well, one afternoon we were an extra large party, and had reached the extreme end of the Monte Rosa Glacier (far away from our hotel), when suddenly a dense fog sprang up, enveloping us in darkness that could be felt. But the Dean was equal to the emergency; he shouted to us to come quite close to where he was standing, lighting at the same time his electric torch, which just gave out a faint glimmer of light in the prevailing darkness. As we got near him he roped us in double file, with himself at the head. We all safely traversed the whole length of the glacier. When we got to the other end the fog suddenly lifted, and we were once more in bright sunshine. A small electric railway starting from Zermatt, down below, and calling at the Riffelalp, the Riffelberg, and the Riffelhaus, reaches the summit, foot of the Gorner Grat, at an elevation of 9,908 feet, the Gorner Grat itself being 10,290 feet high, and 4,975 feet above Zermatt. It is a rocky ridge, with the Hotel Restaurant Belvedere at the top, where we lunched, after a sturdy tramp all the way from the Riffelalp, for we none of us cared to go by train; even our ladies walked. We sat down to lunch with the late Duke and Duchess of Devonshire, who had come up by train from Zermatt, where they were staying. This Gornergrat Railway is the highest mountain railway in Europe; it is a rack and pinion line, propelled by electricity. Its length is 6¼ miles, with an average gradient of 16 per cent., the maximum being 20 per cent. (or 1 in 5). One morning, after early "café au lait complet," I walked with Ernest Ford from the Riffelalp down to Zermatt, where I saw him off in his train. I then walked up again to our hotel in time for lunch. Immediately after lunch I tramped with a select party right up to the top of the Gorner Grat, where we had tea at the Restaurant Belvedere. After tea I tramped down with the rest of the party, having thus walked 12½ miles (6¼ up and 6¼ down), or practically the whole way from Zermatt up to the Gorner Grat and down again to Zermatt.

An easy morning or afternoon excursion which we were able to do by ourselves (Dean Lefroy smiled at it) was to the Findelen Glacier. I remember on one occasion Mr. T. P. O'Connor, M.P., joined our party; he was the life and soul of it, so courteous and pleasant all round, full of wit and small talk. As we were all out for a real holiday we barred politics and "shop" of every description. This pleased him. We found in casual conversation that he stood very well with the Conservatives, who in all non-contentious matters were always ready to lend him a helping hand, to the extent very often of 50 votes all in his favour. I can well believe it, for he is a real good sort, and, as far as I could judge, the best of the whole lot of them put together.

When I went to Mürren with the Harveys I was without my ladies. We put up at the Grand Hotel. I simply loathed Mürren, and so did my friends. Mr. Harvey told me in confidence he had made a mistake, but begged me not to give the show away, which I did not. The only one whom Mürren suited was Mrs. Harvey, who, with an interesting book and easy chair, enjoyed the restful quiet of the place. It certainly, without question, was both restful and quiet.

Mr. Harvey, at the time of his death, on Friday, 10 March, 1905, was an active member of The Royal Commission on Food Supply in Time of War. The President of the Commission was Lord Balfour of Burleigh, while our present King, then Prince of Wales, formed one of the Committee. The last meeting Mr. Harvey attended was on the Wednesday, 8 March, 1905, two days only before his death, and he had proposed attending on the Friday, 10 March, the very morning of his death. Mr. George Street, a member of the Committee of Lloyd's, told me that, on the last occasion that he attended, Mr. Harvey appeared to be the life and soul of the meeting, full of practical sound advice, to which his colleagues paid the deepest attention.

At his special request Mrs. Harvey wrote me that her husband would like to see me, specifying the afternoon of Friday, 3 March, 1905. When I accordingly called, Mrs. Harvey told me he was just recovering from a severe attack, but that he had made up his mind to attend the next meeting of the Council the following Wednesday, dead against the doctor's advice.

When I went into his library I found him propped up in his easy chair, with a pile of papers, books, and documents on a table beside him, all relating to this Royal Commission. He was as bright and cheerful as ever, full of this Commission, of which he had evidently mastered every detail. He told me that he and the Prince (our present King) got on splendidly together. The Prince managed to sit next to him both at the meeting and at lunch, a very simple repast, for which they were each allowed 1s. 6d. per head out of the public purse; that had to include everything, both in the way of eatables and drinkables.

Lord Balfour of Burleigh, the President of the Royal Commission, was a strict martinet; he allowed a bare half-hour for lunch, and would not hear of anyone smoking. One day, however, he had to attend a Court function, so just before lunch he left the Council chamber, saying he would not return that afternoon. When he had gone the Prince, heaving a sigh of satisfaction, said: "Thank goodness, we can lunch in peace for once and have time for a smoke afterwards," which, in fact, they all did. The Prince smoked a short pipe, Mr. Harvey a mild cigar, the rest all following suit. The lunch and subsequent smoke combined occupied just one hour, and no more, so that, after all, they were very moderate.

Mr. Harvey told me that, like myself, the Prince was a firm believer in Joe Chamberlain. This I had heard before, so I know it is true.

On the very day of the death of her husband Mrs. Harvey telegraphed me the sad news, and that the funeral was fixed for the following Tuesday, 14 March, at St. Michael's, Highgate, when she wanted me to attend at the house and join the family as one of them. This, of course, I was only too ready to do. The one and only hymn sang on that occasion was as follows :—

O God our help in ages past,
  Our hope for years to come,
Our shelter from the stormy blast
  And our Eternal Home.
      &c. &c.

It was the favourite hymn of our late King Edward, and was sung at his funeral also, as well as at all the memorial services held that day throughout the whole of the United Kingdom and its dependencies.

The service was solemn in its impressive simplicity. The whole of the partners of the banking house attended to pay their last respects to their honoured secretary.

Shortly after Mr. Harvey's death, his son, my friend Baldwin, set about compiling the memoirs of his late father, in which he had the hearty co-operation of Mr. R. H. I. Palgrave and of Lord Welby, his former chief at the Treasury. The obituary notices from *The Bankers' Magazine* of April, 1905, as also of *The Times* of 13 March, 1905, were both of them also very touchingly sympathetic.

Baldwin's memoirs of his father are splendidly compiled. They form a handsome volume of 527 pages, replete with matters of deep interest, at any rate to me, who can almost imagine I am hearing my dear old friend talking all the time.

The volume is handsomely bound in blue Russia leather. At the foot of the title page are the three lines :

LONDON:
PRINTED FOR PRIVATE CIRCULATION.
1907.

Shortly after its completion I received a copy of it, with the following touching letter from the widow :—

The Grove,
Highgate, N.
4 March 1907.

Dear Mr. van de Linde,

I am sending you a book containing some of the writings of my dear husband, and I know you will keep it as a memento of one whose friendship you valued.

With kind regards.

I am,
Yours truly,
Jane Harvey.

I do indeed value this sacred memento very highly. He was always a real, true friend to me, and even now, after the lapse of ten years, I often look back upon the loss I sustained when he died.

As a leading City man said to me at the time : "Mr. van de Linde, I look upon Mr. Harvey's death as a national calamity," as, indeed, it was. I am sure this sentiment is reciprocated by all who knew him.

Mr. Harvey, like his friend, the late Mr. Bertram Wodehouse Currie, was a staunch supporter of the "Gold Standard," having a supreme contempt for "Bi-metallism." I may mention in this connection that when I was in India in 1866-1867 the silver rupee varied in value from 2s. to 2s. 3d., while its present value is only 1s. 4d. Two banks, the Oriental Bank and the Chartered Mercantile Bank of India, favoured the silver basis, and it led to the collapse of the Oriental Bank, and nearly so of the other bank, which lost its charter and is now known as the Mercantile Bank. When I was in India I invariably used these two banks to remit home by. A third bank, the Chartered Bank of India, Australia, and China, would have nothing to do with silver, but pinned its faith upon gold. It is at the present day stronger than ever, and likely to remain so.

CHAPTER XIII.

Mr. John Peter Gassiot, "The Culvers," Carshalton.

IT was through the introduction of Mr. Harvey that I got to know the late Mr. John Peter Gassiot, of "The Culvers," Carshalton, who became my good client and staunch friend. Mr. Gassiot was a keen observer, full of pungent wit. He once said to me: "van de Linde, in former days they used to hang thieves upon crosses, but now it appears that they hang crosses upon thieves." Once a month I used to drive over on a Saturday morning from Bromley to "The Culvers," spending the week end with my dear old friend, who was kindness itself. "The Culvers" (Mr. Gassiot's freehold property) stood in a beautiful park, with the River Wandle running through it. There was a large, roomy boat on it, in which we had much enjoyment rowing up and down its peaceful shores. He was always most kind to my wife and daughter, making the former a present of a Rudge Whitworth tricycle, which she still uses in our quiet country lanes, my daughter accompanying her on her bicycle. I have got very deaf in recent years, so I have reluctantly had to give up this pleasure; the motor cars rushing by are too much for me.

Mr. Gassiot had any amount of carriages and horses, so we had lovely long drives together in his open, roomy landau. One of our favourite drives was along the River Thames to Hampton Court and back. But we often drove over to my house at Bromley and back, taking up a whole afternoon in doing so.

CHAPTER XIV.

SCOTLAND AND SAINT ANDREW'S DAY.

I HAVE travelled a great deal in Scotland, and I simply love the Scotch, and all connected with them. Dean Ramsay's "*Scottish Life and Character*" is hard to beat. I know it pretty well by heart. The Scotch, owing to their long-continued military alliance with the French in years past, have adapted several French words, and this is especially the case with old-fashioned Scotch people, as witness the following instances :—

ENGLISH.	SCOTCH.	FRENCH.
Leg of Mutton.	Gigot.	Gigot.
Crystal Jug or Decanter.	Caraff.	Carafe.
Gooseberries.	Groserts or Grossarts.	Groseille,
Partridges.	Pertricks.	Perdrix.
Plate.	Ashet.	Assiette.
Troublesome.	Faschious.	Facheux.
Draughts (the Game).	Dams.	Dammes.
Skirt.	Jupe	Jupe.
Oil.	Ule.	Huile.
Slippers.	Pantufles.	Pantoufles.
Hashed Meat.	Haggis.	Hachis.
Obstinate (Hard).	Dour.	Dur.
Mild (Soft).	Douce.	Doux,
Cupboard.	Aumrie.	Armoire.
Portmanteau.	Walise.	Valise.
Sugar.	Sucker.	Sucre.
In the old Edinburgh streets, where the houses are high, with several flats, the households in the higher flats used to dispose of their foul water by throwing it out of the window. This operation was limited to certain hours, and the well-known cry preceding the missile to warn passers-by was	Gardeloo.	Garde l'Eau.

Two other of my favourite Scotch books are *"Our Ain Folk"* and *"The Humour of the Scot,"* both by the late James Inglis (" Mavie "); a copy of each has been given to me by my friend and neighbour, Colonel Sir Robert Inglis.

Hear land o'cakes and brither Scots,
Frae Maiden Kirk to Johnny Groat's,
If there's a hole in a' your coats,
I rede ye, tent it;
A chiel's amang ye takin' notes,
An' faith he'll prent it!

Copied from the title page of *"The Humour of the Scot."*

This brings me to St. Andrew's Day, the great Scotch Saint's day of 30 November, observed rigidly by all good Scotchmen all over the world.

On two occasions, by special invitation, I have been privileged to be a favoured, honoured guest at a St. Andrew's dinner.

The fare is always simply delicious; the favourite dishes are "singed sheep's head," "Haggis," preceded by good Scotch broth (with plenty of pearl barley and leeks), the predominant drink being good Scotch whisky (" Auld Reekie," as it is affectionately called).

The wonderful grace composed by Robert Burns invariably precedes the annual banquet. It runs as follows:—

Some hae mait who canna ate.
Some can ate that want it;
But we hae mait and we can ate,
So let the Lord be thankit.

The banquet concludes by everyone standing up and, with crossed hands, singing the beautiful Scotch melody entitled "*Auld Lang Syne*," which was also composed by Robert Burns.

I make no apology for reproducing it *in extenso*. I am sure that my Scotch readers, at any rate, will welcome it. It runs thus :—

I.

Should auld acquaintance be forgot, And never brought to mind;
Should auld acquaintance be forgot, And days o' lang syne.
For auld lang syne, my dear, For auld lang syne;
We'll tak' a cup o' kindness yet, For auld lang syne.

II.

We twa hae run about the bıaes, And pu'd the gowans fine,
But we've wandered mony a weary foot, Sin auld lang syne.
For auld lang syne, my dear, For auld lang syne;
We'll tak' a cup o' kindness yet, For auld lang syne.

III.

We twa hae paidl'd in the burn,
Frae morning sun till dine;
But seas between us braid hae roar'd,
Sin auld lang syne.

IV.

And here's a hand, my trusty friend,
And gie's a hand o' thine
And we'll take a richt-gude-williewaught,
For auld lang syne.

I have had very pleasant times in Scotland. I remember on one occasion starting with my bicycle and golf clubs. My first stop was Crieff, with a good nine-holes golf course, where I played some good games. But I simply loathed the hydro. I stopped at; everything connected with it was most unpleasant. The Drummond Arms Hotel, Crieff, is all right, and can be highly recommended as an agreeable change to the other. From Crieff I cycled on to Saint Fillans, on Loch Earn, where they made me especially comfortable at the hydro. there, and where I also got excellent golf.

The long days, with apparently endless twilight, reminded me of Westport, Connemara, Ireland. It was so enjoyable sitting out after dinner, smoking my cigar and sipping my black coffee, while I watched the others playing a good game of bowls, a game for which the Scotch are as famed as they are for golf.

I then cycled on to Elgin, Macbeth's country, where I visited his castle at Dunsmane, Birnam Wood, and Cawdor, of which Macbeth was the Thane, following strictly the text of the play. From there I cycled along the coast all the way to Forres, where I lunched. I had tea at Nairn, getting that same evening to Inverness, a most enjoyable day's spin from Elgin. I was the whole time in the Macbeth country, with all its romantic, weird reminiscences. I dined comfortably at the hotel at Inverness, and then went on board one of David Macbrayne's celebrated steamers for a trip down the Caledonian Canal, and upon which Mr. Macbrayne had already kindly booked me a comfortable, roomy state-room, which I had all to myself right away to Oban. The porridge and Finnon "haddies" for breakfast were most acceptable, as, indeed, was all the food at all the meals. I confined myself to the wine of the country, good old Scotch Highland whisky; in fact, that was my favourite beverage the whole time I was in Scotland. It was the safest drink procurable, being always reliable.

The trip down the Canal was throughout most enjoyably restful. It was replete with interest; as I had my bicycle with me I often rode upon it between one loch and another, having heaps of time and to spare to manage this. The run to Fort Augustus, on to Fort William, with Ben Nevis on my left, was fine. I finished up for the time being at Oban, putting up at one of the comfortable hotels (I forget now which it was). The town is an ideal place for yachting; the bathing, too, is excellent, for I sampled it, as usual.

The next morning I caught the early steamer (8.20 o'clock), which brought me at 2.40 p.m. to Tighnabruaich, lunching first on board the steamer, and then spending the week end at the comfortable hotel there. A young bank clerk from London, who had accompanied me all the way from Inverness, joined me. He had come out by steamer to Aberdeen, and was returning by steamer from Glasgow, so that we really were together the whole way from Inverness to Glasgow. He was a cheery young chap, with a love, like myself, for golf, so, hearing that there was a golf course quite handy, we started after lunch for a game, he using my clubs, of which I had a good supply. There was no caddie in sight, so we started playing without one. We found the holes rather rough, but we did not mind. Just then we heard a voice shouting to us. It turned out to be the caddie master, caddie, and keeper of the ground all rolled into one. We asked him what he wanted to shout at us like that; we were not deaf. At which he shouted all the louder: "Them's not golf holes; them's rabbit holes." "Then show us the proper holes," we replied, and he showed them us. "Thanks," we replied, "but we prefer the rabbit holes," and we went on with our game. He went off, not shouting this time, but muttering, and calling us "daft lunies," at which we smiled, and this shut him up.

The next day, Sunday, we attended the Scotch church in the village, and in the afternoon we strolled on to Ardlamont Point, where we went over Ardlamont House, of tragic interest, for it was at Ardlamont that a young fellow was capsized and drowned from a boat. Whether it was an accident or a murder on the part of his companion remains still a mystery, upon which opinions appear to be divided.

The next day (Monday), after another game at golf and lunch at the hotel, we caught the 2.40 p.m. steamer from Tighnabruaich, which, steaming along Wemyss Bay, Gouroch, and Greenoch, landed us at 6.45 p.m. at Glasgow, in the River Clyde, where my young bank friend caught his steamer for London, while I went on to the St. Enoch Station Hotel, returning to London the next morning by the Glasgow and South Western Railway to Carlisle, and thence by the London and North-Western Railway to Euston. I might have come on from Carlisle by the Midland Railway to St. Pancras, but I prefer the first named line of the two, always travelling by it when I possibly can do so in preference to the competing lines.

CHAPTER XV.

Continental Mountain Passes.

SHORTLY after my return my business called me away for a Continental round. I combined pleasure with it, so when I had completed my Swiss visit I went by way of Coire (1,935 feet high) to the Hotel Steinbock, where they gave me a bottle of delicious red wine, "Perla di Sassela." The next day I drove on to Thusis (2,450 feet high), stopping at the delightful Hotel Via Mala, surrounded by a lovely garden. After an early cup of tea I tramped to the celebrated Via Mala by the Boval Wood, walking as far as the third bridge (2,903 feet high), where the Via Mala ends. It is the route to the Splugen Pass, leading to Chiavenna. I have been by it once or twice. The Hotel Conradi is very good. At my hotel they brought me a grand bottle of Alt Valtellina wine. The next morning I secured a banquet seat on the diligence by the Albula Pass to Samaden—a distance of 38 miles, through the Schyn Pass, to Tiefenkastell, to Alveneu Bad (3,115 feet high); thence up to Bergün (4,550 feet high), where we changed horses and lunched; on to Ponte (5,548 feet high), and thence to Samaden (5,670 feet high), where I left the diligence, had tea at the Hotel Bernina, and then took another diligence to Pontresina, a distance of 3¼ miles. Although we passed the Hotel Kronenhof and Bellavista I was not allowed to alight, but had to continue on to the post office, which is also the diligence office. There the hotel porter met me with a truck, upon which he placed my luggage, and we walked together to our hotel (5,915 feet above sea level). I only stayed a couple of days this time at Pontresina, as I had to push on. I was the only passenger on the diligence from there to Nauders, a lovely drive down the River Inn, past Zernetz (4,910 feet), Süs (4,689 feet), Bad Tarasp (3,946 feet), a famous bath establishment, where I stopped on a subsequent occasion at the Curhaus; on to Schuls (3,980 feet), and then Nauders (4,470 feet), where I put up at the Hotel Post. The next morning I continued on to Landeck, a distance of 27 miles, but as I was the only passenger they sent me on by a carriage and pair (a "bei wagen").

The road through the Finstermunster Pass runs high above the River Inn. We passed through two avalanche galleries. The highest point is Hoch Finstermünz (3,630 feet high). Then, gradually descending through three short tunnels, we crossed the river again, and reached Pfunds (3,185 feet), on to Ried (2,875 feet). Shortly afterwards we again re-crossed the river by the Pontlatz Bridge (2,830 feet high). I then reached Landeck, Austria (2,670 feet high), where I left my carriage, after a delightful drive of two days all along the grand River Inn. At Landeck I lunched at the Post Hotel, and then was driven in an "Ein spänner" (a one-horse Victoria) to the Alberg Railway—on our way the coachman pointed out the interesting old "Schloss Landeck," an ancient castle which stands on high ground—a distance of a mile. I there took the train to Innsbruck (44 miles off). The whole of the run was most interesting, as we passed through lovely country.

When I reached Innsbruck I found my train awaiting me in the station, with not a soul in it. All the passengers were finishing their lunch at the restaurant adjoining. I looked for a seat, not an easy job, as the carriages were littered with shawls, rugs, handbags, books, and papers. At last I found a likely compartment, where I deposited my Gladstone in the rack overhead and took an empty seat.

Just then the passengers came crowding out to resume their places. The sole other occupant of my compartment was a bright, pleasant, youngish lady, who, on taking her seat, addressed me in German, just using the single word "Pardon," a common expression with the Teutons. So we began talking German together until I saw her take out of her bag a French book, so I said to her, "Madame, parle Français n'est ce pas?" to which she replied, with a perfect French accent, "Oui, monsieur," upon which we continued our conversation in French.

Soon after we entered a rather long tunnel, when I heard her say "Oh! My!" with a distinct American twang, so I said to her, "Madame speaks English also?" to which she replied, "Waal, I am English." "No," said I; "pardon me, I think you are American," at which we both laughed. At Munich she got out, so I had the whole compartment to myself, right away to my destination, Berlin. I dined at the Station Restaurant at Munich, and then had a comfortable long sleep. Munich is 407 miles distant from Berlin.

The next morning my Berlin client met me at the station called the Anhalt Bahnhof, where, having already had " Café au lait complet," which the guard brought me to my carriage, we crossed over the way to the Hotel Excelsior, where he had secured me an excellent bedroom, with a bath room attached, where, after depositing my Gladstone, we drove to his office. We very shortly disposed of our business there, and then he drove me to his charming villa at Charlottenburg, standing in its own lovely garden, surrounded by lofty trees. His wife, daughter, and three sons greeted me warmly, like old friends. We had a capital lunch, and then sat out in the shady garden, where we had our coffee, with real Havana cigars of the choicest quality.

After lunch we strolled on to the Royal Palace at Charlottenburg (close by), admiring the pleasant Palace Garden, laid out by the eminent French landscape gardener (Le Notre), who also laid out the extensive gardens and grounds at Versailles.

We then visited the Mausoleum where Queen Louise (who died in 1810) and her husband (who died in 1840) repose. The recumbent figures, executed in Carrara marble, are strikingly impressive. The heart of Frederick William IV is placed in a marble casket at the feet of his Royal parents. After visiting the Palm Garden and Winter Garden we returned for afternoon tea at my client's house, after which we drove to Berlin, where we had an early tasty dinner in a celebrated restaurant in the famous fashionable quarter known as Unter den Linden, after which we went to the Hippodrome, where we saw some wonderful feats of horsemanship.

The next morning I was off to Cologne, where I invariably stop at the comfortable English hotel known as the Hotel du Nord. Our English Royal family always go there, and in the spring of 1914, when my nephew and I were there, we found that our Prince of Wales had been stopping there for some days, and had only just left. We always have the same comfortable, lofty, roomy bedrooms adjoining on the first floor, and overlooking the lovely garden, where during the summer time we have all our meals in the verandah surrounding it.

One day, just as I was going to lunch, I met the agent of the South Eastern Railway, who asked me whether he could do anything for me. I told him I was leaving that afternoon by the mail train to Brussels. It had two portions—that in front for the Calais passengers went right through from Verviers (without examination of luggage) to the Midi Station, arriving there an hour before the second portion with the ordinary passengers arrived at the Nord Station. Fortunately my return through ticket was via Calais, so I was all right. When I got to the station I found him waiting for me by the side of a large empty saloon compartment labelled "Sir Myles Fenton" (the General Manager of the South Eastern Railway). He told me that the Calais portion was so full that that was the only way. I accordingly wired to the Hotel Bellevue, Brussels, for the hotel 'bus to meet me at the Midi Station and to have supper ready for me on my arrival.

Just then I met the late Sir George Henry Lewis, taking the last seat in his crowded compartment in the Nord portion. I invited him to join me, saying I had heaps of room in my reserved saloon compartment; and knowing that he, too, was going to the Bellevue Hotel,

I told him that by so doing he would arrive an hour earlier.

But he refused to change his seat, saying that as we were travelling by the same train we were bound to arrive at the same time, to which I laconically replied, "All right, we shall see." I had a good wash in the lavatory attached to my saloon, and a brush up, so that when I reached the hotel I was ready for my supper. The porter sent my bag up into my room, while I sat down at once to my meal. I told the head waiter to write me out an elaborate menu of my supper, including every course.

This I kept by me, with an excellent bottle of red Assmannshausen wine, after which (German fashion) the waiter brought me at my table my black coffee and a good Havana cigar.

Just as I was beginning my cigar in came Sir George Lewis, who, on seeing me, exclaimed, "Why, Mr. van de Linde, is that you? How long have you been here?" To which I replied, "Oh! about an hour, Sir George. I have finished my supper, and am now going to have a quiet smoke, if you don't mind." I showed him at the same time the elaborate menu of my supper. This finished him. He could not understand it, and said he was sorry he had not taken my advice. I told him I was equally sorry. Sir George asked me to move up my chair to his table with my coffee and cigar (he did not mind my smoking), and I did so.

He then told me he was just back from Homburg, where he had been staying at the same hotel with the Prince of Wales (afterwards our King Edward VII), where at the same hotel were staying three City solicitors whom he named. They were all leading high-class solicitors, and personal clients of my firm. The Prince and these four solicitors used to sit over the fire in the smoking room after dinner comparing notes and telling racy stories. This is one of them :

A rather bumptious old gentleman, having died, was reposing in the celestial regions.

One day he thought he detected a smell of lucifer matches, so he sent a polite message down below requesting the gentlemen down there to kindly stop striking lucifer matches, as the smell of the sulphur affected his throat. A polite answer came up from below saying that they had not been striking any lucifer matches.

But the old gentleman, fancying he still detected the smell of sulphur burning, sent down a second message to the same effect, but not quite so polite this time.

The same reply came up from below, also rather less polite than the first.

A third time the gentleman sent down, but this time it was a peremptory message ordering them to stop the nuisance at once.

To which the reply came up that he might take whatever measures he thought fit, for they were not going to trouble about it any more. This stumped the irascible old gentleman upstairs, for he perfectly well knew that *there are no lawyers in Heaven* !

This story was categorically confirmed to me by the other three lawyers, and that separately the one after the other. It appears that the Prince very much enjoyed the joke.

A day or two afterwards I returned from Brussels via Calais to Dover, intending to be met at Cannon Street by my office commissionaire with my letters. When our steamer got to Dover my friend, Mr. W. T. Lord, the station-master there, told me he had reserved me a compartment for Cannon Street, but he strongly advised me to go on by the portion to Charing Cross, for which he had also reserved me a compartment, as this portion was starting at once, whereas the other portion would have to wait for the Ostend steamer to arrive, entailing a delay of at least an hour.

I told him I was very sorry, but that I could not change my plans, so I would just wait. He told me he would see what he could do, and went off. Soon after he returned, saying it was all right. He had just seen the agent in charge of the mails, with whom he had arranged to send off at once the Calais portion, and that a special first-class compartment would be attached to the mail vans to take me straight away to Cannon Street. In this way I reached my destination without any delay, met my man at Cannon Street Station, who gave me my letters, and I then comfortably caught my 5.35 p.m. train down to Bromley in excellent time.

CHAPTER XVI.

Opening of the Tower Bridge: We Receive Two Royal Salutes.

ON 30 June, 1894, the then Prince of Wales (afterwards our King Edward VII) was deputed by his mother, Queen Victoria, to open the Tower Bridge. At the time I had in my office two splendid young fellows. The one was Reginald Trotter (now a distinguished officer in the Cameron Highland Regiment, fighting at the front). His mother (a sister of Lord Gifford) was Lady Trotter, while his father was Colonel Trotter, who was to be in command of the troops at the opening ceremony.

The other was Edward Treffry (now Lieutenant-Colonel Treffry, in command of the H.A.C., also at the front). His mother was sister to Lady Garvagh, daughters of the Baroness le Bretonne, a distinguished Danish family, intimate friends of the then Princess of Wales. My office was then at 50 Gracechurch Street, a corner house with three large balconies and French windows.

We also looked upon Eastcheap, where I had my own private office, an immense room with three large French windows. As the Royal Procession was to pass by Gracechurch Street, along Eastcheap, we decided to have a large party of friends to view it, and it was arranged that my wife and daughter should attend. Our guests included the four ladies already referred to. In order that everything should be complete I arranged with my friend Captain Gordon, the secretary of the Grosvenor Club (of which my son Sidney and I were members), that he would kindly undertake the catering for us. The previous day he sent to my office a large van containing the necessaries for lunch and tea, while early the next morning he sent a small van with sweets, ices, fruit, cream, &c., and half a dozen club servants in livery, who laid the cloth, put everything straight, and eventually waited at table.

The afternoon previous (29 June, 1894) the Prince and Princess of Wales gave a garden party at Marlborough House, at which were present the old Duke of Cambridge and the four ladies already referred to.

The Duke, in shaking hands with Lady Trotter, said he supposed that as her husband, Colonel Trotter, had charge of the military arrangements she would have a good seat to view the opening ceremony. To this she replied that she was seeing it as guest of her friends, the van de Lindes, and at the Duke's request she gave him our office address. At the same time the Prince and Princess of Wales asked the Baroness and her two daughters the same question, and received the same answer, they, too, by Royal request, giving our office address.

The next day, while these four ladies were sitting by my wife and daughter at a large open window facing Eastcheap, we heard a flourish of trumpets. "This is my show," said Treffry to Trotter, to which the latter replied, "No, Trotter, it is mine"; and, sure enough, it was, for just then the old Duke rode up on horseback, stopped the procession, and at the same time, recognising Lady Trotter and the ladies sitting by her, saluted her and them, upon which, with a second flourish of trumpets, the procession galloped by.

Very soon after a second flourish of trumpets; this time it was indeed Treffry's show, for the Prince and Princess of Wales stopped the Royal carriage just opposite our open window, and, smiling graciously to the three Danish ladies, saluted the whole party of six ladies, after which, with a second flourish of trumpets, the Royal procession drove past.

Our lunch was a grand success. An old friend of mine who had hoped to be present was prevented at the last moment, so he sent me instead a hamper containing a dozen bottles of choice French champagne, which, together with claret cup and other cooling beverages, came in very acceptably and was highly appreciated.

Just as we were finishing lunch two strangers came in. They said they were Justices of the Peace from the North, and asked to be allowed to sit down. As we did not like their appearance we were just about telling them to make themselves scarce when we were saved the trouble, for four policemen turned up at the moment, handcuffed and marched them off, explaining to me, aside, that the two intruders were "cracksmen" who were wanted at Bow Street for picking pockets. When they had been marched off we breathed more freely and enjoyed our afternoon tea, after which our guests, warmly thanking us for the treat we had given them, left us. We were in all a party of quite fifty, but, having plenty of room, we were not a bit crowded.

The Treffrys have a lovely seat called "Plas," at Fowey, Cornwall; it has been in their family ever since the eleventh century. My wife and I spent a very pleasant week there with the family, enjoying their unbounded hospitality. I have in my library a splendid large photograph of the venerable pile, and alongside an excellent portrait of my dear old friend, Lieutenant Colonel Edward Treffry, in full war paint of the H.A.C.

Early in 1895 a young Indian nobleman, Jiggiram Bagaram Mohite, the son of a high-placed official at the court of the Guicowar of Baroda, came over to this country, accredited by the India Office to Sir George Birdwood, to study business ways, and at Sir George's request we took him into our office. He turned out a splendid fellow, and became a great favourite with my staff, who christened him "Jiggi," saying, "Now then, Jiggi, buck up," to which "Jiggi" replied in a sepulchral tone, "Bock up yourself." When he lunched with me at the club he made his meal off mutton and plain water. When my second and remaining son Sidney died on 28 March 1896, he was soon after buried in Bromley Cemetery, when my whole staff attended, and with them Mohite, who stood with us all at the open grave.

Considering that in doing so he lost caste for the time being, until he returned the following year to Baroda and did *poojah,* thus being restored to his caste, we all felt his self-denial very deeply. He visited us a few years later, when he was in a splendid position, and is now a leading man out in the East. He tells me he owes it all to us and the training he got in the office.

On 10 February 1899 my dear cousin Eugéne Monteuuis died at the age of 62. I attended his funeral at Highgate Cemetery, where a great number of his old friends and colleagues of the London Rowing Club were also present.

In May, 1901, Lord Kitchener, of Khartoum renown, came over to this country to found the Gordon Memorial College at Khartoum, for which he required £100,000. The money was practically raised in one day. A very strong committee, consisting of Lord Kitchener, Lord Rothschild, Lord Revelstoke, Lord Cromer, Sir Reginald Wingate (the then Sirdar of Egypt), Sir Ernest Cassel, and Mr. Hugh Colin Smith (a Director and afterwards Governor of the Bank of England), was at once formed, and their first meeting was at the Bank of England, at which the Governor presided. Mr. Alfred Spalding Harvey and I were invited to be present, when Lord Hillingdon was appointed Honorary Treasurer; Mr. Alfred Spalding Harvey, Honorary Secretary; and my firm (Gérard van de Linde & Son), Honorary Auditors, with the full supervision and charge of the accounts, both at home and abroad, an honorary post which we have ever since held. On the death of Mr. Alfred Spalding Harvey on 10 March 1905 his son, Baldwin Sidney Harvey, succeeded his father as Honorary Secretary.

A year after the formation of the College a very successful meeting was called at the Mansion House, at which the late Lord Salisbury presided, and I sat in front, between the Baroness Burdett Coutts and her husband. I very much enjoyed seeing the dear old lady again. She was very bright and cheerful, talking of old Highgate days. Her portrait hangs over the mantelpiece of the dining room at 440 Strand, while mine hangs by the side. It was put up there by my dear old friend the late Lord Archibald Campbell. That meeting at the Mansion House was the last occasion on which I saw the late Baroness Burdett Coutts.

CHAPTER XVII.

CONTINENTAL TRIP WITH MY WIFE AND DAUGHTER.

IN the beginning of the year 1901, feeling rather run down, I consulted Dr. Joseph Kidd to prescribe for me. He advised me either to take a sea trip (which he would prefer my doing), or else to go south with my ladies in order to get out of the inclement weather. We chose the latter alternative, and the following is our itinerary.

We left London on 18 February, and were back 18 May 1901, having been away three calendar months exactly.

We put up in Paris at the Hotel du Chemin de fer de Lyon—very poor, but handy. Next morning we reached Marseilles (Hotel Teminus du Chemin de fer de Lyon). We stayed at Marseilles three days, being so very comfortable. While there we took steamer excursions to the Chateau d'If (the scene of Monte Cristo's adventures in prison, and where we were shown the dungeons) and to the small islands adjacent.

We lunched at the Restaurant Basso, where they gave us excellent "Bouillabaisse," a speciality. Another day we lunched at La Reserve, where they showed us our lobster alive, which was then specially boiled for us.

We had delightful drives along La Route de la Corniche (extending all the way from Marseilles, along both the French and the Italian Rivieras), visiting on our way, three miles out, le Prado Plage, a seaside resort with excellent bathing, of which I availed myself.

After that we took the train on to Nice, and from there a carriage and pair, with our luggage, up to Cimiez, stopping at the Grand Hotel de Cimiez, where our late Queen Victoria stayed. The hotel is charmingly situated in a large, well-cultivated garden, and adjoins the celebrated Roman amphitheatre, a Temple of Apollo, and other interesting antiquities.

On other occasions we stopped both at Cannes and at Mentone, but this time we pushed straight along the Italian frontier till we came to San Remo, stopping at the Grand Hotel Bellevue, next door to the Villa Sirio, where the German Emperor Frederick (Unser Fritz), the father of the present Kaiser, died.

The hotel was excellent, but the visitors decidedly Teutonic. It was at San Remo that I first saw and took an electric light bath. From San Remo we went over to Bordighera, lunching at the Hotel Augst there.

We then went to Genoa, stopping at the Hotel Savoy, handy for the station, but not good. We should have fared much better had we gone either to the Hotel Isotta, in the Via Roma, or else to the Eden Palace Hotel (run by the former proprietors of the Hotel Isotta, and standing in a large park; in fact, its old name was the Park Hotel). I have stayed at both these latter hotels, and have found them very good. I know Genoa very well, as I very often go there.

We then went on to Rome, stopping at the old Hotel Granelli (now the Savoy Hotel). It is not bad, but we much preferred the Hotel Continental, opposite the railway station, where we always now go to.

From Rome (avoiding Naples, then rather plague infected—it is all right now) we went straight on to Castellamare di Stabia, an ideal spot on high ground, overlooking the Bay of Naples, putting up at the Hotel Quitisana, and from there taking delightful excursions to Herculaneum, Pompeii, and, myself alone, to Vesuvius—a wonderful experience. Castellamare di Stabia itself is built on the ruins of the old town of Stabia, which was also destroyed with the lava of Vesuvius at the same time as Herculaneum and Pompeii were. One evening, just as we were finishing dinner, three huge omnibuses drove up to Quitisana. The landlord was quite excited, but the hall porter simply said " Tutti Cooki " (not " Tutti Frutti "), meaning that they were simply Cook's tourists, and nothing more.

It was pouring with rain, and they were wet through, but they dined in their damp clothes, writing their individual names in the visitors' book, after which they went to bed.

Next morning, at 4.30 o'clock, they were up in the pouring rain to do Pompeii, Vesuvius, and Naples, all personally conducted by Cook's agent.

We spent a delightful week end at the Island of Capri, putting up at the Savoy Hotel, as the Quisana there was full up. Capri is overrun by German artists, so that the English painters have left the island and have migrated to Newlyn, in Cornwall. The German hotel in the island is called Pagano, very primitive but very cheap. Board and lodging all included cost only 6 lires (4s. 9d.) a head per day. The white plain walls of the dining room are adorned by wonderfully realistic frescoes of all descriptions; they are the work of the German artists.

On our way back by steamer from Capri we stopped at Sorrento, putting up at the Hotel Victoria. It is excellent, with an English garden. I have been there several times since. The other one, Tramontane, is, perhaps, more select, but we preferred the Victoria for many reasons.

From Sorrento we drove up to Amalfi, an ideal place. Our hotel was Grand Albergo Cappuccini Convento, formerly an old monastery. The bedrooms (old cells, but very comfortable) look on to a lovely covered terrace dominating the valley below. It has been painted over and over again by enthusiastic artists.

From there we drove up to Ravello, lunching at the excellent Hotel Palumbo. It was chock full, so on our way down to Sorrento we hired a carriage and pair, which drove us with our luggage to Salerno. The Hotel d'Angleterre, where we stopped, is simply vile, but the only one in the place. From there we took train to Paestum, where we saw the wonderful Greek temple, still well preserved, in its noble ruins. I subsequently visited Girgenti, in Sicily, abounding in similar ruins of grand old Greek temples, but the one at Paestum impressed me the most. I suppose it was because I saw it first.

We spent that night at the Hotel de Londres at La Cava dei Tirreni (an ideal hotel in an ideal spot). The brother of the landlord at Amalfi kept it. They were both splendid fellows, and very original.

La Cava abounds in antiquities, besides being charmingly situated. From La Cava we took the train straight back to Rome, stopping this time at the Hotel Continental.

From there we went on to Florence (Hotel Paoli—nothing could be better). The galleries at Florence are just unique. We spent a long time admiring the masterpieces in them. We drove up to Galileo's old castle, where we saw many of the philosopher's old relics, for the place is now a State museum.

From there we went to Venice (Grand Hotel). The landlord began by charging us 43 lires a day for our three rooms, including board and lodging. This we thought most reasonable, but at dinner he told me he had made a mistake; it was 40, not 43, lires. For our first breakfast (café au lait complet) he gave us the table by the window of Princess Battenburg, who, with her daughter Princess Ena (now Queen Victoria of Spain), was staying at the Grand Hotel.

We stayed a long week at Venice, seeing fresh beauties at every turn. I often have been there since, and always go to the Grand Hotel. The landlord and I are bosom pals; he always gives my nephew and me our same old rooms. Once my other nephew joined us, bringing with him their two respective wives—a merry party of five, with a suite of rooms all to ourselves.

We stopped two days at Verona (Grand Hotel de Londres et Royal deux Jours), and visited this wonderful old world city. Of course, we paid a pilgrimage to the tomb of Juliet. We were rather sceptical about it being the real tomb of our heroine, for if it was she must either have been a remarkably short young lady, or else her legs must have been packed over her body. Over the tomb is a deep stone tray crowded with visiting cards, all in deep mourning, from sentimental American and other visitors. Many of them have written on them touching (?) sentences, of which the following is an example :—

"*To dearest Juliet, with deepest sympathy from her sincere friend Mary Washington Snooks.*"

We were also shown Juliet's balcony, and the spot at the foot where Romeo serenaded her. But what are really well worth seeing are the imposing Arche degli Scaligeri (the tombs of the Scaligers), with the stern Gothic forms immortalising the masculine genius of the dynasty. The "ladder" which is their crest (hence their name) recurs frequently on the elaborate railings. The Piazza delle Erbe, containing the ancient Forum, is one of the most picturesque squares in Italy. The marble column bears on it the Lion of Saint Mark, Venice, while the ancient fountain, besides being antique, is also unique of its kind. The palaces, churches, and cathedrals (12th century), too, are very grand. But what, after all, impressed us most was the famous Amphitheatre (Arena), erected A.D. 290 by Diocletian, a grand old relic of bygone barbaric days.

Leaving Verona, we continued our railway journey to Milan. Between the two stations, Peschiara and Desenzano, we skirted the lovely Lago di Garda. To my mind it is the grandest of all the Italian lakes, for only the extreme north of it, Riva, is Austrian, and even that, by the time these "Reminiscences" are in the hands of my readers (both numerous and intelligent "*cela va sane dire*"), will no doubt also belong to the kingdom of Italy. We have frequently since stayed on this grand lake, our principal stopping places being Salo (the Hotel Metropole is excellent, with a steamer landing stage adjoining) and Riva, where we put up at the Lido Palace Hotel (a regular palace, with large garden overlooking the lake). We took several excursions, both by water and in carriages, exploring this magnificent oasis, so little known by English travellers. We also did some very respectable tramps, including negotiating a small mountain or two.

At Milan we put up, as usual, at the Hotel Continental, where I am well known, and always have the same suite of rooms adjoining on the first floor.

It is close to the celebrated gallery known as the Galleria Vittorio Emanuele, which contains splendid shops and restaurants of the highest order. The one known as Salvini we often take lunch at, while a favourite place for dinner is Cova, close to the Scala Theatre. In winter we dine indoors, while in summer we dine al fresco in the garden. These two outside resorts we frequent when we are with our Italian friends, but when we are alone or with our ladies we prefer taking all our meals at our hotel. The menus, both for lunch and dinner, at the Hotel Continental, are excellent, while the prices for each meal are decidedly more reasonable than those charged at the restaurants, where every separate dish is *à la carte,* instead of the whole meal being at a fixed *table d'hôte* price. This, however, is the general rule everywhere, both at home and abroad.

While at Milan we, of course, visited the celebrated cathedral, both the interior as well as the exterior of which are of surpassing magnificence. I climbed right up to the roof to the highest gallery of the tower, ascending 194 steps inside and then 300 outside. The view from the top is simply marvellous.

The celebrated statue of Leonardo da Vinci is in the Piazza della Scala, and adjoining the Galleria Vittoria Emanuele. We then went to the masterpiece of this great artist, namely, "*The Last Supper,*" which is in the refectory of the suppressed monastery of Sancta Maria delle Grazie. This picture is unfortunately in a very deplorable state, from the fact of it having been painted in oils on the damp wall of the refectory. The large fresco of the "Crucifixion," by Giovanni Donato Montofarno, painted on the opposite wall, is in a much better condition. Additional interest attaches to this last picture from the fact that the kneeling figures of the Duke Ludovico Il Moro and his wife, Bianca Maria, with their children, are the work of Leonardo da Vinci.

We then went to the Palazzi di Brera, the wonderful art gallery, comprising twelve rooms, all replete with priceless works by such celebrated masters as Luini, Raphael, Bellini, Titian, Rembrant, Van Dyck, Paolo Veronese, Tintoretto, Corregio, Guido Reni, Salvator Rosa, Jordaens, Poussin, Thorwaldsen, and other great artists.

To my mind the gem of the whole collection is Raphael's far-famed "*Sposalizio*" (or the "*Nuptials of the Virgin*"). Although painted as far back as 1504 the colours remain as fresh as ever. This masterpiece stands by itself in Room No. V, and is numbered 270.

In the centre of the handsome court leading to the gallery is the bronze statue of Napoleon I as a Roman Emperor, executed by Canova, and considered to be one of his finest works.

After leaving Milan we took the train to Turin, where we alighted in the Albergo del Europa, an immense building with enormous bedrooms, situated in the spacious Piazza Castello, in the centre of the city. The charm of Turin consists in its numerous covered ways running alongside all the principal streets, and affording agreeable shade from the hot glare of the sun's rays, besides affording shelter in inclement weather. The principal shops abut on to these covered ways, which are thus rendered very attractive, and generally thronged with people of all sorts and conditions.

I have always been most favourably impressed with Turin, which I have visited on and off repeatedly for more than a quarter of a century, having during the whole of that time had important business relations there. One of my clients, a leading Italian merchant, hearing of our arrival, went out of his way to show my ladies every attention, thus rendering their visit a very interesting one.

The River Po, which runs through the city, gives an additional charm to it. The Superga (2,205 feet), dominating this river., is the burial church crowned with a dome, and stands out conspicuously on the lofty eminence. My Italian client drove us up there in his carriage and pair, pointing out to us when we reached the summit of the dome itself the wonderful view of the

Alps. The numerous palaces and churches with which this city abounds are replete with interest.

The Pinacoteca, or picture gallery, is very fine. It contains masterpieces of very many celebrated artists, among whom my friend pointed out to us pictures by Botticelli, Fra Angelico, Raphael, Memling, Van Dyck, Andrea del Sarto, Bellini, Hobbema, Holbein, Teniers, Snyders, Poussin, Wouverman, Guido Reni, and Paolo Veronese. This celebrated picture gallery contains in all 21 rooms, and vies with the Brera Gallery in Milan in its general excellence, also in the wonderful scope and variety of schools represented therein.

We left Turin by the Mont Cenis route. It preceded its rival, the St. Gothard, by many years, while the Simplon route is of quite recent date.

I have not only travelled repeatedly through all these three tunnels, but I have also driven over them, once over the Mont Cenis and the St. Gothard, and several times in both directions over the Simplon, the scene of "*No Thoroughfare,*" a Christmas tale written jointly by Charles Dickens and Wilkie Collins. Of the three I think the St. Gothard is the grandest to travel through, while I much prefer the Simplon to travel over. Our route was via Modane, the combined French and Italian frontier, with Custom House officers of both nationalities working harmoniously together; the French officials looking after the homeward bound traffic and the Italian after the outward bound.

At Modane we had to change into other railway carriages.

After passing Chambery we stopped at Aix les Bains, putting up at the Hotel de l'Europe, where our late Queen Victoria stayed, and where we were very comfortable in every respect.

On my previous visit I stopped at the Hotel Splendide, and, because it was then out of the season, they rooked me most unmercifully at every turn. When I left I gave the landlady a bit of my mind.

Aix les Bains is a very celebrated watering place, with sulphur springs (113 degrees Fahrenheit). I, of course, sampled them freely by taking the baths and drinking the waters. The town contains remains of old Roman baths, also the Arch of Campanus, a Roman tomb of either the third or fourth century, built to represent a triumphal arch—hence its name.

We took a delightful circuitous drive of some length, finishing at Le Lac de Bourget, where we dismissed our carriage and got on to the steamer, which took us right round the lake. On leaving our steamer we walked back to our hotel, a distance of between 1¼ and 1½ miles, certainly not more.

Another day we took a lovely coach drive up to the summit of Mont Revard (5,000 feet high). From its plateau we got a grand view of Mont Blanc and its sister Alps. We only paid 5 francs (or 4s.) each for this magnificent drive. We went in the morning, immediately after our early breakfast, and got back in time for table d'hôte lunch at our hotel.

Another time we had a whole day's excursion to La Grande Chartreuse. There we paid 15 francs (12s.) each for our seat on the coach, but it was well worth it.

After leaving Aix les Bains we went straight on to Paris, putting up at the Hotel ——. (No, thank you, I am not going to let out the name; it is already so much sought after that, although I go there regularly at least twice a year, I have to book rooms well in advance.) The charges are tolerably high, but the bedrooms are simply palatial; everything is simply all right, and we are always most comfortable.

At Folkestone we stopped at Wampach's Hotel, delightfully situated on Castle Hill Avenue. It is an ideal hotel to stop at. The managing director, Mr. C. Wampach, is a personal friend of mine, for whom I have the greatest respect, as also for Mrs. Wampach.

The hall porter, too, is a regular good sort. He knows a good cigar when he sees it, and thinks my "Partagas Brevas" are not half bad.

As I mentioned at the outset, we left London on 18 February and got back again on 18 May 1901, being away exactly three calendar months on this most enjoyable health recuperating trip.

CHAPTER XVIII.

Sicily Alone.

ON my return to England I gave Dr. Kidd a full account of what we had accomplished, when he at once exclaimed :

" But what about Sicily. I thought I particularly told you to go to Sicily. You have just left out the pearl or gem of the whole setting."

This was a floorer for me, but I thought I would rise to the occasion by calmly replying, though really boiling over all the time :

" You see, I quite meant going to Sicily, and, in fact, I started with that intention, but, having my two ladies with me, I was not exactly a free agent. They lingered on the way, so we got no further than Paestum."

To this he replied :

" Well, mind you go there this autumn, alone this time, for you must see Sicily, and that the sooner the better."

So I at once went to my old friends, Messrs. Keller, Wallis & Co., the agents of the Batavier steamers from London to Rotterdam, who offered me a splendid deck cabin to myself in the "*Rhein*" steamer (10,200 tons regular and 17,700 tons displacement). She was commanded by Captain H. Walter, and due to leave Southampton on Monday, 16 September 1901 (special train from Waterloo to Southampton). She was timed to reach Genoa on Sunday night, 22 September, leaving again on Tuesday, 24 September, and reaching Naples Wednesday, 25 September 1901.

Nothing could possibly have fitted in better, for this would give me a few days at Naples, when I could visit Ischia, Baia, Procida, Posilipo, Puteoli (see Acts XXVIII., verse 13), now known as Pozzuoli, as also Reggio, or Rhegium (same verse), Cumae, and other places of interest north and west of Naples, which were out of my reach when we were staying at Castellamare de Stabia that spring, so I accordingly closed with their "*Rhein*," where I was given the corner cabin No. 2 on the promenade deck, with the promise of an equally good reserved cabin all to myself on the homeward journey, my friends (the London agents) giving me at the same time a letter to their Naples agents (Messrs. Aselmeyer Pfister & Co., 10, Piazza San Siro, Naples), who looked after me splendidly.

The secretary (the late Colonel Sir Henry Montagu Hozier) gave me letters of introduction to Lloyd's agents and sub-agents all along my route. These letters all came in most useful. My bankers kindly gave me a comprehensive letter of credit, with a list of their correspondents, so that I started fully equipped in every respect.

It now rests with my indulgent readers to decide for me the knotty point as to whether (in the quaint but incisive words of the old North Country proverb, I have "made a spoon or spoilt a horn." My nephew Freddie saw me off as far as Southampton; while during my absence my two ladies, with a friend, were off the next morning, via Newhaven and Dieppe, on a cycling tour through Normandy, for which I mapped them out an interesting, easy itinerary.

In our carriage we made the acquaintance of two, two young ladies going out all the way to Australia. We soon became close friends. Strange to say, on a subsequent homeward trip from Naples I again met them with their father, and the following summer we all again met on the Orient steamer "*Cusco,*" when we were making a pleasure trip to Norway. The "*Rhein*" is a fine vessel, built in 1899. This was her maiden trip as a passenger steamer, for up to then she had been a cargo, or what is known as a tramp, steamer.

I have already so fully described our life on board ship that I will not bore my readers with any further reiteration. Suffice it to say that we had a nice, genial set of passengers on board, so that we all got on splendidly together. The Bay of Biscay behaved very well. This was my first trip round, so it was extra interesting. I have since done it out and home over 30 times, and have always enjoyed it immensely. My first impression of Gibraltar was great. We were up that morning at 5.30 o'clock, when we saw the sun rise in all its glory over Tarifa, with the famous Rock of Gibraltar facing us. We had Tarifa on the Spanish (European) coast, while on our starboard we had on the other side Cape Espartel on the African coast.

As the Bay of Gibraltar opens out we pass Punta de Europa (Europe Point), the southern extremity of the

Rock, which contains 70 miles of galleries, all cut out for purposes of defence, while the place is provisioned at all times so amply that it can stand a five years' siege.

A few years subsequently, while on a pleasure trip in the P. & O. yacht "*Vectis,*" I again visited Gibraltar, spending three days there on the yacht. On that occasion I brought out with me a letter of introduction to a leading military officer, who kindly allowed me to be shown over these wonderful galleries containing the necessary provisions to last at least five years.

When I was in the island of Malta in the spring of 1903 I was shown a similar arrangement, only in Malta the provisions are stored in huge vaults underground, while access is gained to them by large round caps let into the ground, with rings to lift them, all tightly secured in the meanwhile. I believe in the case of Malta the provisioning is for three years, as against five years for Gibraltar.

At Gibraltar the officer pointed out to me the spot on the opposite Spanish coast (somewhere about Algeciras) where the old Spanish Queen sat in her armchair on a rocky eminence facing Gibraltar, declaring she would not move from her seat (even if she perished with hunger and exposure) whilst the English troops remained in sight. This was reported to the English officer in command, who, being a good sort of fellow, placated the dear old lady by suddenly remembering it was time for a meal of some sort, so, to the sound of the bugle, the regiment suddenly disappeared as if by magic, any few remaining (for emergency's sake) discreetly concealing themselves round the corner. Then, with all the majestic dignity of a Spanish dame of the first water, the old Queen leisurely retired in full regal state, and when she was gone our soldiers reappeared.

Her Chamberlain after this took care to let her have her exercise in another direction in future, fearing lest the English officer might not be so complacent on a second occasion. Algeciras is a fashionable Spanish watering-place, delightfully situated on an eminence at the mouth of the River Nuel, and offering a picturesque view from the sea. The excellent Hotel Reina Christina is always well patronised. I had lunch and tea there, and found everything excellent. The town has a good name as a rest cure; it is one of the healthiest in Spain, with a perfect supply of pure drinking water. I wish I had had the same when I stayed at Carthagena that summer of 1876.

Our run on to Genoa was very pleasantly interesting. The Balearic Islands, Formentera, Iviza, Majorca, and Minorca stood out fine as we passed by them quite closely. On that "*Vectis*" trip we landed at Palma, in Majorca, having lunch and tea at the Grand and Victoria Hotel. There is a magnificent broad road leading from the shore to the hotel. Majolica pottery derives its name from the island. In the Calle de la Palma I was shown the ancient house of the Bonaparte family until they migrated in 1411, when they left the island to migrate to Corsica, where Napoleon I was born. While at Palma we visited Valldemosa, one of the loveliest spots in Europe, also Miramar, a grand domain of the Austrian Archduke Luĩs Salvator, whilst the Castle of Miramar, finely placed on the Adriatic coast five miles north of Trieste, was in former days the property of Maximilian, Emperor of Mexico, who was also an Austrian Archduke. My nephew and I, while staying at Trieste a couple of summers ago, spent a charming day there. The Gulf of Lyons gave us a bit of a dusting. Although touching neither at Marseilles nor at Toulon, we gave it a tolerably wide berth. As soon as we had steamed further up in a north-easterly direction we skirted the coast of the French Riviera so closely that we quite clearly " spotted " the hotels of the various towns as we went by them. We anchored in the harbour of Genoa at 12.30 on the morning of Monday, 23 September 1901. We all had an early breakfast, so that by 9 a.m. we were ashore. We went by electric tram to Pegli, where we visited Palazzo Pallavicini, with its wonderful tropical garden, where that previous spring we met the American woman who complained to her daughter Maria at having to pay 1 lire to see a banana. A river flows through the grounds, crossed by numerous bridges, with summer houses and garden seats, upon all of which (namely, bridges, summer houses, and garden seats), as soon as you crossed, entered, or sat down, jets of water squirted from the surface, drenching you in no time, a gruesome joke which I judiciously avoided my party falling a victim to by our promising the guide a handsome tip not to turn any taps on; which he did not, thus gaining a tip "beyond the dreams of avarice." The Campo Sancta (cemetery) at Pegli is very grand. We then took an electrical tram along the coast from Pegli, past Genoa, to Nevvi (on the Riviera di Levante), lunching in the shady garden of the Eden Hotel. We then hired a carriage and pair, taking that wonderful drive along the Via di Circonvallazione à Mare, passing close by the lighthouse (Lanterna) standing on a rock to the extreme south-western extremity of the harbour. After that we were driven back into the city, where we had afternoon tea in the Galleria Mazzini, after which we took the funicular to the summit of the Righi, where stands a fine plateau 1,253 feet above sea level, with an extensive view all round. We had a very good dinner at the restaurant, and then walked down and rejoined our steamer, which was lying alongside the Dogana (Custom House). She had been coaling all day, but, the coaling being over, the sailors were washing down the decks in the bright moonlight, making everything ship-shape again.

The next day, after breakfast, we visited the more celebrated Pallazos, the first the Palazzo Ducale, the grand old residence of the Doges, dating from the 13th century. From there we visited the Palazzo Durazzo Pallavicini, on the first floor of which is the Galleria, with nine rooms full of masterpieces by Van Dyck, Rubens, Memling, Tintoretto, Guido Reni, Ribera, David, and other celebrated artists. We then visited the Palazzo Balbi-Senarega, with six rooms with masterpieces by the same artists, as well as by Titian, Michael Angelo, Botticelli, Velasquez, Bassano, and Schiavone. Then the Palazzo Rosso, with another unique Galleria of masterpieces of Leonardo da Vinci, A. Durer, Paolo Veronese, and other well-known artists, in its nine rooms replete with pictures of fabulous value.

Our last Galleria was the Palazzo Bianco, containing nine large rooms full of similar masterpieces. (*Note.*—

"Rosso" stands for red and "Bianco" for white, the distinctive names of these two palaces, standing opposite each other.)

We returned to our steamer for lunch, and then visited the wonderful cathedral of San Lorenzo, dating from A.D. 985, and restored in the years 1307, 1567, 1617, and finally in 1896. The treasury contains relics of great value, while the cathedral is beautified by canopies, frescoes, and statues of great antiquity, including relics of St. John the Baptist, brought from Palestine during the time of the Crusades.

We then visited the small Gothic church of San Matteo, dating from 1278, and lastly the Capuchin Church of Santissima Anunziata del Vastato, erected in 1587, with magnificent inlaid marble columns and fine frescoes. It is considered to be the most sumptuous church in Genoa. When I got back to the steamer I found that my pet easy boots, which I had put out to be cleaned, had disappeared, but I got no sympathy from anybody. One passenger declared they had gone to the Christopher Columbus Museum as a prehistoric relic; another declared they were being used by the sailors for baling purposes; while a third christened me on the spot "Pussenas" (or "Puss in Boots"). Just then the first officer came up beaming; he had just unearthed three stowaways, and felt happy in consequence. Just before dinner on Tuesday, 24 September 1901, we weighed anchor and were off again. The passengers had taken a fancy to calling me "Your Royal Highness," declaring that I was the image of the Prince of Wales. Now (since 22 January 1901)

King Edward VII and others have told me the same thing. With reference to my supposed likeness to our late King I may mention that a few years previously he then, as Prince of Wales, with the Princess of Wales (now the Dowager Queen Alexandra) attended a bazaar at the Alexandra Hospital, of which my firm are auditors. I was present on the occasion. The Prince walked up to close where I happened to be standing, and then stopped. A Kodak was snapped, and next morning the *Daily Graphic* reproduced us thus standing together alone, with no one else. I remember at the time that one or two of my friends noticed the resemblance, so that there must be something in it after all. That same night, at 11 o'clock, we passed on our starboard the Island of Elba, the first prison of Napoleon I, and later on the Island of Corsica, his birthplace. I have often passed both these islands, generally by daylight, so getting a good view of them.

On the afternoon of Wednesday, 25 September 1901, as we approached Naples, I got very excited, seeing once more the old familiar scenes, including, *inter alia,* Vesuvius (smoking his pipe), Capri, Sorrento, Castellamare di Stabia, &c. &c. Our last dinner on board was extra recherché. As soon as we had finished our cigars and our black coffee the tender came alongside and took us ashore, where I was met by Mr. F. Da Costa (a friend of Mr. A. G. Dryhurst, the Secretary of Lloyd's Register of Shipping, and himself one of their Surveyors). This gentleman kindly looked after me the whole time I was in Naples, going everywhere with me, and showing me all that he felt I ought to see, the great attraction being the marvellous Museo Nazionale, with its unique collection of Royal antiquities and pictures, in which, too, the excavated treasures of Herculaneum, Pompeii, Stabiae, and Cumae now form the very finest collection in the whole civilised world; with, as regards sculptured figures, the two celebrated works of antiquity, namely, "*The Farnese Hercules,*" discovered in 1540 in the Roman baths of Caracalla, where was also found in 1546 "*The Farnese Bull,*" in a sadly mutilated condition, its restoration being superintended by Michael Angelo himself. The Pompeian Frescoes are simply uniquely beautiful. The picture gallery contains a marvellous collection of masterpieces, mostly of the schools generally known as those of Rome, of Parma, of Lombardy, of Genoa, and of Venice.

We had some grand drives together, scouring the country around for miles, visiting (*inter alia*) the famous Grotta del Cane (or the "Dog Grotto"), strongly impregnated with carbonic acid gas, rendering dogs insensible, but they soon recover when brought out again. This gas is so densely heavy that I walked upright in the grotto with impunity, while dogs were at once affected by it. We also visited the celebrated Lago Averno (or Lacus Avernus), regarded by the ancients as the entrance to the infernal regions.

Charon rowed us in a boat through this River Styx into the Grotta d'Averno. Its poisonous exhalations in those days prevented any bird flying across it and living. Close to the entrance to the infernal regions is a chamber with mosaic pavement containing a sulphur warm bath; it is called the Bath of the Sibyl. I had one, which I very much enjoyed. We then had a look in at the

Amphitheatre of Nero, investing at the same time in delicious green figs and grapes from an adjoining orchard, both at a ridiculously low price. From there we drove on to Baia (the ancient Baiae), lunching at the Restaurant Vittoria, celebrated by Horace, who exclaims, "Nothing in the world can be compared with the lovely Bay of Baiae" (see his Epistle I, 85). Our lunch was grand. It consisted of oysters, red mullet, and sardines, all fresh from the adjoining lake, with one small devil fish thrown in, and very good it was, too. Then veal from the Beccherin Municipale, fried potatoes, delicious bread and butter, Falernian grapes and figs, washed down with a bottle of old Falernian wine. After this excellent lunch we had our coffee and cigars overlooking the lovely Bay of Baia, with Cape Miseno on our right and the Isla di Nisida on our left, used as a penitentiary prison and quarantine station combined. From Baia we drove along the coast past the Bagui di Nerone, and along the Cantiere Armstrong (Armstrong's gun factory), with the ruins of Cicero's Villa on the opposite side of the road. On to Pozzuoli (the ancient Puteoli in the days of St. Paul, vide Acts XXVIII., verse 13, and where the Apostle on his journey to Rome, A.D. 62, spent seven days). From there, still driving along the coast, with, on our right, the small rocky island of Nisida (an extinct volcano), we came to Posilipo, standing prominently on a hill, where close by we visited the Tomb of Virgil (an ancient Roman Columbarium buried among vineyards), and from there back to the Grand Hotel on the Piazza Principe du Napoli, very well situated facing the sea, where I was very comfortable in Room No. 28, first floor front, facing the sea, but as the hotel closes during the summer months I left it, for I have to be in Naples twice a year. I then moved to the Hotel Savoy, where I was all right for the time being, when the old proprietor had the hotel, but when he left, the new management did not appeal to my nephew or to myself, so we moved into the celebrated Hotel del Vésuve, where we have been ever since, and where we are extra well looked after. We have been able to influence to the hotel very many visitors, who have all been thoroughly well pleased, thanking us warmly for sending them there. Before leaving Naples we took a combined railway and steamer day excursion to the island of Ischia, lunching at the Grand Hotel Jasolini. The earthquake of 28 July 1883 (displacing a large mass from the mountain) has given the whole place a very dismal appearance, the hotel where we lunched, like most dwellings there, being just nothing but a rough wooden shanty of a very primitive nature, reminding me very much of Barège, in the Pyrenees, which is also subject to similar upheavals, leaving behind them sinister results of a gloomy nature.

There were always plenty of excellent victorias for hire at the carriage stand adjoining the Grand Hotel, where I stayed at. I fancied one of the drivers particularly, so I engaged him permanently the whole time I was in Naples. Not knowing his real name, I christened him "Don Pasquali," and then "Fra Diavolo." His real name is Guiseppi Migliardi, but as a child he was nicknamed "Masaniello," since which he answers to no other, though his coachman's licence, costing him lire 1.40 (1s. 1½d. a year), is made out in his proper name. Being, therefore, used to nicknames, he quite enjoyed the new names I gave him. I remember once during a drive we came across a rather dangerous bit, which he negotiated all right by going very slowly, so I said to him, "Che va piano va sano" ("He who goes slowly goes safely"), and he replied "Che va sano va lontano" ("He who goes safely goes a long way"), which I thought very clever of him. We were great pals.

And now for just a friendly word of advice. When Dr. Kidd knew I was going to Italy and Sicily he told me that the drivers are miserably paid by their masters. He therefore begged me always to tip the poor fellows adequately, for it made all the difference to them, without hurting me much. I duly acted upon this kind hint, and my good friend Don Pasquali was the first to benefit by it. I have ever since carried out this precept both at home and abroad. It really pays to do so.

The French word for a tip is "Pourboire," while the Italian is "La Mancha," or "Macaroni," and the German is "Drinkgeld."

On the evening of Saturday, 28 September 1901, I left Naples by the "*Marco Polo*" steamer for Palermo. She is 1,663 tons register, belonging to the Navigazione Generale Italiana (the old Florio Rubbatini line), and the manager my very good friend Roberto Consiglio. This gentleman was introduced to me by Mr. F. Da Costa. We at once took to each other, and have been fast friends ever since. Both these gentlemen saw me off in the "*Marco Polo,*" where Mr. Consiglio had reserved me a three-berth cabin, "D," No. 12, all to myself, charging me only one single first-class fare, say lire 34.30 (about 27s.). My faithful Masaniello drove Mr. Da Costa and myself to the steamer, where our parting was most touching.

As soon as we had steamed out of Naples we had a comfortable dinner on the "*Marco Polo,*" and the next morning, Sunday, 29 September 1901, at 5.30 o'clock, we were safely anchored in Palermo Harbour, alongside the Galileo, and at 7 a.m. we were all on deck and passed the medical officer; my name was called out as Gérardo. I was given a permit to get into a boat, and was rowed ashore, when, on giving up my permit, I found I was described in it as being "Gérardo," the "figlio di Gérardo" (the son of "Gérardo"), my father's and my Christian name being the same. Having passed my luggage at the Custom House (without anything being opened), I was driven away in a landau to the Hotel Trinacria, on La Marina, where I was given a large front bedroom, No. 11, with a balcony to myself, at the inclusive "*en pension*" terms of lire 12 a day (or 9s. at the exchange then ruling). My floor consisted of stone flags, but they brought in mats, and later on the whole room was carpeted for the winter. After a comfortable "café au lait complet" on my balcony, overlooking the Golfo di Palermo, I attended morning service at 11 o'clock at the Church of the Holy Cross (Chaplain Dr. Dixon). My landlord, Ernesto Ragusa, is a real good sort, but he has since given up his hotel, and now owns the Restaurant Gambrinius at Naples, where my nephew and I, when in Naples, always lunch, while we dine at our hotel, the Vésuve, which, being open all the year round, we prefer to the Grand Hotel, which is not open in summer. The brother, Enrico Ragusa, used to own the Grand Hotel des Palmes, but has moved to the Excelsior Palace Hotel, where, with my nephew and his wife, I went in the spring of 1914, when we did the tour of Sicily, beginning with Palermo. The driver of my victoria, No. 513, who took me to church, fetched me in the afternoon to take me to the Prefecture, where my certificate of health was duly registered and stamped (free of charge). On our way back I peeped in at the Reale Palazzo, and then visited the Reale Capella Palatina, a superb chapel in mosaic Byzantine, with pillars from Constantinople. From there I was driven to San Giovanni degli Eremite. It was from the belfry or campanilla that the "Sicilian Vespers" rang, and the massacre began at the Campo Sant Orsola. Walter of the Mill in 1173 founded this monastery, where, on 31 March 1282, the massacre took place. From there I was driven to La Favorita, a small palace built by Ferdinand IV in the Chinese style. The rooms on the ground floor contain pictures by the celebrated English artist George Morland, with a white horse and a pig in nearly every one of the pictures. It was by this characteristic that I spotted the artist. On the first floor is the dining room, with dishes for four persons. These dishes are let into the table, and slide up and down on a lift, so the repasts are all served with no servants in the room.

At dinner that night two Austrian gentlemen told me that brigands just then were at a prohibitive premium in Sicily—there were none to be had. I consoled them by saying that we had just brought over from Naples in the "*Marco Polo*" a fresh batch of two gangs of 10 and 11 (in all 21), with a chain connecting the gang, each prisoner being handcuffed with folded wrists.

The next morning, Monday, 30 September 1901, carriage No. 513 was at the door at 9.30 o'clock, when my Jehu drove me to call on Mr. John Mackinnon, Lloyd's agent, who welcomed me cordially. He told me he had a splendid secretary (Mr. Edwin Payne), to whom he introduced me, so that he (John Mackinnon) would see that all the time I was under his jurisdiction I should be personally conducted by himself, his secretary, or his agents, not only at Palermo, but also at Trapani, Marsala, and everywhere else in his jurisdiction. Talking about the Mafia in connection with brigands, he assured me I was all right; ordinary travellers were never molested, it was only a big local man such as Florio (of Florio and Rubbatino) who not only owned the big steamship company but also immense vineyards, saltpans, and other industries, who found it paid him to subsidise these ruffians rather than see his crops all suddenly destroyed in one night.

Mr. Jehu drove me along the lovely Foro Umberto Primo, along the sea front, which my balcony looked down upon, and then on to the Botanical Gardens, where the celebrated papyrus grows luxuriantly. He then drove me to the cathedral (Duomo), built in 1169 by Archbishop Walter of the Mill (Gualterio offamilio). I was shown the Tomb of the Kings; the sarcophagi of porphyry are most imposing.

I then passed the square Quattro Canti, an eight-sided Piazza built in 1609, with columns, statues of the four (quattro) seasons, the Spanish kings, and the holy virgins. I dismissed my Jehu for the day at the Museo Nazionale. Driving in Palermo is prohibited on Good

Fridays. On all other days the tariff for one to four persons is as follows :—

	Carriages with 1 Horse	Carriages with 2 Horses
A drive within the walls	50 c. ..	80 c.
A drive within the suburbs	Lire 1 ..	Lire 1^{50}
By the hour—First hour	Lire 1^{80} ..	Lire 2^{20}
Subsequent hours ..	Lire 1^{60} ..	Lire 2^{0}

After midnight these charges are raised one half. I had No. 513 a full hour and a half. He asked the exact fare, and when I added to it " la mancha " (the tip) he was delighted.

The museum is very fine, full of choice antiquities. In the second court is a basin with papyrus in full growth. I drove to Mackinnon's office for 50 c. Mackinnon introduced me to Monsieur le Baron Albert de Gavres, and we three were then driven in my friend's open carriage to the Chalet delle Sirene, on a wooden pier out at sea, where Mr. Mackinnon gave us a choice lunch, after which we were driven to the catacombs of the Convento di Cappuccini, in the subterranean corridors of which are preserved the mummified bodies of wealthy inhabitants. The sight is gruesome, many standing up in their grave clothes only, instead of reclining in a coffin. This mode of sepulture is now prohibited, so that the body of the latest celebrity, Crispi, is there in a solid coffin since July, 1901, to be removed later on to the cathedral and there immured. We then drove on to the electric tram, which took us up to Monreale, a grand hill, with fine sea views, 980 feet above the sea, where we visited the beautiful cathedral, one of the wonders of the world. The pointed vaulting inside is supported by 18 columns of Egyptian granite, while the walls are entirely covered with mosaics, reminding me of San Marco, Venice, with three screens: the first screen representing prophecies of Christ from the Old Testament, the second screen representing the life of the Saviour himself, and the third screen representing the lives of the Apostles; while in the centre of all there is a huge mosaic of our Lord Himself.

The cloisters are marvellous—the pillars are chaste, and all different; there are 216 columns in pairs, the capitals and shafts are all different. We then returned by the electric tram to Mr. Mackinnon's carriage, and were driven to the Trattoria Caflisch, where we had excellent afternoon tea. When I asked the waiter, "Darf ich hier ranchen?" ("May I smoke here?"), he answered, quite surprised, "Warum nicht?" ("Why not?"), so we all three indulged.

Tips in Sicily are quite the exception; they are, in fact, strictly forbidden by the State, and notices to that effect are placed everywhere about.

Next morning, Tuesday, 10 October 1901, Mr. Edwin Payne (Mackinnon's private secretary) called to take me up to Monte Pellegrino. We left at 7 a.m. sharp, when he drove me in his carriage to the foot of the mountain, where (at 7.20 a.m.) we began the ascent. At 8.30 a.m. we reached the Grotto of Santa Rosalia (the patron saint of Palermo). Between the night of 3 September and morning of 4 September a vast pilgrimage annually visit her shrine. At 8.45 we moved upward, reaching the summit (2,065 feet) at 9.5 a.m., where we rested to drink a glass of delicious water, and smoked a cigarette while we admired the extensive view. We began descending at 9.30 a.m., reaching once more the Grotto at 9.45 a.m., and after another five minutes' rest we again started walking down. Mr. Payne told me that the emigration from Palermo to the United States of America was enormous, some 20,000 a month being the average.

Mr. Mackinnon told me recently that he was once taking a country walk when an evil-disposed looking man suddenly asked him, "Pardon, Senor, but do you happen to carry firearms about you?" to which Mr. Mackinnon replied, "Yes, I do, and loaded, too," presenting two revolvers at his face. The man bowed and bolted. My waiter worried me to buy cigars of him "duty free." I shut him up by saying, "I can quite believe that, my friend, seeing that they are made either of cabbage leaf or else something worse."

The local doctor called at the hotel twice a day to enquire about my health, and as I was never in he had to accept the hall porter's assurance that I was all right.

After another hour's pleasant tramp we reached the foot of the mountain at 10.50 a.m., where Payne's carriage drove us back. On our way we noticed some prickly pears. Our Jehu alighted, seized six, and a knife from the owner, peeled them skilfully, and then paid the man uno solde (one halfpenny) for the six; they were delicious. Payne put me down at the hotel at 11.15 a.m., where I had a refreshing warm bath and change. At 12.30 p.m. Mackinnon and Payne came and lunched with me. We had our coffee and cigars outside on my balcony facing the sea. Mackinnon was hard at work elaborating a wonderful programme for me. Meanwhile he lent me his carriage, with his secretary, for the afternoon, when we had a grand drive all over and round this magnificent city, returning to the hotel at 4.45 p.m. for afternoon tea.

Wednesday morning, 2 October 1901, Payne fetched me at 9 o'clock in an open carriage and pair to drive to Solunto along the sea coast on the high road to Messina. It is a wonderful drive. We admired the bamboos, papyrus, prickly pears, peaches, pears, grapes, also the olive groves, the lemon groves, and Indian corn—all growing in rich profusion. After driving about eight miles we came to Bagheria, and then two miles further on to Santa Flavia, where we noticed in passing several ancient tombs of the Phœnicians and Carthagenians. We then drove to the ruins of Solunto through an archway marked "Antichita di Solunto." At the foot of the hill we alighted and, preceded by the custode, we climbed it (1,000 feet high). This Solunto had three separate occupants, Phœnician, Roman, and Saracen, thus accounting for its varied ruins around. We admired a huge stone cistern fed by stone conduits, which carry the water into it down to the present day. We had brought our lunch with us—eggs, fowl, beef, salami, cheese, bread, butter, grapes, pears, peaches, and wine, our custode bringing us, in an ancient porous "amphora," deliciously cold water drawn fresh from an ancient well, some 2,000 years old.

We had plenty of lunch left, which we shared between our coachman and the custode, making the latter also a gift of 2 lires (about 1s. 6d.). He was supremely happy, having only expected 50 c. (a quarter of the sum we gave him). Leaving Mr. Payne on the way, I drove back to my hotel.

Thursday, 3 October 1901. Up at 4.20 a.m., dressed, packed, and early breakfast, with fruit, at 5.10 a.m. Mr. Payne fetched me in Mr. Mackinnon's carriage, and we drove to the station, taking our tickets by the 5.45 a.m. train for Alcamo Calatafimi, where we alighted at 8.26 a.m. We there took a carriage, in which we were driven to the ruined temple of Segesta (a Doric structure with 36 columns), the grand old amphitheatre, and the ancient Campo Sancto. Here we met the custode, who conducted us to his cottage, where we spread out our lunch, he providing crockery, with all other necessaries, including water brought, as yesterday, in a porous "amphora" and drawn from an ancient well, also rather inferior wine. Having settled with our custode, we drove back to the station, where we invested in a huge pink water melon costing 2 soldi (one penny), deliciously refreshing. After a pleasant run of 1½ hours we reached Castelvetrano at 5.30 p.m., and drove to the Albergo Bixio. Our dinner was a poor one, but the dog by our side helped us through with it. Two other tourists sitting at our long table shovelled everything into their mouths with their knife.

Friday, 4 October 1901. Up quite early, so that by 7.30 a.m. we were comfortably away in our one-horse shay to view Selinus, among whose ruins are the grandest ancient temples in Europe; but, after all, not in our one-horse shay, which belonged to an eminent divine, but in a landau and pair. Suddenly Selinus burst upon our gaze, opening out to us its colossal ruined temples, not one stone standing upon another—a scene of absolute desolation.

We drove on to the Acropolis and viewed the gigantic ruined Temple of Hercules, and beyond the ancient Necropolis on to the ruined temples of Apollo, Minerva, and Juno, after which we ate some delicious black grapes. We got back to our hotel to lunch, and then caught the 2.8 p.m. train back to Palermo, reaching my hotel at 5.20 p.m., in time for tea and a smoke on my balcony, after which a refreshing warm bath, followed by a really good dinner and bed. The refreshing thunderstorm had come at last, cooling everything and laying the dust.

Saturday, 5 October 1901. A lovely cool morning after last night's storm. Up by 8 a.m., packing for another excursion. Mr. Ragusa was kindness itself, for although the hotel was filling fast, and I had one of his best rooms, he allowed me to retain it while away, declining to make any charge for it during my absence. My friends came up, and we drove to the steamer office, where we took our tickets for Payne and myself by the steamer "*Tirzo*" (1,411 tons), bound for Trapani. Before leaving us Mackinnon introduced us to the captain, giving me various letters of introduction to his various sub-agents on our route, after telling us he was wiring to Mr. Serrano, Lloyd's agent at Trapani (where we were due to arrive that afternoon at 5 p.m.), to look after us. The captain invited us up to his sanctum, "riservato al comando," adjoining the "sala nautica" (steering house).

This vantage was lovely. Overhead a thick awning open at the sides. A sailor brought us two deck chairs, and we enjoyed a grand view all round. It was a perfect day. On our port side was the bold coast of Sicily, while on our starboard side was the sea, studded with many white sails and a few steamers. They don't steer here "port" and "starboard," but "sinistra" ("left," which is our "port"), and "destru" ("right," our "starboard"). At 12 noon the steward reminded us that the "collazione" awaited us—not a cold collation, but a nice hot lunch, eggs, hors d'œuvres, fresh fish, mutton cutlets, bread, cheese, butter, fruit, wine, and coffee, "*tout complet*" in our passage ticket. After lunch we resumed our seats up above. At 4 p.m. the steward brought us up afternoon tea, with slices of lemon "*à la Russe*" instead of milk—not half bad. Our tea, which was excellent, quite refreshed us.

The entrance into Trapani Harbour interested us immensely, with its two lighthouses, the "lazzaretto" (hospital), and two islands—everything there white and clean; the esplanade, a boulevard planted with trees. We drove along the broad avenue to the Grand Hotel in Mr. Serrano's carriage; he had met us in his private boat, and taken charge of us right away from the steamer. We had excellent rooms—mine (No. 22) with two windows, one facing west, the other south, both windows looking on to the sea. Mr. Serrano took us for a splendid drive along the sea front, constituting the new city. The old city is up on the mountain (Monte San Giuliano). Seven brigands were captured yesterday, and were marched to-day through the city as a terror to evil-doers. We got back to our hotel, where at 7.30 p.m. we had an excellent dinner—the fish, red and grey mullet, deliciously fresh.

Sunday, 6 October 1901. The mosquitoes here, owing to the salt pans around, average, I should say, 2,000 horse power in ferocity and strength.

The sun arose in all its glory as if to blot out the reminiscences of the past night, but unfortunately two swollen wrists, two limping ankles, and a rubicund, knotty headpiece told a different tale. The consequent run on vinegar threatened to create a corner in that article of daily consumption. The staple industry of Trapani is salt, which is manufactured by evaporation.

When I got down to breakfast Payne met me with awful news. Last night he looked out of his bedroom window and saw a free fight going on between some fishermen on the quay in front. Knives were freely brandished, two men being killed, while a third was desperately wounded; all this arising out of the men demanding of the masters higher pay for the fish they had brought than the latter would agree to. All this tragedy, with the fact of the capture of the seven brigands, decided us to curtail our stay in these parts, so instead of going to Marsala the following day we arranged to return to Palermo by a mid-day train. Marsala, it appears, is a hotbed of sedition, so we did well to give the place a wide berth.

At 9 a.m. Mr. Serrano turned up in an open carriage drawn by three horses abreast, and took us up to Monte San Giuliano, the Eryx of antiquity (2,485 feet above sea level). The men up here mostly wear the "cappa," or hood, while the women, who are noted for their beauty, wear the long black silk "mantilla." The cathedral is very fine. We left our wraps at the Nuovo Albergo

Cordici, which a few years ago had the honour of providing lunch for the late Duc d'Aumale. It really was a very good lunch. After lunch we visited the ancient city of Eryx, the sacred city of Venus. We then returned to our inn, and at 4 p.m. we all three drove back to Trapani, where we had a wash and a change, being fetched by Mr. Serrano in his carriage, which took us to his house for 7.30 p.m. dinner to a regular dinner party. Mr. Serrano gave me, to fumigate my bedroom, "fidibus." The fumes, pretty powerful, sent the mosquitoes off into gentle sleep, and allowed me to enjoy a good night's rest.

Monday, 7 October 1901. A lovely morning. We enjoyed a fine row on the sea, and then visited "la Catedrale de San Lorenzo," containing "*The Crucifixion,*" by Van Dyck. We returned to our hotel to a wretched lunch—everything stale. Mr. Serrano saw us off by the 12.30 p.m. train, which landed us at 5.5 p.m. at Palermo once more safe and sound, for which we were indeed thankful.

Tuesday, 8 October 1901. A lovely day, which I employed in taking an excursion to Corleone (Cœur de Lion), supposed to be where our King Richard was confined by the Saracens. The rule of the road with us in England is summed up by—

> If you go to the right you are sure to go wrong,
> If you go to the left you are sure to go right.

while here, like everywhere else abroad, it is just the contrary, as we found to our cost when cycling in foreign parts.

On our drive I admired the way in which the dwellers of the fifth, sixth, and seventh stories of the high houses get up their provisions by a basket attached to a rope, reminding me of the Apostle St. Paul being let down in a basket, as also of myself when I went down that Bohemian coal mine in 1884. I took a single first-class to Corleone. In the train I got into conversation with an intelligent Sicilian talking English perfectly. Arrived at Corleone, I visited the old dungeon of Saracenic origin, and then hired a carriage to Ficuzza to visit the Royal hunting lodge and park there. On my way I stopped to lunch by the roadside, having brought my provisions with me. I then drove on to the station to take the train back to Palermo. In my compartment I found the same Sicilian, who on seeing me said:

"Of course, you met no brigands at Corleone. They have given up that trade, and are now established in business at Palermo. Are you established in business at Palermo?"

I told him I was not, and asked him whether he was. His reply was: "I am established in business at Palermo."

Wednesday, 9 October 1901, I took the early train to Girgenti, visiting the wonderful temples there, the finest in the world, all in a magnificent state of chaotic ruin. Porto Empedocle, on the sea shore adjoining, is the great place for shipping sulphur wherever there are vineyards. In fact, all the time I visited the temples the smell of the sulphur was very overpowering. I put up at the Hotel des Temples, owned by my Mr. Ragusa, where I stayed on till Saturday night, 12 October 1901, fully exploring this interesting old city, when I embarked in the steamer "*Pachino*" (1,049 tons), leaving Porto Empedocle Sunday, 13 October 1901, at 1 a.m., for Syracuse. My cabin was a roomy one, with two berths and a sofa. All the time I was at Girgenti the British Consul and Lloyd's agent there (Mr. Oates) looked after me splendidly, finishing up by giving me dinner at his club at Porto Empedocle, and seeing me on to my steamer, recommending me to the captain. Ours was a coasting cargo steamer, so we stopped at any amount of ports, discharging and taking in cargo, but there were no passengers except myself, so that the captain and I chummed along very comfortably; he gave me the full run of the steamer. The food on board was excellent, and the eggs served in various forms all quite fresh. They are great egg eaters abroad.

This reminds me of the German lady who, replying to enquiries concerning her husband, who had been very ill, said: "Thank you, he is much better since he has eaten both his eyes." Consternation! followed by explanation. She meant "eggs"; the German for "egg" is "ei."

The sea being a bit rough and choppy by the coast, we missed one or two ports where we had cargo to discharge and to take in, the captain saying it was too rough to enter these small ports, but he hoped that on the next trip it would be all right. On my asking him when that would be he calmly answered, "Oh! in about five or six weeks." The consignees were used to this, so as we passed these ports they were on the jetty waving their hands in assent to the captain's shout of "Next trip."

I always had a sea bath on board. When Lord Rosebery was in Naples for the first time he, too, wanted a salt-water bath in his room, but the landlord explained that, salt being a Government monopoly, he had to get official leave first. The permission was granted on the condition that after the bath the water was to be taken back again through the Custom House, to be duly verified and then poured back again into the sea.

Kindly understand, please, the meaning of these two all-important words—"Collazione" stands for "lunch," while "pranzo" does duty for "dinner."

By the by, when I took those headers into deep water, why did I do so? Answer, "For divers reasons." And why do I come out? Answer, "For sundry purposes." We were off Scoglitti, where we ought to have taken in a lot of wine, but we were in the midst of a heavy thunderstorm, with forked lightning, thunder, and a perfect torrent of rain, so had to leave it alone. This made the fourth port we had not touched since we left Porto Emperdocle. At our dinner we had butter for the first time, served up in a round pat on a folded napkin. We also had bringals, the first I had tasted since I had them in India in 1866-67. Here they are served up sliced with macaroni in gravy, making an excellent separate vegetable course. On board these steamers capital red and white wine is served at lunch and dinner, free of charge, with a glass of excellent Marsala afterwards with our cheese. Florio, the owner of these steamers, is the great Marsala wine producer of the island. When Nelson was around with his fleet he wanted a wine resembling sherry for his officers and himself, so Woodhouse, of Marsala, made him up this wine, which has ever since been held in high repute.

All through the night the storm raged furiously; impossible to have my porthole open, so I slept with the door wide ajar instead. On the morning of Monday, 14 October 1901, after a delightful sea run of eight days, we weighed anchor at Syracuse, where I first stopped at the Casa Politi, but, finding I had made a mistake, I went on to the Villa Politi, where I was more comfortable. On my way up I passed the Temple of Diana; the Palazzo Montalto, a fine old ruin; the cathedral; an old Doric Temple of Minerva, mentioned by Cicero; the celebrated Fountain of Arethusa, adorned with papyrus plants, growing luxuriantly; and the Passegiata Arethusa, a fine promenade overlooking the fountain and the harbour. My landlady, Madame Politi, was an English widow, a regular brick. I visited the adjacent catacombs of San Giovanni, where St. Paul preached when he tarried three days in Syracuse (see Acts XXVIII., verse 12). I stood on the spot where he preached, admiring the symbols of the four Evangelists—St. Matthew, the eagle; St. Mark, the lion (vide Venice); St. Luke, the bull; and St. John, the lamb.

Our hotel stood in a lovely garden, the ancient Latomia de Cappuccini, a wild, grand, disused quarry. It was from its heights that 7,000 captive Athenians were hurled alive to perish in the depths below, Syracusan females (they cannot be called ladies) sitting out on the top gloating over their agony, and throwing them coarse food so that they should not die too quickly, thus spoiling the afternoon's enjoyment. I had a splendid bedroom

(No. 3), with a fine balcony overlooking the sea. The hotel was full of English visitors, making it all the more pleasant. Syracuse is certainly, without exception, the freshest, brightest place I have ever yet been to. I have visited it several times since, *inter alia,* from 14 to 18 February 1914, in all five days on that occasion, and the place appeals to me more and more each time I go there.

At 2.30 on the afternoon of Tuesday, 15 October 1901, we made up a party of four (two ladies and two gentlemen) for a row up the River Anapo to Olympieum and Cyane and back, a lovely 3½ hours' trip. We drove in Madame Politi's carriage to the small harbour (Porto Picolo), where Madame Politi's boat took us the remainder of the way. Rowing right across the harbour, we entered the narrow, shallow river. About half way up the river goes underground, so we alighted, crossed an embankment, and joined the river in another boat on the other side. We passed along groves of papyrus and bamboo, after which we obtained a good view of the two single columns of the Olympieum (a temple of Jupiter). It is here that I got my first view of Mount Etna. We rowed to the very end of the river, which stops abruptly at the Fountain of Cyano, the azure spring in which the nymph of that name was metamorphosed for opposing Pluto when he was carrying Proserpine down to the infernal regions. The clear spring, abounding with fish and bordered all round with lofty papyrus, is called La Pisina. We rested awhile to take a draft of Etna wine, eating bread and butter, our substitute for afternoon tea. After a pleasant smoke of a mild Havana cigar we started back at 4.30 p.m., reaching our small harbour at 5.45 p.m., and were driven back, reaching our hotel at 6 p.m., sitting down at 7 p.m., a merry party, to dinner. Three officers from H.M.S. "*Cruiser,*" then lying in the harbour, joined us. Captain Tufnel (one of them) is cousin to my Dalkey friends, while Lieutenant Forbes is a first cousin to Reginald Trotter, who was in my office. After dinner we all strolled down into the Latomia garden with lighted candles. Two sisters (one married, the other a spinster) knowing the way, took me in hand. The spinster sister kept saying, "Mr. van de Linde, you do remind me so of my father—he is 81." What could she mean? I was barely 61 (20 years younger).

On Wednesday, 16 October 1901, we started exploring the city. We first came across the old Roman Palvestra Ginnasio Romano, excavated in 1864, with entablatures of the Colonna family (their crest is an upright column), a marble coat of arms of Charlemagne, also a Roman bath with the wall of the Roman neapolis alongside; after which the sight of all others, namely, the Roman Amphitheatre, holding 60,000 spectators, with the places where the crocodiles and the wild beasts were kept for purposes of sport. Further on we came to the great Altar of Heiro II, where 450 oxen were annually sacrificed to commemorate the expulsion of the tyrant Thrasybulus.

After this the Latomia del Paradiso, where Dionysius had his famous prison, the captives being let down from a sliding trap into a grotto below, and dominated by the Ear of Dionysius, so arranged that the tyrant, sitting up in the roof 210 feet above, could hear the slightest whisper of the prisoners quite distinctly. I visited both the prison below and then the one above, sitting down where the tyrant sat, so that I can fully vouch for the wonderful acoustic powers here displayed. We then visited the Greek Theatre, holding 40,000 spectators, and the Nymphæum, a grotto with two old Roman water conduits, still in active use. It is the water we drank at the Villa Politi (simply delicious). It was from up here that we reached the Ear of Dionysius. We then went through the rock-hewn street of tombs (Via delle Tombo), with its cavities (tomb chambers of ancient catacombs). We finished up by inspecting the old Roman baths, which are in a lovely garden, full of luxuriant vegetation.

After dinner Captain Tufnel and Lieutenant Bowie took me down the Latomia (each with a lighted candle) to show me the graves of various English officers and of a British Consul buried here; they had all of them perished in duels, being buried just where they fell. One poor young English officer was only 18 years old.

Thursday, 17 October 1901, I drove to Fort Euryelus, the west extremity of the ancient Epipolue, with its five massive towers and two deep fosses, through which I entered subterranean passages, formerly magazines and storehouses. I then drove to the tomb of Archimedes, rediscovered by Cicero. Then, passing along the Catania Road north, I came to the ancient fortifications of the Tyche, descending to the Scala Greco on the sea coast. From there I got a grand view of Mount Etna. Before lunch I visited the crypt of the Cappuccini Church at the Convent adjoining our hotel, a gruesome sight, showing the skeletons in their grave clothes hanging from niches in the wall. After lunch we descended the bathing place and rowed to the island of Ortygia, the oldest part of the city, called the Achradina, with its far-famed caverns. On our tramp a lady asked me this riddle—

"If a lady kissed you, would you kiss her back?"

Answer: "I should prefer to kiss her face."

Friday, 18 October 1901. Good-bye for the present, being off to Catania, which I reached at 1.15 p.m., just in time for lunch at the Hotel Grande Brelagne (very good indeed). After lunch I drove along the sea coast to Aci Castello, a grand old castle of the 13th century, passing on my way the Portus Ulixis (see Virgil Aeniad III), filled by a lava stream in the 15th century. During my drive I passed a lot of these Etna streams. Out at sea are the famous seven Scogli de Ciclope, the rocks which the blinded Polyphemus hurled at Ulysses. The highest, Isola d'Aci, rises 230 feet.

Saturday, 19 October 1901, 4 a.m. Catania is an awful fever den, full of mosquitoes from the salt pans around. I got up, packed everything, had café au lait complet, and caught the 6 a.m. train for a 91 miles circuit of Mount Etna, rising up to an elevation of 3,810 feet, the highest point we reached. A wonderful trip through wild beds of lava from former eruptions, and then, on turning a corner, we got into grand vegetation, abounding with ripe fruit and the splendid Etna grapes. We pass Bronte, belonging to the Duc de Bronte (Lord Bridport), whom later on I have travelled with once or twice. He is a very genial man. Once, on reaching Naples by steamer, he cleared all our luggage for us by simply calling out "Niente." The Custom House people all know him. I got back to Catania all right, telegraphed Hotel Timeo at Taormina that I was arriving that afternoon, had lunch with the British Consul, Mr. Elford, and then drove round with him exploring the city.

(*a*) *The Cathedral,* built in 1091, destroyed by earthquake 1169—parts only still remain; the granite façade is of columns from the ancient theatre.

(*b*) *Fontana dell Amenano,* another beautiful fountain.

(*c*) *Pescheria,* or fish-market, with an ancient and a fish-like smell, reminding one of Adelina Patti's voice—the one is "smell odious," the other is "melodious."

(*d*) *Castel Ursino,* a grim old castle, erected by Frederick II., destroyed by lava during the eruption of "Aetna" in 1669.

(*e*) *Græco Roman Theatre,* a magnificent ruin, visited by torchlight, most of it being underground, overwhelmed by lava, but all extremely interesting.

(*f*) *Benedictine Monastery of San Nicolo,* the organ by Donato del Piano, containing 2,916 pipes, and is one of the finest organs in Europe. Monastery has a beautiful garden with lovely flowers and a fine view.

(*g*) *The old Roman Amphitheatre,* partly demolished, rest a ruin.

(*h*) *Villa Bellini,* with an exquisite garden and lovely exotics.

We then drove on with my luggage, and I caught the 4.16 p.m. train for Taormina, which, after a pleasant run all along the sea coast, I reached at 5.31 p.m. The station is called Giardina Taormina. I hired an open carriage and pair, in which I was driven up the hill to the Hotel Timeo, where I was given a fine room (No. 27), with a balcony overlooking the sea. The hotel backs on to the "Teatro Greco," a fine old ruin. From the hill on which it stands is one of the most beautiful views in Italy. The hall porter carried me up into the doorway, sheltered from the sun, a table and an easy chair, where I sat after my meals, enjoying my "*dolce far niente,*" with, after lunch and dinner, a cup of coffee and an excellent cigar. The hotel was full of very good people, among others my two lady friends from the Villa Politi. The food was excellent, my café au lait complet a dream. Taormina is a quaint old place with only one long street, full of "salones" (barbers' shops), consisting of one single large room open to the public gaze. They are always full, for no one seems to shave himself in the Latin countries. At the end of the street is the Grand Hotel San Domenico, an old Dominican Convent, an interesting old place with a fine garden looking sheer down the cliff on to the sea, 700 feet below. Adjoining the hotel is the old Dominican Chapel, where Mass is still regularly conducted. I had afternoon tea in the garden, after which the manager showed me over the hotel. It is all very well got up, but the bedrooms are gloomy and very small—they are the cells of the former inmates, the monks of old.

By moonlight the hills to the right of my hotel stand out so sharp and distinct that they remind one of scenes at the theatre cut out of cardboard. The Gothic Palazzo Corvaia has an interesting court; on the staircase is a relief of the 14th century, representing Adam delving while Eve is spinning. Adjoining it is the Roman theatre, excavated in 1894. I took a lovely walk up to Mola (2,080 feet high). It contains rock tombs of pre-Hellenic origin, with the Torrente di Fontana Vecchia leading to the old Castle of Taormina, formerly the Acropolis Tauromenium, a venerable pile, founded 396 B.C. I then climbed Monte Venere (2,834 feet), lunching on the summit. I wanted to climb Mount Etna, but, finding it to be out of the question, I gave up the idea, though with great regret.

My two Villa Politi ladies were Australians, and half sisters; they gave me the four distinguishing names by which the various inhabitants out there are known, namely:—Those from Victoria are known as "Crow-eaters," those from New South Wales are known as "Cornstalks" (tall), those from Western Australia are known as "Gum Suckers," those from Queensland are known as "Banana Landers." The married sister was a "Croweater," while the spinster was a "Cornstalk." She looked it, too.

In order to climb Monte Venere comfortably I had taken a guide with me, a frisky young rascal who, on our descent, skipped down the mountain like a goat. I had christened him "Fra Diavolo," so I shouted out, "Piano, piano, Fra Diavolo." He stopped at once, and in the clearest Italian, with a merry twinkle, replied:

Che va piano, va sano; va lontano.
Che va forte, va à la morte.

Who goes gently, goes safely; goes far.
Who goes swiftly, goes to the death.

The second line was new to me; it is splendid.

The next morning I had a delightful walk down to Giardini Taormina. On my way I passed along the road some open disused catacombs, or rock tombs, similar to those up at Mola. Both groups are of pre-Hellenic origin, that is, before the Greeks settled here, which they did 735 B.C., or 2,652 years from the present date, so that they are at the very least as old as that. The ancient Naxos, founded by Theocles 735 B.C., was destroyed 403 B.C. by our old friend Dionysius, of Syracuse fame. Naxos was the first Greek settlement in the island of Sicily. All that remains to mark the site of Naxos is its old castle, Castello di Schiso, now converted into a farm dwelling. The old square tower remains, also a small castle, Piccolo Castel, adjoining. A flourishing vineyard at Giardini Taormina marks the site of the ancient city, with the remains of old lava walls covered with prickly pears in full bloom. I reached the point of the promontory forming the Bay of Giardini Taormina; it is now called Capo Schiso, while in ancient times its name was Capo Naxo. The huge boulders are just Etna lava, jet black, with seaweed creeping over them. I walked back all along the sea shore of the lower town; the sand, which is hard, makes excellent, firm walking. At the station an open landau with two horses took me up to my hotel. The driver's charge was lire 2. I gave him lire 2.50 (2s.), and he was in the seventh Heaven. His number was 4. I engaged him to drive me the following Monday morning, 28 October 1901, straight from the Hotel Timeo to the Hotel Trinacria, Messina, a distance of 32 English miles, or a little over 51 kilometres.

My Latomia Vestal asked me: "Why didn't Eve catch the measles?" Answer: "Because she had Adam."

Taormina, or Tauromene, is a corruption of "Taurus" (bull) and "Homo" (man).

The arms of Sicily are a head between three legs, resembling those of the Isle of Man; while Trinacria, as also Sikelia, are the old Greek names for the island, Trinacria, like the three legs, evidently referring to the shape of the island.

Monday, 28 October 1901, after a dull morning, turned out into a perfect day. I had an early lunch at 10.15 a.m., and at 11 a.m. my open landau and pair loaded up, and off we started, after many pleasant "Good-byes" all round. I had thoroughly enjoyed my nine days' pleasant stay up there in this restful place. The drive, mostly along the coast, is simply grand. We crossed some five or six magnificent fiumari (mountain torrents). We reached the Hotel Trinacria, Messina, at 4.30 p.m., a drive of 5½ hours, covering 32 miles without one single stop. I thoroughly enjoyed my delicious afternoon tea in my cheerful bedroom, No. 34, nicely carpeted, large, but yet cosy. It overlooks the Marina. While I was indulging in a cigar after, my friend Mr. Moore turned up, with his partner Mr. Alec Bennett, the nephew of my old Bromley friend, Tom Bennett. I sat at dinner next to Mr. Herbert Oates (the brother of Mr. G. E. Oates, Lloyd's agent). He took his meals at my hotel. He introduced me to his friend, Mr. G. Sanderson, and also to Mr. and Mrs. Gerald C. Lascelles. Mr. Lascelles is the new Vice-Consul there, and the son of

Sir Francis Lascelles, the late British Minister at Berlin, cousin to the Earl of Harewood, whose daughter (Lady Louisa Lascelles) my banker, Lord Hillingdon, married. After dinner Mr. Moore joined us, and we all had coffee together. Mrs. Lascelles reminded me that the previous Saturday week she saw me having afternoon tea at the hotel San Domenico, Taormina, when I was coaching up two English officers about Etna. She told me that Messina was then the greatest town in Sicily, rather a contrast to when it was founded, B.C. 732 (just 2,649 years ago), by Cumean pirates on the site of a Sikelian town called Zancle (a sickle), when in those ancient days this city was the scene of repeated carnage and bloodthirsty warfare.

Next day, Tuesday, 29 October 1901, Mr. Herbert Oates called at 9.30 a.m. and took me to his office, after which we looked round the town, and then, accompanied by Mr. G. Sanderson, we both caught the 12 o'clock steamer, "*Christofo Colombo*" (1,662 tons) for Reggio ("Rhegium," see Acts XXVIII, 13). We two were off, immediately sitting down to lunch—soles, red mullet, devil fish (octopus), chicken, potatoes, cheese, bread, butter, fruit, wine, and coffee constituted our frugal repast. By the time we had finished we found ourselves anchored off Reggio. We got into a small boat, and were rowed to the place. We entered the cathedral; it has on its façade a Latin inscription which, translated, reads, "And from thence we fetched a compass and came to Rhegium" (Acts XXVIII, 13). Our guide lighted a candle and showed us at the high altar a round granite column called St. Paul's Stone. The legend is that when St. Paul preached that day at Rhegium it was by the sea shore, and, getting dark, he lighted a candle and put it on a stone (this very granite column now before us). The people refused to hear him, so St. Paul said to them, "Well, wait at all events, and hear me while the light lasts." Seeing that it was but a small bit of candle end they agreed to wait. But when the candle end was consumed the stone took light, so St. Paul preached on till daylight.

We rowed back to our steamer, which left at 3 p.m. for Messina, passing Scylla, a rock on the mainland, facing Charybdis, the whirlpool opposite. We landed in a small boat at the fish market. A frightful storm set up, stopping for the time being all traffic, both by land and sea, quite a record storm, in fact.

Wednesday, 30 October 1901. The thunder and lightning had stopped, but the gale raged as furiously as ever, spreading desolation everywhere. The line from Taormina to Messina was quite destroyed, and the cemetery on the hill sloping down became a lake, for the strong walls around kept the water in. The coffins floated down to the bottom wall, remaining there three or four deep. Bridges were torn away. At 12, just as we were sitting down to lunch, the rains began again, a torrential downpour, lasting the whole afternoon. Mr. Oates told me that in 1880 (21 years previous) they had a similar storm, but it lasted only a few hours, while the present storm seemed likely to last 48 hours, which, indeed, it did. Passengers for Catania to Messina, a direct distance by rail of 95 kilometres, had to go from Messina to Palermo, thence inland to Catania, a distance of 415 kilometres, making a detour of 320 extra kilometres, that is to say, close upon 200 English miles. This wholesale devastation was accompanied by a heavy loss of human lives and property. The olive, the citron, and lemon crops were all destroyed, entailing untold poverty to the small growers, for not only were the crops done for, but the trees themselves were mostly uprooted or hopelessly damaged.

Thursday, 31 October 1901. The storm at last had abated. Mr. Oates' nephew was being married. He hoped to spend his honeymoon at the Hotel Timeo, Taormina, travelling via Palermo and Catania to Taormina, a distance of 450 kilometres, or, say, 281 miles, as against the direct route of 50 kilometres, or, say, 31 miles, a detour of 400 kilometres, or, say, 250 miles.

I had just heard from the agents that the steamer "*Hamburg*" would be leaving Naples for Southampton at noon on Friday, 15 November 1901 (sixteen days thence), and that they would keep me duly advised both at the Hotel Trinacria, Palermo, as also at the Grand Hotel, Naples, as the time for departure drew nearer. They meanwhile promised me as comfortable a cabin on the return journey as I had coming out on the "*Rhein,*" so that they felt sure that my trip homewards would be equally pleasant in every respect. With this satisfactory letter, giving me my actual date for leaving Naples, I could now make all my intermediate arrangements with ample time for everything.

The morning being fine, the public writers were driving a roaring trade in the Via del Nettuno. There were six of them on each side of the street, say twelve in all, with their desks, writing implements, and two chairs to each (one chair for the writer, the other chair for the customer). I noticed that the customers were all men; there were no women. Possibly the women made different arrangements or came at another hour.

At 10.45 a.m. Mr. Oates fetched me in his carriage to drive me along the Marina to the Faro Lighthouse, the extreme north-east point of the city and of Sicily, a glorious drive of 16 miles there and back. On our way we passed ten or twelve fiumari (mountain torrents), which had brought down huge masses of alluvial soil from the hills above. They made big cones right across our road, thus converting our drive into a series of switchbacks. We both offered to get out and walk, but the coachman would not hear of it, declaring it would offend the horse, so we kept our seats, sitting tight as the horse galloped up the hill, to tear down the other side at breakneck speed. It certainly was an exciting drive. We passed on our right the far-famed whirlpool, Charybdis, while just opposite, on the mainland of Calabria, rose the steep Scylla, the ill-famed rock with a castle on the top.

"Incidis in Scyllam, cupiens vitare Charybdin." ("You split upon Scylla, wishing to avoid Charybdis.")

We stopped at the Ristoranti della Napoletana, at the interesting village of Pace, where we ordered our lunch to be served outside, on the borders of a lovely salt lake, connected by a channel with the sea, and surrounded by hills. This lake contains excellent fish, including oysters. We then continued our drive to Ganzirri, alighting at the Faro, or lighthouse. This is the narrowest part of the Straits of Messina, about two miles across, or even less. The place opposite, on the mainland of Calabria, is called Alta Furnara. One can hear the cock crow across. We got back to our Ristoranti, where the landlord gave us for lunch oysters and fish, both fresh caught, fillet, vegetables, bringal (our English egg plant, the French name for it is aubegine), cheese, pears, and the largest black grapes I ever saw; they were the size and shape of egg plums, sweet and fleshy; red and white wine, café noir, and an excellent cigar, for all of which (including the drive) I am the guest of my bountiful host, Mr. Oates. "Me don't like it," as my sister used to say when her god-mother began singing in a high key. I don't think it is fair; it looks like involuntary sponging on my part. Returning, our horse was not quite so fresh, so that he was not a bit offended when we got out at each of the ten or twelve fiumari and walked, while our Jehu coaxed his jaded steed up the hills and down the dales. The children would get in the way; to avoid turning our carriage into a sacrificial car of Juggernaut the horse had to stop dead just as he had got a little impetus. We eventually reached the hotel safe and sound.

An Italian lady told me that I reminded her very much of Verdi; to which I replied: "Indeed, but was not Verdi very nearly 100 when he died quite recently?" Her answer was: "I am not referring to his age, but to his intellect. You have just got his look about you."

Friday, 1 November 1901 (All Saints' Day), a general holiday. All the offices and warehouses were closed. Mr. Moore fetched me at 9 a.m. to drive me to the Campo Santo (cemetery), where everybody went this day to deposit votive offerings at the graves of their relatives.

But on this occasion it was a gruesome sight, with those coffins washed out of the graves and shattered against the wall. Mr. Moore and his friend, Mr. Barrett, lunched with me at the hotel at 11 a.m., and at 11.45 a.m. we took a carriage to the ferry, starting at 12 noon for the mainland opposite, which we reached at 12.35 p.m., after a pleasant run across. Arrived at our destination, the Villa San Giovanni, Mr. Barrett chartered a Victoria and pair, in which we were driven along the lovely coast to the celebrated Scylla, a grand rock jutting sheer out of the sea, surrounded by low rocks and reefs, which makes it all so desperately dangerous. The huge fortress on the summit is now dismantled. There is on the shore the cosy little fishing village of Scilla, in a darling little bay, while the high town above, nestling among the rocks, starts from the Forti di Scilla, the fortress itself. We then ascended to the summit of the high town. Descending to the level, we regained our carriage, driving on another three miles in order to get another view of Scylla from the north side. We reached Villa San Giovanni at 4.30 p.m., stopping at the Trattoria, where, under the personal superintendence of Mr. Barrett, the landlord brewed us a pot of excellent tea; but there was no milk, so Mr. Barrett rushed out, seeing a herd of goats being slowly driven along the road. A nanny goat was put under contribution, and in less than no time Mr. Barrett returned with a foaming jug of fresh goat's milk. This the landlord boiled, to avoid accidents by destroying all noxious germs.

Our return steamer, "*Caridi,*" came alongside, we went on board, and by 5.35 p.m. were off for Messina in a thunderstorm, with torrents of rain. We got shelter down below, thus reaching Messina, at 6.10 p.m., quite dry. We jumped into a closed carriage, which took us to our respective ségours, and here the iniquity of these two young men (Moore and Barrett) comes in. I had allowed them to be paymasters pro tem. But when it came to settle up they politely but firmly told me that I was "odd man out, and not in this show at all." However, to show that I bore no ill-feeling, I dined with Mr. and Mrs. Moore at their comfortable house, where, after an excellent dinner, we all three adjourned to Mr. Barrett's flat, where we indulged in black coffee and a cigar.

Saturday, 2 November 1901. At 10.30 a.m. Mr. Moore drove round in a carriage and pair for a day's outing in the mountains. The hotel had packed up for us a sumptuous lunch in a basket, with all accessories, while Mrs. Moore had kindly looked after our tea. We drove to the War Office for a permit, which the Lieutenant-Colonel himself made out and handed me. It authorised Mr. Gérard van de Linde and friend to drive in their carriage along the military road by the English camp.

Armed with this precious document, the carriage climbed the mountain by a lovely winding road, past beautiful valleys abounding with richest vegetation. We passed the hillside village of La Scala, where Mr. and Mrs. Moore have their eight-roomed country house overlooking this lovely scene. For this he paid an annual rent of lire 200 (£8 sterling), occupying it all May and all October, besides two or three days each month in between. His children simply ran wild in this charming solitude, where the nightingale sings all night. "Parva domus, magna quies" ("a poor house, great quiet").

At 1 p.m. we reached Castanea, a beautifully situated village (2,000 feet), on the slope of Monte Cicci, where we adjourned to a cottage for lunch, away from the madding crowd (beggars, children, goats, and pigs). Our coachman lunched on a seat outside, thus minding his carriage and horses at the same time. After enjoying the grand view all around we returned by the coast road constructed by the English during their occupation of the island in the early part of the last century. We passed right by the Campo Inglese, where our permit was requisitioned. Twelve Sicilian soldiers surrounded our carriage, but upon its production we were at once allowed to pass. Half way down, at Curcurace (La Sirzzera di Messina), we stopped for tea (with lemon instead of milk), and delicious tea it was. We returned by the main Faro road, and got back to the hotel at 5.30 p.m.

After an excellent dinner at the hotel Mr. Barrett and I went on board the steamer "*Toscana*" at 11 p.m. for the following excursion next day:—

Sunday, leaving Messina at 1.10 a.m.

reaching	Isola di Lipari at	6.0 a.m.,	leaving again	7.0 a.m.
,,	Isola de Salina ,,	8.10 ,,	,, ,,	8.40 ,,
,,	Rinella (do.) ,,	9.5 ,,	,, ,,	9.20 ,,
,,	Malfa (do.) ,,	10.10 ,,	,, ,,	10.25 ,,
,,	Isola di Panaria	11.25 ,,	,, ,,	11.40 ,,
,,	Isola di Stromboli	1.0 p.m.	,, ,,	1.30 p.m.
,,	Isola di Lipari	4.0 ,,	,, ,,	5.0 ,,

Arriving back at Messina at 9.50 p.m.

We each had an excellent cabin on the "*Toscana.*" It was blowing a gale, and the steamer rolled horribly, so that we got little, if any, sleep. We reached Lipari at 6.30 a.m., when we got up and dressed. The same happy thought struck us both :

" Why not land here? It is useless going on to Stromboli in this gale; it is so rough that they are neither discharging nor taking in cargo."

We had so far taken no tickets, so we only paid singles to Lipari, lire 11.50 each. Our steward had laid in a basketful of provisions. This we purchased of him for lire 9. We took it away with us. Our fellow passengers were ten convicts, handcuffed and connected together with one chain. We were rowed ashore; the sea was rough, but it was a lovely fresh morning. We were piloted by our boatman, who spoke English, to a decent " Albergo," kept by Francesco Traina. Lipari is a lovely island, its industries being the pumice stone mines, also the cultivation of sultanas and currants. They have neither springs nor wells; the only water they get is rain water collected on the deep, flat roofs, with conduits leading down to storing cisterns. Our Albergo was peculiar, consisting of three parlours, each containing, besides the dining table with chairs, three beds, one washstand, one brush, and one comb. We secured a parlour, where we had our café au lait complet, and arranged with our hostess for lunch at 12.30 p.m. sharp. We sallied forth at 8.30 a.m. to explore the island, first noting our address, " Albergo, Francesco Traina, Via Lazzaro 53." Our first visit was to the convict settlement, where the convicts walk about freely all day long. They have their own shops, salone, cafés, and churches. At night they are locked up in their cells, while bloodhounds roam about guarding the roads. They sleep all day, so as to be fresh at night. Able-bodied convicts get work outside at lire 1 a day, upon which they live. Their masters answer for them, seeing that they return at night to be locked up. Those who cannot work stay in the settlement, being allowed 50 c. (under fivepence) a day to keep themselves.

The officer invited us to return at noon to see them mustered to draw their daily pay (some 200 of them). We then visited the convict church. Mass was going on. The officiants consisted of three priests and one small boy. We then visited the Cathedral of St. Bartholomew, whose bones we were shown, as also those of St. Mark. They are kept labelled in a glass case. It is an imposing edifice, with fine mosaics; the panels in front of the high altar are of solid silver, as is also the life-size figure of St. Bartholomew over it. We ascended the belfry, which commands a fine view of the town, the mountains, the sea, and the adjacent islands, especially of Stromboli, of Vulcano, Salina, Filicuri, and Panaria. Stromboli is always in eruption. The cone of its crater is 3,020 feet high. We descended to the sea shore; Mr. Barrett suggested donkeys to ride over the mountain. There being only one available, he made me have it. I had a meal sack for a saddle, the same as I had at Tangiers a few years before. There were no stirrups or bridle, only a rope round its neck to hold on by, not even a bit. I rode up a mule track while he walked. We came to a lovely little fishing village called Canneto, where we visited Signor Carboni, a wealthy pumice stone merchant. After sitting awhile to rest we returned to Lipari to lunch—a great success. Just before lunch, however, the officer fetched us to see the convicts being paid. One of them, having served his time, was paid his 50 c. and then discharged. He did not like going away; he kissed the convicts and bowed to the officer.

The convict was neatly dressed in clean dark clothes. After lunch a "faquino" (porter) asked to carry my Gladstone to the steamer. When I agreed he handed it on to his wife's shoulders, "Mia Madame," as he called her. "Faquino" in Italian means "porter," while "Faquin" in French means a "rascal," similar to our English "knave," while the German equivalent, "knabe," means a "boy," without any sinister meaning attaching to it, as in "faquin" or "knave." I have come across similar instances, but the above two exemplify my ideas on this point.

Our steamer, the "*Milazzo,*" was late in starting, arriving just too late at Milazzo for us to catch the direct steamer on to Messina. Our remaining fellow passenger was a handcuffed convict, who lay down full length on deck while two soldiers guarded him. The "*Milazzo*" was half the size of the "*Toscano,*" but twice as lively. We eventually reached Milazzo, which is on the mainland of Sicily, 16 miles from Messina, which we reached by train at 9 p.m., driving on to the hotel for supper and bed.

Monday, 4 November 1901, I caught the 10 a.m. train taking my hotel lunch in my first-class compartment, which I had all to myself. Mr. Herbert Oates kindly saw me off. It was a lovely railway journey, all along the coast. I got a grand view of the Lipari (or Aeolian) Islands. I had sent on my kit direct to Palermo, but I left the train at Cefalu, 42 miles this side of it. I chartered a carriage, and was driven to the cathedral, a noble pile of Norman architecture, dating from A.D. 1148. I then drove on to Termini, a distance of 20 miles, through lovely country, where at 6.56 p.m. I caught the Catania express to Palermo, getting there at 8.30 p.m. Mr. Payne met me at the station; I got my luggage, and we drove on to my Hotel Trinacria, where my kind landlord, Mr. Ragusa, welcomed me cordially, giving me a good supper in Room No. 12, adjoining my old one, No. 11 (now occupied by the High Admiral and his family, all in one room).

Some people were here from Lipari who complained to Mr. Ragusa, "You call yours a first-class hotel, with electric light in each room, and yet you do not even provide your guests with a comb and brush. We never heard of such a thing." To which Mr. Ragusa added, with a smile, "Nor with a toothbrush either." They did not understand him, for they have never heard of or seen such a thing, which, in fact, apparently does not exist in Lipari.

I spent the next few days quietly with Mackinnon and Payne, who took me about everywhere in comfortable, luxurious ease, and at 8 p.m. on Thursday, 7 November 1901, Mackinnon and Payne saw me off in the "*Caridda*" (1,231 tons) for Naples. Through their friendly intervention I got cabin 30, with four berths to myself. As soon as we weighed anchor, at 8 p.m. sharp, we sat down to an excellent dinner. After dinner I arranged about sleeping. My cabin was "midships," berths 5 and 6 running crossways, while 7 and 8 were fore and aft. The wind was east on the starboard side, while my cabin was on the port side. The steward unslung the top berth, No. 5, and I had No. 6 (crossways), where I was pretty comfortable, sleeping on till 7.30 o'clock next morning. I turned in again till 8.45 a.m. We anchored alongside in Naples at 10 a.m., soon after going ashore, so that I reached my Grand Hotel at 11 a.m., bathed and dressed, lunching at 12. I spent a week, from Friday, 8, to Friday, 15, November 1901, in Naples, occupying the time revisiting old haunts, such as Castellamare de Stabia, Capri, Vesuvius, Sorrento, and Ischia, all very lovely; also the Aquarium, one of the finest in the world, on the sea front, close to my hotel.

My friend, Mr. Da Costa, looked after me, and we had pleasant excursions by land and sea together. The place I enjoyed most was the Hotel Quisisana at Castellamare de Stabia, where my wife, daughter, and I were so comfortable in the spring. I went there without Mr. da Costa. The landlord, Mr. Cannavale, treated me like an old friend, gave me my old bedroom, No. 23, and an entire change while my own clothes were drying, for I arrived in a thunderstorm. He provided me a recherché lunch, with all the delicious accessories. When I asked for my bill he smiled and said, "Niente." I was his honoured guest, he told me. Just before leaving he gave me afternoon tea, and then bade me an affectionate farewell as I resumed my carriage to the station below, taking the train back to Naples.

After a comfortable lunch at the Grand Hotel, Naples, I went quietly on board the "*Hamburg,*" where I got an excellent, roomy cabin, No. 116, port side, on the promenade deck, all to myself, as usual. Nothing could be better. I had an enormous electric fan in the ceiling of my cabin, which I could switch off and on from my berth, also a sliding Venetian blind to my port-hole, which I hoped thus to keep open all night. Table, camp stool, sofa, carpet, four large drawers, two hanging wardrobes, four small lockers, a huge plate-glass mirror, plenty of nets to put things in, three sets of hooks (four hooks to each set), and a curtain across the entrance to my cabin in case I wanted to keep my door open. In fact, I had every comfort, including a glorious hot sea-water bath, and by far the biggest cabin I have ever yet had. It certainly would easily accommodate the High Admiral and all his family, so, having it all to myself, I felt simply luxuriated, and was perfectly happy.

We reached Genoa early on Sunday morning, 17 November 1901, in time to attend 11 o'clock morning service at the Church of the Holy Ghost. I then took the funicular up to the Restaurant du Righi de Genes, with a splendid terrace and grand view. My lunch, including white wine (ad lib.), one dozen oysters, and delicious black coffee, cost me lire 5.10 (or 4s.). I then walked down some grassy slopes, and, striking the regulation drive, "Circouvallazione à Mare," I took further short cuts down till I got back into the city and to my steamer. We left Genoa Monday afternoon, 18 November 1901, and came across a big whale (rather rare in the Mediterranean), reaching Gibraltar on the night of Wednesday, and leaving on the morning of Thursday, 21 November 1901, at 2 o'clock. We anchored on the afternoon of Sunday, 24 November 1901, in the Southampton Waters. At 5.50 p.m. a tender took us into the Southampton Docks, where I got my luggage cleared at once, so that by 7.15 p.m. I reached the South-Western Hotel, and at 7.30 p.m. sat down to table d'hôte dinner with three fellow passengers, Captain Glossop, Lieutenant Crawley, and Mr. Rose Innes, of Brabant's Horse, all three seriously wounded in the Boer War. They were excellent fellows. When we got back to

London they lunched with me at the City Carlton Club, while I dined with them the same evening at their West End Club. Strange to say, I have a nice young fellow at my office whose name is J. F. Rose-Innes. He (like a lot of my office staff) is now out at the front fighting for his King and his country.

Monday, 25 November 1901, I had a pleasant journey up to London, and then home, after a most enjoyable trip.

No more go to sea (until next time)
In a great big overgrown shippio.
Master he say you be
Ugly bad son of a gipsio.

CHORUS.—Hi chingarin cum chie,
Hi chingarin cum chokee oh;
Hi chingarin rin can cha,
Chin a rin a chokee oh.

—Pidgin English.

CHAPTER XIX.

Golf.

IN the spring of 1902 the Sundridge Park Golf Club was started. Our first captain was Mr. William Hardy. I was one of the original members, and assisted at the opening ceremony.

I am a tolerably keen golfer. When living at Bromley I thought nothing of doing three rounds of 18 holes each in one day, the first between breakfast and early lunch, the second between lunch and early afternoon tea, and the third from tea to 7.30 p.m., cycling home to 8 o'clock dinner.

My firm were elected first honorary auditors, and are so still. I generally do the audit myself with an intelligent Lieutenant (also a golfer, "*cela va sans dire*"). In November 1904 I was elected a life member, a great honour. My colleague is the Hon. A. J. Balfour, M.P., a very keen golfer. Although I am now living at Reigate Hill, a good distance from Bromley, I still manage to get over there four or five times a year. I keep myself in form by practising on my two lawns, where I have nine sporting putting holes, besides "golf clock" on the top lawn. I know the lie of my holes thoroughly, having come to Reigate in Michaelmas, 1909 (eight years ago). My wife is a good player, so she and I are very evenly matched.

CHAPTER XX.

Gibraltar, Genoa, Naples, Sicily, Malta, Tunis, and Carthage.

EARLY in the year 1903 I decided upon taking another sea trip similar in some respects to the previous one of 1901, but on this occasion, through the assistance of my friends, Keller, Wallis & Co., of London, and Mr. Roberto Consiglio, of Naples, I arranged that from first to last my present trip should be entirely by sea from the moment I took the steamer at Southampton until my return to Southampton, my only railway journey being from London to Southampton and back.

I found a big North German Lloyd steamer, whose ultimate destination was Australia, shortly leaving Southampton for Genoa, where she would stay two days, and on the same night that she was leaving for Naples a large Florio Rubbatini steamer was leaving Genoa for Bombay, calling at Naples, Messina, Catania, and Syracuse, my destination. I accordingly secured a roomy cabin to myself in both these steamers, and started accordingly. On arrival at Genoa I retained my cabin those two days, having my meals on board. On the evening of the second day, after a comfortable dinner, I was transhipped with my luggage from one steamer to another, thus avoiding having to go ashore or to having my luggage examined at Genoa. My first steamer had excellent real Havana cigars on board, so I laid in a good stock at a very reasonable price. The next afternoon, after leaving Genoa, we put in at Naples, where we stayed 24 hours. This enabled me to look up my old friends, Mackinnon and Payne, with whom I spent my time ashore very pleasantly. We left the following night. There was no moon, so that I had a grand view of Vesuvius, which was in full eruption, "smoking his pipe," as the saying is. The next morning we put in at Messina, where I again had a good time with my friends, Oates and Alec Bennett.

When we left Messina that night I had a fine view of the Aeolian Islands, the volcanoes of Vulcano (with its constantly smoking crater) and Stromboli were blazing away. Later on in the night, or, rather, early morning, while it was still dark, I had a grand view of Etna blazing away, which I saw again even to better advantage the next night as we were leaving Catania. We stayed a few hours at Catania, where my old friend Mr. Elford took me to lunch at his club, looking after me all the time I was ashore.

The next day we landed at Syracuse. Madame Politi, who was expecting me, had sent on her carriage and pair to meet me at the steamer. I was thus driven up comfortably to the Villa Politi, where I had my old comfortable bedroom. The hotel was so full that Colonel Barlow (of the Royal Engineers), stationed at Malta, who arrived that evening just in time for dinner, had to put up with the largest of the bathrooms, where a bed and other accessories were put up for his convenience.

We got to be very intimate. I told him I was going in a couple of days to Malta, showing him at the same time my various letters of introduction to the Admiral of the Port, to Major M. A. Boyd, of the Royal Engineers, to Captain R. S. Lowry, and to Lloyd's agents. I intended staying a week or so at Malta, and from there going on to Tunis. Colonel Barlow said he knew all my friends, that he, too, would look after me as well, so that I should be all right.

We accordingly left together a day or two after in the Hungarian steamer "*Carola.*" We left Syracuse at 4 p.m., had an excellent dinner on board, reaching Malta at 11 p.m. that night. We both put up at the Royal Hotel, where I had engaged my bedroom. Next morning Colonel Barlow very kindly invited me to put up at his own place across the harbour, close to the breakwater, then in course of erection. I thanked him, but said I thought I had better stay in Malta. To this proposition he reluctantly agreed, on the understanding that we were to see a good deal of each other. That morning he took me across the harbour in his own steam launch to his comfortable, palatial residence the other side.

He had given over the whole of the ground floor as mess quarters to his regiment. Major Boyd happened to be there, so we all lunched together. A young Lieutenant Cavendish was also of our party, a great polo player. In Malta they play polo in the trenches. I watched the game one afternoon, when Cavendish scored splendidly. The next year, when he came over on leave to England, he was my guest at "Glebe Knoll," Bromley, for two or three days, and we played golf together at my club. The roof of Colonel Barlow's mansion was entirely flat, very spacious, with a stone coping all round. On this roof a long strip of carpet was laid, the stumps were placed at each end. This was their cricket ground; it was a bit primitive, but it answered its purpose.

After lunch, followed by a comfortable smoke in the verandah, Colonel Barlow took me back in his steam launch to his club, called "l'Auberge de Castille," the headquarters of the Royal Engineers and of the Royal Artillery, where we dined. The other club is the military Malta Union Club, situated in l'Auberge de Provence, the former "House" of the Provence Knights, where I also was taken to lunch one day.

Colonel Barlow introduced me to his chief, General O'Brien, who dined with us at our table. He and the Colonel had a lot to talk about, for the following week our late King Edward VII was coming over to lay the foundation stone of the new breakwater adjoining Colonel Barlow's place. The ceremony was fixed for 20 April. They both wanted me to stay, but I thought I could hardly spare the time, much as I should have liked to do so.

The next morning I called upon the Admiral of the Port, to whom I presented my letter of introduction. He was courtesy itself; showed me all over the arsenal, and then, hearing that I was lunching with Colonel Barlow, he had me taken over there in the Admiralty steam launch. I was wearing a blue reefer suit, with cape to match, so that the sailors in the men-of-war in the harbour took me for the late King Edward, and gave me a Royal salute, much to Colonel Barlow's and

General O'Brien's amusement, when I told them the incident at lunch at the mess there.

General O'Brien and Colonel Barlow took me back to the city after lunch, when the latter showed me the famous cathedral, the site of the former house of Publius, who, when Governor of the Island, accorded a hospitable reception to St. Paul, as duly recorded in Acts XXVIII., verse 7, and at whose house the Apostle lodged three days. In front of the cathedral are planted two cannons, as in the days of the Maltese Order. The interior contains fine tombs of coloured marbles; in one of the chapels is a Byzantine image of St. Paul, covered with a cloth of silver, while in the choir stands a silver crucifix from Rhodes. We then visited the adjacent catacombs of St. Paul, also, a short distance inland, the Grotta di Calipso, with a clear spring of deliciously cold water.

I also visited (this time alone) the Island of Gozzo, by a small steamer from the Great Harbour; the passage took 1¼ hours each way. I lunched at the Victoria (Duke of Edinburgh) Hotel. On our way back we visited the islet of Comino, lying between Gozzo and Malta, after which we passed St. Paul's Bay, the scene of his shipwreck, as fully described in Acts XXVII.

I stayed over Sunday in Malta, when I was the guest of Major Boyd. We went to the cathedral together. I sat in his pew, lunching with him afterwards at his club in the Auberge de Castille, where I dined that night with General O'Brien and Colonel Barlow, as the guest of the latter. Colonel Barlow saw me off when I left Malta shortly after by the French mail steamer of the Compagnia Générale Transatlantique for Tunis, where

I put up at the Grand Hotel, Avenue de France. The entrance to Tunis is through a narrow passage, La Goulette (330 feet wide and 26 to 33 deep), which leads into the wide Lac de Tunis, with the city, protected by a breakwater, at the extreme end. Tunis is essentially a French city, as is also Algiers, which I know very well, having visited it repeatedly, and, in fact, on this trip on my return journey.

The interior of Tunis is, however, thoroughly Oriental. I took an open carriage to visit the Ruins of Carthage. It occupied a whole day. I lunched at the Grand Hotel de Carthage. It is a grand excursion; I think I did it thoroughly. The city was founded by the Phœnicians (Dido) about 880 B.C. It was the scene of the celebrated Punic Wars. At school we were taught the well-known sentence, "Carthago delenda est" ("Carthage must be destroyed"). I visited the hill, the site of the temple dedicated to Aesculapius, the god of healing. While tramping over the old ruins I was accosted very deferentially by a Bromley friend—my next-door neighbour, in fact—who for the moment took me to be the Bishop of Dover. When he discovered his mistake his deference passed away, and we became very pally, talking of home and its associations. He and a friend also had a carriage, so we three remained together the rest of the day, visiting various wonderful scenes of former glory and of present devastation, and then returned together to the hotel I was stopping at, which also happened to be theirs.

From Tunis I took the French direct mail steamer of La Compagnie de Navigation Mixte, bound for Marseilles, with its first stop at Palermo, where I landed, taking that same evening the Florio Rubbatini steamer for Naples, where I found my return steamer awaiting me, so I went straight on board from one steamer to the other, thus again avoiding examination of luggage. We started from Naples that very afternoon, calling at Genoa and Algiers, where we stayed a whole day in that lovely Oriental French Colony. Messrs. Thomas Cook and Son were on the look out for us, so I joined one of their personally conducted excursions ("Tutti Cooki"), where they showed us all there was to be seen in this old Arab city, giving us a good lunch at the Grand Hotel Continental, followed by a breakneck drive in char-à-bancs all along the high ground skirting the coast. It was, indeed, a grand drive, which we all thoroughly enjoyed. Our next stop was Gibraltar, where, everything being favourable, we landed. I had a good drive all round, and bought some delicious fruit, which I found very refreshing. For a wonder our steamer came alongside a quay outside, but adjoining the harbour, so we were able to land straight from our steamer on to *terra firma*.

CHAPTER XXI.

HINDHEAD.

I REACHED Southampton all right quite early one morning, where I found a telegram awaiting me from my wife. They had taken a bungalow at Hindhead, where I was to join them, telegraphing my coachman at home to send me on my bicycle, which reached me all right that very afternoon. Hindhead is an ideal spot. Our bungalow, all among the heather, was simply charming. We had one maid from home at a time to look after our simple wants, and my dear little Welsh terrier, " Scamp," a charming companion. He died three years ago of old age, 27 December 1914, and I have put over his grave a stone monument: " Scamp, 27 December 1914." The grave, surrounded by a little square garden, with stone coping, stands under a chestnut tree.

We scoured the country round about Hindhead very thoroughly, my wife on her tricycle, my daughter and I each on our bicycles, a most enjoyable sequel to my lovely sea trip, out in the fresh air all the time, except for our meals.

CHAPTER XXII.

Lisbon, Cintra, Tangiers, Onwards.

At the end of January, 1908, my nephew Henry and I left Dover in the Deutsch Ost Afrika steamer, "*Kronprinz,*" bound for Naples, stopping *en route* at Lisbon, Tangiers, and Marseilles. We reached Lisbon on the morning of Sunday, 2 February 1908, where we learnt that afternoon that, on the previous day, (Saturday) the King and Crown Prince of Portugal were foully assassinated, and when we arrived, it being Sunday (a holiday), the whole city was in an uproar. Having already landed, probably an imprudent act on our part, we put ourselves under the protection of a friendly policeman, who, seeing we were English, escorted us to the railway station, where we took the train up to Cintra (18 miles away), a town set amidst beautiful surroundings—mountain, sea, and luxuriant vegetation—at the base of the Sierra de Cintra. We went straight to the Central Hotel, where, after ordering our lunch, we procured a guide, who showed us the Palacio Real, of the fourteenth and fifteenth centuries; then up to the rocky height of Pena (1,735 feet), and the Castello da Pena below, which is the ancient Castello dos Mouros, whence a lovely road (Caminho de Collares) leads to the Quinta de Monserrate, the property of Sir F. Cook, who is also Visconde de Monserrate. His grounds are a wealth of vegetation. A two miles' walk took us back to our hotel, where we enjoyed an excellent lunch.

After lunch we interviewed the landlord about returning to Lisbon. He said it was simply impossible, the whole city being in a state of revolution, the military were out, and it was a free fight between them and the infuriated mob. So we just stayed where we were for the time being, awaiting further developments. Later on he came to us with the welcome news that the Lord Chamberlain and his wife, who were up at the Royal Palace, were returning shortly by a special train down to Lisbon, and kindly invited us to join them, which we did. On arrival at Lisbon they drove us in one of the Royal carriages to the Avenida Palace Hotel, where they put us under the special care of the landlord, telling him to give us tea and everything we needed at their expense, for we were their honoured guests. Later on, when it was dark, and the streets comparatively quiet, the landlord himself conducted us through quiet back streets to our steamer, and did not leave us till he had seen us safely on board the "*Kronprinz.*"

The next morning, Monday, 3 February 1908, everything was once again normal. The revolution had spent itself out, and we were told by the police that we might safely go ashore. As our steamer was not leaving till late that afternoon we took advantage of the fact and went ashore.

Our first visit was to the Avenida Palace Hotel, where, after ordering our lunch, we procured a guide for the morning to show us over the city. He first took us to the Praço do Commercio, a handsome square with one side open to the River Tagus, showing us at the north-west corner the spot where the murders had taken place that previous Saturday afternoon, in broad daylight, before a crowd of involuntary spectators who happened to be passing to and fro at the time. We then visited the cathedral close by, several other churches, various museums, and the Jardin Botanico, the finest botanical garden in Europe, full of tropical plants and magnificent palms. He then took us to Belem, where we saw the Royal Mausoleum, and where the two Royal victims would shortly be buried. He finished up by taking us to the Church of Santa Maria, where Vasco de Gama and Camoens are both buried.

Our next stop was Tangiers, which we reached a day or two after. Here we were in luck's way, for Sir Harry Maclean had that morning been released, and the whole place was rejoicing.

As it was hardly considered safe to wander about this Moorish place alone we joined a party of Cook's tourists, and were thus personally conducted everywhere in perfect safety, thus seeing everything comfortably. Our first visit was to the native town, with its narrow, crooked, uneven streets, crowded with Moors, Jews, and negro slaves in quaint, many-coloured attire. We visited the Market, where we found an assortment of mules and asses awaiting us, which we all mounted. We had no saddle, bit, or bridle, just a sack to straddle our legs across, with a bit of rope to hang on by. We passed two English young ladies riding splendid Arab steeds. They were the Misses Maclean, looking so bright and happy. After that we came across some camel caravans, a most interesting spectacle. We then had a pleasant jog-trot ride along the ridge of hills overlooking the town and sea beyond, finishing up with a comfortable lunch at the Hotel Cecil, after which we went on board our steamer.

Our next stop was Marseilles, where some friends invited us to lunch at the Grand Hotel du Louvre et de la Paix, where I stopped when going out to India in December 1866, as also on my return in 1867.

We reached our destination, Naples, on the following Monday, 10 February 1908, pursuing thence the even tenor of our way.

Our final trip on the North German Lloyd's line was in February, 1909, by the "*Prince Ludwig,*" Southampton to Naples, calling at Gibraltar, Algiers, and Genoa. We had by that time given up the Grand Hotel at Naples, and had moved to the Hotel Savoie, where we were very comfortable while the old proprietor was there, but when he left we moved to the Grand Hotel du Vésuve. Our first visit there was on 12 August 1911, and we have always been there since. We are much too comfortable there to think of going anywhere else. We remember, too, the good old saying, namely, "Third time fair."

CHAPTER XXIII.

ORIENT LINE HALF-YEARLY FROM 6 AUGUST 1909 TO 31 JULY 1914.

THE same applies to our steamers, for it was exactly on the same trip that we began travelling by the Orient Line. There, too, we are always so comfortable that we never want to change. This is our summary so far by that excellent line.

6 August 1909:	"Osterley,"	12,129	tons,	twin screw.
4 February 1910:	"Orsova,"	12,036	,,	,,
5 August 1910:	"Osterley,"	12,129	,,	,,
3 February 1911:	"Otway,"	12,077	,,	,,
4 August 1911:	"Orontes,"	9,023	,,	,,
16 February 1912:	"Osterley,"	12,129	,,	,,
2 August 1912:	"Orsova,"	12,036	,,	,,
31 January 1913:	"Osterley,"	12,129	,,	,,
1 August 1913:	"Orvieto,"	12,130	,,	,,
30 January 1914:	"Orama,"	12,928	,,	triple screw.
31 July 1914:	"Otway,"	12,077	,,	twin screw.

All these steamers, with the exception of the "*Orontes,*" have passenger lifts from the lowest deck right up to the highest deck. They are all comparatively new. The "*Osterley,*" which we started with on 6 August 1909, was then making her first trip. Strange to say, we have so far been on her four times; on the "*Orsova*" twice; as also twice on the "*Otway.*" On every one of them I have had an excellent roomy cabin all to myself, and latterly a bedstead cabin with two beds (not berths) to choose from.

By the by, I suppose you all know the story of the empty bed? You don't! Well, that's where you lie!

The advantage of all these 12,000 tons steamers, from the "*Osterley*" onward, is that, being, comparatively speaking, sister ships, their arrangements are all generally alike. Being old stagers, my nephew and I manage to secure our same seats for meals in the dining saloon (always the second dinner when there happens to be two going, if the steamer is full), and our seats up in the lounge, where we have coffee and are allowed to smoke.

When we came out in the "*Osterley*" on her first trip we had a number of naval officers on their way to Australia. Among others was Post Captain (now Admiral) Wemyss, with whom we got to be very friendly. Captain W. J. Jenks, R.N.R., our commander, noticing this, called my nephew aside to tell him that if Capt. Wemyss and he saw their way to get up any entertainment on board he would tell the ship's carpenter and the store keeper to help in every way possible, as, indeed, they did.

The entertainment chosen was taken from Charles Dickens' "*Old Curiosity Shop,*" and entitled, "*Mrs. Jarley's Waxworks.*" Captain Wemyss took the part of "Mrs. Jarley"; my nephew, a great big strapping fellow, was attired in a short pair of drawers, socks, pumps, and a narrow jacket (purposely much too tight for him). He was "Mrs. Jarley's Boy," and, armed with a long stick, explained the various figures. One of the scenes was called "The Babes in the Wood." The two ruffians in top boots, slouched sombrero hats, and armed with a couple of carving knives apiece, looked true villains of the deepest dye, while the babes were two dear little passengers. "Little Nell" was charmingly personified by a sweet young lady. She really ought to have had the wand and explained the various figures, but, being rather bashful, she got my nephew to replace her. He did it splendidly, never missing an opportunity of giving the two ruffians a whack over the head, which they returned whenever they got the chance, Mrs. Jarley every now and then exclaiming in a rich staccato voice, "'Enery, 'Enery, my boy, do behave yourself." This set Master 'Enery misbehaving himself all the more. We prevailed upon "Little Nell" to go round with a plate to collect for various seamen's charities. With her winning ways she secured a substantial amount, which she handed to "Mrs. Jarley" with a sweet smile, the latter passing it on to Captain Jenks. The whole thing was a great success, as were also the games on deck, and the early morning drill of the ship's officers, in which, by common consent, my nephew was appointed "boss." He always saw that they were up to time. The drill began at 6.30 a.m., lasting half an hour, after which there was a rush for hot sea baths.

We found out that the gallant Post Captain's nickname was "The Jackdaw of Rheims," by which, with his full consent, we called him ever afterwards.

CHAPTER XXIV.

Chartered Accountants' Annual Meetings.

AS my readers are by this time doubtless aware, I have, from the very outset, taken the deepest interest in everything connected with the Institute of Chartered Accountants. It is indeed a noble Institution, fulfilling its mission thoroughly.

The spirit of "camaraderie" and good fellowship is simply splendid. This has been very fully fostered by the establishment of the various Students' Societies and the lectures regularly delivered to the members. It will be seen on reference to page 435 of the present work that I have been privileged to contribute my fair share to the papers read on these occasions.

Another spur to this good feeling thus prevailing among the members arises from the Autumnal Meetings, at which a goodly number of members make a point of attending. I attach so much importance to these social functions that I invariably arrange to be present. I am just about to briefly outline three of them, as being typical of the many that I have been privileged to attend.

The first took place at Sheffield, 29, 30 September and 1 October 1910, given under the auspices of my old friend, Alderman George Franklin, Litt.D., the President of the Sheffield Society of Chartered Accountants.

Our headquarters were at the Cutlers' Hall, where the ladies' lounge and reading room was No. 15 first floor and the gentlemen's reading and smoke room No. 14 first floor.

The following was our programme :—

Thursday, 29 September 1910.—11 a.m.: Reception of the members of the Institute at the Cutlers' Hall by the Lord Mayor (the Right Hon. Earl Fitzwilliam, D.S.O.) and the Master Cutler (Herbert Barber, Esq.). After the vote of thanks was proposed to these two gentlemen the presidential address was given by Mr. (now Sir) William Plender, our President, after which, at 1 p.m., we all adjourned to luncheon at the Cutlers' Hall, on the invitation of the Sheffield members, Alderman George Franklin presiding.

The lunch was followed by two papers read by Mr. J. G. Griffiths and Mr. A. Duncan Barber respectively. The latter, an exceptionally good paper, was entitled "Recent Financial Legislation in Some of its Bearings on Professional Accountancy."

At 7 for 7.30 p.m. the banquet took place at the Cutlers' Hall, Alderman George Franklin presiding.

Extract from *The Sheffield Daily Telegraph,* Friday 30 September 1910 :—

> "Mr. Gérard van de Linde mentioned that during the next three days they were partaking of the boundless hospitality of Dr. Franklin and others; and he was sure that Dr. Franklin would take it as a very great compliment if they sent up to him a large donation to their Benevolent Association."

This appeal of mine simply worked wonders. Donations came pouring in from all sides. These were all handed to me in the first instance, when I had the pleasure of passing them on to Dr. Franklin, who in his turn (after himself adding a substantial cheque to this improvised collection) gave over the whole to the Hon. George Colville, our Honorary Secretary, to deal with in due course.

During the banquet our President (Sir William Plender), in the course of his speech, said "that a little learning is a dangerous thing. That reminds me of the story of a fond mother who had a large family. To her another child was born, in whom she was anxious that the clergyman of the parish should show a little interest. She said to him, 'You see, sir, he is our eighth child, so we will call him Octopus.'"

After the banquet there was a musical entertainment for the ladies in the drawing room, on the invitation of the Master and Mistress Cutler (Mr. and Mrs. Herbert Barber). Songs by Miss Eva Rich and Mr. William Foxon; musical sketches by Mr. Ernest Hastings. Accompanist, Mr. Edmund S. Skinner.

The fact that ladies honoured us by attending and sitting down to the banquet gave additional charm to our very pleasant social evening.

Friday, 30 September 1910.—10 a.m.: Visit to Messrs. Vickers, Son & Maxim's works, or Messrs. John Brown & Co.'s works. I attended the latter works, very much enjoying everything I saw there. We were taken to and from in special tramcars.

1.15 p.m.: Luncheon at the Cutlers' Hall, on the invitation of the Sheffield members, my friend, Alderman George Franklin, presiding.

2.30 p.m.: Visit to the works of Messrs. Walker & Hall or to Messrs. Mappin & Webb, Limited. I attended the latter works under the personal care of my esteemed friends, Mr. W. Holmes and Mr. J. W. Merryweather, who both looked after me splendidly. After seeing the works my friends took me to the Weston Park Museum and to the Mappin Art Gallery, both most interesting, after which, at 4.30 p.m., I attended afternoon tea at the University, on the invitation of Alderman George Franklin, LITT.D. (Pro-Chancellor), and Mrs. Franklin, both very old and valued friends of mine. My host (the Pro-Chancellor) himself very kindly took me round and showed me everything of interest.

That evening I attended his dinner at the Grand Hotel, when he entertained the members of the Council and a few friends. Early that evening, prior to the function that followed, namely, 8.30 p.m., At Home at the Town Hall, on the invitation of the Lord Mayor (the Right Hon. Earl Fitzwilliam, D.S.O., and the Lady Mayoress. Her Ladyship being, however, indisposed that evening, her place was taken by Mrs. George Franklin, who discharged her duties admirably.

There was dancing to the accompaniment of the band of the Fourth Hallamshire Battalion of the York and Lancaster Regiment. The music, too, was very good. Refreshments were provided in the ladies' drawing room, while supper was held in the Council Chamber. The whole function was simply brilliant; hospitality was extended with a generous hand. The flowers and plants lavishly adorning the entrance hall, noble massive marble staircase, corridors, and rooms gave a most entrancing effect to the whole bright scene of splendour.

Saturday, 10 October 1910.—At 9 a.m. prompt we left the Cutlers' Arms for an excursion by coach to Ashopton, and thence to Castleton, visiting the Peak Cavern, and returning to Bamford for lunch; a very charming excursion indeed, full of interest connected with "Peveril of the Peak" by Sir Walter Scott. Then at 2.30 p.m. we had lunch at the Marquis of Granby Hotel, Bamford, on the invitation of the Sheffield members, Alderman George Franklin presiding. At 4.15 p.m. afternoon tea was served on the lawn of the hotel, and the return to Sheffield was made at 5.30 p.m. via Hathersage and Fox House. I rode back with my old friends, Mr. and Mrs. William Holmes, who very kindly took me back to their home to dinner.

Our second function was a banquet given 18 July 1911 by the London members of the Institute, at the Guildhall, in celebration of the Coronation of His Majesty King George V. President, Sir William Plender.

Our guests included the Right Honourable Earl Brassey, G.C.B., the Right Honourable Winston S. Churchill, M.P., the Right Honourable Lord Justice Sir John Fletcher Moulton, the Right Honourable the Earl of Halsbury, and Sir Francis C. Gould.

All these gentlemen spoke at the banquet. The speech of the Earl of Halsbury, who evidently thoroughly enjoyed himself, was most brilliant, while that of Sir Francis C. Gould simply sparkled with bright wit.

We had a splendid programme of music, provided by the band of the Royal Regiment of Artillery, finishing up with "*God Save the King.*"

The Guildhall makes a noble banqueting hall, with the monuments of Nelson, Wellington, and Chatham at one end, while at the other end, opposite, are the monuments of Beckford and Pitt.

On Wednesday, 19 July 1911, from 9 to 12 p.m., there was a Conversazione at the Natural History Museum, South Kensington—a very brilliant function. We had the same military band as on the previous evening, while in the Shell Gallery there was, at 9.30 p.m., a vocal and instrumental concert of a bright, sparkling nature.

Light refreshments were served at the various buffets in the North and South Corridors. Altogether this conversazione was a great success, ladies being present, whereas on the evening previous only gentlemen attended the banquet.

The third function to which I now propose drawing attention has reference to the Autumnal Meeting held at Leeds 9, 10, and 11 October 1913, under the auspices of the Leeds and District Society of Chartered Accountants (President Mr. John Gordon, F.C.A.). The following is the programme :—

Thursday, 9 October 1913.—11 a.m.: Reception at the Philosophical Hall by the Right Hon. the Lord Mayor (A. W. Bain, Esq.), and the Presidential address; vote of thanks being duly proposed and seconded.

1 p.m.: Luncheon at the Great Northern Hotel, on the invitation of the local members, Mr. John Gordon, F.C.A., presiding.

At the meeting that morning I had mentioned to Mr. Gordon the claims of our Benevolent Fund upon its members, asking him at the same time to say a word in its favour. He promised me he would do his best if I would leave it to him.

Judge, then, of my surprise when, at the lunch, Mr. Gordon, who presided, rose and in most eloquent terms pleaded the cause of the Chartered Accountants' Benevolent Association, at the same time handing me his own cheque for £100. The effect was simply magical. Right and left contributions kept pouring in, which were handed over to me, and which I duly passed on to our Honorary Secretary.

After lunch two papers were read, but as I had my nephew Freddie with me we slipped out quietly to pay a pilgrimage to Kirkstall Abbey, a venerable old pile.

On our return to the Queen's Hotel, where we were stopping, a letter was handed me from Mr. John Gordon inviting me to an early dinner at the Queen's to meet a few friends, so, letting Freddie dine by himself in the coffee room, I accepted. It was a very genial function, which I thoroughly enjoyed.

8.30 p.m.: Reception at the Leeds City Art Gallery, on the invitation of the Right Hon. the Lord Mayor and the Lady Mayoress (Mr. and Mrs. A. W. Bain). It was a splendid affair, everything very choice and in first-rate taste.

Friday, 10 October 1913.—10 a.m.: Special train to Harrogate, and thence by motors, leaving Harrogate at 10 a.m. for Ripon.

11.30 a.m.: Personally conducted over Ripon Minster by Mr. E. W. Winser, the Dean's Verger.

12.30 p.m.: Luncheon at the Spa Hotel, Ripon, on the invitation of the local members, my old friend, Mr. J. Hartley Blackburn, presiding.

1.30 p.m.: Motors to Fountains Abbey, personally conducted and described by Mr. W. Wainwright, returning to Ripon afterwards, where, at 4 o'clock, we had afternoon tea in the lovely grounds of the Spa Hotel, Ripon.

4.30 p.m.: Motors to Ripon Station.

5.15 p.m.: Special train from Ripon to Leeds, which we reached in good time for the

7.30 p.m. banquet at the Queen's (my) Hotel, Mr. John Gordon presiding.

Sir George Alexander at the Grand Theatre, where seats were reserved for those ladies who preferred visiting the theatre instead of attending the banquet. The piece, called "Bella Donna," by Robert Hichens, proved a great success, as I was told.

Saturday, 11 October 1913.—9.30 a.m.: The choice of a visit to four different factories or a motor drive to Farnley Hall, Otley, where a fine collection of Turner's masterpieces may be seen. Needless to say we went to Farnley Hall, Otley, where we had a real treat, both in the motor drive through charming country and the grand old hall, with its priceless contents.

We motored back to Leeds in good time for 1.30 p.m. luncheon at the Hotel Metropole, on the invitation of the local members, Mr. George P. Norton presiding.

After lunch Freddie and I caught an afternoon train to Harrogate, putting up at the Prospect Hotel. Freddie just spent the week end there, but I stayed on a further week to drink the waters, have the baths, and enjoy the lovely motor drives all about.

I rather fancy that the reason Freddie made such a short visit was that the following (Sunday) morning, before breakfast, I beguiled him to drink, on an empty stomach, a tumbler of hot, strong sulphur water, which nearly settled him. I revel in it. I find that that water taken twice during the morning, and followed in the afternoon by a tumbler of magnesia water, just suits me, but Freddie thought otherwise, and consequently bolted incontinently.

I am very fond of the old-fashioned four-horse coach drives. One of my favourites is :—

Leaving	Hotel Victoria, Northumberland Avenue	10.25 a.m.
,,	Broadway, Hammersmith	10.55 ,,
,,	The King's Head, Roehampton (change horses)	11.20 ,,
,,	The Griffin, Kingston	11.45 ,,
,,	The Bear, Esher (change horses) ..	12.15 p.m.
,,	The White Lion, Cobham	12.35 ,,
,,	The Talbot, Ripley	1.5 ,,
,,	The Lion, Guildford	1.4 ,,

A distance of 29 miles, or of 58 miles there and back.

We have lunch at the Lion, Guildford, starting back the same way as we came at 3.10 p.m., stopping for ten minutes at 4.45 p.m. at the Bear, Esher, for afternoon tea, while we changed horses, and reaching the Hotel Victoria at 6.30 p.m. sharp. I strolled over to Charing Cross Station, where I took a train to Cannon Street, changing there into the 7.28 p.m. for Reigate, getting home comfortably to supper at 9 p.m., after a delightful day's excursion, which I can thoroughly recommend. The coach is called the " New Times." Its proprietors are my old friends, Messrs. Wimbush and Co., Limited.

I had given a copy of my work, "Bookkeeping," to the London manager of a Japanese firm, whose head office was in Tokio, Japan, where the firm had been established over 200 years. This gentleman sent my book to his firm out there. A few months after he came round to my office to say that two of the partners were on their way to this country, and were expected to arrive in London the following week, when he wanted to bring them on to my office to make my acquaintance. As soon as they saw me they told me how much they had benefited by perusing my book, so much so that they had come over on purpose to adopt the principles advocated by me in it—namely, the system of double entry in lieu of single entry.

They then asked me to make it a matter of business to go round to their London office and remodel their books upon that basis, which I did, the two Tokio partners and their London manager closely watching my procedure throughout. When they returned to Japan they took back with them full specimens of the improved system. This enabled them to start their books out there upon the same basis, which they did, to their entire satisfaction.

After having lived over 20 years at "Glebe Knoll," Bromley, Kent, we moved, on 29 September 1909, to our present house, "Beech Hill House," Reigate Hill, Surrey, beautifully situated right among the Surrey Hills, with grand views all round, including Leith Hill and Box Hill. We often go over Leith Hill, standing 1,000 feet high; it is the highest hill in the south-east of England. From the summit the whole circumference of the horizon exceeds 200 miles. In 1844 the

Ordnance surveyors counted the spires of 41 London churches. Ships, too, can be seen out at sea through Shoreham Gap. At the foot of the hill is a comfortable inn, where you can get afternoon tea out in the open. At Burford Bridge, adjoining Box Hill, there is an excellent inn belonging to the Surrey Trust, where we have either lunch or afternoon tea, the latter on the lawn. We generally take a day, driving over in an open carriage and pair, past King's Wood and Walton Heath. The descent down from there over Box Hill to Burford Bridge is truly romantic; it is called "Little Switzerland." Our recreation ground is on the site of old Reigate Castle, underneath which are wonderful caves, called "The Barons' Caves," for it was there that "Magna Charta" was drawn up by the Barons, who presented it later to King John for signature at Runnymeade. Our house and grounds stand on high ground (420 feet above sea level). We are just under the "Pilgrims' Way" and Colley Hill, recently acquired by the town in perpetuity, in the same way as Box Hill has been presented to the county by a generous benefactor (Mr. Goldschmidt).

We have two disused old windmills on Reigate Heath. One is on the golf links; the interior is now used every Sunday for Church of England service, being fitted up for that purpose with pulpit, Communion table, benches and chairs; in fact, all complete.

On Kingswood, about two miles from our house, on the borders of Walton Heath, is the celebrated Greek Church, the gift of Dr. Edwin Freshfield, with Church of England service twice every Sunday, Dr. Freshfield generally reading the lessons. It is a magnificent structure, replete with valuable mementoes brought over from the East by the learned Doctor. Whenever I have visitors to " Beech Hill House " I make a point of taking them to all these places of interest in our neighbourhood and around.

Another charming excursion is to the Silent Pool. Shirebourne Pond is its old name, which is, after all, best; it is identified with Shere, the prettiest of all the Surrey villages. The old White Horse Inn has a splendid fireplace, with iron dogs for a wood fire, and cosy seats inside the chimney, quite in the olden style. We often have afternoon tea there, or else at Gomshall, another of the Surrey Trust Inns, with wide verandahs and a fine lawn.

I lived 40 years in Kent (20 at Bexley Heath and 20 at Bromley). I then used to consider Kent the county par excellence, but since I moved to Reigate in 1909 I have had to change my allegiance in favour of Surrey, an ideal county, with its hills, dales, and large open commons in every direction.

Our favourite seaside resorts at home are Deal, Westgate-on-Sea, Bexhill, St. Leonards-on-Sea, and Herne Bay, with convenient golf links at each place. Until recently, and when we lived at Bromley, I thought nothing of cycling to all these places. By making an early start from home I managed the run comfortably in the one day, with a good hour at least for lunch. We hired a furnished bungalow one winter at Westgate-on-Sea, taking our servants and " Master Scamp " with us.

He got to be knowing in the way of electric trams, jumping on them up to the top of his own accord. The conductors all knew him, so when he came up they were on the look-out for us to follow.

When we stayed at Bexhill-on-Sea we often cycled over to Pevensey Bay, with its fine old castle, an imposing ruin. In the village is the old Mint House, containing an interesting collection of curiosities, some of them really unique of their kind.

In the autumn of 1909 I paid a visit to Eugene Sandow in St. James's Street, who beguiled me into paying a year's subscription to his famous institution, giving me the right to 52 visits during the year, whenever I was free to go there. The course was somewhat trying, but I think it did me good, on the whole.

In November, 1909, we spent a fortnight with some friends at Llanishen, near Cardiff, where I again got good golf. My friends took me to their respective clubs at Cardiff, the University and the County, paying me, as usual, every kind attention. On our return we all went for a month to the Riviera. On our way we stopped a couple of days at the celebrated Hotel de la Cloche, Dijon, where we are well known, always getting our same bedrooms, with private bath rooms attached.

Dijon (formerly the capital of Burgundy) is a most interesting old city. The Hotel de Ville, the ancient Palace of the Dukes of Burgundy, contains a wonderful museum and picture gallery. The collection of pictures is of rare excellence; in fact, it is one of the best provincial ones in France. The antiquities and archives are also very fine. In "la Salle des Gardes" are two splendid marble tombs of Philippe le Hardi and of Jean Sans Peur (his son).

Close by is the Church of Notre Dame, of the thirteenth century, with a three-storied porch. The old clock bears the date of 1383.

The Botanical Garden and the Public Park are both well kept up; they form an agreeable promenade.

After leaving Dijon we stopped first at the Hotel Terminus, Marseilles, where we were very comfortable, and from there we went on to the Grand Hotel, Grasse, where we were most uncomfortable, so we very soon moved down to l'Hotel Prince de Galles, at Cannes, a first-rate hotel, full south, in a large sunny park, beautifully situated. The hotel is well sheltered, and quite up to date. There are good golf links at Cannes belonging to the Grand Duke Michael of Russia, but I did not play on them; there was so much to interest us the fortnight we were there. From there we moved on to Mentone Garavan, putting up at the Hotel de Belle Vue. The hotel was crowded, but some friends living close by just managed to secure us very comfortable rooms, where the proprietor, Mr. Churchman, looked after us splendidly, giving us a good suite of rooms on the first floor, with a large sitting room in it, where we always burnt a bright wood fire. I practised my Sandow exercises on the floor, as I was keen to get on with them.

Mentone is simply perfect. We revelled in the place and its surroundings. We spent Christmas Day and New Year's Day there, starting back the following Monday, 3 January 1910, and reaching home the evening of Thursday, 6th.

My nephew and I caught, on Friday 4 February, the "*Orsova*" (12,036 tons) steamer from Tilbury, landing us at Naples Saturday, 12th. On Monday afternoon, 14th, we caught the "*Sardegna*" (6,000 tons), arriving Genoa 7 o'clock on the morning of Wednesday, 16th. Our steamer waited the afternoon of the previous day (Tuesday, 15th) at Leghorn, where we went ashore. We had a grand drive all along the sea front, having afternoon tea there. The hotel where we had it rooked us so shamefully that for once we were disgusted. This was quite a novel experience, for as a rule we find Italian hotel keepers most reasonable and obliging. We went on by our steamer to Genoa, whence we caught a morning train to Milan. From Milan we visited Lake Maggiore, stopping at a small hotel by the landing stage, for, being out of the season, the regular hotels were not open. We had a splendid time at Verona (Grand Hotel de Londres et Royal deux Tours), and from there on to our dear old Grand Hotel, Venice. From there, via Monfalcone, we went on to the Hotel de la Ville Trieste. The new one, Excelsior Palace Hotel, was in course of construction; as soon as it opened we went to it. It is indeed palatial.

From there we went on to Gratz (Hotel Erzeherzog Johann), and thence to Vienna. We put up at the Grand Hotel, but were so very uncomfortably neglected that we moved to the Hotel Angst, where we could not be better, and have been there ever since. The present war between Italy and Austria is especially interesting to us. We know so many of the places mentioned in the despatches such as Riva, Udine, Monfalcone, Nabresina, Trieste, Laibach, Gratz, and Vienna. On our way to Vienna we stopped a couple of nights at Semmering (Hotel Sudbahn). It is a favourite resort both in summer and winter, amidst grand scenery. We made some very fine hilly excursions during the week end we were there.

Before I forget it I want to mention a fine steamer excursion we took one summer on the River Danube. We left the train from Nurnberg one afternoon at Passan, where at 3 o'clock we boarded our steamer, passing on our way the famous Gorge and reaching Linz that evening at 6.35, putting up at the Hotel Erzherzog-Karl, where we were very comfortable. It is a magnificent city, the capital of Upper Austria.

The next morning we caught the 9 o'clock steamer, reaching Vienna at 5.50 p.m., sleeping there. The following morning we caught the 7 o'clock steamer, reaching Budapest, the capital of Hungary, at 8 p.m. We put up at the Hotel Hungaria, a big, showy place, but full of discomforts, attendance wretched, and charges exorbitant. The next morning we explored this fine old city, and after lunch at the railway station, the restaurant of which is excellent, we caught the 2 p.m. train back, reaching Vienna at 6.25 p.m. It was a restaurant corridor train, so we were able to get afternoon tea on board.

That spring trip my nephew and I, being at the time in Switzerland, quite handy, broke off to visit my wife and daughter at the Pelerin Palace Hotel, Mont Pelerin (3,855 feet above sea level). The country all around is very fine. We spent Easter there, and then resumed and went on to the Jura and Vosges Mountains, returning via Paris, where I met my wife and daughter, reaching home Thursday, 7 April 1910.

Near Redhill is Fronsham, the smallest model village in England. The Philanthropic Schools occupy the whole site. It is just a toy village, with a miniature church, windmill, and railway station, also a canal which turns the mill. The canal has a lock. Everything complete, in fact.

On Monday, 12 December 1910, I took my wife and daughter out to Vevey, putting up at the Park Hotel, Mooser, our usual comfortable headquarters, where I stayed over Christmas and the New Year with them. When I left they went on to Chateau d'Oex, taking up with them two sledges, a pair of skis, and a pair of skates for the winter sports there.

On Friday, 27 January 1911, I gave my annual dinner at the Trocadero to my office staff.

My fellows are great adepts in getting up a musical entertainment on these occasions, so that we always spend a pleasant evening together.

That summer my nephew and I reached Hotel Metropole, Salo, on the Lago di Garda, on Monday, 21 August 1911, where we stayed till the following Friday, 25th. The whole of this lake is Italian except the extreme northern portion, Riva, which is Austrian. Riva possesses a splendid hotel on the shores of the lake, the Lido Palace Hotel. We took the day steamer there from Salo, had lunch, and then returned by the steamer. We were so impressed with Riva and its excellent hotel that we went there the following spring. It is open from 15 February to 15 November. We got there on

Sunday, 3 March 1912, staying on till Friday, 8th, when we went on via Mari to the Tiroler Hof, Innsbruck, a favourite hotel of mine. The landlord, Mr. C. Landsee, is an old friend. He is the principal shareholder in the hotel at Riva; in fact, it was there that we came across him, travelling on with him to Innsbruck.

I went out again about the middle of April, 1912, and joined my ladies at Chateau d'Oex.

CHAPTER XXV.

Chateaux d'Oex, Basle, Heidelberg, Baden Baden, Wiesbaden, The Rhine to Cologne, Amsterdam, The Hague, and Brussels.

THE Hotel de l'Ours at Chateau d'Oex is thoroughly good; it is opposite the Post Office, and adjoins the railway station. We stayed on there till the 30th April, when we took the restaurant 12.6 p.m. train, reaching Basle that evening at 7.35, putting up at the celebrated Hotel des Trois Rois, kept by my old friend, Mr. L. A. Bossi, who gave us splendid rooms on the first floor, including a private bath room. After staying there a couple of days we went on to the Pension Nagel, Baden Baden, a poor place, where we just managed to exist. Baden Baden itself is a fine city, with grand promenades and drives in the lovely country around. We found it, however, very relaxing. From there we went on the Schloss Hotel, Heidelberg, an old favourite of mine, where we simply revelled in the lap of luxury. Being on very high ground, we soon forgot our Baden Baden feelings of languor. We took lovely excursions over the hills, generally finding a welcome "restauration" at the top, as usual.

From there we went on to the Hotel Metropole, Wiesbaden, where we got splendid rooms, with private bath rooms attached. The water is supplied by the celebrated

Kochbrunnen Bad. I took my ladies a lovely carriage drive on the Neroberg, a grand place for a fine view all round. We stayed at Wiesbaden till Wednesday morning, 15 May 1912, when we took the 9.25 a.m. Rhine steamer from Biebrich to Cologne (4.45 p.m.). It was a perfect day, so that my ladies thoroughly enjoyed being on deck the whole time, except for table d'hôte lunch, feasting their eyes on the lovely scenery on all sides. We put up, as usual, at the comfortable Hotel du Nord, where my old friend, Mr. Friederichs, had reserved us extra fine quiet rooms overlooking the lovely garden, where we had afternoon tea, taking dinner on the sheltered terrace overlooking the garden.

The next day, Thursday, 16th, being Ascension Day, we attended morning service in the English church standing in the grounds of the hotel.

We left Cologne on Friday, 17th, by the 10.6 a.m. restaurant car, arriving that afternoon at 2.53 at the Central Station, Amsterdam. At the Dutch frontier, Livenaar, where the luggage is examined, the Custom House officer, seeing our name, "van de Linde," on our eight pieces, touched his hat, passing everything unopened. He also saw us into a comfortable first-class compartment, which he ordered to be kept reserved for us. At Amsterdam we put up at my old Amstel Hotel, where excellent sunny rooms, facing the River Amstel, had been reserved for us.

The following morning, Saturday, 18th, we took an open carriage and drove round the city, visiting the Niewe Kerk, a Gothic edifice dating from 1408, and after that the Oude Kerk, dating from 1300. Then Het Paleis (the Royal Palace), erected in 1648.

We then went over the Ryks Museum, with the picture gallery on the first floor, full of the masterpieces of Rembrandt, Rubens, Jan Steen, Gérard Dow, Paul Potter, Bakhuisen, Van de Velde, Wouverman, Ruysdael, A. Cuyp, A. Vàn Ostade, Hobbema, F. Hals, and other celebrated artists. After that the Fodor Museum, with a unique collection by French masters, such as by Meissonier, Ary Scheffer, Rosa Bonheur, Decamps, and others. This collection, with the exception of that at The Hague, is the finest in Holland.

In the afternoon we took the steamer to Zaandam, a busy town on the River Zaan, with the houses painted either green or red. Innumerable windmills are very conspicuous. It was here that we saw the hut of Peter the Great, where, taking the name of Peter Michaeloff, this young Czar lived for about a week in 1697, while he worked as a carpenter in the shipyard of Mynheer Kalf.

The next morning, Sunday, 19th, we attended at 10 o'clock English Episcopal Church service. In the afternoon we went out to call on some Dutch friends. Monday, 20th, my ladies devoted to shopping in the morning. In the afternoon I took them for a grand drive through the Vondelspark, and then on to the Zoological Gardens and to the Botanic Gardens, finishing up with afternoon tea at the Paviljoen Café.

Tuesday, 21 May, we caught an early steamer for a day's excursion on the Zuyder Zee, having lunch on deck at the stern, and very good it was too. We landed at Volendam. From there we steamed on to the Island of Marken, where my daughter took some excellent snapshots of some fisherfolk (male and female), attired in their quaint costumes. They were all ready grouped waiting to be photographed *for a consideration,* the fact being that in this way they make a lot out of tourists. The women's attire, with their caps with turned-up corners and golden ornaments, is singularly picturesque, as also is that of the men, who wear coloured knickerbockers made very full, and quaint, broad, blue caps, with a button on the top.

Their sleeping accommodation is a mystery. It mostly consists of a cupboard in the wall, with drawers where the beds are laid. We then steamed on to Edam, where we went over a cheese factory, investing in two of the celebrated Edamer cheeses, which we took home with us. We also touched at Monnickendam, finishing up with Broek. This last named village has such a reputation for cleanliness in the past that its present inhabitants are ever in a state of fever to live up to it. It is really more like a toy town than a real home for serious folk. The main streets are spotlessly clean, for no horses or cattle are allowed there; a bar prevents them from entering at either end. No one may smoke a pipe or a cigar in the streets for fear of the ashes dropping. No one enters a house in his boots, so a collection of sabots and shoes are seen outside the doors. Should a banana skin or a leaf be dropped some one at once picks the same up, to be thrown in the canal. The doors of the houses are left open to display a goodly array of shining pots within, the bright tiles, and the spotless tablecloths.

The next afternoon, Wednesday, 22 May, we had tea with some friends, and then took the 5.15 p.m. fast train bringing us to The Hague at 6.6 p.m., where we put up at le Vieux Doelen Hotel, where my father and I lodged in 1852, the old hotel porter well remembering our name. He is part proprietor, and practically bosses the show, including the visitors, who must obey him.

We stayed at The Hague till the following Tuesday, 28 May, spending a very happy time visiting the wonderful picture gallery, Koninklyk Kabinet van Schilderyen, with free admission everywhere.

Rembrandt stands first in the collection, then Paul Potter, with his far-famed bull, the most popular picture in the whole collection. After that what struck us most were the masterpieces of Gérard Dow in Room VIII, No. 28, "The Young Housekeeper," a lady with a child in the cradle, and an attendant. This work, also known as "The Household," is one of the gems in the collection. It is dated 1658. Also No. 29 in the same room, and by the same master, "Woman with a Lamp." The light cast upon the scene by the lamp is simply realistically marvellous.

The collection is housed in twelve rooms, every one of them full of priceless masterpieces.

One of our favourite excursions was by steam tram to Scheveningen, the fashionable Dutch watering place. I far prefer it in every respect to its Belgian rival, Ostend.

It was in 1673 that Admiral de Ruyter defeated the united fleets of England and France off the coast near Scheveningen.

A friend drove us out into the country and showed us his wonderful flower gardens of choice tulips and other bulbs in full bloom. He is a wholesale tulip grower, but he told me he could not sell me any bulbs direct;

he could only sell through the trade. We spent a very pleasant afternoon at Leyden, visiting the University and the Club Minerva. In my library I have a large engraving of this celebrated club, with my father standing full face on the right, talking to his friend, Heinrick Veder, brother of Aart Veder, who also comes out very prominently in the centre of the engraving.

As I have already mentioned in the early part of this book, our visit both to the University and to the Club was a gala day for both the students and ourselves. The students were simply frantic with delight at entertaining us.

We left The Hague in the morning for Rotterdam, leaving our luggage at the Delft Railway Station. There we took an open carriage, and were driven along De Boompjes, the broad quay on the River Maas, to the Park close to the river, then on to the Botanical and the Zoological Gardens, all three in their prime. We then visited de Groote Kerk (Church of St. Lawrence) and Bowman's Museum, where we saw a fine collection of pictures by old and modern Dutch masters. We were then driven to the station, where we lunched in the restaurant, catching the 2.39 p.m. train to Brussels, arriving there at the Nord Station at 5.56 p.m., where the hotel omnibus took us to the Grand Hotel.

The next morning, Wednesday, 29 May, we visited some friends in l'Avenue Louise, who took us for a drive in their automobile to La Bois de la Cambre. They saw us off by the 11.20 a.m. train (Midi Station), whence, after lunching in the train, we reached Calais (Gare Maritime) at 3.21 p.m., putting up for the night at the Hotel Terminus.

The next morning, Thursday, 30 May, we went all over the quaint old city, catching the 3.45 p.m. steamer, which landed us at 5 p.m. at Dover, where we stopped the night at The Lord Warden Hotel, having our comfortable old rooms.

On Friday morning, 31 May 1912, we caught the 11.5 through train to Redhill, reaching there at 1.4 p.m., where a carriage and pair and a cart for our luggage met us. We reached home at 1.30 p.m., just in time for lunch.

On Thursday morning, 6 June 1912, we all three went up the river by Salter's steam launch to Oxford and back, reaching home the following Wednesday, 12th, in time for dinner.

The following Saturday morning, 15 June, I had a fall and broke my arm. Our local medico, my dear friend Dr. Gilbert, assisted by the expert surgeon, Dr. Johnston, set it very skilfully, making me keep my bed for the following twelve days, when by special favour they allowed me to get up that afternoon to assist entertaining the inmates of the Brabazon Home of Rest, who came over in two large brakes to spend the afternoon and have tea on our lawn.

I entered so fully into the spirit of the whole thing that I forgot all about my broken arm, and walked about the whole afternoon and evening with our interesting visitors, who on arrival, soon after 3 p.m., were grouped on the lawn and photographed. I sat in the middle with my dear old dog "Scamp" in my arms.

This has become ever since an annual treat for us, for we do indeed esteem it a great privilege to entertain them.

On Thursday, 1 August 1912, I saw my wife and daughter off by the 1.20 p.m. train from Euston. They reached Holyhead at 6.55 p.m., sleeping at the Station Hotel there, having their regular rooms, 61 and 62. Next day they caught the 2.5 p.m. mail steamer, arriving at Kingstown 5 p.m., where Sir Robert and Lady Gardner met them and drove them to Killiney, close by, where they stayed a month as the guests of our kind friends.

CHAPTER XXVI.

PORT SAID, CAIRO, BATH ON RETURN.

MY nephew and I slept that Thursday night at the St. Pancras Hotel, leaving next morning, Friday, 2 August, by special train for Tilbury, whence we embarked on the "*Orsova*" for Port Said, *en route* for Cairo (Shepheard's Hotel), my nephew and I each having a comfortable cabin to ourselves on the C. deck.

On the steamer we got to be very friendly with Dr. Percy Wilde, the eminent specialist, of Bath, a great personal friend both of Dr. Gilbert and Dr. Johnston.

Seeing that I was still more or less seedy, he moved to our table and looked after me thoroughly. He went on with us to Cairo, putting up at Shepheard's Hotel, and doing the Pyramids with my nephew.

He then returned with us by the Italian steamer "*Syracusa*" to Genoa, calling on the way at Syracuse, Catania, Messina (after the earthquake of 28 December, 1908, a perfect scene of desolation still), Naples, and Leghorn. At Genoa Dr. Wilde went on with us to Milan, putting up at the Hotel Continental. He stayed on with us there till Saturday, 24 August 1912, when, seeing that I looked more myself again, he left us to go on by ourselves to Venice, while he went home by the Simplon route.

I discovered afterwards by the merest accident that he bossed the private hospital and nursing home, "Lansdown Grove House," Bath, so by the advice of Dr. Gilbert (after reaching home from the Continent on Wednesday, 25 September 1912—my ladies returning from Ireland the following afternoon), I started with my nephew Freddie on Saturday, 28 September, reaching Bath that afternoon. Dr. Wilde met us at the station and drove us to the Home, where he gave me Room No. 28 on the ground floor, overlooking the garden, where I stayed till Monday, 4 November. I then went home for a fortnight, returning with my wife and daughter Tuesday, 19 November, where we stayed till Tuesday, 17 December 1912, when we all three returned home, wonderfully recuperated by our visit to Bath, under the personal supervision of Dr. Percy Wilde and his partner, Dr. Beville. While I was down there Dr. Gilbert and Dr. Johnston came down to see me, so there was a consultation of four learned sympathetic doctors over me. While at Bath I motored over with a lady patient on Tuesday, 22 October, to the Bristol Musical Festival at Colston Hall, where we had the grand oratorio of "*Elijah,*" and on the following Friday, 25th, I again motored over with Nurse Alice (Dr. Wilde's lady housekeeper), when we had Wagner's "*Siegfried.*" On both occasions we lunched very comfortably on arrival at the St. Stephen's Restaurant at 12 noon, before the oratorios, having tea there afterwards before we returned to Bath.

The drives about Bath are simply grand. I used to have treatment in the morning and drive out in the afternoon, just as I do when I am at Harrogate.

We got to know some very nice people at Bath, among others Major and Mrs. Aikenhead, Mr. and Mrs. Jones, Mrs. Champney, and the Rev. Charles Green, all patients at the Home. I also got to be very friendly with the Reverend L. J. Fish, Archdeacon of Bath and Rector of the Parish Church of St. Stephen's close by.

The year 1913 was more or less uneventful. My nephew and I did our usual half-yearly trip, starting on 31 January in the "*Osterley,*" and on 1 August in the "*Orvieto,*" from Tilbury to Naples. When we reached the Hotel du Nord, Cologne, on 20 September, the head porter, Herr Bruno Urban, showed us the German Emperor's silver medal which His Imperial Majesty had bestowed upon him for 30 years' faithful continuous service at the hotel. As a token of my personal esteem, having known him well over a quarter of a century, if not more, I bestowed upon him the *gold* medal of our gracious King George V., which I believe he prizes far more than the other medal, for, strange to say, the Germans, high and low, do not esteem their own Imperial Royal Family as we do our Royal Family; in fact, taking very little interest in all that concerns the German Emperor and his belongings.

On 30 January 1914 my nephew and I left Tilbury for Naples in the "*Orama,*" when all went well, as usual.

On Thursday, 23 July, we again entertained the inmates of the Brabazon Home of Rest, as we had done annually previously, while on Thursday, 30 July, we entertained the children of the Ward Convalescent Home, taking a photographic group of them on our lawn, with myself in the middle and my dear old "Scamp" on my knees, as usual. It was a very happy afternoon, the dear children enjoying themselves thoroughly, as did we also.

CHAPTER XXVII.

"OTWAY" TO GIBRALTAR, THENCE PER "MOLDAVIA" BACK.

I HAD to leave them at 5.40 p.m. to catch my 6.2 p.m. train to London, as I was dining and sleeping that night at the St. Pancras Hotel, catching on the Friday morning, 31 July, the "*Otway*" steamer for Naples, an eventful trip indeed, for when we reached Gibraltar on Tuesday, 4 August 1914, we found war had been declared, so that we could go no further, nor were we even allowed to land or leave our steamer. Each evening the Admiralty yacht came round with the latest news, for as soon as we reached Gibraltar our own Marconi communication was cut off.

We were kept three days at Gibraltar, during which time we had the felicity of seeing various German ships brought in as prizes.

On Friday, 7 August, we were suddenly transhipped on to the P. & O. steamer "*Moldavia*," where I had a small single cabin, No. 7, allotted to me for that night, but the next morning I was changed into a large double cabin (berths 8 and 9), a great improvement. Before the "*Moldavia*" would take any of us on board they made the purser of the "*Otway*" hand them over several carcases of meat (beef and mutton). They also required payment in cash (notes or gold) for our passage money, absolutely refusing to take any cheque. Fortunately I had by me an ample supply of notes and gold, so I was not only able to pay my nephew's and my fare, but also turn banker for two or three passengers, giving them ready cash in exchange for their cheques.

We were somewhat startled on reading the following notice prominently posted up on the various green notice boards of our steamer :—" NOTICE.—The night current of lights on deck and in the public rooms will only be in use to-night and throughout the ship. Passengers are requested to screen off the cabin scuttles on the outside windows of their cabin" ; while a second notice was posted up restricting the food, observing the greatest economy, so as to be prepared for every eventuality, as it would be impossible to obtain more.

Considering that we had only just taken on board from the "*Otway*" an enormous quantity of frozen carcases, we were somewhat at a loss to know what it all meant. However, on reaching Lisbon shortly after we found that Portugal had unreservedly declared itself for the Allies, so that both these notices suddenly disappeared, and nothing further of a disquieting nature was put up in their place.

Soon after passing Lisbon we were held up by a French cruiser, who demanded to see our ship's papers. As my nephew spoke French he was asked to go alongside to help our officers explain matters, which he did.

When the French naval officers found we were all right they ordered their band to play "God Save the King," at the same time shaking our officers and my nephew warmly by the hand. They then told us that only two hours before they had held up a steamer flying the P. & O. flag and painted exactly to imitate one of these steamers, but when she was overhauled it was discovered that it was a German armed cruiser sailing under false colours, and for which it was captured as a prize.

So long as I put my own full name and address, as also those of the recipients (a rather costly affair), I was able while waiting at Gibraltar to telegraph regularly home and to receive replies in exchange. But when I transhipped to the "*Moldavia*" and wished to do the same my telegram was refused; I was told that telegrams could not be accepted from the "*Moldavia,*" as she was homeward bound from the East. Just then a ship's officer came up and said, "But Mr. van de Linde is not from the East; he has just come off the '*Otway,*' as you ought to know, having already sent off several of his telegrams." This put everything all right, and my message went off. Just as the "*Moldavia*" was casting off from the "*Otway*" my steward brought me a final telegram from home, saying that they were much relieved on receiving mine, and that they were all well.

We reached Plymouth all right, where several of the passengers disembarked, returning to London by special train. My nephew and I stayed, however, on the "*Moldavia,*" going up with her to her final destination, Tilbury, as I wired my people. We were to have left that night again, but were delayed, having the Indian mail on board, which was very heavy, so we only got off late the next morning.

At midnight a squad of soldiers and an officer boarded us and took off two German spies. The soldiers held loaded pistols to their heads while they were disarmed of a loaded revolver which each was found to carry in his hip pocket. They were given ten minutes to pack up (the loaded pistols still at their heads); they were then handcuffed and taken ashore.

The next morning our skipper pointed out to us some German prizes that had been brought into the harbour. The following morning we landed at Tilbury, where our luggage (bearing the "*Otway*" labels) was not examined. We went up to Fenchurch Street by a special train, and got back home safe and sound for 1.30 p.m. dinner.

I found that already two Belgian Refuges were started in Reigate. I went to see them, taking the men pipes, tobacco, and cigarettes, and to the women plum cakes and sweets.

CHAPTER XXVIII.

Red Cross Hospitals at Reigate.

TWO Red Cross hospitals were also being started, one "Highfield," a big mansion lent by a lady, in which she also became a hospital nurse. This cost the town £50 a week to run. Of this the War Office contributed 14s. a head a week for the 50 patients, making £35, leaving only £15 a week to find, and this we (the inhabitants) raised among ourselves.

The other Red Cross hospital was the old "Ward Convalescent Home." The children had all been sent home, and the Hon. Mrs. John Ward was filling it up entirely at her own expense, not even receiving the Government grant.

Later on, when the patients came in, I was privileged to supply them with papers, books, "baccy," and limp Russia leather pocket Testaments. These latter I gave also to the nursing staff of both these hospitals. The number of Red Cross hospitals at Reigate is now increased to four, in all of which I take great interest. When I went to the office the next morning I found our office staff very much denuded; so many of our fellows had gone to the front. We found it difficult to replace them. However, those who stayed on (mostly married men with families) worked away with a will, and we were able to secure competent lady clerks to replace those who had gone.

On the afternoon of Tuesday, 29 September 1914, we were privileged to entertain a party of Belgian Refugees to tea and games on our lawn. My daughter kodaked us all in a group on our top lawn, with Colley Hill and the Pilgrims' Way as a background. My wife and I sat by each other in front, and I had, as usual, dear old "Scamp" on my knees.

It made a splendid group. All our guests looked so intelligent. I gave them each a copy.

On Friday, 2 October 1914, we went down to Sidmouth, where we found comfortable quarters on the sea front, and where we stayed till close upon Christmas, when we returned home just in time for me to send out some ten large Christmas cakes to the several local and other institutions in which we are interested. These were all very much appreciated.

CHAPTER XXIX.

Non-commissioned Officers Billeted on us.

On 2 January 1915 we had billeted upon us Sergeant William Ewart Goldring, Sergeant Arthur James Goldring, and Corporal Frederick Potter, all three of the 2/19th Battalion London Regiment. They stayed with us till 30 March 1915, and we were, indeed, very sorry when they had to leave us. They were all three real good fellows, with whom we all got to be very "pally." Just before they left, my daughter photographed us four (the three and myself) in my verandah —a very pleasing memento of their stay with us.

In the early part of last February, 1916, my firm was asked by a client to investigate a matter for him in Amsterdam, and my nephew and partner, Freddie van de Linde, arranged to take it up. But owing to stringent passport arrangements he was only ready to start by the end of the month, and then he received strict instructions from the Foreign Office not to take out any letters, notes, papers or written particulars of any description whatever. He secured his passage by the Dutch steamer "*Mechlenburg,*" first signing at the office of the Company a declaration that he travelled at his own risk and that the steamship company was in no way responsible for anything that might occur.

He went on board at Tilbury the evening of Saturday, 26 February 1916, but the steamer did not leave till 10 o'clock the next morning, Sunday, 27th. At about 12 noon she struck a mine, and in half an hour after went to the bottom. Fortunately a Holland-America steamer came alongside and rescued the passengers and crew, with part of their baggage.

The captain of the steamer first talked of taking them to New York, but he was stopped in time by a Marconi message from the Admiralty to put in at Deal, landing the passengers and crew there, which he did on the Monday morning, 29 February 1916. So "all's well that ends well," but rather a painful experience at the first.

Since Corporal Potter left us he has been busily engaged enlisting, having already secured 1,500 recruits. He recently sent me a splendid photographic group of his recruiting staff, with himself in the middle. On the top of the photograph is a large placard with the words:

"If you really want to smash up the Germans join the 19th.
There are still plenty of Germans left in Belgium,"

while at foot appeared the inscription:

"19th Batt. London Regt. Recruiting Staff."

They are indeed a splendid set of men, of whom Corporal Frederick Potter may well feel proud to work with.

Corporal Potter told me that the way they get to work is to perambulate during the day the streets with their band playing, and then stop all of a sudden and look up fixedly in the sky. This at once draws a crowd. They also in the evenings do a lot of recruiting from the platforms of various music halls. All this is hard work, for they begin at 9 in the morning, and seldom finish before midnight.

The officers, too, are simply splendid, taking such care of their men. We got to be very friendly with them all when they were billeted at Reigate.

In this connection I think the following comes in appropriately, and will be read with interest by my readers :—

"THE ACCOUNTANT," 30 JANUARY 1915.

NATIONAL HYMN.

(*To the Editor of The Accountant.*)

SIR,—I hope you will kindly find space to insert the enclosed in your this week's issue. Although composed in 1873 (forty-two years ago) it is so splendidly appropriate at the present day that it might well have been written only yesterday.

Your obedient servant,

GÉRARD VAN DE LINDE.

Reigate Hill, Surrey, 26th January 1915.

NATIONAL HYMN.

Written by request to music by Rossini, by Frances Ridley Havergal, Switzerland, 1873.

O Lord most high,
Who art God and Father,
Hear Thou our cry,
While Thy children gather!
Lord of Peace, oh hearken,
Though war clouds darken!
Do thou our labours bless,
And crown them with success!

Bend from Thy glory now,
Hear each suppliant vow!
And on our children pour
Blessings evermore.
Guarded by Thee,
England shall be
Bright in Thy light,
Strong in Thy might,
Glorious and free!

Hero and saint,
Victors at last,
Bid us not faint,
But follow, follow fast.
Make us we pray,
Loyal as they,
Faithful and brave,
Our country to save!

When in the grim fight,
Pierceth the dim light,
Through the cleft ranks that [shall close no more,
Fearfully flashing,
Awfully crashing,
Death-furrows follow the [cannon's roar.
When wounded lie,
Ready to die;
When death is braved,
That life may be saved;
Teach us to show
Mercy with might,
Pardon the foe,
Crown Thou the right!

Father, hear us!
Thou art near us!
Guard and cheer us
By Thy strong hand!
Thou art resplendent,
Labour attendant
Shall bless our land!

Lord bless the land we love,
God save our Queen!

On 16 October 1915 I lost my old Havana friend, Sir Lionel Gresley Carden, K.C.M.G., late British Minister in Mexico. He died at Basil Mansions, Knightsbridge, in his 65th year. Only a few days previously I called on him at his special request, but found him very feeble, but still bright and cheerful.

Reigate is a favourite place for recruits. We often have 4,000 billeted in the town, and I am very friendly with them all, both officers and privates. They often pay us a friendly call, staying to tea and a smoke afterwards.

In the same way we have four Red Cross hospitals in the town, and we often have contingents of wounded to spend the afternoon with us. Notwithstanding their wounds and sufferings, they are always bright and cheerful. One of them recently with us told us that the Prince of Wales worked in the trenches close by him.

CHAPTER XXX.

APPENDIX.

A MONSOON AND SHIPWRECK.

AFTER the foregoing was in print I came across the following. As it was then too late to insert it in its proper place I now add it as an Appendix, thinking that it may prove of interest to my readers. It is a copy of a letter of mine dated Bombay, 22 July 1867, addressed to the Editor of *The Times*, who printed it *in extenso* in the issue of 23 August 1867. It was also reproduced in *The Kentish Mercury*, Canterbury, 29 August 1867, and reads as under :—

To the Editor of *The Times*, London, E.C.

SIR,—The monsoon after holding back for a long time and being at least a month overdue, has at length burst upon us with great force, and the violence of the wind and of the waves has resulted in the total loss of the ship *Tirzah* on the night of the 17th inst., off Kennery Island and Lighthouse, under the following circumstances.

The captain of the vessel, which sailed from Newcastle, N. S. Wales, bound to this port, it appears had not heard of the erection of the Kennery Lighthouse, and observing a bright fixed light before him, mistook it for the light of Colaba Lighthouse (which by-the-bye is a revolving light). The result was obvious—he was soon among the rocks in a very heavy sea and terrific wind, and his ship soon became a total wreck.

Mr. Allen F. Shuttleworth, late of the Indian navy and at present Deputy Conservator of Forests, has stationed himself this monsoon (as he did last monsoon) at the Collector's bungalow at Alibarg, and from the beach adjacent early on the morning of the 18th he noticed that a ship was in distress off Kennery Island. He immediately collected a crew from among the native fishermen of the village of Alibarg and started off with them in the life-boat to the rescue. The surf was very heavy and the breakers rough, and they were soon drenched with spray. Eventually they came up to the vessel and succeeded in throwing a line on board. Several lines were thrown from the ship, but the tide was running so strong that they were swept away. All on board the *Tirzah* who could swim jumped overboard and swam to the boat or were hauled on board, with the exception of a boy, who, although a strong swimmer, could not reach the boat, so strong was the tide. He, however, managed to swim to the Island of Kennery (or Oondari), and next morning, having recruited his strength, swam across to the mainland. A man who never swam before in his life jumped from overboard the *Tirzah* and paddled while the tide drifted him down to the boat, when he was pulled in. Another, not so fortunate, lashed himself to a plank, and when near the boat a heavy breaker swept him away. A life-buoy was thrown out to him, but he would not leave his hold of the plank to seize the buoy, and he was lost. The captain was the last of the swimmers who left the ship. As soon as he got on board the boat he told Mr. Shuttleworth that none of those remaining on board could swim, so he had ordered them to tie themselves to the line which made the lifeboat fast to the ship, and jump overboard. The men tied themselves as directed, but some jumped inside the chains and others jumped outside—the sea rolling them round and round. Two were thus drowned, their bodies hanging on the back ropes, and two went down like stones. As the tide made the sea rose until round the ship it became a mass of broken water. The boat was knocked about like a cork, and the people inside tumbled about as if tossed in a blanket. Considering the crowded state of the boat the inmates stood imminent risk of being capsized, and as there was no chance of rendering further help to the men on the wreck, and that by staying there longer they jeopardised the lives of the 27 men who were in the boat—the last steering oar being smashed—the sea increasing in fury, they were reluctantly compelled to cut the line holding them to the wreck, and run into Thull Creek, and landed at the village of Thull. On reaching the shore a consultation was held, and Mr. Shuttleworth was very anxious to go off again to the wreck, with a crew composed of but ten men of the survivors to rescue the remainder; but as meanwhile not a vestige of the wreck remained, as both the steering oars and four of the pulling oars were gone, and as there seemed to be no hope of doing any good when they got there, with every probability of the men landing on pieces of wreck which covered the water, the proposal was abandoned as a useless risk. The result was as they had anticipated: the chief officer and seven men floated in on pieces of planking, &c. The captain and 13 men were brought in shore by Mr. Shuttleworth, and the boy who drifted on to the Kennery (or Oondari) Island, bringing the total number of saved up to 23. The crew all told amounting to 31, 8 are therefore missing, of whom 4 were seen to drown alongside the ship, one floated away on a plank, and, being an old man, no hopes are entertained of finding him alive. It is feared that the other three have also met with a watery grave. The boat is not a self-relieving one, and it took three men with buckets baling as fast as they could to keep the water from swamping her.

Twelve of the men, including the captain, reached the shore in a state of nudity. The fishermen who manned the life-boat showed the utmost consideration for the unfortunate men, and threw off their own clothing to cover the nakedness of the officers as soon as they were taken into the boat.

On reaching the shore they proceeded to the bungalow set apart for the reception of shipwrecked seamen, and were served with blue guernsey trowsers and red worsted night-caps, and supplied with a substantial meal, which they had scarcely finished when the chief officer made his appearance. As soon as he was perceived by the men they broke out into an involuntary cheer, as he was supposed to be lost. The coast is now strewn for miles with débris of the wreck. The survivors all came over to Bombay on Saturday evening last, by the steam ferry from Rewas and were conveyed to the Sailors' Home, where they are now well taken care of, and a subscription is being got up in Bombay on their behalf.

I should mention that on Thursday, the 18th inst., during a temporary lull in the heavy rain, the men at the watch at Colaba Lighthouse saw the ship in distress, and two attempts were made to send off assistance, but owing to the violence of the storm they both failed.

On the morning of the 19th inst. the steam-tug *Elephanta*, under the command of Captain Morland, and the *Lind*, under Commander Robinson, left Bombay at 2 a.m. They had each a life-boat on board. The *Lind* put out her life-boat, which instantly capsized, and threw the entire crew of 13 into the water. With the exception of two who were instantly picked up, and two others—who, having put on their life-belts, floated off in Alibarg and were picked up there after being 26 hours in the water—the whole crew were drowned; that is to say, nine out of the thirteen. Every effort was made to rescue them, but owing to the darkness of the night and the severity of the weather nothing could be done. About an hour later the life-boat in tow of the *Elephanta* capsized and three of her crew fell into the water, but were rescued. When daylight appeared all signs of the *Tirzah* had disappeared, and the tugs returned to Bombay. So great was the force of the hurricane that the *Elephanta* was compelled to anchor her life-boat off Kennery (which eventually got knocked to pieces), and returned to Bombay without her.

The two tugs reached Bombay at 11 a.m. on the night of the 19th inst., and as the *Lind* put her ensign half-mast high, it was at once known to those on shore that a bad disaster had happened.

Regarding the actual fate of the *Tirzah* and her crew, we were ignorant until the evening of the 19th, when the steam ferry brought a letter from Mr. Shuttleworth to the authorities here detailing the facts.

There is a life-boat attached to Kennery Island and Lighthouse, but she met with an accident some time since, and is unavailable for service. Without, therefore, the aid of Mr. Shuttleworth, I fear (humanly speaking) the crew of the *Tirzah* would have had but a poor chance of being saved.

This is at present the first time this season that Mr. Shuttleworth has had an opportunity of displaying his bravery and humanity in saving life, but if anyone will take the trouble of referring to the files of last year's local papers of about this date he will find repeated instances of Mr. Shuttleworth's successful and gallant efforts. I will just cite the *Die Vernon.* I might mention many others. At this wreck, Mr. Shuttleworth *directly* saved the captain and many other men, and *indirectly* saved the lives of *all* the survivors, for when the life-boat crew were dispirited and disinclined to face the elements in their frail boat, it was he who, by his gallantry and undaunted mien, led them on and kept them at the task—he is always the first everywhere. In many other wrecks last year did he equally distinguish himself.

The Royal Humane Society, in recognition of his services, have presented him with the *bronze* medal of their society, the same medal which they presented to all his life-boat crew, forgetting that these men were instiuments in Mr. Shuttleworth's hands, and that at nearly every wreck a new crew had to be formed by Mr. Shuttleworth, so that whereas they individually went out once, he went out about a dozen times.

No other recognition of his services has been made by the home authorities. Mr. Shuttleworth is quite unattached ; he no more belongs to the Alibarg life-boat than any other man in Bombay. It is his sole anxiety to save life that induces him to peril his own life.

Is not such a man—Allen F. Shuttleworth, I.N., Deputy Conservator of Forests—deserving of the Albert Medal, and of the thanks of the community of Underwriters at Lloyd's, and of the whole world ?

I remain, Sir, your obedient servant,

GÉRARD VAN DE LINDE.

Bombay, 22 July 1867.

My task is ended and I lay down my pen, commending my labour of love to the sympathetic consideration of my indulgent readers. I trust that my efforts will result in a ready sale for my "*Reminiscences,*" thereby adding materially to the funds of the Chartered Accountants' Benevolent Association, in which I take the deepest interest.

GÉRARD VAN DE LINDE,

The Author.

THE DEVELOPMENT OF CONTEMPORARY ACCOUNTING THOUGHT

An Arno Press Collection

Baldwin, H[arry] G[len]. **Accounting for Value As Well as Original Cost** *and* Castenholz, William B. **A Solution to the Appreciation Problem.** 2 Vols. in 1. 1927/1931

Baxter, William. **Collected Papers on Accounting.** 1978

Brief, Richard P., Ed. **Selections from Encyclopaedia of Accounting, 1903.** 1978

Broaker, Frank and Richard M. Chapman. **The American Accountants' Manual.** 1897

Canning, John B. **The Economics of Accountancy.** 1929

Chatfield, Michael, Ed. **The English View of Accountant's Duties and Responsibilities.** 1978

Cole, William Morse. **The Fundamentals of Accounting.** 1921

Congress of Accountants. **Official Record of the Proceedings of the Congress of Accountants.** 1904

Cronhelm, F[rederick] W[illiam]. **Double Entry by Single.** 1818

Davidson, Sidney. **The Plant Accounting Regulations of the Federal Power Commission.** 1952

De Paula, F[rederic] R[udolf] M[ackley]. **Developments in Accounting.** 1948

Epstein, Marc Jay. **The Effect of Scientific Management on the Development of the Standard Cost System** (Doctoral Dissertation, University of Oregon, 1973). 1978

Esquerré, Paul-Joseph. **The Applied Theory of Accounts.** 1914

Fitzgerald, A[dolf] A[lexander]. **Current Accounting Trends.** 1952

Garner, S. Paul and Marilynn Hughes, Eds. **Readings on Accounting Development.** 1978

Haskins, Charles Waldo. **Business Education and Accountancy.** 1904

Hein, Leonard William. **The British Companies Acts and the Practice of Accountancy 1844-1962** (Doctoral Dissertation, University of California, Los Angeles, 1962). 1978

Hendriksen, Eldon S. **Capital Expenditures in the Steel Industry, 1900 to 1953** (Doctoral Dissertation, University of California, Berkeley, 1956). 1978

Holmes, William, Linda H. Kistler and Louis S. Corsini. **Three Centuries of Accounting in Massachusetts.** 1978

Horngren, Charles T. **Implications for Accountants of the Uses of Financial Statements by Security Analysts** (Doctoral Dissertation, University of Chicago, 1955). 1978

Horrigan, James O., Ed. **Financial Ratio Analysis—An Historical Perspective.** 1978

Jones, [Edward Thomas]. **Jones's English System of Book-keeping.** 1796

Lamden, Charles William. **The Securities and Exchange Commission** (Doctoral Dissertation, University of California, Berkeley, 1949). 1978

Langer, Russell Davis. **Accounting As A Variable in Mergers** (Doctoral Dissertation, University of California, Berkeley, 1976). 1978

Lewis, J. Slater. **The Commercial Organisation of Factories.** 1896

Littleton, A[nanias] C[harles] and B[asil] S. Yamey, Eds. **Studies in the Historv of Accounting.** 1956

Mair, John. **Book-keeping Moderniz'd.** 1793

Mann, Helen Scott. **Charles Ezra Sprague.** 1931

Marsh, C[hristopher] C[olumbus]. **The Theory and Practice of Bank Book-keeping.** 1856

Mitchell, William. **A New and Complete System of Book-keeping by an Improved Method of Double Entry.** 1796

Montgomery, Robert H. **Fifty Years of Accountancy.** 1939

Moonitz, Maurice. **The Entity Theory of Consolidated Statements.** 1951

Moonitz, Maurice, Ed. **Three Contributions to the Development of Accounting Thought.** 1978

Murray, David. **Chapters in the History of Bookkeeping, Accountancy & Commercial Arithmetic.** 1930

Nicholson, J[erome] Lee. **Cost Accounting.** 1913

Paton, William Andrew and Russell Alger Stevenson. **Principles of Accounting.** 1918

Pixley, Francis W[illiam]. **The Profession of a Chartered Accountant and Other Lectures.** 1897

Preinreich, Gabriel A. D. **The Nature of Dividends.** 1935

Previts, Gary John, Ed. **Early 20th Century Developments in American Accounting Thought.** 1978

Ronen, Joshua and George H. Sorter. **Relevant Financial Statements.** 1978

Shenkir, William G., Ed. **Carman G. Blough: His Professional Career and Accounting Thought.** 1978

Simpson, Kemper. **Economics for the Accountant.** 1921

Sneed, Florence R. **Parallelism in Two Disciplines.** (M.A. Thesis, University of Texas, Arlington, 1974). 1978

Sorter, George H. **The Boundaries of the Accounting Universe** (Doctoral Dissertation, University of Chicago, 1963). 1978

Storey, Reed K[arl]. **Matching Revenues with Costs** (Doctoral Dissertation, University of California, Berkeley, 1958). 1978

Sweeney, Henry W[hitcomb]. **Stabilized Accounting.** 1936

Van de Linde, Gérard. **Reminiscences.** 1917

Vatter, William J[oseph]. **The Fund Theory of Accounting and Its Implications for Financial Reports.** 1947

Walker, R. G. **Consolidated Statements.** 1978

Webster, Norman E., Comp. **The American Association of Public Accountants.** 1954

Wells, M. C., Ed. **American Engineers' Contributions to Cost Accounting.** 1978

Worthington, Beresford. **Professional Accountants.** 1895

Yamey, Basil S. **Essays on the History of Accounting.** 1978

Yamey, Basil S., Ed. **The Historical Development of Accounting.** 1978

Yang, J[u] M[ei]. **Goodwill and Other Intangibles.** 1927

Zeff, Stephen Addam. **A Critical Examination of the Orientation Postulate in Accounting, with Particular Attention to its Historical Development** (Doctoral Dissertation, University of Michigan, 1961). 1978

Zeff, Stephen A., Ed. **Selected Dickinson Lectures in Accounting.** 1978